DEMOCRACY AND DIFFERENCE

DEMOCRACY AND DIFFERENCE

CONTESTING THE BOUNDARIES

OF THE POLITICAL

Edited by Seyla Benhabib

PRINCETON UNIVERSITY PRESS   PRINCETON, NEW JERSEY

Library of Congress Cataloging-in-Publication Data

Democracy and difference : Contesting the boundaries
of the political / edited by Seyla Benhabib.
p.   cm.
Includes bibliographical references and index.
ISBN 0-691-04479-1 (cl : alk. paper).—
ISBN 0-691-04478-3 (pb : alk. paper)
1. Democracy.   2. Ethnicity.   3. Nationalism.
4. Social movements.   I. Benhabib, Seyla.
JC423.D43979   1996
321.8—dc20   96-2189

This book has been composed in Berkeley Book

Princeton University Press books are printed
on acid-free paper and meet the guidelines
for permanence and durability of the Committee
on Production Guidelines for Book Longevity
of the Council on Library Resources

Printed in the United States of America
by Princeton Academic Press

10   9   8   7   6   5   4   3   2

Contents

Nineteen
Democracy, Philosophy, and Justification

Twenty
Foundationalism and Democracy

DEMOCRACY AND DIFFERENCE

Introduction _____

The Democratic Moment and the
Problem of Difference

SEYLA BENHABIB

TWO HUNDRED YEARS after the French Revolution, in 1989, a different set of walls came crumbling down. With the end of authoritarian communism in East Central Europe, the Baltic countries, and the former Soviet Union, and with the earlier transitions from dictatorship to democracy in the Philippines, Argentina, and Brazil, the worldwide movement toward democracy has been celebrated. Like Alexis de Tocqueville, who in 1833 prophesied the "irresistible revolution advancing century by century," contemporary thinkers have greeted the "democratic moment."[1] Francis Fukuyama, in *The End of History*, proclaimed that we have reached "the end point of mankind's ideological evolution and the universalization of Western liberal democracy as the final form of human government."[2]

History, however, always proves wrong those who claim to have solved its riddle. The ink had hardly dried on Fukuyama's triumphalist words when political realities and experiences different from the ones prophesied by his theory erupted: the civil war and ethnic genocide in Bosnia-Herzegovina; the Russian destruction of Chechnya; the simmering nationality conflicts in Azerbaijan, Armenia, Macedonia, and Greece; the devolution of democracy and the rise of Moslem fundamentalism in Algeria and elsewhere among the countries of North Africa and the Middle East. These trends indicate that "the universalization of liberal democracy" is far from complete. Yet in the heart of the West as well, in France and Italy, and perhaps even in the United States neofascist movements have emerged on a scale unprecedented since the end of World War II.[3] The global trend toward democratization is real, but so also are the oppositions and antagonisms asserting themselves against this trend in the name of various forms of "difference"—ethnic, national, linguistic, religious, and cultural.[4] Throughout the globe a new politics for the recognition of collective identity forms is resurging.

Since every search for identity includes differentiating oneself from what one is not, identity politics is always and necessarily a politics of the creation of difference. One is a Bosnian Serb to the degree to which one is not a Bosnian Moslem or a Croat; one is a Gush Emmunim settler in the West Bank to the extent that one is not a secular Zionist; one belongs to the "European anthro-pological-cultural community" to the degree that one is not from the Maghreb, the Middle East, or Asia. What is shocking about these developments is not the inevitable dialectic of identity/difference that they display but rather the atavistic belief that identities can be maintained and secured only by eliminat-ing difference and otherness. The negotiation of identity/difference, to use William Connolly's felicitous phrase,[5] is the political problem facing democra-cies on a global scale.

I

Under the title *Democracy and Difference: Contesting the Boundaries of the Politi-cal*, the essays collected in this volume seek to articulate and come to grips with forms of identity/difference politics that were particularly salient in West-ern liberal democracies throughout the 1970s and 1980s. Referred to at times as "new social movement politics," these developments were seen as express-ing "postmaterialist values" (Ronald Inglehart)[6] and were interpreted as signal-ing a shift from "issues of distribution" to a concern with "the grammar of forms of life" (Jürgen Habermas).[7] Through the experiences of new social movements, major transformations occurred in the nature of issues defined as being political concerns. The struggles over wealth, political position, and access that characterized bourgeois and working-class politics throughout the nineteenth and the first half of the twentieth century were replaced by strug-gles over abortion and gay rights, over ecology and the consequences of new medical technologies, and the politics of racial, linguistic, and ethnic pride (colloquially referred to in the U.S. context as the "politics of the Rainbow coalition"). These new issues have been represented by novel groups of politi-cal actors: instead of political parties, there was a shift to movement politics and to loosely coalesced groups of activist women, people of color, gay indi-viduals, and concerned citizens.[8]

Viewed in a global context, the emergence of this new politics in Western democracies partially overlapped with the worldwide movement toward de-mocratization. But the politics of "identity/difference," emerging out of the experience of new social movements in liberal capitalist democracies, and the politics of racial, ethnic, linguistic, and religious difference developing in for-mer communist countries, North Africa, and the Middle East are radically different. Whereas the former kind of identity/difference politics focuses on the negotiation, contestation, and representation of difference within the pub-lic sphere of liberal democracies, the politics of ethnonationalisms seek to redefine the constituents of the body politic, and aim at creating new politi-cally sovereign bodies. In fact, the expression of cultural, religious, national, and ethnic homogeneity through a sovereign state-form is the desideratum of these latter movements. The essays in this volume, in discussing the democratic politics of difference, share the assumption that the institutions and culture of liberal democracies are sufficiently complex, supple, and decentered so as to allow the expression of difference without fracturing the identity of the body politic or subverting existing forms of political sovereignty.[9]

The phrase "democracy and difference" was an invitation to the contributors to reflect upon the theory and practice of democracy after the experiences of identity politics in their "new social movement" form. Does democracy rest on homogenizing models of identity? What does the "body" of the body politic look like? Can the ideal of universal citizenship accommodate difference? What theories of rationality and motivation govern our conceptions of the democratic citizen and the legal person? Does democracy need philosophy? If so, which kind: rationalist, contextualist, postmodernist, critical, or neo-Kantian? What institutional, cultural, representational channels are there for the expression of difference? How much difference is compatible with the ideal of the rule of law under fair and equal conditions?

Within this context, the term "difference," and its more metaphysical permutations, "différance" in the work of Jacques Derrida, and "le différend" in the work of Jean-François Lyotard, have become rallying points for two issues: a philosophical critique of Enlightenment-type rationalism, essentialism, and universalism, and a cultural battle cry for those who insist on the experience of alterity, otherness, heterogeneity, dissonance, and resistance.[10] Contemporary Western liberal democracies are being challenged by groups who insist upon their unassimilatable difference and who want to use their experience of alterity to demystify the rationalist and identitary illusions of these liberal democracies.

As is often the case in periods of momentous transformations such as the ones we have been living through since 1989, old and new definitions, presuppositions, currents of thought, assumptions, and values mix, mingle, and clash in inchoate ways. The purpose of this volume is to contribute to a self-clarification of our times by analyzing the conceptual, cultural, and institutional quandaries and puzzles of the present "democratic moment" in the face of the questions of identity/difference.

II

In his contribution to this volume, Sheldon Wolin writes: "Thus democracy is too simple for complex societies and too complex for simple ones." The question of social complexity and democracy is also in the forefront of Habermas's lead essay, "Three Normative Models of Democracy." Habermas distinguishes among the liberal, republican, and proceduralist-deliberative views of democratic politics. According to the liberal model, the democratic process has the function of transmitting to the political apparatus the interests of an autonomous civil society; the task of politics is the coordination of divergent interests among private persons. According to the republican model, politics is viewed as the articulation of a "common good," of a substantive vision of the ethical life of a community. The good of politics is not the administration of the interests of civil society as much as it is the creation of solidarity among citizens.

Habermas objects that both the liberal and the republican models "presuppose a view of society as centered in the state—be it as guardian of a market-society or the state as the self-conscious institutionalization of an ethical community." The discourse theory of democracy (used by Habermas interchangeably in this context with a "deliberative model of politics") proceeds from the image of a decentered society. The political system is considered neither the peak, nor the center, nor even the formative model of society in general, but as one more "action system," to borrow a phrase from Niklas Luhmann, among others. Habermas seeks to recast concepts like legitimation and popular sovereignty in the terms of this proceduralist model: "Discourse theory works instead with the *higher-level intersubjectivity* of communication processes that flow through both the parliamentary bodies and the informal networks of the public sphere. Within and outside the parliamentary complex, these subjectless forms of communication constitute arenas in which a more or less rational opinion- and will-formation can take place." Habermas shares with the civic republican tradition of J.-J. Rousseau, Thomas Jefferson, Hannah Arendt, and among the contributors to this volume, Benjamin Barber, an insistence "on the original meaning of democracy in terms of the institutionalization of a public use of reason jointly exercised by autonomous citizens." The challenge is not only how to reconceptualize the ideal of such a public sphere under conditions of societies "too complex for democracy," but it is to give it a philosophically more adequate formulation which does not run together questions of justice with those of the good life, the way in which civic republicans do. Habermas maintains, on the basis of arguments he has developed much more explicitly elsewhere,[11] that the republican tradition "overburdens" the democratic process by assimilating "politics to a hermeneutical process of self-explication of a shared form of life or collective identity." He distinguishes such ethical discourses on collective forms of life from political discourses proper that would involve both *moral questions of justice* and *instrumental questions of power and coercion.*

Although a large number of contributors to this volume defend a version of "deliberative democracy" as providing the most adequate conceptual and institutional model for theorizing the democratic experience of complex societies (Benhabib, Joshua Cohen, Iris Young, Jean Cohen, Amy Gutmann), none would subscribe to all aspects of Habermas's sociological and philosophical arguments on behalf of this model. Joshua Cohen believes that the substantive presuppositions of procedural democracies need to be taken much more seriously. Citizens' autonomy needs to be protected and expanded through the guarantee of certain social and economic rights that would enable participation in democratic deliberative processes. Even under conditions of a reasonable value pluralism among competing conceptions of the good and of value in general, Joshua Cohen believes that a more substantive conception of democracy can be defended.

In my contribution, "Toward a Deliberative Model of Democratic Legitimacy," I also defend the model of a decentered public sphere, but refuse to follow Habermas's sharp distinctions among ethical, political, and moral discourses. In fact, as Iris Young argues in her article entitled "Communication and the Other: Beyond Deliberative Democracy," the version of deliberative democracy proposed by Habermas cuts political processes too cleanly away from cultural forms of communication. Even if we consider some distinction between the right and the good at the philosophical and institutional levels as being essential to preserving democratic freedoms in societies in which multiple visions of the good compete, this distinction does not commit one to building a *cordon sanitaire* around political discourse such as to block off the articulation of issues of collective identity and visions of the good life. Young focuses on three sociocultural practices which, in her view, "a broader conception of communicative democracy requires in addition to critical argument: greeting, rhetoric, and storytelling."

Very broadly stated, there is a tension in this volume among defenders of the proceduralist-deliberative model of democracy and a fourth type, not named by Habermas. I will call this the "agonistic model of democratic politics." Sheldon Wolin provides a succinct and compelling account of this vision. Strains of this view, in different ways, also animate the contributions by Jenny Mansbridge, Chantal Mouffe, Bonnie Honig, and Benjamin Barber. "I shall take the *political*," writes Wolin, "to be an expression of the idea that a free society composed of diversities can nonetheless enjoy moments of commonality when, through public deliberations, collective power is used to promote or protect the well-being of a collectivity. *Politics* refers to the legitimized and public contestation, primarily by organized and unequal social powers, over access to the resources available to the public authorities of the collectivity. Politics is continuous, ceaseless, and endless. In contrast, the *political* is episodic, rare."

The development of the modern state in Western industrial societies created a specific kind of politics; a politics of domestication, containment, and boundary drawing. Advanced industrial democracies are heirs to this tremendous controlling power of the state, which defends and exploits "the labor, wealth, and psyches of the citizens." Any conception of democracy grounded in the citizen-as-actor and politics-as-episodic models, argues Wolin, is incompatible with the "modern choice of the State as the fixed center of political life." Instead of exploring the alternative of a non–state-centered vision of the political, however, Sheldon Wolin concludes that "democracy needs to be reconceived as something other than a form of government: as a mode of being that is conditioned by bitter experience, doomed to succeed only temporarily, but is a recurrent possibility as long as the memory of the political survives."

This conceptualization of the democratic project as a certain "mode of being," not just a form of government, is shared by Chantal Mouffe, Bonnie Honig, Joan Landes, and Benjamin Barber. Both Mouffe and Landes appeal to Claude Lefort's concept of "the dissolution of the markers of certainty"[12] to characterize the specific form of social-symbolic power that is the core of democracy. "Liberal democracy," writes Mouffe, "is not the application of the democratic model to a wider context. . . . Understood as a *regime*, it concerns the symbolic ordering of social relations." This symbolic ordering is characterized not just by a pluralism of values and worldviews, as John Rawls would maintain; rather, this is a pluralism "at the axiological level," which recognizes the impossibility of ever adjudicating without contest and without residue among competing visions of the good, of justice, and of the political.

Bonnie Honig sums up a similar perspective of agonistic politics: "To take difference—and not just identity—seriously in democratic theory is to affirm the inescapability of conflict and the ineradicability of resistance to the political and moral projects of ordering subjects, institutions, and values. . . . It is to give up on the dream of a place called home, a place free of power, conflict, and struggle, a place—an identity, a form of life, a group vision—unmarked or unriven by difference and untouched by the power brought to bear upon it by the identities that strive to ground themselves in its place."

Agonistic visions of democratic politics inevitably invite the question, How can we be so sure that the agon of episodic politics, or the contest of pluralisms that cannot be adjudicated at the higher levels, will all be instances of good and just democratic politics as opposed to being instances of fascism, xenophobic nationalism, right-wing populism? Are the people always wise? Are their decisions always just? Is the will that guides them always worthy of respect? Radical visions of agonistic politics are subject to the kinds of objections which liberal-constitutional theory articulates so well: the democratic *demos* may be unjust, racist, fickle, and capricious. How can theorists of agonistic democracy safeguard freedom and justice, respect for the rights of citizens as equal and free beings, if they are unwilling to place some constraints that bind, trump, limit, and otherwise confine the will of the sovereign people?

In his contribution to this volume, Benjamin Barber articulates the standpoint of the strong democrats: "What is required is not foundational mandates or individual mental acumen in rigidly applying fixed standards to a changing world but such political skills as are necessary to discovering or forging common ground. What is right, or even what a right is, cannot in itself determine political judgment. Rights themselves . . . are both constantly being redefined and reinterpreted *and* dependent for their normative force on the engagement and commitment of an active citizen body." Barber speaks of the self-correcting mechanisms of democracy. Surely though among such self-correcting mechanisms are not just the will of the people but the institutions of the Bill of Rights, constitutionalism, the interplay of the highest court of the land with the elected representatives of the people, processes of constitutional review, and the like. Where deliberative-democratic politics, in its strong proceduralist form defended by Habermas, immunizes politics against the forces of cultural and ethical life, theorists of agonistic politics view democracy as the incessant contestation over such ethical and cultural questions. At the theoretical level the desirable alternative is clear: a deliberative vision of democratic politics which can also do justice to the agonistic spirit of democracy so well articulated by its defenders.

The contributions by Jenny Mansbridge, Anne Phillips, Will Kymlicka, and Jean Cohen approach the old conflict between liberalism and democracy in novel ways. In fact, it would be fair to state that even for the defenders of agonistic democracy represented in this volume, there is little question that the historical legacy of liberalism—respect for the rule of law, for individual rights, for value pluralism, for constitutional guarantees—must be upheld in one way or another. The issue is rather the right mixture, theoretically and practically, between the legacy of liberalism and the conflictual and contestatory nature of all democratic politics. It is the virtue of Jane Mansbridge's essay, "Using Power/Fighting Power: The Polity," that it focuses precisely on this mix. Arguing that no democratic polity can wholly eliminate the need for the use of coercive power, or attain full legitimation, Mansbridge maintains that along with the institutional safeguard of institutional rights, free speech and association, the rule of law, political parties, and interest groups, "democracies also need to foster and value informal deliberative enclaves of resistance in which those who lose in each coercive move can rework their ideas and strategies, gathering their forces and deciding in a more protected space in what way or whether to continue the battle."

According to Mansbridge none of the criteria for legitimating coercion, "whether based on assessments of hypothetical consent, the substantive justice of outcomes, the freedom from coercion or closeness to agreement of the deliberative process that resulted in a decision to coerce, or the equal power that participants exercised in the decision process—can produce in cases of ongoing disagreement an incontestably legitimate result." Theoretically, this observation leads Mansbridge to express sympathy for those agonistic theorists of democracy, who maintain that there is no full-proof rational justification without a remainder. Actual democracies can only produce "good enough" legitimacy.

At the level of institutional proposals, Mansbridge joins a number of other contributors to this volume, who, following a decentered public sphere and pluralistic civil society model, would like to combine the virtues of deliberative politics with a sociological realism adequate to the complexity of modern societies (Joshua Cohen, Benhabib, Jean Cohen, and Nancy Fraser). Mansbridge utilizes the term "enclave politics," and also drawing from an essay by Nancy Fraser,[13] she writes of "subaltern counterpublics." For groups and social movements seeking to express diversity, the goals of such counterpublics would include "understanding themselves better, forging bonds of solidarity, preserving the memories of past injustices, interpreting and reinterpreting the meaning of those injustices, working out alternative conceptions of self, of community, of justice and of universality . . . deciding what alliances to make both emotionally and strategically, deliberating on ends and means, and deciding how to act, individually and collectively."

A sympathy for hybrid institutional solutions for representing differences within democracies also governs the essays by Anne Phillips and Will Kymlicka. After a brief examination of thoughts about "representation" within the liberal tradition, Phillips observes that liberalism has focused on diversity and conflict of ideas within pluralist polities. "But when the politics of ideas is taken in isolation from what I will call the politics of presence, it does not deal adequately with the experiences of those social groups who by virtue of their race or ethnicity or religion or gender have felt themselves excluded from the democratic process. Political exclusion is increasingly—I believe rightly—viewed in terms that can be met only by political presence." However, if what are to be represented are groups rather than ideas, views, and belief systems, this model of representation raises another set of quandaries: can groups be treated as homogeneous entities? If principles of representation are distributed along group lines, which aspects of group identity should be given the most preference in public modes of representation? Say you have a group of Francophone women of African descent within the Province of Quebec: what aspect of their group identity is the one that should be represented in the political process? Since all identities, individual and collective, are riven by multiple, complex, and heterogeneous allegiances, does not the "politics of presence" run the risk of reinforcing a form of identity-essentialism, a defunct metaphysics of group presences, as it were? Phillips concludes that the road leading in contemporary liberal democracies from a politics of ideas to a politics of presence is irreversible, and that "mechanisms should be—and can be—devised that address the problems of group exclusion without fixing the boundaries or character of each group."

Will Kymlicka, in his contribution to this volume, "Three Forms of Group-Differentiated Citizenship in Canada," deals with the general question of group rights within the liberal-democratic state by looking at the special case of Canada. Since Canada, in its historical development, has involved the

federation of three distinct peoples or nations (English, French, and Aboriginals), Kymlicka is sympathetic to the view that such differences at the level of
national identity may require special legal or constitutional measures to be
sustained and honored. Also, Canada is a polyethnic state through immigration, being the home to individuals from India, Africa, Asia, and Europe, as
well as from the Middle East and other countries. Kymlicka lists three forms
of differentiated citizenship rights: self-government rights claimed by the original nations (in particular the Québécois and the Aboriginal nations); polyethnic rights and special representation rights. Kymlicka thinks that it should be
possible to accommodate such differential rights with the liberal guarantees
of individual rights of freedom and equality. He does acknowledge, however,
that conflicts can and do occur, as, for example, in the case of the Inuit Indian
women.[14]

Carol Gould, in "Diversity and Democracy: Representing Differences," is
critical of what she names "group essentialisms," namely the view that the
identities of groups are given and historically unchanging essences. Instead
she pleads for a form of voluntary social pluralism or multiculturalism. Such
representation would have to be compatible with the priority of equal rights.
Within the framework of a nonessentialist and social pluralist vision of group
differences, as well, questions as to how and by whom group identities are to
be defined and established remain open. In the final analysis, Gould thinks
that increased participation at all levels in a polity is the most viable mechanism for the representation of difference.

The quandaries of a politics of presence (Phillips) derive principally from
the difficulties of establishing a theoretically defensible and politically viable
concept of "group identities." In his essay, "Peripheral Peoples and Narrative
Identities: Arendtian Reflections on Late Modernity," Carlos Forment com-
pellingly illustrates the internal rifts of all political identities by focusing on
"peripheral peoples." This term refers "to 'ex-colonials' who, since the postwar period, have been emigrating in unprecedented numbers and settling in
postimperial countries (England, Spain, Italy, France, Germany, the U.S.) of
the North Atlantic basin. While their legal status is relatively assured, their
experience of citizenship remains ambiguous." Not only are there categories
of dual nationality, but also large groups of such individuals, for example,
Turks, Greeks, and members of ex-Yugoslavian states, are neonomads, working in European capitals for certain portions of the year and then returning to
their home country. But the term "peripheral peoples" also refers to the experiences of discrimination, marginality, and nonrepresentations experienced by
these individuals.

Forment focuses on the construction of narratives of identities in order to
explore how peripheral peoples enter late modernity through the language of
liberalism, and "like master bricoleurs, peripheral groups tinkered with those
elements that liberalism had left behind as refuse, cobbling them together with

unexpected results." Hybrid narratives of individual and collective experience, opposed to purism of all forms, and revealing another Enlightenment and modernity, were the result.

Whereas Forment concentrates on the hybridity and fracture that result from the encounters of democratic liberalism with "peripheral peoples," Fred Dallmayr, drawing on Tzvetan Todorov's account of the conquest of the Americas,[15] reminds us of the following tension: "The opposition between the egalitarian universalism of modern Western culture and the array of particular ethnic cultures and religious traditions, that is, between a rationalized worldview and indigenous life-worlds," is not merely accidental but has a basic or paradigmatic status, he argues. Dallmayr seeks to illustrate this point by discussing Charles Taylor's position as articulated in the book *Multiculturalism and "The Politics of Recognition."*[16] The controversy over the status of Quebec, and, in particular, conflicts between the Canadian Charter of Rights and Freedoms and the indigenous rights demanded by the separatist Québécois movement become the backdrop for Dallmayr's exploration of this cultural opposition.

An issue that is to haunt discussions concerning difference for the foreseeable future is the use of analogous reasoning in constructing accounts of the position of social groups. Are all social groups discriminated against or positioned in the hierarchy of oppression in the same way? Are linguistic forms of discrimination analogous to discrimination based on gender and race? Are race and gender discrimination really analogous? The term "difference" must thus be viewed as an invitation to further reflection rather than as an analytically useful tool for describing the multifarious issues identified by the contributors so far.

Undoubtedly, the form of difference that is in the forefront of the majority of contributions in this volume is the oppression and discrimination of women. Even in those essays like Mansbridge's, Benhabib's, Young's, and Gould's, where it is not the exclusive focus of attention, gender discrimination and the experience of the women's movements are in the background. Three essays address different aspects of the gender question through different methodologies: Jean Cohen's essay, "Democracy, Difference, and the Right of Privacy," examines the controversy over abortion rights in recent U.S. political thought and jurisprudence; Nancy Fraser looks at the way in which the late-capitalist, postindustrial welfare state implicitly enforces gender-dualistic models of citizenship; and Joan Landes examines the gendered character of the bourgeois public sphere by focusing on the "performance of citizenship" by women of the French Revolution.

Building on her work in *Women and the Public Sphere in the Age of the French Revolution*,[17] Joan Landes acknowledges the existence of competing discourses in enlightened thought on the position of women. However, she maintains "that neither liberals, rationalists, nor republicans wholly met the challenge of gender equality, nor was this a consequence of some lapse of attention or traditional prejudice on their part. From the outset, democracy in the modern world produced not only a discourse but a practice of gender difference." In particular, Landes concentrates on the representation of the subject considered capable of occupying the public sphere of bourgeois democracies. "Only men's bodies," she concludes, "seemed to fulfill the ideal requirements of this contained form of subjectivity. In contrast, women were deemed to inhabit bodies that, rather than guaranteeing political liberties, were marked by their physically distinctive sexualities and irrational, hence apolitical, qualities."

Feminist theorists interested in retrieving a concept of the public sphere for contemporary debates around democracy and difference are more confident than Landes about the continuing viability of this project. Jean Cohen begins her article by examining recent attempts by feminist theorists, like Young, Fraser, and Benhabib, to rethink the normative conception of public space with an eye to empowering and representing difference. While Cohen is sympathetic to these approaches, she objects that it is no longer enough to exercise the feminist "hermeneutics of suspicion" (Paul Ricoeur), in deconstructing the public/private split, but that feminist theory must take the next step and "bring the private back in." The feminist critique of the traditional public/private split requires a reconceptualization of privacy.

Cohen's essay moves at several levels at once: first and foremost, it is an intervention in recent U.S. debates about abortion rights, and an examination of the various positions articulated by the communitarian critics of *Roe v. Wade*; second, it is an attempt to reconstruct a conception of privacy without reviving the "paradigm of property rights" that has traditionally been taken as the model of privacy rights *tout court*; finally, Cohen wants to maintain that the goods protected by privacy rights include "one's inviolate personality, bodily integrity, psychic processes of identification, and decisional autonomy." She concludes that "to cast the rights to abortion as a privacy right is to acknowledge women's 'difference' while leaving it up to each individual woman how to define this difference."

Whereas Cohen is concerned to reconstruct the right of privacy, Nancy Fraser undertakes a reconstructive feminist thinking about the welfare state. She proceeds from several social facts: in the labor markets of postindustrial capitalism, few jobs pay sufficient wages to support a family singlehandedly; postindustrial families are less conventional and more diverse; "gender norms and family forms are highly contested." In this new world of less stable employment and more diverse families, there will still be a need for a welfare state that will ensure people against uncertainties of the labor market and life circumstances. But, Fraser asks, "what should a postindustrial welfare state look like?" Such a welfare state, she maintains, should uphold *gender equity*. Among available responses to this question, Fraser distinguishes the "universal breadwinner" and the "caregiver parity" models. The first model seeks to universalize the condition of gainful employment to both men and women; the second model takes into account that gender equity in the labor markets cannot be achieved until and unless the "caregiver" function of most women (to children, to the elderly, to the sick and the disabled) is restructured in some way or another. Fraser runs through certain thought experiments, exploring a possible combination of these visions, but maintains that neither of those approaches can deliver full gender equity.

This volume concludes with a series of answers to the question, Does democracy need foundations? Richard Rorty begins by suggesting that one should distinguish between idealizations and foundations. Whereas idealizations answer the question, How can we make our practices more coherent? the search for foundations are supposed to answer the question, Should we be engaging in our present practices at all? For Rorty, to be antifoundationalist about a practice is to urge that criticism or commendation of it be confined to a comparison with other actual and possible social practices. Rorty acknowledges that this coherentist appeal to an ever-widening network of social practices may not convince the exclusivists, the racists, the bigots. He thinks that a theoretically convincing answer to such individuals does not exist, but that democracy is not necessarily enfeebled unless such premises can be shared. Rorty, like Mansbridge, Mouffe, Barber, and Honig in their contributions, is skeptical that the project of justifying democracy is an enterprise with a rational solution. Rather, there is always "more than reason," whether this be power, nonnegotiable and axiomatic value differences, or the never-ending assertions of conflict and alterity. Postmodernist bourgeois liberalism[18] and agonistic politics meet at certain levels.

Robert Dahl suggests that the question, Does democracy need foundations? can be interpreted in three very different ways: 1) do democratic systems, regimes, or government need foundations in order to exist and to function properly; 2) does democratic theory need foundations; and 3) do democratic systems need democratic theory as a foundation? Dahl observes that it is extremely difficult, maybe even impossible, to answer the first question. Even restricting ourselves to modern democratic systems, since 1993 at least thirty more countries have attained democratic political systems, adding to the twenty-one that were defined as having reached that "somewhat arbitrary threshold" by 1950. Furthermore, there are also instances of nondemocratic regimes replacing democratic governments fifty-two times between 1900 and 1985.

Concluding that the question cannot be posed as a purely empirical one, Dahl observes that whether democratic theory needs foundations will largely depend on one's strategy for theory construction. Nonetheless, if by foundations one means "a reasonable set of assumptions that provide grounds for believing that democracy is desirable, for judging whether and to what extent a given system is democratic, and for judging what practices and institutions

are compatible or incompatible with the assumptions," then we want foundations to help improve "our political judgments and choices." In conclusion
Dahl observes that whereas it is hard to know whether a democratic system
needs a democratic theory, it is clear that if in a country with democratic
political institutions the intellectual elites are in the main convinced that democracy *cannot* be justified on reasonable and plausible grounds, then in
times of serious crisis, "those who try to defend democracy will find the going
much harder, while those who promote nondemocratic alternatives will find
it that much easier."

Amy Gutmann picks up the gauntlet dropped by Dahl and asserts that
"democracy needs justifications, not foundations. . . . Justifications need not
be foundationalist or antifoundationalist." If practices of justification must rest
upon truths about human nature, human rights, rationality, or politics "that
are self-evident, rationally incontestable, or axiomatic," then such justifications are implausible and hard to deliver. Gutmann defends a moderately
pragmatic conception of justification that goes beyond the Churchillian view
that democracy may be the worst form of government except that a better one
has not been invented. According to Gutmann, political philosophers aspire to
something more than the defense of nonideal democracy. "We try to construct
out of our inheritance, and imagine beyond it, a more fully justifiable set of
social and political institutions, which we can call democracy without qualification, or at least without neologism." Gutmann also proposes a model of
deliberative democracy as such a political ideal, which, she observes, is bound
to be not only incomplete and controversial but also reasonably contested.

Benjamin Barber, whose essay has been referred to in the preceding, formulates his own version of strong democracy, privileging, we may say, citizens'
deliberative processes of collective participation and judgment building. Barber considers the question, Does democracy need foundations? to mandate a
discussion on the turf of epistemology; refusing to engage at this level, he
argues that democratic politics is "practical, not speculative, about action
rather than about truth. It yields but is not premised on an epistemology and
in this sense is necessarily pragmatic." For Barber democracy is not about
difference, primarily or even secondarily; rather it is a "regime/culture/civil
society/government in which we make (will) common decisions, choose common conduct, and create or express common values in the practical domain
of our lives in an ever-changing context of conflicts of interests and competition for power." Democratic politics, thus conceived, has certain normative
attributes, like its revolutionary spirit, its autonomy, and the commonality or
publicness of democratic judgment. Admittedly, a full exploration of these
criteria of democratic politics may lead back to the turf of epistemology that
Barber is anxious to avoid. A number of other contributors, like Habermas,
Joshua Cohen, Iris Young, Jean Cohen, and Benhabib, argue for a closer link
between epistemology and politics, between philosophy and democracy.

It will be clear to the reader of these essays that they do not express a *consensus omnium*. However, it is my hope that the intensity and liveliness of the debates presented in these contributions can guard us against the kind of situation identified by Robert Dahl in his sagacious observation that unless intellectuals are convinced that democracy can be defended with rigorous argument, and not only with good faith and pious wishes, in times of crisis, "those who try to defend democracy will find the going much harder, while those who promote nondemocratic alternatives will find it that much easier."

III

The essays collected in this volume originated in the annual meetings of the Conference for the Study of Political Thought, held between April 16 and 18, 1993, at Yale University. They were substantially revised for inclusion in this volume, and they represent a selection of papers delivered on that occasion. The conference was made possible by the generous support of the Edward J. and Dorothy C. Kempf Fund and the Robert and Louise Olmsted Fund. The Ethics, Politics, and Economics Program at Yale University and the Graduate Faculty of the New School for Social Research provided logistical, secretarial, and financial assistance, which I gratefully acknowledge.

I owe a special debt of gratitude to Jeffrey Wengrofsky from the Department of Political Science of the Graduate Faculty of the New School for Social Research. He was a dedicated, diligent, and competent conference assistant who saw through the early stages of this volume. Special thanks are also due to Patchen Markell of the Department of Government at Harvard University for his sure hand in finalizing this volume with me.

Notes

1. Alexis de Tocqueville, *Democracy in America*, trans. George Lawrence, ed. J. P. Mayer (New York: Doubleday, 1969), "Author's Introduction," 12; and Marc Plattner, "The Democratic Moment," in Larry Diamond and Marc Plattner, eds., *The Global Resurgence of Democracy* (Baltimore: Johns Hopkins University Press, 1992). For a thoughtful assessment of the contradictory forces at work, see Adam Przeworski, *Democracy and the Market: Political and Economic Reforms in Eastern Europe and Latin America* (Cambridge: Cambridge University Press, 1991).

2. Francis Fukuyama, "The End of History?" *The National Interest* (Summer 1989): 4. See also *The End of History and the Last Man* (New York: Free Press, 1992).

3. See Umberto Eco, "Eternal Fascism," *New York Review of Books* 42, no. 11 (June 22, 1995): 12–16.

4. See the special double issue of *Telos* (nos. 98–99, Winter 1993–Spring 1994) on

"The French New Right," and in particular the article by Pierre-Andre Taguieff, "From Race to Culture: The New Right's Vision of European Identity," on the evolution of this movement's views of "Europe and its others," and the "culturalist" defense of Europe against the Third World "others."

5. William E. Connolly, *Identity\Difference: Democratic Negotiations of Political Paradox* (Ithaca: Cornell University Press, 1991); cf. Ernesto Laclau, ed., *The Making of Political Identities* (London: Verso, 1994).

6. Ronald Inglehart, *Culture Shift in Advanced Industrial Society* (Princeton: Princeton University Press, 1990).

7. See Jürgen Habermas, "Dialectics of Rationalization: An Interview," *Telos* 49 (Fall 1981): 5–33, and *Theory of Communicative Action*, trans. T. A. McCarthy, vol. 1: *Reason and the Rationalization of Society* (Boston: Beacon Press, 1984), 339–403.

8. See Claus Offe's essays collected in *Contradictions of the Welfare State*, ed. John Keane (Cambridge, Mass.: MIT Press, 1984), 147–62, 179–207, 292ff.

9. The term "multiculturalism" has been used in recent discussions to refer to phenomena ranging from the integration of migrant workers and postcolonials into European nation-states like France and Germany, to the right of the Francophone community in Quebec to assert its cultural, linguistic, and political autonomy, to debates about teaching the "canon" of the Western tradition in philosophy, literature, and the arts. Because of its confusing deployment in all these instances, the term has practically lost meaning and is not used widely by the contributors to this volume. In its most important manifestations in the U.S.A. context, the politics of multiculturalism is a direct outgrowth of the new social movements of the 1980s. The debates around the canon, however, raise a different set of issues that touch on questions of research methodologies as well as pedagogical philosophies. I have dealt with some of these issues in "What Is Culture?" in Marjorie Garber, ed., *The Work of Culture* (New York: Routledge, forthcoming).

The contribution by Carlos Forment begins to look at some of the issues generated by the politics of multiculturalism in homogeneous nation-states, while Will Kymlicka discusses the specificities of the Canadian case.

10. See Jacques Derrida, "The Other Heading: Memories, Responses, and Responsibilities," *The Other Heading: Reflections on Today's Europe*, trans. Pascalle-Anne Brault and Michael B. Naas (Bloomington: Indiana University Press, 1992); and Jean-François Lyotard, *The Différend: Phrases in Dispute*, trans. Georges Van Den Abbeele (Minneapolis: University of Minnesota Press, 1988). See my essay "Democracy and Difference: Reflections on the Metapolitics of Lyotard and Derrida," *Journal of Political Philosophy* 2, no. 1 (1994): 1–23.

11. See the essays collected under the title *Moral Consciousness and Communicative Action*, trans. C. Lehnhart and S. Weber Nicholsen (Cambridge, Mass.: MIT Press, 1990); see also "On the Pragmatic, the Ethical, and the Moral Employments of Practical Reason," in Habermas, *Justification and Application: Remarks on Discourse Ethics*, trans. C. Cronin (Cambridge, Mass.: MIT Press, 1993).

12. Claude Lefort, "The Question of Democracy," *Democracy and Political Theory*, trans. David Macey (Minneapolis: University of Minnesota Press, 1988), 19.

13. Cf. Nancy Fraser, "Rethinking the Public Sphere: A Contribution to the Critique of Actually Existing Democracy," in Craig Calhoun, ed., *Habermas and the Public Sphere* (Cambridge, Mass.: MIT Press, 1992).

14. See Will Kymlicka, *Multicultural Citizenship* (Oxford: Clarendon, 1995).

15. See Tzvetan Todorov, *The Conquest of America: The Question of the Other*, trans. Richard Howard (New York: Harper Perennial, 1992).

16. Charles Taylor, "The Politics of Recognition," in *Multiculturalism and "The Politics of Recognition,"* ed. Amy Gutmann (Princeton: Princeton University Press, 1992). An expanded edition of this anthology appeared under the title *Multiculturalism: Examining the Politics of Recognition* (Princeton: Princeton University Press, 1994).

17. Joan Landes, *Women and the Public Sphere in the Age of the French Revolution* (Ithaca: Cornell University Press, 1988).

18. See Richard Rorty, "Postmodernist Bourgeois Liberalism," *Journal of Philosophy* 80 (October 1983); reprinted in *Objectivity, Relativism and Truth*, vol. 1 of *Philosophical Papers* (Cambridge: Cambridge University Press, 1991), 197–202.

Part One

DEMOCRATIC THEORY:
FOUNDATIONS AND PERSPECTIVES

One

Three Normative Models of Democracy

JÜRGEN HABERMAS

I WOULD LIKE to sketch a proceduralist view of democracy and deliberative politics that differs in relevant aspects from both the liberal and the republican paradigm. Let me delineate the opposing features of these two established models. I will then introduce a new proceduralist conception by way of a critique of the "ethical overload" of the republican view. The last part of the essay further elaborates the three normative models of democracy by comparing their corresponding images of state and society.

The Two Received Views of Democratic Politics

According to the "liberal" or Lockean view, the democratic process accomplishes the task of programming the government in the interest of society, where the government is represented as an apparatus of public administration, and society as a market-structured network of interactions among private persons. Here politics (in the sense of the citizens' political will-formation) has the function of bundling together and pushing private interests against a government apparatus specializing in the administrative employment of political power for collective goals. On the "republican" view, however, politics involves more than this mediating function; it is rather constitutive for the processes of society as a whole. "Politics" is conceived as the reflective form of substantial ethical life, namely as the medium in which the members of somehow solitary communities become aware of their dependence on one another and, acting with full deliberation as citizens, further shape and develop existing relations of reciprocal recognition into an association of free and equal consociates under law. With this, the liberal architectonic of government and society undergoes an important change: in addition to the hierarchical regulations of the state and the decentralized regulations of the market, that is, besides administrative power and individual personal interests, *solidarity* and the orientation to the common good appear as a *third source* of social integration. In fact, this horizontal political will-formation aimed at mutual understanding or communicatively achieved consensus is even supposed to enjoy priority, both in a genetic and a normative sense. An autonomous basis in civil society, a basis independent of public administration and market-mediated private commerce, is assumed as a precondition for the praxis of civic self-determination. This basis preserves political communication from being swallowed up by the government apparatus or assimilated to market structures. In the republican conception, the political public sphere acquires, along with its base in civil society, a strategic significance. These competing approaches yield two contrasting images of the citizen.

According to the liberal view, the citizen's status is determined primarily according to negative rights they have vis-à-vis the state and other citizens. As bearers of these rights they enjoy the protection of the government, as long as they pursue their private interests within the boundaries drawn by legal statutes—and this includes protection against government interventions. Political rights, such as voting rights and free speech, have not only the same structure but also a similar meaning as civil rights that provide a space within which legal subjects are released from external compulsion. They give citizens the opportunity to assert their private interests in such a way that by means of elections, the composition of parliamentary bodies, and the formation of a government, these interests are finally aggregated into a political will that makes an impact on the administration.

According to the republican view, the status of citizens is not determined by the model of negative liberties to which these citizens can lay claim *as* private persons. Rather, political rights—preeminently rights of political participation and communication—are positive liberties. They guarantee not freedom from external compulsion but the possibility of participation in a common praxis, through the exercise of which citizens can first make themselves into what they want to be—politically autonomous authors of a community of free and equal persons. To this extent, the political process does not just serve to keep government activity under the surveillance of citizens who have already acquired a prior social autonomy in the exercise of their private rights and prepolitical liberties. Just as little does it act as a hinge between state and society, for administrative authority is not at all an autochthonous authority; it is not something given. Rather, this authority emerges from the citizens' power produced communicatively in the praxis of self-legislation, and it finds its legitimation in the fact that it protects this praxis by institutionalizing public liberty. So, the state's raison d'être lies not primarily in the protection of equal private rights but in the guarantee of an inclusive opinion- and will-formation in which free and equal citizens reach an understanding on which goals and norms lie in the equal interest of all.

The polemic against the classical concept of the legal person as bearer of private rights reveals a controversy about the concept of law itself. While in the liberal view the point of a legal order is to make it possible to determine in each case which individuals are entitled to which rights, in the republican view these "subjective" rights owe their existence to an "objective" legal order that both enables and guarantees the integrity of an autonomous life in common based on mutual respect: "For republicans rights ultimately are nothing but determinations of the prevailing political will, while for liberals some rights are always grounded in a 'higher law' of . . . reason."[1] Finally, the different ways of conceptualizing the role of citizen and of law express a deeper disagreement about the *nature of the political process*. In the liberal view, the political process of opinion- and will-formation in the public sphere and in parliament is determined by the competition of strategically acting collectivities trying to maintain or acquire positions of power. Success is measured by the citizens' approval, quantified as votes, of persons and programs. In their choices at the polls, voters give expression to their preferences. Their voting decisions have the same structure as the acts of choice made by participants in a market. They license access to the positions of power that political parties fight over in the same success-oriented attitude.

According to the republican view, the political opinion- and will-formation occurring in the public sphere and in parliament obeys not the structures of market processes but the obstinate structures of a public communication oriented to mutual understanding. For politics, in the sense of a praxis of civic self-legislation, the paradigm is not the market but dialogue. This dialogic conception imagines politics as contestation over questions of value and not simply questions of preference.

Proceduralist vs. Communitarian Views of Politics

The republican model as compared to the liberal one has the advantage of preserving the original meaning of democracy in terms of the institutionalization of a public use of reason jointly exercised by autonomous citizens. This model accounts for those communicative conditions that confer legitimating force on political opinion- and will-formation. These are precisely the conditions under which the political process can be presumed to generate reasonable results. A contest for power, if represented according to the liberal model of market competition, is determined by the rational choice of optimal strategies. Given an indissoluble pluralism of prepolitical values and interests that are at best aggregated with equal weight in the political process, politics loses all reference to the normative core of a public use of reason. The republican trust in the force of political discourses stands in contrast to the liberal skepticism about reason. Such discourses are meant to allow one to discuss value orientations and interpretations of needs and wants, and then to change these in an *insightful way*.

But contemporary republicans tend to give this public communication a communitarian reading. It is precisely this move toward an *ethical constriction of political discourse* that I call into question. Politics may not be assimilated to a hermeneutical process of self-explication of a shared form of life or collective identity. Political questions may not be reduced to the type of ethical questions where we, as members of a community, ask who we are and who we would like to be. In its communitarian interpretation the republican model is too idealistic even within the limits of a purely normative analysis. On this reading, the democratic process is dependent on the virtues of citizens devoted to the public weal. This expectation of virtue already led Rousseau to split the citizen oriented to the common good from the private man, who cannot be ethically overburdened. The unanimity of the political legislature was supposed to be secured in advance by a substantive ethical consensus. In contrast, a discourse-theoretic interpretation insists on the fact that democratic will-formation draws its legitimating force not from a previous convergence of settled ethical convictions but both from the communicative presuppositions that allow the better arguments to come into play in various forms of deliberation and from the procedures that secure fair bargaining processes. Discourse theory breaks with a purely ethical conception of civic autonomy.

According to the communitarian view, there is a necessary connection between the deliberative concept of democracy and the reference to a concrete, substantively integrated ethical community. Otherwise one could not explain, in this view, how the citizens' orientation to the common good would be at all possible. The individual, so the argument goes, can become aware of her co-membership in a collective form of life, and therewith become aware of a prior social bond, only in a practice exercised with others in common. The individual can get a clear sense of commonalities and differences, and hence a sense of who she is and who she would like to be, only in the public exchange with others who owe their identities to the same traditions and similar formation processes. This assimilation of political discourses to the clarification of a collective ethical self-understanding does not sit well with the function of the legislative processes they issue in. Legal statutes no doubt also contain teleological elements, but these involve more than just the hermeneutic explication of shared value orientations. By their very structure laws are determined by the question of which norms citizens want to adopt for regulating their living together. To be sure, discourses aimed at achieving self-understanding—discourses in which the participants want to get a clear understanding of themselves as members of a specific nation, as members of a locale or a state, as inhabitants of a region, and so on; in which they want to determine which traditions they will continue; in which they strive to determine how they will treat one another, and how they will treat minorities and marginal groups; in short, discourses in which they want to get clear about the kind of society they want to live in—such discourses are also an important part of politics. But these questions are subordinate to moral questions and connected with pragmatic questions. Moral questions in the narrow sense of the Kantian tradition are questions of justice. The question having *priority* in legislative politics concerns how a matter can be regulated in the equal interest of all. The making of norms is primarily a justice issue and is gauged by principles that state what is equally good for all. And unlike ethical questions, questions of justice are not related from the outset to a specific collective and its form of life. The politically enacted law of a concrete legal community must, if it is to be legitimate, at least be compatible with moral tenets that claim universal validity going beyond the legal community.

Moreover, compromises make up the bulk of political processes. Under conditions of religious, or in any way cultural and societal pluralism, politically relevant goals are often selected by interests and value orientations that are by no means constitutive for the identity of the community at large, hence for the whole of an intersubjectively shared form of life. The political interests and values that stand in conflict with each other without prospects of consensus are in need of a balancing that cannot be achieved through ethical discourses—even if the outcomes of bargaining processes are subject to the proviso that they must not violate a culture's agreed-upon basic values. The required balance of competing interests comes about as a compromise between parties that may rely on mutual threats. A legitimate kind of bargaining certainly depends on a prior regulation of fair terms for achieving results, which are acceptable for all parties on the basis of their differing preferences. While debates on such regulations should assume the forms of practical discourse that neutralize power, bargaining itself well allows for strategic interactions. The deliberative mode of legislative practice is not intended just to ensure the ethical validity of laws. Rather, one can understand the complex validity claim of legal norms as the claim, on the one hand, to compromise competing interests in a manner compatible with the common good and, on the other hand, to bring universalistic principles of justice into the horizon of the specific form of life of a particular community.

In contrast to the ethical constriction of political discourse, the concept of deliberative politics acquires empirical reference only when we take account of the multiplicity of communicative forms of rational political will-formation. It is not discourse of an ethical type that could grant on its own the democratic genesis of law. Instead, deliberative politics should be conceived as a syndrome that depends on a network of fairly regulated bargaining processes and of various forms of argumentation, including pragmatic, ethical, and moral discourses, each of which relies on different communicative presuppositions and procedures. In legislative politics the supply of information and the rational choice of strategies are interwoven with the balancing of interests, with the achievement of ethical self-understanding and the articulation of strong preferences, with moral justification and tests of legal coherence. Thus "dia-, logical" and "instrumental" politics, the two ideal-types that Frank Michelman has opposed in a polarizing fashion,[2] do in fact interpenetrate in the medium of deliberations of various kinds.

Images of State and Society

If we start from this proceduralist concept of deliberative politics, this reading of democracy has implications for the concept of society. Both the liberal and the republican model presuppose a view of society as centered in the state—be it the state as guardian of a market-society or the state as the self-conscious institutionalization of an ethical community.

According to the *liberal view*, the democratic process takes place in the form of compromises between competing interests. Fairness is supposed to be granted by the general and equal right to vote, the representative composition of parliamentary bodies, by decision rules, and so on. Such rules are ultimately justified in terms of liberal basic rights. According to the *republican view*, democratic will-formation takes place in the form of an ethical-political discourse; here deliberation can rely on a culturally established background consensus shared by the citizenry. Discourse theory takes elements from both sides and integrates these in the concept of an ideal procedure for deliberation and decision-making. Weaving together pragmatic considerations, compromises, discourses of self-understanding, and justice, this democratic procedure grounds the presumption that reasonable or fair results are obtained. According to this proceduralist view, practical reason withdraws from universal human rights, or from the concrete ethical substance of a specific community, into the rules of discourse and forms of argumentation. In the final analysis, the normative content arises from the very structure of communicative actions. These descriptions of the democratic process set the stage for different conceptualizations of state and society.

According to the republican view, the citizens' political opinion- and will-formation forms the medium through which society constitutes itself as a political whole. Society is, from the very start, political society—*societas civilis*. Hence democracy becomes equivalent to the political self-organization of society as a whole. This leads to a *polemic understanding of politics directed against the state apparatus*. In Hannah Arendt's political writings one can see where republican argumentation directs its salvos: in opposition to the privatism of a depoliticized population and in opposition to the acquisition of legitimation through entrenched parties, the public sphere should be revitalized to the point where a regenerated citizenry can, in the forms of a decentralized self-governance, (once again) appropriate the power of pseudo-independent state agencies. From this perspective, society would finally develop into a political totality.

Whereas the separation of the state apparatus from society elicits a polemical reaction from the republican side, according to the liberal view it cannot be eliminated but only bridged by the democratic process. The regulated balancing of power and interests has need of constitutional channeling, of course. The democratic will-formation of self-interested citizens is laden with comparatively weak normative expectations. The constitution is supposed to tame the state apparatus through normative constraints (such as basic rights, separation of powers, etc.) and to force it, through the competition of political parties on the one hand and that between government and opposition on the other, to take adequate account of competing interests and value orientations. This *state-centered understanding of politics* can forego the unrealistic assumption of a citizenry capable of collective action. Its focus is not so much the input of a rational political will-formation but the output of sensible and effective administrative accomplishments. Liberal argumentation aims its salvos against the potential disturbance of an administrative power that interferes with the spontaneous forces of a self-regulating society. The liberal model hinges not on the democratic self-determination of deliberating citizens but on the legal institutionalization of an economic society that is supposed to guarantee an essentially nonpolitical common good by the satisfaction of private preferences.

Discourse theory invests the democratic process with normative connotations stronger than those found in the liberal model but weaker than those of the republican model. Once again, it takes elements from both sides and fits them together in a new way. In agreement with republicanism, it gives center stage to the process of political opinion- and will-formation, but without understanding the constitution as something secondary; rather it conceives the principles of the constitutional state as a consistent answer to the question of how the demanding communicative forms of a democratic opinion- and will-formation can be institutionalized. Discourse theory has the success of deliberative politics depend not on a collectively acting citizenry but on the institutionalization of the corresponding procedures and conditions of communication. Proceduralized popular sovereignty and a political system tied in to the peripheral networks of the political public sphere go hand-in-hand with the image of a *decentered society*. This concept of democracy no longer needs to operate with the notion of a social whole centered in the state and imagined as a goal-oriented subject writ large. Just as little does it represent the whole in a system of constitutional norms mechanically regulating the interplay of powers and interests in accordance with the market model.

Discourse theory altogether jettisons certain premises of the *philosophy of consciousness*. Either these premises invite us to ascribe the praxis of civic self-determination to one encompassing macrosubject, or they have us apply the rule of law to many isolated private subjects. The former approach views the citizenry as a collective actor that reflects the whole and acts for it; in the latter, individual actors function as dependent variables in system processes that move along blindly. Discourse theory works instead with the *higher-level intersubjectivity* of communication processes that flow through both the parliamentary bodies and the informal networks of the public sphere. Within and outside the parliamentary complex, these subjectless forms of communication constitute arenas in which a more or less rational opinion- and will-formation can take place.

Informal public opinion-formation generates "influence"; influence is transformed into "communicative power" through the channels of political elections; and communicative power is again transformed into "administrative power" through legislation. As in the liberal model, the boundaries between "state" and "society" are respected; but in this case, civil society provides the social basis of autonomous public spheres that remain as distinct from the economic system as from the administration. This understanding of democracy suggests a new balance between the three resources of money, administrative power, and solidarity, from which modern societies meet their needs for integration. The normative implications are obvious: the integrative force of "solidarity," which can no longer be drawn solely from sources of communicative action, should develop through widely expanded and differentiated public spheres as well as through legally institutionalized procedures of democratic deliberation and decision-making. It should gain the strength to hold its own against the two other mechanisms of social integration—money and administrative power.

This view has implications for how one understands legitimation and popular sovereignty.

On the liberal view, democratic will-formation has the exclusive function of *legitimating* the exercise of political power. Election results are the license to assume governmental power, whereas the government must justify the use of power to the public. On the republican view, democratic will-formation has the significantly stronger function of *constituting* society as a political community and keeping the memory of this founding act alive with each election. The government is not only empowered to exercise a largely open mandate but also programmatically committed to carry out certain policies. It remains bound to a self-governing political community. Discourse theory brings a third idea into play: the procedures and communicative presuppositions of democratic opinion- and will-formation function as the most important sources for the discursive rationalization of the decisions of an administration constrained by law and statute. Rationalization means more than mere legitimation but less than the constitution of political power. The power available to the administration changes its aggregate condition as soon as it emerges from a public use of reason and a communicative power that do not just monitor the exercise of political power in a belated manner but more or less program it as well. Notwithstanding this discursive rationalization, only the administrative system itself can "act." The administration is a subsystem specialized for collectively binding decisions, whereas the communicative structures of the public sphere comprise a far-flung network of sensors that in the first place react to the pressure of societywide problematics and stimulate influential opinions. The public opinion that is worked up via democratic procedures into communicative power cannot "rule" of itself, but can only point the use of administrative power in specific directions.

The concept of popular sovereignty stems from the republican appropriation and revaluation of the early modern notion of sovereignty initially associated with absolutist regimes. The state, which monopolizes all the means for a legitimate implementation of force, is seen as an overpowering concentrate of power—as the Leviathan. This idea was transferred by Rousseau to the will of the united people. He fused the strength of the Leviathan with the classical idea of the self-rule of free and equal citizens and combined it with his modern concept of autonomy. Despite this sublimation, the concept of sovereignty remained bound to the notion of an embodiment in the assembled, physically present people. According to the republican view, the people are the bearers of a sovereignty that in principle cannot be delegated: in their sovereign character the people cannot have others represent them. Liberalism opposes this with the more realistic view that in the constitutional state any authority originating from the people is exercised only "by means of elections and voting and by specific legislative, executive, and judicial organs."[3]

These two views would exhaust the alternatives only if we had to conceive state and society in terms of the whole and its parts—where the whole is constituted either by a sovereign citizenry or by a constitution. To the discourse theory of democracy corresponds, however, the image of a decentered society. To be sure, with the political public sphere the proceduralist model sets off an arena for the detection, identification, and interpretation of those problems that affect society as a whole. But the "self" of the self-organizing legal community here disappears in the subjectless forms of communication that regulate the flow of deliberations in such a way that their fallible results enjoy the presumption of rationality. This is not to denounce the intuition connected with the idea of popular sovereignty but to interpret it in intersubjective terms. Popular sovereignty, even if it becomes anonymous, retreats into democratic procedures and the legal implementation of their demanding communicative presuppositions only in order to make itself felt as communicatively generated power. Strictly speaking, this communicative power springs from the interactions between legally institutionalized will-formation and culturally mobilized publics. The latter, for their part, find a basis in the associations of a civil society quite distinct from both state and economy alike.

Read in procedural terms, the idea of popular sovereignty refers to a context that, while enabling the self-organization of a legal community, is not at the disposal of the citizens' will in any way. Deliberation is certainly supposed to provide the medium for a more or less conscious integration of the *legal community*; but this mode does not extend to the whole of society in which the political system is *embedded* as only one among several subsystems. Even in its own proceduralist self-understanding, deliberative politics remains a component of a complex society, which as a whole resists the normative approach practiced in legal theory. In this regard the discourse-theoretic reading of democracy has a point of contact with a detached sociological approach that considers the political system neither the peak nor the center, nor even the formative model of society in general, but just one action system among others. On the other hand, politics must still be able to communicate, through the medium of law, with all the other legitimately ordered spheres of action, however these happen to be structured and steered.

Notes

1. F. I. Michelman, "Conceptions of Democracy in American Constitutional Argument: Voting Rights," *Florida Law Review* 41, no. 3 (July 1989): 446f.
2. Ibid.
3. Cf. *The Basic Law of the Federal Republic of Germany*, article 20, sec. 2.

Two

Fugitive Democracy

SHELDON S. WOLIN

> . . . beyond all civil bounds.
> *Shakespeare,* Twelfth Night, *1.4.21*

> Democracy seems to revive in a scene of wild
> disorder and tumult . . .
> *Adam Ferguson,* An Essay on the History of Civil
> Society, *part 1, sec. 10*

BY WAY OF preliminaries I want to set out my own understanding of some basic concepts so that the reader may have some notion of the orientation that guides my discussion.

I shall take the *political* to be an expression of the idea that a free society composed of diversities can nonetheless enjoy moments of commonality when, through public deliberations, collective power is used to promote or protect the well-being of the collectivity. *Politics* refers to the legitimized and public contestation, primarily by organized and unequal social powers, over access to the resources available to the public authorities of the collectivity. Politics is continuous, ceaseless, and endless. In contrast, the political is episodic, rare.

Democracy is one among many versions of the political, but it is peculiar in being the one idea that most other versions pay lip service to. I am reluctant, for reasons to be discussed later, to describe democracy as a "form" of government or as a type of politics distinguished by its "experimentalism."[1] In my understanding, democracy is a project concerned with the political potentialities of ordinary citizens, that is, with their possibilities for becoming political beings through the self-discovery of common concerns and of modes of action for realizing them.

I

The notion of boundaries is a rich and complex one. Boundaries proclaim identity and stand ready to repel difference. They may signify exclusion— "keep out!"—or containment—"keep inside!" Those who guarded the Berlin

Wall were as much concerned to keep their citizens in as to keep foreigners out. In most modern political discourse, boundaries are commonly identified with frontiers, frontiers with nation-states, and the state with the bearer of the political.

This cluster of notions can be illustrated by Hobbes's striking metaphor of sovereign authorities that are "in the state and posture of gladiators" standing guard at "the frontiers of their kingdoms." In Hobbes's formulation, the frontier protected by "forts, garrisons and guns" separates the antipolitical state of nature from political society and from "the industry of their subjects," from, that is, a private condition that the power of the sovereign is constructed to secure and that Hobbes fondly hoped would serve to sublimate the political passions that might otherwise challenge the sovereign's monopoly upon the political.[2] There is no public or legitimized politics in Hobbes's scheme; each has been squeezed between the absolute political in the form of the sovereign on the one hand and, on the other, the private domain of absolute, competitive self-interested men protected by it.

Both as container and as excluder, boundaries work to foster the impression of a circumscribed space in which likeness dwells, the likeness of natives, of an autochthonous people, or of a nationality, or of citizens with equal rights. Likeness is prized because it appears as the prime ingredient of unity. Unity, in turn, is thought to be the sine qua non of collective power. During the nineteenth century, however, boundaries were associated with collective identity defined in historical and cultural terms and identified with a nation. Nationalism was, and is today, an avid proliferator of boundaries. Nationalism absorbs the political into the pursuit of a homogeneous identity that is sometimes quickened through such purgatives as ethnic cleansing or the imposition of religious orthodoxy.

As the twentieth century winds to a close, the preoccupation with boundaries has not diminished. If anything it has become intensified. Postmodern cultural politics follows in the footsteps of nationalism in insisting upon boundaries that establish differences (as in gender or racial politics) but proclaims identities as well. Here, too, the political becomes associated with purification or, more precisely, a reversal in which the stigma of impurity as well as the badge of purity are switched so that the pariah or victimized group is now pure, even innocent, while the dominant group is impure.[3] Politics centers around the unmasking of the various disguises of oppression regardless of whether the alleged act has occurred yesterday, or in the distant past, or in an ancient text of philosophy, a nursery fable, a textbook, a modern novel, or a Senate confirmation hearing. Here the quest for boundaries has been closely linked with a myth of homogeneity that seeks to establish cultural perimeters within which oppression disappears. Dwelling amid similars, human beings will now be free at last to enjoy a good that is truly common. The vision is of a political in which similarities are treated as commonalities and purity/innocence is adopted as a prophylactic against the politics of mere power.[4]

II

Boundaries are the outlines of a context; or, more precisely, boundaries signify the will to contextualize. Politically, contextualization signifies the domestication of politics in a double sense. A domestic politics is established with its distinctive practices and forms and distinguished from those of similarly bounded societies and from international or intercontextual politics. But the domestication of politics also corresponds to one dictionary definition of domestication, "to tame, bring under control." The "native country" (*domus*) is the site of *domitus* or "taming."

What do boundaries bound? How is the space circumscribed by boundaries filled in or structured? And how does that "fill" or structure relate to democracy and, most importantly, to its prospects? Boundaries are a metaphor of containment. I shall try to show that the reality cloaked in the metaphor of boundaries is the containment of democracy and that the crucial boundary is a constitution.

For some of the familiar exemplars of modern theory—Hobbes, Hegel, Weber—the answer to the question of what is bounded by boundaries was: the constitution that founded the authority and power of the state. The political in this reading is the active element, concentrated in those who lead. Political leadership is both the management of collective desires, resentments, anger, fantasies, fears, and hopes and the curatorship of the simulacra of democracy.[5] The political is focused upon an organization of power that guarantees domestic peace and security, including the security of the state; that promotes, guards, oversees, and interlocks with the corporate powers upon which the citizenry is dependent for their material well-being; that adjudicates social conflicts, punishes lawbreakers, and keeps the whole of society under a watchful eye; and that is continually trying to reconcile or conceal the contradiction between the state as the symbol of justice, impartiality, and the guardian of the general welfare—the steady state—with a dynamic politics that registers the intense competition that pervades not only the economy but cultural formations as well.[6] To contain that contradiction, the state cultivates the political education of its citizens to instill the virtues of loyalty, obedience, law-abidingness, patriotism, and sacrifice in wartime. Through the practice of those virtues, the state encourages identification of the self with the power of the state, the surrogate of participation and the sublimate of self-interest.

It is easy to think of democracy and constitution as "naturally" belonging together and each as incomplete without the other; to refer unself-consciously to a "constitutional democracy"; and to assume that democracy is the sort of political phenomenon whose teleological or even ideological destination is a constitutional form.

What this means, literally, is that democracy as we know it in the self-styled "advanced industrial democracies" has been constituted, that is, given forms, structure, and boundaries. Constitutional democracy is democracy fitted to a constitution. It is not democratic or democratized constitutionalism because it is democracy without the demos as actor. Its politics is based not, as its defenders allege, upon "representative democracy" but on various representations of democracy: democracy as represented in public opinion polls, electronic town meetings and phone-ins, and as votes. In sum, a constitution regulates the amount of democratic politics that is let in.

The crucial institution is the Presidency. As chief executive the President symbolizes the modern hope that politics may be regularized as policy and rationalized as administration; at the same time he is, as the textbooks constantly remind, the one politician elected by the whole body of the people. Thus he is the tribune who administers; he is democracy *and* rationality. He is also the cruelest symbol of the impotence of the demos and, fittingly, the highest office of constitutional democracy. The demos has no effective voice in what the President does, yet once the election is over their mythical act is carefully preserved as ritual and invoked whenever a President feels the need of courting public support. Voting merges into a fluent process whose illusory connection with the demos is prolonged by the periodic election of senators and representatives and by the continuous commentary manufactured by the media. The result is an illusion of perpetual political motion launched initially by democratic elections. Meanwhile a parallel politics of process—legislative, administrative, judicial, and military—flows continuously of its own accord. Electoral campaigns are preserved as the lessons that consultants huckster. For the demos they are soon forgotten. It must now get its politics vicariously and passively through the pronouncements of television oracles, talk-show babble, and the political burlesque hustled by the pundits.

Thus a constitution in setting limits to politics sets limits as well to democracy, constituting it in ways compatible with and legitimating of the dominant power groups in the society. Not only are constitutions about what is legal and what is illegal political activity, but they regulate the amount of politics, the temporal rhythms or periodicity of politics, and they give it ritualistic forms—for example, every four years the "voice of the people" is given the opportunity to "speak" by entering an appropriate mark beside the name of one or another Presidential candidate. In the political economy, elections are "free" in the double sense that no one coerces the citizen into voting, and the voter does not pay directly for the privilege of voting; that expense is footed by the dominant powers that organize, operate, and finance campaigns. For them elections are investment opportunities from which they hope to reap a return.

III

But for reasons diametrically opposed to Hobbes, the idea of boundaries as frontiers is anathema to some postmodern writers. Boundaries signify that the state has predetermined that the primary locus of the individual's concerns and commitments should be within the boundaries presided over by the state when, in fact, the contemporary individual may consider that her deepest concerns are with certain groups of foreign women rather than with her fellow citizens. The Hobbesian notion of "frontiers" has also been disputed on other grounds: as anachronistic by those who claim that all mankind now inhabits an electronic "Global Village"; or as obstructionist by those who point to the grave problems whose causes and solutions defy political boundaries; pollution, famine, abuses of human rights, nuclear weapons, and epidemics. Thus whereas boundaries signified to the early modern the limits of the political, to the postmodern they are a sign of its limitations.[7] In the attempt to transcend boundaries these views strain to enlarge the political by retaining the core notion of shared concerns and values while extending them to include humanity. But that conception of the political reproduces the conception associated with representative government, a trustee or stewardship notion of acting on behalf or in the interests of others with the tacit assumption—also held by modern champions of representative government—that the vast majority of the "others" had an "interest" but not a coherent, that is, well-informed opinion about how to protect or promote it. The highest political expression of the postmodern ideal is of a Rio Conference where the representatives of boundary-transcending human interests meet face-to-face with representatives of sovereign states.

IV

The modern state as the guardian of boundaries has been rendered paradoxical, if not anachronistic, because of the problematical status of boundaries. The many phenomena that seem to escape or transcend boundaries, for example, electronic communications, are often cited as confirmation of the real existence of the postmodern. If such is the case, then that development may shed some light not only on the future of the state, and its conception of the political, but also on the democratic or nondemocratic tendency of the postmodern.

Postmoderns are not alone in being indifferent to boundaries. The forms of power upon which the modern state has come to depend are notoriously cavalier about boundaries. Thus modern state-power is inseparable from modern science and technologies; both are boundary-leapers, and to an important extent both carry their own contexts. Further, modern state-power is deeply dependent upon the market. Market activity too has its share of indifference to national boundaries and its own ethos-creating context. Then, too, from its beginnings the modern state was indelibly shaped by those who claimed to possess systematic forms of knowledge that would advance the power of the state and place it on firmer foundations. Lawyers, financiers, administrators, and then economists shaped state bureaucracies; but as their skills became more systematic, even scientific, they too assumed a universalist character. Like the ancient royal courts, the modern state also aspires to intellectual and artistic embellishment to its power. It subsidizes and honors writers, artists, actors, musicians, and scholars who then respond with contributions. The Kennedy Center is as much the symbol of state power as the Bell Laboratories. But the contemporary artist, scholar and intellectual is also a multinational operative, at home in any performance center.

Finally, the state itself, though the boundary-keeper par excellence, is also a great boundary-defier that seeks to project its power abroad, carrying with it the contributions of the components just described. In passing, we might note that each of the components of state power—scientific, technological, economic, and cultural—is a representation and perpetuation of elitism.

The *domus* has thus become the equivalent of a home base of operations, a launching pad for projecting the modern forms of power. The constitution of the *domus* provides a stable foundation that guarantees to the state a steady supply of human and material resources. The democratization of "advanced industrial democracies" comes down to this: the labor, wealth, and psyches of the citizenry are simultaneously defended and exploited, protected and extracted, nurtured and fleeced, rewarded and commanded, flattered and threatened.

V

The democracy we are familiar with is constitutionalized democracy, democracy indistinguishable from its constitutional form. Its modern ideological justification can be found in Harrington, the English republicans, *The Federalist*, and Tocqueville. Each was a critic of democracy. Each records a reaction to revolution, although not a reactionary reaction. Each of their constitutions is constructed against democracy; while each seeks to repress democracy none seeks to suppress it. It is to be given a "place," as the American framers did in the House of Representatives, otherwise the legitimacy allegedly bestowed by "the sovereign people" would lack all credibility.

The representation of democracy that the theorists of modern constitu-tionalized democracy have sought to counteract is as old as the classical theo-ries of Plato and Aristotle and was a staple of early modern political thought. It is the specter of democracy as lawless and prone to fits of violence. "A popular state," according to Jean Bodin, "is always the refuge of all disorderly spirits, rebels, traitors, outcasts who encourage and help the lower orders to ruin the great. The laws they hold in no esteem."[8] Madison warned that "[pure] democracies have ever been spectacles of turbulence and contention; have ever been found incompatible with personal security, or the rights of property; and have in general been as short in their lives, as they have been violent in their deaths."[9]

Tocqueville once complained of there being no example of a democracy introduced without revolutions; and he proceeded to invent one, claiming that the reason for the stability of American democracy was that, unlike France, democracy in America was not the creature of revolution.[10] Tocque-ville's eagerness to dissociate democracy from revolution and his concern over not finding supporting examples invite the question of how the two phenom-ena became associated in the first place and what that association reveals about democracy.

The truth contained in those images of democratic disorder is that histori-cally modern democracy and ancient Athenian democracy all emerged in combination with revolution. In each case (the fifth century B.C.E., the 1640s, 1776, and 1989) revolution inspired the creation of democratic ideas and radically enlarged the circle of political participants to include the active in-volvement of social classes hitherto excluded or marginal.

Revolution might be defined for our purpose as the wholesale transgression of inherited forms. It is the extreme antithesis to a settled constitution, whether that constitution is represented by documents ("basic laws") or by recognized systems or practice. Democracy was born in transgressive acts, for the demos could not participate in power without shattering the class, status, and value systems by which it was excluded.

VI

What we tend to think of as systematic political philosophy is conventionally said to have begun with Plato and Aristotle in fourth-century Athens. The modern tendency for philosophy to set the terms for interpreting Plato and Aristotle has obscured another achievement of the ancient thinkers. They also invented constitutionalism, the theory and political science of constitutions. They intended it to be a measured, antidotal response to the democratic revo-lutions of the fifth century B.C.E. and the consequent democratization of the Athenian constitution. Constitutional theory was distinctive for its urge to use the political to synthesize the entire life of the polis, to encapsulate it within a form, and then to distribute/enclose the varieties of political life within a classificatory scheme of constitutions. Yet that enterprise harbored an inner tension that was evident even in the ideal form of Plato's *Republic*. At one juncture of the dialogue Socrates declaims: "The object on which we fixed our eyes in the establishment of *our* state was not the exceptional happiness of any one class but the greatest possible happiness of the city as a whole" (420c). But having posited that ideal of solidarity, Socrates then proceeds to sketch an ideal society in which class divisions are etched in the sharpest possible lines of superiority/inferiority. The same problem of combining commonality with exclusivity crops up in Aristotle's three well-ordered constitutions. The identity of each form was dependent upon excluding some distinct social elements from political citizenship.[11] In the end Aristotle concedes that each constitutional form embodies the values and interests of a ruling class and hence in one way or another each is deficient in commonality.[12]

These tensions were strikingly preserved in some passages in Cicero's *De Republica*. Cicero has his own Socrates in Scipio Africanus who recites the arguments for each of the conventional forms of rule, monarchy, aristocracy, and democracy. In the surviving manuscripts, the longest and most systematic discussion is devoted to that *civitas* "in which the power of the people is the greatest" (1.31.47). In presenting the case for democracy, Scipio declares that only the *res populi* deserves to be called a *res publica* (1.32.48). *Res publica* was not only the phrase designating the political identity of the Romans of Cicero's day but also the quintessential rendering of what Romans understood as the political: that which was of common concern and belonged to all. Those connotations linked it more closely to the Latin for democracy, *res populi*, than to the exclusivist language associated with aristocracy, oligarchy, or monarchy.

Centuries later, Karl Marx remarked that democracy was the basis of every constitution in the sense that each pays its respects to the principle of commonality but without allowing the people to rule.[13] But throughout history it is not difficult to identify the social groups whose interests have been consistently exploited so as to render commonality a mockery; it has been the same groups that have been excluded from active participation in the political.[14]

Democracy is not about where the political is located but about how it is experienced. Revolutions activate the demos and destroy boundaries that bar access to political experience. Individuals from the excluded social strata take on responsibilities, deliberate about goals and choices, and share in decisions that have broad consequences and affect unknown and distant others. Thus revolutionary transgression is the means by which the demos makes itself political. It is by *stasis*, not *physis*, that the demos acquires a civic nature.

For the very idea of equality is transgressive of the social and political boundaries that have formed the precondition for political exclusion, which, in turn, is the precondition for legitimizing economic exploitation. Those boundaries have been formed around highly prized scarce values, such as noble birth, wealth, military prowess, and certain forms of arcane knowledge, the possession of which forms the basis of a claim to power, that is, to office. The excluded—farmers, artisans, mechanics, resident foreigners, women, slaves—represent values and virtues that are, at best, minimally valued even though, as Aristotle recognized in the case of manual workers and slaves, their activities were "necessary" to the being if not the excellence of a society.

The story of Athenian democracy was of a succession of popular uprisings that succeeded in transforming the so-called ancestral constitution and its various boundaries so that eventually, in the words of Apollodorus, "the Athenian demos has supreme authority over all things in the polis and it is in its power to do whatever it wishes" (59.88).

But the democracy carried along by revolution comes to appear as surplus democracy when revolutions are ended and the permanent institutionalization of politics is begun. Consider the narrowing of the political that is represented in the contrast in Locke's *Second Treatise* between, on the one hand, the state of nature, where each individual has to use his own judgment in executing the law of nature—where, in other words, participation is universal, obligatory but fluent—and, on the other, the three prerequisites of a political society postulated by Locke: "an established, settled, known Law," "a known and indifferent Judge," and an effective executive.[15] The political has become specialized, regularized, and administrative in character and quality. Institutionalization marks the attenuation of democracy: leaders begin to appear; hierarchies develop; experts of one kind or another cluster around the centers of decision; order, procedure, and precedent displace a more spontaneous politics: in retrospect the latter appears as disorganized, inefficient.[16] Democracy thus seems destined to be a moment rather than a form. Throughout the history of political thought virtually all writers emphasize the unstable and temporary character of democracy.[17] Why is it that democracy is reduced, even devitalized by form? Why is its presence occasional and fugitive?

VII

In an attempt to throw some light on those questions I want to turn to that workhorse of modern political theory, the state of nature, especially in its Lockean formulation. Although the Hobbesian state of nature is clearly one where the idea of boundaries does not operate and where a prepolitical condition reigns, for Locke it is a condition that is "bounded" by the law of nature. What that law "bounds" is a condition of commonality and "Equality . . . without Subordination or Subjection." We might call Locke's construct a democracy without form. In that "one community of nature," each is under an obligation "to preserve the rest of Mankind" by enforcing the law of nature (2.4, 6). Originally, too, all men hold the earth in common, including its natural "fruits" and "the Beasts it feeds" (2.26). Thus, insofar as these elements of commonality exist and each man performs the public role of guardian of the law of nature, the condition could be described as political and democratic.

But the "natural" commonality of Locke's state of nature seems artificial because of its near absolute homogeneity. To the modern, Madisonian eye it appears as a condition lacking that most modern of phenomena, conflicts between different interests. Notwithstanding the suggestion of heterogeneous elements in Locke's description of the origins of private property and money in the state of nature, once his argument begins to crystallize around the main event, the contract, heterogeneity is suspended and plays no part in the consensus—with one exception, as we shall see shortly. When contract time approaches, distinctions of property, class, religion, gender, race, ethnicity, or language are blacked out; or, more precisely, the distinctions previously acknowledged, as between husband and wife, parents and child, master and servant, are treated by Locke as special cases because they are nonpolitical (2.80–86). Those differentia are ignored by Locke when he prepares his argument for the contract, because without a postulate consisting of the homogeneity of democratic commonality Locke would have lacked the mechanism needed to operationalize an agreement among similar individuals.

What homogeneity makes possible is a species of power based upon non-differentiation. The power of homogeneity is most strikingly evident in the language that Locke used to introduce the idea of a majority constructed from the consent of single but unsingular men: "For when any number of Men have by the consent of every individual, made a 'community,' they have thereby made that Community one Body, with a Power to Act as one Body, which is only by the will and determination of the majority" (2.96). The assumption behind Locke's claim that a community has "a Power to Act as one Body" is that it was composed of equal and undifferentiated units, each of whose act of consent was a registry of similar units of power. When added together their sum enabled the community to act as one body: " 'The Body should move whither the greater force carries it' which was 'the will and determination of the majority' " (2.96). Yet when Locke attempted to meet the argument that "one body" seemed to imply unanimity rather than a majority and that the mere notion of a majority was a confession that heterogeneity rather than homogeneity—inequality/difference rather than equality/similarity—had prevailed in the state of nature, he fell back on a commonsense rationale that casts doubt upon the homogeneity of interests in the state of nature. Unanimity is an impossible basis of action because "the Infirmities of Health and Avocations of Business, which a number, though much less than that of a Common-wealth, will necessarily keep many away from the publick Assembly" (2.96).

But Locke then continues his retreat from the homogeneity of the state of nature: "To which if we add the variety of Opinions and contrariety of Interests which unavoidably happens in all Collections of Men," then "insistence upon unanimity can only end in the dissolution of the community" (2.96). Thus, the homogeneity of the state of nature turns out to have been the suspension of heterogeneity.

Yet the state of nature is not so much a fiction as a metaphor of lost commonality, an exceptional moment that keeps returning in times of revolutionary crisis when power returns to "the Community" and agency to "the People." The democratic moments in revolutions have been the carriers of commonality, the perduring conscience of the political: "The Power that every individual gave the Society, when he entered it, can never revert to the Individuals again, as long as the Society lasts, but will always remain in the Community" (2.243).

Homogeneity might then be reinterpreted. When Locke's individuals place themselves under an obligation to observe the law of nature and to treat others as free and equal beings, they create homogeneity not as a description but as a norm.

VIII

> If any democracy has ever flourished, it has been at
> its peak for only a brief period, so long as the
> people were neither numerous enough nor strong
> enough to cause insolence because of their good
> fortune, or jealousy because of their ambition.
>   *Dion Cassius 44.2*

That heterogeneity should emerge in Locke's state of nature is not a tribute to its universality or naturalness. Rather, heterogeneity is a consequence of liberty and equality, the two values that since antiquity have been associated solely with democracy.[18] As Tocqueville observed of Jacksonian America, democratic equality results in an extraordinary release of human energies, the net result of which is social inequalities arising from individual differences of natural endowment, luck, and circumstance.[19] Add the peculiarity of democratic liberty that it shields antidemocratic forms of power—corporations are "persons" that enjoy some of the same rights as individuals while its officers acquire immunities denied to ordinary citizens, and the fugitive character of democracy is no mystery. For whereas democratic freedom encourages the expression of diversity and its attendant fragmentation of the homogeneity signified by "the people," some fragments are less fragmented than others. Multiculturalism and multinational corporations are not equivalences.

The surrogate of lost homogeneity and of the power of the demos is majority rule; but constitutionalism, especially in its Madisonian version, is designed to strew as many barriers as possible to democratic power.

IX

I have been attempting to retrieve aspects of democracy that suggest a tension with the organizational impulses of ancient and modern constitutionalism. A reflection of that tension is the fact that democracy has no continuous history following the absorption of Athens into the Macedonian empire. From 322 B.C.E. to the political experiments launched by the American and French revolutions of the eighteenth century, there were examples of city-state republics in which the "people" sometimes had a small share, but the evidence overwhelmingly indicates that these were oligarchies dominated by the rich and well-born. That hiatus ends in the destruction of democratic hopes by the failure of modern revolutions and in the creation, instead, of the modern representation of democracy, the nation-state organization. Today democracy is universally acclaimed as the only true criterion of legitimacy for political systems, and its real presence is said to consist of free elections, free political parties, and free press. And, of course, the free market. The specifications are so precise that the United States periodically dispatches experts to Central America to determine whether those requirements have been met.

Paradoxically, while hardly anyone questions that the self-styled "advanced industrialized democracies" really are democracies, fewer still care to argue that "the people" actually rule in any one of them, or that it would be a good idea if it did. For in societies where managerial rule is widely practiced, democracy appears as inherently crude and hence unsuited for the task of governing complex and rapidly changing societies. At the same time in those quarters, it is often declared that democracy demands such a high level of political sophistication from citizens as to make it doubtful that it can be mastered by Third World peoples. Thus democracy is too simple for complex societies and too complex for simple ones.

What is actually being measured by the claim of democratic legitimacy is not the vitality of democracy in those nations but the degree to which democracy is attenuated so as to serve other ends. The most fundamental of these is the establishment and development of the modernizing state. The so-called problem of contemporary democracy is not, as is often alleged, that the ancient conception of democracy is incompatible with the size and scale of modern political societies. Rather it is that any conception of democracy grounded in the citizen-as-actor and politics-as-episodic is incompatible with the modern choice of the state as the fixed center of political life and the corollary conception of politics as continuous activity organized around a single dominating objective, control of or influence over the state apparatus.

Democracy in the late modern world cannot be a complete political system, and given the awesome potentialities of modern forms of power and what they exact of the social and natural world, it ought not to be hoped or striven for. Democracy needs to be reconceived as something other than a form of government: as a mode of being that is conditioned by bitter experience, doomed to succeed only temporarily, but is a recurrent possibility as long as the memory of the political survives. The experience of which democracy is the witness is the realization that the political mode of existence is such that it can be, and is, periodically lost. Democracy, Polybius remarks, lapses "in the course of time" (6.39). Democracy is a political moment, perhaps *the* political moment, when the political is remembered and re-created. Democracy is a rebellious moment that may assume revolutionary, destructive proportions, or may not.

Today it is no longer fashionable to appeal to cycles of government or to states of nature. Yet it might be argued that a belief in the restorative power of democracy is still part of the American political consciousness. Certain events support that belief: the recurrent experience of constituting political societies and political practices, beginning with colonial times and extending through the Revolution and beyond to the westward migrations where new settlements and towns were founded by the hundreds; the movement to abolish slavery and the abortive effort at reconstructing American life on the basis of racial equality; the Populist and agrarian revolts of the nineteenth century; the struggle for autonomous trade unions and for women's rights; the civil rights movement of the 1960s and the antiwar, antinuclear, and ecological movements of recent decades.

Just what constitutes a restorative moment is a matter of contestation. Ancient historians claimed that the hegemony which Athens established over Greece as a result of her leadership in the war against Persia was due to the energies and talents encouraged by democracy. In the most recent Persian war, American leaders hailed the triumph of American arms as a new restorative moment. "Desert Storm" was represented not as the restoration of democracy, nor as the taking back of power by the people, but as a certain kind of healing, one that meant "kicking the Vietnam syndrome" and thus restoring America's unity and its status as Number One. That understanding of the restorative moment represents a perfect inversion in which the state of war, rather than the state of nature, serves as the condition of renewal.

"Desert Storm," or constitutional democracy's Persian War, demonstrates the futility of seeking democratic renewal by relying on the powers of the modern state. The possibility of renewal draws on a simple fact: that ordinary individuals are capable of creating new cultural patterns of commonality at any moment. Individuals who concert their powers for low income housing, worker ownership of factories, better schools, better health care, safer water, controls over toxic waste disposals, and a thousand other common concerns of ordinary lives are experiencing a democratic moment and contributing to the discovery, care, and tending of a commonality of shared concerns. Without necessarily intending it, they are renewing the political by contesting the forms of unequal power that democratic liberty and equality have made possible and that democracy can eliminate only by betraying its own values.

But renewal also must draw on a less simple fact: a range of problems and atrocities exists that a locally confined democracy cannot resolve. Like pluralism, interest group politics, and multicultural politics, localism cannot surmount its limitations except by seeking out the evanescent homogeneity of a broader political. Recall the remarkable phenomenon of Polish Solidarity, a movement composed of highly disparate elements—socialists, artists, teachers, priests, believers, atheists, nationalists, and so on. Yet one of the literal meanings of solidarity is "community or perfect coincidence of (or between) interests."[20] Clearly homogeneity was not then and need not now be equated with dreary uniformity, any more than equality need be mere leveling. What it does require is understanding what is truly at stake politically: heterogeneity, diversity, and multiple selves are no match for modern forms of power.

Notes

1. I have discussed this topic at greater length in "Norm and Form," in J. Peter Euben, John R. Wallach, and Josiah Ober, eds., *Athenian Political Thought and the Reconstruction of American Democracy* (Ithaca: Cornell University Press, 1994).

2. Thomas Hobbes, *Leviathan*, ed. Michael Oakeshott (Oxford: Blackwell, 1946), 83.

3. Mary Douglas, *Purity and Danger: An Analysis of Concepts of Pollution and Taboo* (Harmondsworth: Penguin, 1970), esp. 137ff.

4. For a fuller discussion, see my "Democracy, Difference, and Re-Cognition," *Political Theory* 21 (1993): 464–83.

5. The concept of technē will be treated at full length in John Wallach's forthcoming *The Platonic Political Art*.

6. The classic discussion of this contradiction remains Marx's "On the Jewish Question."

7. See William E. Connolly, *Identity\Difference: Democratic Negotiations of Political Paradox* (Ithaca: Cornell University Press, 1991).

8. Jean Bodin, *Six Books of the Commonwealth*, trans. M. J. Tooley (Oxford: Blackwell, n.d.), book 6, chap. 4, 192–93.

9. *The Federalist*, ed. Jacob Cooke (Middletown, Conn.: Wesleyan University Press, 1961), 61 (no. 10).

10. For Tocqueville's complaint, see Jean-Claude Lamberti, *Tocqueville et les deux démocraties* (Paris: Presses universitaires de France, 1983), 180. For Tocqueville's dissociation of American democracy from revolution see his *Oeuvres Complètes*, ed. J.-P. Mayer (Paris: Gallimard, 1969–), 1.14.

11. I have discussed Plato's and Aristotle's treatment of democracy more fully in my essay "Norm and Form." The quotation from Plato's *Republic* follows the Shorey translation in the Loeb series.

12. Aristotle, *Politics*, 3.5–6.1278b6–15: "Now in every case the citizen body of a state is sovereign; the citizen body is the constitution. Thus in democracies the people are sovereign, in oligarchies the few." Trans. T. A. Sinclair, revised Trevor J. Saunders (Harmondsworth: Penguin, 1981).

13. "Democracy is the generic constitution. . . . [It] is the resolved mystery of all constitutions." Karl Marx, *Critique of Hegel's "Philosophy of Right,"* ed. Joseph O'Malley (Cambridge: Cambridge University Press, 1970), 29–30.

14. On this topic in the ancient world see G.E.M. de Ste. Croix, *The Class Struggle in the Ancient Greek World* (London: Duckworth, 1981), 278–300.

15. Locke, *Two Treatises of Government*, 11:124–26. The enlarged political reemerges when Locke discusses the right of revolution in terms of "the Majority of the People" (11.209).

16. Athenian democracy of the fifth century resorted to heroic measures—lot, rotation, ostracism—to preserve direct democracy, but in the next century it, too, began to exhibit symptoms of Michels's Iron Law of Oligarchy. See Josiah Ober, *Mass and Elite in Democratic Athens* (Princeton: Princeton University Press, 1989).

17. See, e.g., Plato, *Republic* 7.563e–564a; *Laws* 701a; Polybius, *The Histories* 7.9; Philo, *De Confusione Linguaram* 23.108; *De Fuga et Inventione* 2.10, John Calvin, *Institutes of the Christian Religion* 4.20.8; Sir Thomas Elyot, *The Book named The Governor* 1.1; Claude de Seyssel, *The Monorchy of France* 1.1; David Hume, "Of the Populousness of Ancient Nations," in *Essays Moral, Political and Literary* (Oxford: Oxford University Press, 1963), p. 374; and *The Federalist*, no. 10, p. 61, and no. 14, p. 84.

18. Plato, *Republic*, 8.557e–58a; and see Laws, 3.693d.

19. Tocqueville, *Journey to America*, ed. J. P. Mayer (New Haven: Yale University Press, 1959), 51, 156.

20. *Oxford English Dictionary*, entry 2 s.v. "solidarity."

Three

Using Power/Fighting Power: The Polity

JANE MANSBRIDGE

Coercion and Persuasion

In the last two decades, theorists of deliberative democracy have stressed the democratic potential for reasoned persuasion to the almost complete exclusion of the independently justifiable arguments for power as coercion in democratic life. Yet democracies must have their coercive as well as their deliberative moments.

Against deliberative theorists who associate the coercion in democracy with "violence" and make that coercion at best tangential to the democratic process, this essay argues that coercion must play a large, valuable, and relatively legitimate role in almost any democracy that functions well. But against those who assume the full legitimacy of coercion in conditions of lasting disagreement, this essay argues that any justification for coercion will necessarily be incomplete. In conditions of lasting disagreement there is no unquestionably fair procedure for producing a decision to coerce. Moreover, much coercion in existing democracies will be far from fair, and policies requiring coercion will often have features that are far from just.

Recognizing the need for coercion, and recognizing too that no coercion can be either incontestably fair or predictably just, democracies must find ways of fighting, while they use it, the very coercion that they need.

Democracies usually fight their own coercive power by girding that power about with the institutional safeguards of individual rights, free speech and association, and other features of the "rule of law," sometimes including constitutional requirements that every policy have at least a nominal "public purpose." Along with these safeguards, democracies need political parties, interest groups, and other traditional institutions that can serve as instruments of formal opposition. Less obviously, this essay argues that democracies also

I would like to thank Joshua Cohen and Thomas McCarthy for comments at and after the conference on "Democracy and Difference" at Yale University, and Nancy Fraser, Jürgen Habermas, Bonnie Honig, David Kahane, Cass Sunstein, Iris Young, and participants in a seminar at the London School of Economics for helpful comments and criticisms on an earlier draft of this essay.

need to foster and value informal deliberative enclaves of resistance in which those who lose in each coercive move can rework their ideas and their strategies, gathering their forces and deciding in a more protected space in what way or whether to continue the battle.

Why Democracies Need Coercion

By "power" in this essay I mean coercion. In other contexts I would define power more broadly as "the actual or potential causal relation between the interests of an actor or set of actors and the outcome itself." This broad definition usefully focuses on cause; it is neutral regarding intent; it includes anticipated reactions; and, unlike the narrower meaning of power I will adopt here, it covers what Mary Parker Follett, William Connolly, and many feminists like to call "power to" or "power with" as well as "power over."[1]

In contrast to this broader definition, I will use the word "power" in this essay, interchangeably with "coercion," to mean an actual or potential causal relation between the interests of an actor or set of actors and an outcome, in which cause operates specifically through the use of force or the threat of sanction.[2]

Democracies need coercion primarily to take action without overly privileging the status quo. When individual interests[3] come in what gives every indication of being an irreconcilable conflict, a democratic polity must either reinforce the status quo by taking no action or, by taking action, force or threaten (coerce) some of its citizens into situations or actions not in their interests. Majority rule is one standard mechanism for achieving a relatively fair form of democratic coercion.

Democracies can undoubtedly settle some or many of their conflicts through deliberation. Deliberation can help transform interests and reveal previously unrealized areas of agreement. It can also sharpen participants' understandings of their conflicts. In a good democracy, large or small, the deliberative arena should ideally be equally open to all, and power—in the sense of the threat of sanction or the use of force—should not interfere with the impact of the better argument.

At some point and on some issues, however, deliberation will not lead to agreement. Good deliberation will have opened areas of agreement and will have clarified the remaining areas of conflict. The participants will have come to understand their interests, including their conflicting interests, better than before deliberation. But material interests, and interests in one's deepest values, cannot always be reconciled with the interests, material and ideal, of others. At this point, when conflict remains after good deliberation, a democracy has two choices—to remain at the status quo or to act, by coercing some to go along with others.

When a new highway destroys an old neighborhood or when a government takes a symbolic stand that some citizens find deeply abhorrent, the coercion inherent in democratic decision lets some citizens or their representatives use force or the threat of sanction to cause outcomes that other citizens oppose. Members of the losing group will henceforth, for example, unwillingly live across a noisy highway from their past neighbors or have to dissociate themselves from stands that others attribute to them as members of that polity. In the quintessential example of enforced taxation, a strong welfare state requires coercion to collect taxes from those who are unalterably opposed to extensive social welfare policies, both in principle and as a result of pursuing their own material interests.

Even regulations that succeed primarily because citizens cooperate freely from public-spirited motivation usually need some coercion around the edges to keep the occasional defector from turning the majority of cooperators into suckers.[4] Democracies need to use coercion not only for the reasons of security that Thomas Hobbes recognized and that finally even Robert Nozick, after the most extraordinary twists and turns, recognized as well, but also for the hundreds of thousands of occasions, in a complex, interdependent society, in which collective action requires some degree of coercion to attain even unanimously approved collective ends. And because in a large society with a number of conflicting interests the requirement of unanimity will give almost total power to those who benefit from the status quo, democracies committed to some rough approximation to equal power will require some forms of nonunanimously approved coercion to attain ends that most of their citizens approve.

Coming to Grips with Coercion

Many of the best contemporary political theorists have not faced squarely the role of conflicting interests, and consequently of coercion, in any democratic polity. Thinkers as diverse as Hannah Arendt, Sheldon Wolin, Michael Walzer, and Jürgen Habermas have conceived of democracy in ways that extol the role of democratic deliberation in discovering, creating, and maintaining commonality, while implicitly or explicitly denigrating the role of democratic coercion when interests conflict.

Hannah Arendt is the least subtle and, I believe, the most misguided of these deliberative theorists. Arendt denounced as illegitimate, calling it "violence," the kind of coercion I consider a critical tool of democracy. She contrasted this coercion, or "violence," of which she disapproved, to what she approvingly called "power," defined to mean the power of a united people moving to achieve common ends.[5]

Arendt joined her denunciation of coercion as violence to an insistence that private and material interests should not "invade the public domain."[6] In her view, a voter who uses public coercion (through pressure groups, for example) "out of concern with his private life and well-being" acts as a "blackmailer," not a member of the public (273).

Against Arendt, I contend that concerns with one's private life and well-being, including one's "interest and welfare," are appropriate, important, and valuable material for political deliberation and decision (see n. 36). Such concerns do not constitute the only material for political deliberation and decision. But they have a legitimate place in politics and public life. When such concerns conflict irreconcilably, as when values conflict irreconcilably, and when inaction would unfairly sustain the status quo, democracies need the kind of coercion by which, in Arendt's derogatory phrase, voters "force their representatives to execute their wishes at the expense of other groups of voters" (273). By simply defining any such coercion as violence and ruling it out of the democratic process, Arendt forestalls democratic attempts both to make the coercion as legitimate as possible and, after accepting its necessity, to find ways of containing, restricting and fighting it at the very moment of using it.

The other deliberative theorists to whom I now turn have positions less strong than Arendt's and more subtle. These positions are also sometimes less well worked out, in part because the theorists were not centrally concerned with the problems I address in this essay. With these theorists more than with Arendt I have primarily a disagreement in emphasis.

In *Politics and Vision*, Sheldon Wolin defined the "political" along Arendtian lines as "uniquely concerned with what is 'common' to the whole community."[7] Like Arendt, Wolin also considered material interests "essentially private," "radically individual," and "fundamentally unsharable" (277). But Wolin stopped short of excluding material interests from the public domain. Rather, he objected reasonably to placing these interests "at the center of the political association" (277) and making them "supreme" (280). For Wolin, interests were "*least* capable of representation at the public level" (277, my emphasis), not, as for Arendt, *in*capable of such representation.

Wolin wanted to integrate "politics" (his word for "the struggle for competitive advantage" [42, 10]) with the "political," defined by commonality. His vision of integration takes conflict and antagonism as "the raw material for creating areas of agreement, or, if this fails, to make it possible for competing forces to compromise." It confines "imposition . . . to those situations where no other alternative exists" (43).[8] The rest of the book fleshes out this unexceptionable but relatively empty formulation by never portraying "imposition," or coercion, as a valued component of democracy.

A similar normative abhorrence of coercion informs Wolin's understanding of "compromise," which fails to capture the ways that more and less legitimate uses of coercive power, as well as considerations of principle and the common good, lie behind most viable political compromises. When, say, environmentalists compromise with the proponents of growth on a particular policy, the result derives not only from reasoning together on the merits of their various arguments regarding the common good but also from weighing implicitly or explicitly the number of votes each group can muster in the next election, the relative size of their advertising budgets, the efficiency of their relative political organizations, the harm each can do the other in the media, the alliances each has with other groups, and the degree to which each can appeal to different sectors in the ownership of capital. These considerations are not all illegitimate in a normative understanding of democracy. Some, such as the number of votes each can muster in the next election, have strong claims to democratic legitimacy. By taking an overall stance that refuses normative legitimacy to any of these coercion-related contributions to a compromise, we keep ourselves from asking to what degree each factor could be legitimate, and what criteria for legitimacy we might bring to bear in each case. We also keep ourselves from asking what safeguards we need to institute against the coercion involved in and emanating from such compromises.

Although further removed than Wolin from the Arendtian tradition, Michael Walzer also contends that in democracy, "what counts is argument among the citizens. Democracy puts a premium on speech, persuasion, rhetorical skill. Ideally, the citizen who makes the most persuasive argument—that is the argument that actually persuades the largest number of citizens—gets his way. But he can't use force."[9] Through the deft move of defining "force" as "power used in violation of its social meaning" (282), Walzer simply stipulates its illegitimacy. The reader takes, however, the message that force as coercion—and power as coercion—has no valued role in Walzer's understanding of democracy.

Walzer's emphasis on persuasion leaves him, for example, ill at ease with the vote. He wants to conclude that "power 'belongs to' persuasiveness,"[10] and not to coercive institutions like the vote. Asking rhetorically, "But isn't the vote itself a kind of power?" he hedges: "A kind of power perhaps. . . . But choices . . . still depend not on single votes but on the accumulation of votes—hence on influence, persuasion, pressure, bargaining, organization, and so on" (305–6). Walzer never considers the normative justifications for deciding through the coercive powers of a vote alone when persuasion has been exhausted.

Two decades ago Jürgen Habermas addressed some of these issues in a subtle critique and appreciation of Hannah Arendt.[11] In this essay, Habermas first welcomed Arendt's break with Max Weber and others who defined power only in terms of the "purposefully rational agent, who is exclusively interested in the success of his action" (73), that is, an agent who operates in the spheres of "strategic" rather than "communicative" action. He then criticized Arendt

for giving strategic action no role at all in the "realm of the political" (112).[12]
Yet within this criticism Habermas still deliberately withheld the word "legitimate" from strategic action, with its concern for acquiring and exercising political power. For Habermas, the only "legitimate power arises among those
who form common convictions in communication free from coercion" (183).
These "common convictions" (Habermas's reformulation of Arendt's "power")
create the legitimate power for which strategic actors then *compete*. Competition among strategic actors can be "normalized" (182) and "institutionalized"
(183), but it can never become "legitimate power."[13]

One must agree with Habermas that common convictions formed through
mutual communication differ dramatically from decisions arrived at through
mutual coercion. Even democratic coercion can never be fully legitimate.
Only genuine agreement, arrived at in conditions free from coercion, can produce fully legitimate outcomes. I differ with him, however, in one point of
emphasis and one of substance. I would emphasize that in the real world—as
Foucault reminds us and Habermas grants—there are no conditions free from
the threat of sanction or use of force. The ideal of coercion-free deliberation
resembles many important and useful democratic ideals in being impossible to
achieve fully, although possible to approach. If, as I believe, the structure of
language and culture makes it impossible fully to eliminate "illusionary" convictions, produced by the capacity of some to keep others from perceiving
their interests (186, 183),[14] then in Habermas's own terms *fully* legitimate
power, arrived at through deliberation, is a practical impossibility. Polities can
and do differ in the degree to which they approach that ideal. My substantive
disagreement comes in the next section, where I argue that, much like deliberative agreement, coercion and competition among strategic actors can also be
more or less legitimate.

How the Coercion that Democracies Need Can
Be Made Relatively Legitimate

Democratic theorists have tried to legitimate coercion through one or more of
the following lines of thought.

First, we have tried to legitimate coercion explicitly or implicitly through
direct or indirect hypothetical consent. For a few coordination problems, such
as devising rules of the road, or even collective action problems, such as ensuring clean air, we could imagine that every sane citizen would agree directly to
be coerced into doing his or her part in these matters so long as every other
citizen were subjected to a similar coercion. We could even hypothesize that
every sane citizen would agree to some decision-rule, such as majority rule
within appropriate limiting conditions, to settle most other disagreements,
especially if the hypothesized alternative were a war of all against all. This

"indirect" consent would legitimate all forms of coercion emanating from the agreed-on rule. The logic of consent, however, produces a dubious and indeterminate legitimacy, because no citizen ever gives actual consent to every decision, and hypothetical consent is, at the least, always open to contest.

In a more subtle version of this argument, coercion might be legitimated to the degree that it derived from procedures to which all affected would agree in conditions of free, equal, and unconstrained deliberation. This criterion for legitimation from hypothetical deliberation is subject to some of the same problems as the other, however, for citizens are likely to disagree strongly, on the basis of irreconcilably opposed value commitments, about the procedures to which they would agree in such conditions.[15]

Second, we might legitimate coercion primarily or only through an appeal to substantive justice. To argue for the legitimacy of the coercion necessary to establish private property rights, for example, one would first judge the justice of the desired end by some substantive standard (i.e., one would argue that the institution of private property rights benefits the greatest number, deviates from equality only in benefiting the least advantaged, or even conforms to the criteria for justice embedded in a local situation or community). One would then judge how necessary coercion was as a means to accomplishing that just end. In this approach, anyone seeking to use coercion would have to identify some plausible conception of the right or the good by which to defend what they propose. In this approach only substantively just outcomes, including those that derive from particular stands on the good and the right (e.g., anti-discrimination laws, endangered species acts, and antismoking requirements), would legitimate the coercion required to achieve them.[16] Serious disagreements over what is substantively just make this criterion for legitimating coercion also, at the least, always open to contest.

Finally, theorists in what I have called the "adversary" tradition have taken an independent tack, approaching democracy as if coercion were legitimated only, or primarily, through fair aggregative, rather than deliberative, procedures.[17] Fair aggregation in this tradition requires some version of one person/one vote, or in more radical formulations the equal power of each individual in the decision. In this tradition some theorists have even defined democracy as "equal power,"[18] or more cautiously, "the equal opportunity to exercise power."[19] Theorists as different as Carole Pateman and Robert Dahl have made equal power in decisions a central ingredient of the ideal of democracy.[20]

Even in the adversary tradition most theorists consider coercion legitimate only if it is exercised in the context of certain limiting conditions, such as the protection of individual rights, the "rule of law," and perhaps the constitutional requirement of some formal "public purpose" for the decision.[21] Although these limiting conditions figure prominently in the ways democracies must fight the very coercion that they use, they only mitigate, rather than eradicate, the necessary and valuable imposition of democratic coercion.

The legitimacy of one person/one vote, or more radically equal power, in the adversary tradition does not derive from the medieval conclusion that a majority is, all things equal, more likely to be substantively right than a minority.[22] Rather, in a rationale that has developed slowly since the seventeenth century, the legitimacy of majority rule (and of equal power in decisions more generally) derives, independently of any postulated outcome of uncoerced communication, from two sources.

First, when conflicting interests erode the bases for any standard other than equality, equality becomes the only mutually acceptable default position. This essentially negative argument, which Isaiah Berlin makes in general terms, is particularly applicable to majority rule. Berlin points out that all norms or rules (without which there can be no society) have a structure such that within the categories created by the rule all individuals are treated equally. This is the meaning of a rule. Members of any society, asked to justify a rule, give reasons for including or excluding individuals from the relevant categories. When no good reason for a distinction can be given, the default presumption is that individuals will be treated equally. Following this logic, struggles over the franchise have taken the form of struggles over reasons for exclusion. Whenever the underlying rationale for traditional exclusions erodes, more previously excluded individuals gain the vote.[23]

Second, when a political culture includes a value of respect for the equal moral worth of each individual, that respect provides a positive standard to legitimate the equal vote. Features of the Judeo-Christian tradition, as well as features of the cultures of other societies, help to make the equal vote—or, more radically, equal power—a public mark of equal worth.

These two reasons underlie the decision of democratic theorists in the adversary tradition to legitimate coercion by, within limiting conditions, giving participants equal power in the decision to coerce whenever fundamental conflicts of material interests or values prevent agreement.[24]

The problem with this criterion is that even if equal power were fully to legitimate the coercion democracies must use, no democratic decision-rule could guarantee that equal power. No formula—majority rule or any other—can produce a system in which, even in theory, each can equally coerce and be coerced in turn.

The ideal is theoretically unreachable because we hold at least three opposed, but equally valid, conceptions of what it means to have equal power. One definition is that one's resources for coercion—one's weapons—be equal to those of any other individual (as in the example of one person/one vote). Another is that, as a member of a group, one succeed in getting the outcome one prefers in proportion to the number of allies one has on the issue (proportional outcomes). A third is that one succeed in getting the outcome one prefers as often as any other individual (equal satisfaction). Absent perfectly equal cross-cutting cleavages, these goals are not compatible. When issues do not arise such that each individual wins exactly as often as every other, equally weighted votes will lead to those with more allies coercing others more often than those with fewer allies.[25]

In addition, scholars since the late eighteenth century have demonstrated that when preferences are not single-peaked, majority rule can produce several equally legitimate but competing outcomes.[26]

For these reasons among others, democratic theorists who have studied the issue in some depth have concluded that democratic coercion can be legitimated only by what Charles Beitz calls "complex proceduralism," deriving from "the irreducible plurality of substantive interests associated with the idea of political fairness."[27] Although equal resources with majority rule often produces the best contender for a procedurally fair decision rule, "theoretical reasoning evidently cannot be made to yield a firm conclusion that majority rule is necessarily superior or inferior to some alternatives to it."[28] The same is true for any other attempt to count individuals equally in a decision.

More important than these theoretical considerations is the raw fact that no large democracy has ever produced a political system in which every member had anything even approximating equal coercive resources, the equal opportunity to exercise coercion, or the experience of exercising coercion equally with all other members of the polity. All existing nation-states are so far from actual political equality as to dwarf the technical problems of capturing in any decision-rule the conflicting implicit mandates of democratic theory.

Even the most internally democratic small collectives cannot in fact achieve equality of power in their decisions.[29] If coercion is legitimated only by equal power in the decision to coerce, and if no real democracy can achieve equal power, then no real democracy—especially no real large-scale democracy—can ever fully justify the coercion it exercises.

In short, none of the criteria for legitimating coercion—whether based on assessments of hypothetical consent, the substantive justice of outcomes, the freedom from coercion or closeness to agreement of the deliberative process that resulted in a decision to coerce, or the equal power that participants exercise in the decision process—can produce in cases of ongoing disagreement an incontestably legitimate result. Nor has any contemporary standard for determining the substantive justice of an outcome been able to prevail by appealing to the pure truth of its premises or the logic of its derivation. Whatever policy an actual democracy adopts on any contested subject, some citizens can reasonably believe that by their standards the procedures that produced the outcome were unfair, and that by their standards the outcomes themselves—or aspects of those outcomes—were unjust.

In practice, actual democracies can produce at best a "rough" or "good enough" legitimacy, based on citizens' generalizable interests in creating conditions of relatively willing cooperation. They will always create only institutions "that are reasonably just in view of the circumstances" or that do not "exceed the limits of tolerable injustice,"[30] determinations that will always depend in part on relatively local judgments about the mitigating character of different circumstances and the limits of the tolerable. People's willingness to accept some coercion as "legitimate enough" or "reasonably just under the circumstances" in turn seldom derives from an explicit or reflectively achieved consensus formed by unconstrained discussion. That willingness derives largely from a conventional and unreflective consensus rooted in the internalization of social and cultural traditions.[31] The discursive base from which people make their decisions on the reasonableness of deviations from justice is permeated with power. Accordingly, even these ad hoc rough decisions on what is "good enough" must be suspect.

I do not want to suggest, however, that the inevitability of contest over standards means giving up on at least provisional determinations of what is procedurally fair and substantively just. Indeed, my own relative certainty that many policy decisions in today's democracies are neither procedurally fair nor substantively just rests on strongly held, although admittedly provisional, convictions. Although the best we may hope for is an "if . . . then" formulation,[32] that formulation must suffice for the present, to be possibly corrected through further deliberation. For example, if we conclude now that a rough approximation to political equality is one ingredient in democratic fairness, then most policy outcomes in today's democracies do not derive from procedures that even approach that standard of fairness. If we conclude now that one or more of the egalitarian features of competing contemporary standards of justice (the greatest good for the greatest number, say, or the difference principle in justice as fairness) captures an important aspect of substantive justice, then most policy outcomes in today's democracies do not approach those standards.

I also do not want to suggest that the contestability of standards, the inevitable failure of any actual society to live up to its ideals, or even the great failure of existing democracies to live up to their ideals justifies, in most cases, civil disobedience. To the contrary, I will assume here that most acts of democratic coercion in modern Western democracies are sufficiently procedurally fair and their outcomes sufficiently just "under the circumstances" to disallow, in most cases, large-scale civil disobedience, individual major acts of civil disobedience, and even minor individual breaches of either the law or public spirit, such as small-scale cheating on the income tax. This is not the place for a full-scale discussion of political obligation, which I see as deriving from several different sources. In this essay I want to direct attention away from the traditional focus in political theory on political obligation and civil disobedience, toward a recognition of the ongoing imperfection of democratic decision. Democracies need ways short of civil disobedience and the breakdown of normatively based mutual cooperation to recognize and fight the ongoing injustice of their procedures and their outcomes.

How Citizens Must Fight the Very Coercion
that They Need

When delegitimation walks hand in hand with legitimation, sufficient legitimation must remain to let reasonably just coercion do its good work of helping organize social arrangements and redressing the greater injustices that
would emerge without it. Each individual in each society must feel out this
delicate balance for herself. The trick is to recognize the importance, particularly to the most disadvantaged, of having a large number of relatively democratic and relatively unchallenged decisions made (and democratic coercion
imposed) on a daily, monthly, and yearly basis as a matter of routine, and at
the same time to recognize the importance, particularly to the most disadvantaged, of maintaining, in the institutions and culture of the society and in the
minds of its citizens, some ongoing recognition and critique of the ways in
which those decisions (and that coercion) are unfair and unjust.

Most democracies are capitalist as a rule, and capitalism (like many other
economic systems) creates the very inequalities that make decisions in those
democracies far from procedurally fair. All democracies except small voluntary women's communities are patriarchal, and patriarchy also creates inequalities that make decisions in those democracies far from procedurally
fair. Most democracies are also racist, and classist even without reference to
capitalism, with similar results. All real democracies, including the most utopian intentional communities, incorporate inequalities that produce coercive
decisions that are procedurally unequal. All real democracies, including the
most utopian, produce outcomes with aspects that are substantively unjust.[33]
But workers, women, subordinated races, lower classes, and other disadvantaged groups fare far better in those democracies than they would in most
cases if the democracies began to fall apart. Raw power, unmitigated by democratic values, usually hurts the disadvantaged far more than does democratic
power. The disadvantaged need the relatively just coercion that democracies
produce.

To fight that coercion at the same time as using it, democracies can multiply
the available deliberative arenas to vary the kinds of power that permeate
each one. Different arenas facilitate critiques of power from different directions. C. B. Macpherson and other theorists who excoriate political parties fail
to recognize that parties and organized oppositions provide critical arenas for
the losers in any given political interaction to rework their understandings of
the situation and later return to the fray. Jürgen Habermas and other theorists
who deprecate interest groups do not value the deliberative functions these
groups can perform.[34]

Expanding opportunities for democratic participation, both by traditional
efforts like voter registration and by developing new forms in the untraditional

venues of workplaces, neighborhood town meetings, and deliberative refer-enda,[35] helps citizens fight coercion only when that participation itself does not cloud their understanding. For participation to help people understand their interests better, participants often need issues on which they have direct experience. They also often need a variety of different arenas for deliberation. They may need, for example, to oscillate between protected enclaves, in which they can explore their ideas in an environment of mutual encouragement, and more hostile but also broader surroundings in which they can test those ideas against the reigning reality.

Interest groups, political parties, and social movements, as well as churches, workplaces, ad hoc political collectives, and consciousness-raising groups, provide different forms of protected enclaves, in which members le-gitimately consider in their deliberations not only what is good for the whole polity but also what is good for themselves individually (their private lives and well-being, in Arendt's words) and for their group. Members of these groups may legitimately take particularist as well as universalist stands, as they may legitimately challenge the underlying assumptions of the forms of universal-ism they see around them. Only by making material interest and self-interest legitimate in these and other deliberations can the democracy succeed in en-couraging a thorough "probing of volitions," which subjects "every pressing issue to continuous examination and possible reformulation."[36]

The present reigning hostility to "identity politics" does not recognize the value to democracy of deliberative enclaves in which the relatively like-minded can consult easily with one another. Karl Marx saw that capitalist factories, which had the unexpected attribute of bringing workers together in close quarters to share their experiences, helped transform the workers into the "gravediggers" of capitalism.[37] The black colleges that began the sit-ins of the southern civil rights movement in the United States, the early women's consciousness-raising groups and women's centers, and the bookstores and cafés that now support enclaves of identity politics all harbored and still har-bor relatively safe spaces in which the like-minded can make their own sense of what they see.[38] In a more ephemeral example, some working-class citizens in a small town I studied felt the need to meet one night before the town meeting for a session that was one part strategy, including parsing out the dimensions of the problem, and five parts mutual support.[39]

Much contemporary work on civil society recognizes how partial, conflict-ing deliberative spaces, which yield partial and conflicting accounts of self-interest as well as conflicting accounts of the common good, must supplement both mainstream discourse about the common good and the formal delibera-tions that take place in local and national governments. What Nancy Fraser aptly terms "subaltern counterpublics" allow subordinated social groups to "invent and circulate counterdiscourses, which in turn permit them to formu-late oppositional interpretations of their identities, interests and needs."[40]

James Scott writes of the importance for subordinated groups of "sequestered settings where, in principle, a shared critique of domination may develop."[41]

The goals of these counterpublics include understanding themselves better, forging bonds of solidarity, preserving the memories of past injustices, interpreting and reinterpreting the meanings of those injustices, working out alternative conceptions of self, of community, of justice, and of universality, trying to make sense of both the privileges they wield and the oppressions they face, understanding the strategic configurations for and against their desired ends, deciding what alliances to make both emotionally and strategically, deliberating on ends and means, and deciding how to act, individually and collectively.

Even the most just societies need these enclaves of protected discourse and action, because each institution of new forms of power and participation unsettles past patterns of power in ways that are not simply just. Each balance of power creates a new underdog, each settlement a new group who would benefit from unsettling. Each settlement accordingly creates not only the necessary capacity for action but also the need to protect and facilitate in some way those who have lost.[42] Because no democracy ever reaches the point at which justice is simply done, democracies need to recognize and foster enclaves of resistance. Suggestions to improve democracy, such as democratic neocorporatism,[43] therefore need to show not only how well they foster deliberation in general but also how they facilitate or impede enclaves of oppositional discourse.

This "enclave" model of democratic deliberation and action generates at least two problems. First come the dangers that arise when members of any group speak only to one another. When white supremacists speak mostly to white supremacists, Serbs to Serbs, feminists to feminists, and political philosophers to political philosophers, they encourage one another not to hear anyone else. They do not learn how to put what they want to say in words that others can hear and understand. The enclaves, which produce insights that less protected spaces would have prevented, also protect those insights from reasonable criticism. Yet most people, and particularly those disadvantaged in the larger society, need some such protection in order to think more critically and carefully. We also need this protection to help us develop confidence in our ideas, marshal our forces, and feel supported by others.[44]

For most people, spending time both in an oppositional enclave and outside it promotes weighing the lessons of each venue against the other. It allows the straddling individual to gain the confidence of others' support but temper that support against the light and heat of outside opposition. A division of labor also helps, in which some individuals immerse themselves in enclave life and thought while others span the spectrum between the enclave and the outside world. The danger comes when large numbers live only in their conceptual enclaves, reinforcing one another in their mutual *folie*. Then the translators need to work with a vengeance.

The second, and equally important, problem is that facilitating enclaves can contravene other values, such as the triumph of the right and the good. When the Ku Klux Klan loses influence in the deliberative arena and is outvoted in the coercive one, the racism it espouses ought normatively eventually to disappear entirely from the array of conceptual possibilities to which citizens have access. The case for enclaves must be much like that for free speech, which also must be balanced against other rights and goods. Just as a democracy should affirmatively promote enclaves of speech by postal subsidies for magazines and newspapers regardless of their content, along with subsidies of Internet communication, so too, all other things equal, the public culture of democracy should recognize the value of organizational and deliberative enclaves where oppositional thought can grow.

Facilitating opposition in general may be a luxury open only to relatively settled democracies whose populations find most decisions sufficiently just to let the necessary degree of democratic coercion do its work. Each society must work out the relative values of using and fighting power through constant balancing and testing, sacrificing neither. Normative political thought can help by recognizing as democratic values both reasonably just coercion and opposition to the injustice within that coercion.

Living with the Tension

The tensions we should keep alive in democratic practice resemble the tensions we should keep alive within ourselves when we try to use the power that has made us who we are and yet fight that power at the same time.[45] We need worry far less about the compromises we make between the good and the best, or between the bad-but-livable and the better, when those compromises are, roughly speaking, utility-driven—when we are only giving up one good to get another. But when we compromise with justice, we must design our lives and our institutions so that the justice that is compromised remains nagging, in the margin somewhere, in a bracket that does not go away, to pique our souls and goad us into future action.

In the polity we can best preserve these irritants by encouraging "affirmative pluralism" in democratic talk. In our democracies, we need to find ways of removing coercion as much as possible from the arenas in which we struggle to understand what is just and unjust. This means a public discourse not completely overwhelmed with the massive resources of existing forms of domination.

But we must remember that in their decision-making functions democracies need coercion, that the coercion needed is usually far from fully legitimate, and that in using power, we must also fight it at the same time. To fight power means affirmatively encouraging oppositional discourses and oppositional cultures. Those discourses and cultures have evolved in part for the purpose of reminding their participants and, through them, the other members of the society, of the illegitimate coercion and substantive injustice that pervades any existing democracy. These discourses and cultures make it easier to investigate different ends from those the larger polity is pursuing, and different means to similar ends. The different ways the cultures work and the different avenues they explore may later replace or supplement the ways that reign at present.

The injustices we commit as we act collectively—for not to act coercively would in many cases create a greater injustice than to act and coerce some unfairly—should not be forgotten and put behind us. Our collective deliberations should find ways to recognize, store, and rethink our understandings of these actions, so that we do not foreclose the opportunity of making reparation, or of someday understanding how to make the coercion we must use more procedurally fair and its outcomes more substantively just.

Notes

1. I have adapted to systemic power the definition devised by Jack H. Nagel, *The Descriptive Analysis of Power* (New Haven: Yale University Press, 1975), 29, by substituting "interests" for his "preferences" and adding "a set of actors." By focusing on cause, Nagel's definition avoids imputations of intent and allows anticipations of future events (e.g., the next election) to cause present behavior.

For an emphasis on the relatively benign "power to," "power with," "power as energy," and "power-from-within," in contrast to the "power over" that I emphasize in this essay, see Mary Parker Follett, "Power" (1975), in *Dynamic Administration: The Collected Papers of Mary Parker Follett*, ed. Henry C. Metcalf (New York: Harper, 1942); William E. Connolly, "Power and Responsibility," in *The Terms of Political Discourse* (Lexington: D. C. Heath, 1974); Nancy Hartsock, "Political Change: Two Perspectives on Power," *Quest* 1 (1974): 10–25, reprinted in Charlotte Bunch, ed., *Building Feminist Theory: Essays from Quest* (New York: Longman, 1981); and, among more recent feminist theorists, Starhawk, *Truth or Dare* (1987) (New York: HarperCollins, 1990), 8–19.

2. Power therefore means here "power over" other human beings. In this definition I draw not only on Nagel, *Descriptive Analysis*, but also on distinctions in Peter Bachrach and Morton Baratz, "Decisions and Non-Decisions: An Analytic Framework," *American Political Science Review* 57 (1963): 632–44; and Steven Lukes, *Power: A Radical View* (London: Macmillan, 1974). Unlike the threat of sanction, "force" as I use it here involves no element of the will of the other. If I carry you out of the room and your will is irrelevant, my action involves force; if I tell you I will shoot you unless you leave, my getting what I desire (your leaving) involves, to a small degree, your will. (You can always refuse to leave, and although I shoot you, I will not have gained your leaving.) Force, which does not involve will, is implicated in many systemic attributes such as language. Accordingly, although power as the threat of sanction always involves resistance or the possibility of resistance, power as force is sometimes impossible to resist.

(Michel Foucault may not have recognized this distinction.) To keep the argument relatively simple, the definition of coercion in this essay does not encompass positive inducement, although if asymmetries are great enough, positive inducements may count as forms of coercion. See Brian Barry, "Power: An Economic Analysis" (1975), in *Democracy and Power*, vol. 1 of *Essays in Political Theory* (Oxford: Oxford University Press, 1991).

3. I use the word "interest" here to mean a deliberatively considered conclusion on a policy preference. That conclusion may be self-interested or public-spirited. The conclusion is also always open to contest and to the possibility of reaching different conclusions after further thought, action, and political struggle. The word "interest" often connotes both self-interest and objective, static, or eternal states, discoverable through revolutionary action or through reason and revealed by removing the sources of oppression or repression. I want to discard these connotations, while retaining some distinction between surface preferences (or prereflective understandings) and understandings that are more considered, emotionally and rationally, and more thoroughly tested in action. One test of a considered understanding in this sense might be its formation in as close an approximation as possible to free, equal and unconstrained communication. Another test, which I suggest throughout, might be the vitality of the contest for adopting alternatives within which a given understanding developed, including the divergence of opposing ideas in that contest and the degree of life subsequently preserved in the excluded alternatives. European readers uncomfortable with the frequent American usage of incorporating value orientations into the conception of interests are requested mentally to substitute the phrase "interests and value orientations" whenever the word "interests" appears in this text.

4. Jane Mansbridge, "Public Spirit in Political Systems," in Henry J. Aaron, Thomas E. Mann, and Timothy Taylor, eds., *Values and Public Policy* (Washington: Brookings, 1994); Ian Ayers and John Braithwaite, *Responsive Regulation: Transcending the Deregulation Debate* (New York: Oxford University Press, 1992).

5. This opposition of coercion to "power" permeates Arendt's writing. In *On Revolution* (1963; reprint, New York: Viking, 1965), Arendt defined power, in contradistinction to "pre-political natural violence" (181), as follows: "Power comes into being only if and when men join themselves together for the purpose of action, and it will disappear when, for whatever reason, they disperse and desert one another" (174; see also 145, 148–49, 150–52, 155, 162, 163–67, 170, 175, 179, 181–82).

In her later *On Violence* (New York: Harvest/HBJ, 1970), Arendt consistently elided violence and coercion, attributing to all forms of instrumental coercion the psychology and substantive outcomes of physical violence. Her elision of the two in English reflected the double meaning of violence and coercive power inherent in the German *Gewalt*, which Max Weber and others had used to express the power of the state. The book's earliest section sets the pattern by first making violence quintessentially instrumental, "ruled by the means-end category" (4; also 46, 51, 79), then situating it immediately in the context of the battlefield, the sword, war, guns, shooting, extermination camps, genocide, torture, and nuclear doomsday (4, 5, 6, 11, 13, 14, 17). The second section, introducing "the question of violence in the political realm" (35), first identifies violence with coercion in general (36), then associates violence, rule, and command with the specific psychological feelings that come from imposing oneself on others, making others the instruments of one's will, asserting one's own will against the resistance of others, and desiring to exercise power over others. The third, last section links violence again with the imagery of aggressiveness, rage, and the battlefield (59–61, 63, 67). Arendt never explores the everyday nonviolent forms of coercion that I argue make complex and relatively just interdependence possible. (In *On Violence* Arendt's "power" remains the "living power of the people" acting "in concert" [40–41, 44].)

6. Arendt, *On Revolution*, 255. Arendt distinguished sharply between the "political" realm of "opinions," to which public "power" in her definition applied, and the "social and economic" realms of mere material interest (278). In *Contradictions of the Welfare State* (Cambridge, Mass.: MIT Press, 1984) Claus Offe similarly defines politics as having to do *not* with negotiations among interests but rather with "the working out of visions about the just order of social life, and the conflict among visions of that order" (173). See also Iris Marion Young, *Justice and the Politics of Difference* (Princeton: Princeton University Press, 1990), 72–74.

7. *Politics and Vision* (Boston: Little, Brown, 1960), 277, 2; also 3, 9–10, 60–66, 191, 429–34 on the political as "general and integrative." See also Wolin's "Fugitive Democracy," this volume, 31.

8. On politics, interests, and "the primordial fact that the hard core of power is violence" (220), see also *Politics and Vision*, 42, 86–92, 115–18, 201, 214–23, 232–36, 241, 272–85, 338–42.

9. *Spheres of Justice* (New York: Basic Books, 1983), 304.

10. Ibid., 306. Because he wants to make "power" belong only to persuasiveness, Walzer refuses to call television referenda an "exercise of power." He is "inclined to say, instead, that it is only another example of the erosion of value" (307). Similarly, he writes that "democracy requires equal rights, not equal power" (309). Although in one passage he agrees that a citizen can legitimately aim "to win—that is, to exercise *unequaled* power" (309), he does not explore the implications of this thought for a politics of relatively legitimate coercion.

11. Jürgen Habermas, "Hannah Arendt's Communications Concept of Power" (1976), in Jürgen Habermas, *Philosophical-Political Profiles*, trans. Frederick G. Lawrence (Cambridge, Mass.: MIT Press, 1985).

12. As Habermas carefully enunciated his position, strategic action "has taken place also within the city walls" (182). In another careful formulation, "We cannot exclude the element of strategic action from the concept of the political" (183).

13. For Habermas's evolving thought on this issue, see "Further Reflections on the Public Sphere," in Craig Calhoun, ed., *Habermas and the Public Sphere* (Cambridge, Mass.: MIT Press, 1992), 421–61, esp. 446–50, and "Three Normative Models of Democracy" in this volume, 21–30. For a critique, see my "Ugliness in Democratic Life," forthcoming in *Constellations*.

14. Habermas calls the capacity to keep other individuals or groups from perceiving their interests "violence" (183). He calls "structural violence" the capacity to keep others from perceiving their interests that is built into social and political institutions and "blocks in an unnoticed fashion those communications in which are shaped and propagated the convictions effective for legitimation" (186). This is in my terminology a form of "force" (see n. 2).

15. For example, decisions on majority rule vs. unanimity as a decision rule depend in part on commitments to equality as opposed to a conception of liberty that naturalizes the status quo. Seyla Benhabib, in "Toward a Deliberative Model of Democratic

Legitimacy" (this volume), applies this kind of legitimating criterion of hypothetical deliberation not to coercion per se but to "methods for articulating, sifting through, weighing conflicting interests" (73). In context, her "weighing" involves weighing the merits of arguments for different interests, not the numbers of interest-bearers. The criterion of hypothetical deliberation differs from the criterion of hypothetical consent by making the act of agreement collective, mutual, considered, and subject to the strong constraints of the deliberative ideal (see p. 70 in this volume for features of that ideal).

16. I am indebted to Cass Sunstein for these examples and helpful clarifications. Using this criterion for legitimation, one could also define as just whatever outcome a group of affected individuals would agree (or hypothetically agree) was just after uncoerced deliberation in which only the merit of the better argument prevailed; coercion would be more or less legitimate as the outcome was more or less just. Brian Barry, in "Is Democracy Special?" (1979; in *Democracy and Power*), points out that legitimation from substantive outcomes is insufficient for democratic theory, giving several reasons why "a law's having been enacted (or not repealed) by a democratic procedure adds a reason for obeying it to whatever reasons exist independently of that" (25).

17. Jane Mansbridge, *Beyond Adversary Democracy* (1980; reprint, Chicago: University of Chicago Press, 1983). Readers of that book will recognize in this essay a defense of the (partial) legitimacy of adversary democracy.

18. E.g., Jack Lively, *Democracy* (1975; reprint, New York: Putnam, 1977), 8.

19. Robert Dahl, "The Analysis of Influence in Local Communities" (1960), in Bernard J. Frieden and Robert Morris, ed., *Urban Planning and Social Policy* (New York: Basic Books, 1968), 225, 227. In his more recent work, *Democracy and Its Critics* (New Haven: Yale University Press, 1989), Dahl prefers the formulation, "At the decisive stage of collective decisions, each citizen must be ensured an equal opportunity to express a choice that will be counted as equal in weight to the choice expressed by other citizens" (109).

20. For the many theorists who make some version of equal power or the equal opportunity to exercise power a central element in democracy or, more broadly, in political fairness, see my "Using Power/Fighting Power," *Constellations* 1 (1994): 53–73, n. 19.

21. The exact content of these limiting conditions will always be a matter of contention. For English understandings of the rule of law, see A. V. Dicey, *Introduction to the Study of the Law of the Constitution*, ed. E.C.S. Wade (1885; reprint, London: Macmillan, 1939); Geoffrey Marshall, "Rule of law," in David Miller, ed., *The Blackwell Encyclopedia of Political Thought* (Oxford: Blackwell, 1987); and Don Herzog, *Happy Slaves* (Chicago: University of Chicago Press, 1989), chap. 4. For the ways the constitution of the United States prohibits the majoritarian imposition of the "naked preferences" of one group on another without at least nominal deference to a public purpose, see Cass R. Sunstein, "Naked Preferences and the Constitution," *Columbia Law Review* 84 (1984): 1689–1732.

22. For the argument in canon law, see Gierke, "Über die Geschichte des Majoritätsprinzips" (1913), cited in John Gilbert Heinberg, "History of the Majority Principle," *American Political Science Review* 20 (1926): 52–68, 59. The ancient Greeks may also have had a rationale for majority rule as a curtailed form of deliberation. Willmoore Kendall considers this claim implicit in John Locke's argument for majority rule: *John Locke and the Doctrine of Majority Rule* (Urbana: University of Illinois Press, 1941); and

Elaine Spitz (*Majority Rule* [Chatham, N.J.: Chatham House Publishers, 1984]) also upholds a relatively deliberative justification for majority rule, describing it as a complex social practice in which, at least in the early stages, "discussion, not voting, lies at the heart of the procedures" (xiii). For more recent conceptualizations of majority rule as "discursive as circumstances permit [subject to] temporal constraints," see Habermas, "Further Reflections," 449–50, and Benhabib, "Deliberative Rationality," 72.

23. For the general argument, see Isaiah Berlin, "Equality," *Proceedings of the Aristotelian Society* 56 (1955–56). A version of utilitarianism also provides a numerical argument for majority rule, as when even Willmoore Kendall in his later work justified majority rule as simply a lesser evil (producing fewer coerced individuals) than minority rule: Austin Ranney and Willmoore Kendall, *Democracy and the American Party System* (New York: Harcourt, Brace, 1956), 32.

24. This criterion of legitimation is conceptually independent from the discursive criterion, although if equality is the default position inherent in the concept of a rule, one would expect individuals in conditions of free and equal deliberation to agree on this position in the absence of good reasons for exclusion. The point is that discursive agreement would follow from reasons independent of the discursive agreement itself. These reasons are analytically independent of the discursive agreement even though in order to be persuaded that the criterion of equal power has its own internally compelling rationale, we have to point to the results of actual discursive processes, judged according to the criteria for ideal deliberation. By analogy, when we ask why we should believe a given result in the work of the physical sciences we point to social processes whose degree of closeness to a discursive ideal leads us to have more or less confidence in their conclusions. But those social conclusions in turn are based on criteria that are to some degree independent of the discursive process. In the legitimating loop, the deliberative process and the other criteria have independent but reinforcing status.

25. See Mansbridge, *Beyond Adversary Democracy*, 266–68 and accompanying notes, and Charles R. Beitz, *Political Equality* (Princeton: Princeton University Press, 1989), 8–11 and notes. This problem is particularly severe when segmented rather than cross-cutting cleavages produce permanent minorities. See, e.g., John C. Calhoun, *A Disquisition on Government* (1853) (New York: Bobbs-Merrill, 1953); Arend Lijphart, *The Politics of Accommodation* (Berkeley and Los Angeles: University of California Press, 1968); Lani Guinier, *The Tyranny of the Majority* (New York: Free Press, 1994); and commentaries such as Ian Shapiro's "Democratic Innovation," *World Politics* 46 (1993): 121–50.

26. See, e.g., Duncan Black, *The Theory of Committees and Elections* (1958; reprint, Cambridge: Cambridge University Press, 1963), expanding on the work of Condorcet and C. L. Dodgson; Kenneth J. Arrow, *Social Choice and Individual Values* (New York: John Wiley, 1963); William H. Riker, *Liberalism against Populism* (Prospect Heights, Ill.: Waveland Press, 1982).

27. Beitz, *Political Equality*, xiii.

28. Dahl, *Democracy and Its Critics*, 156. Dahl himself generates five criteria for "political equality" or, more generally, for "a democratic process." In "Is Democracy Special?" Brian Barry gives an excellent account of these problems.

29. See Mansbridge, *Beyond Adversary Democracy*, for evidence of systematic unequal power even in a highly egalitarian, highly democratic, and ideologically committed forty-one-person collective.

30. John Rawls, A Theory of Justice (Cambridge, Mass.: Harvard University Press, 1971), 112, regarding obligations to do one's part to maintain just cooperative arrangements in which others are cooperating and from which one benefits. See also "as just as it is reasonable to expect in the circumstances" (115), regarding the natural duty to support and comply with just institutions.

31. I take this formulation from Nancy Fraser, "What's Critical about Critical Theory?" chap. 6 of her Unruly Practices (Minneapolis: University of Minnesota Press, 1989), 120.

32. Compare the celebrated first sentence of H.L.A. Hart's "Are There Any Natural Rights?" Philosophical Review 64 (1958): 175–19.

33. In regard to justice, Iris Young has suggested the example of a universal health care bill that omitted coverage for victims of AIDS. In a country previously without universal coverage, the overall thrust of the policy would be in the direction of social justice, while parts of its operation would be, by most standards, unjust.

34. For a defense of the potential deliberative capacities of interest groups, see Mansbridge, "A Deliberative Theory of Interest Representation."

35. See the suggestions for participatory innovation in Benjamin Barber, Strong Democracy (Berkeley and Los Angeles: University of California Press, 1984).

36. The phrase "probing of volitions" comes from Charles E. Lindblom, Inquiry and Change (New Haven: Yale University Press, 1990); and the mandate to subject every issue to continuous reexamination is from Barber, Strong Democracy, 182. This is not the place for a full defense of my claim that narrow, material self-interest ought to play a role, in some cases an important role, in democratic deliberation (see my "Feminism and Democracy," "A Deliberative Theory of Interest Representation," and "On the Relation of Altruism and Self-Interest," in Mansbridge, ed., Beyond Self-Interest [Chicago: University of Chicago Press, 1990]). My claim derives from two kinds of experience. The first is the experience of "consciousness-raising," which Pamela Allen described as follows: "Although we are not sure that full autonomy is a possible goal, we believe that our hope lies in developing as individuals who understand themselves, their own needs, the workings of our society, and the needs of others" (Pamela Allen, "Free Space" [1970], in Anne Koedt et al., eds., Radical Feminism [New York: Quadrangle Press, 1973], 271–72). We cannot understand our "own needs" better without also understanding better our narrow material self-interested needs as well as other kinds of needs. The second is the experience of collective decision-making, from which I conclude that deliberations that force participants into describing their needs and desires only in terms of the collective "we" gravely distort the process of communication and keep participants from seeing as accurately as possible when they ought to strive for consensus on the basis of discovering or creating common interests and when they ought to deal with the issues by recognizing underlying conflicts and settling those conflicts provisionally through the fairest available "adversary" democratic procedures. See also Laura Stoker, "Interests and Ethics in Politics," American Political Science Review 86 (1992): 369–80.

37. Capital (1867) (New York: International Publishers, 1967), vol. 1, 763; Karl Marx and Friedrich Engels, The Communist Manifesto (1848) (Chicago: Henry Regnery, 1954), 32. Jon Elster, Making Sense of Marx (Cambridge: Cambridge University Press, 1985), 355, points out that Marx did not say explicitly that concentration in the factory rather than in housing and residence was the decisive factor in producing worker soli-

darity, "but from what he says elsewhere about the importance of trade unions this can reasonably be inferred."

38. For examples of such enclaves, see Verta Taylor, "Social Movement Continuity: The Women's Movement In Abeyance," *American Sociological Review* 54 (1989): 761–75, and Verta Taylor and Nancy Whittier, "Collective Identity in Social Movement Communities," in Aldon D. Morris and Carol McClurg Mueller, eds., *Frontiers in Social Movement Theory* (New Haven: Yale University Press, 1992). For an early description of the importance of "a place in which to think," see Pamela Allen, "Free Space," 271–79. On social movements politicizing culture, see Iris Marion Young, *Justice and the Politics of Difference*, 86–88.

39. Mansbridge, *Beyond Adversary Democracy*, 62–63.

40. "Rethinking the Public Sphere: A Contribution to the Critique of Actually Existing Democracy," in Craig Calhoun, ed., *Habermas and the Public Sphere*, 123.

41. James C. Scott, *Domination and the Arts of Resistance: Hidden Transcripts* (New Haven: Yale University Press, 1990).

42. See Bonnie Honig, *Political Theory and the Displacement of Politics* (Ithaca: Cornell University Press, 1993), esp. chap. 1, on both the reality and the affirmative dimensions of "perpetual contest." Honig argues that "every politics has its remainders," or competing possibilities that are "produced by the process of division itself" but are often successfully suppressed by that process (3, 15, and 213, n. 1). Honig's argument has influenced both my own insistence on the need to keep contest alive and my stress, contrary to her overall thrust, on the importance, particularly for the disadvantaged, of ongoing stable coercion.

43. Joshua Cohen and Joel Rogers, "Secondary Associations and Democratic Governance," *Politics and Society* 20 (1992): 393–472; Philippe Schmitter, "The Irony of Modern Democracy and Efforts to Improve Its Practice," *Politics and Society* 20 (1992): 507–12. On group representation see also Young, *Justice and the Politics of Difference*.

44. Scott, *Domination and the Arts of Resistance*.

45. Mansbridge, "Using Power, Fighting Power," 54–55, 65–67.

Four

Toward a Deliberative Model of Democratic Legitimacy

SEYLA BENHABIB

Democratic Legitimacy and Public Goods

Complex modern democratic societies since the Second World War face the task of securing three public goods. These are legitimacy, economic welfare, and a viable sense of collective identity. These are "goods" in the sense that their attainment is considered worthy and desirable by most members of such societies; furthermore, not attaining one or a combination thereof would cause problems in the functioning of these societies such as to throw them into crises.

These goods stand in a complex relation to one another: excessive realization of one such good may be in conflict with and may jeopardize the realization of others. For example, economic welfare may be attained at the cost of sacrificing legitimacy by curtailing union rights, by limiting a more rigorous examination of business accounting practices, or by encouraging the unfair use of protectionist state measures. Too great an emphasis on collective identity may come at the cost of minorities and dissidents whose civil and political rights may be impinged upon by a revival of a sense of collective identity. Thus legitimacy claims and collective identity demands, particularly if they take a nationalist tone, may come into conflict. There can also be conflicts between the claims of economic welfare and the demands of collec-

This essay is a much-revised version of an article that originally appeared in *Constellations* 1, no. 1 (April 1994), under the title "Deliberative Rationality and Models of Democratic Legitimacy." It is part of a manuscript in progress tentatively entitled *In Search of the Civic Polity: Democracy, Legitimacy, and Citizenship at Century's End*.

I would like to acknowledge my thanks to members of the New York University "Law and Social Theory" symposium and the Yale University "Legal Theory Workshop" for comments and criticisms on earlier drafts. In particular, I am thankful to Professors Ronald Dworkin and Thomas Nagel for their rigorous criticisms on the question of the status of basic rights and liberties within the framework of a theory of deliberative democracy. I would also like to thank Stephen Macedo, whose comments on an earlier version of this paper delivered at the Political Theory Colloquium of the Harvard University Department of Government in the spring of 1994 have greatly contributed to my thoughts.

tive identity, as when excessive forms of protectionism and nationalism isolate countries in the world economic context, possibly leading to declining standards of living. Conversely, too great an emphasis on economic welfare may undermine a sense of collective identity by increasing competition among social groups and by weakening the claims of political sovereignty vis-à-vis other states. In a well-functioning democratic society the demands of legitimacy, economic welfare, and collective identity ideally exist in some form of equilibrium.

The present essay is concerned with one good among others which democratic societies must attain: the good of legitimacy. I am concerned to examine the philosophical foundations of democratic legitimacy. I will argue that legitimacy in complex democratic societies must be thought to result from the free and unconstrained public deliberation of all about matters of common concern. Thus a public sphere of deliberation about matters of mutual concern is essential to the legitimacy of democratic institutions.

Democracy, in my view, is best understood as a model for organizing the collective and public exercise of power in the major institutions of a society on the basis of the principle that decisions affecting the well-being of a collectivity can be viewed as the outcome of a procedure of free and reasoned deliberation among individuals considered as moral and political equals. Certainly any definition of essentially contested concepts like democracy, freedom, and justice is never a mere definition; the definition itself already articulates the normative theory that justifies the term. Such is the case with the preceding definition. My understanding of democracy privileges a deliberative model over other kinds of normative considerations. This is not to imply that economic welfare, institutional efficiency, and cultural stability would not be relevant in judging the adequacy of a normative definition of democracy. Economic welfare claims and collective identity needs must also be satisfied for democracies to function over time. However, the normative basis of democracy as a form of organizing our collective life is neither the fulfillment of economic welfare nor the realization of a stable sense of collective identity. For just as the attainment of certain levels of economic welfare may be compatible with authoritarian political rule, so too antidemocratic regimes may be more successful in assuring a sense of collective identity than democratic ones.

My goal in the first half of this article will be to examine the relationship between the normative presuppositions of democratic deliberation and the idealized content of practical rationality. The approach I follow is consonant with what John Rawls has called "Kantian constructivism," and what Jürgen Habermas refers to as "reconstruction."[1] In this context, the differences in their methodologies are less significant than their shared assumption that the institutions of liberal democracies embody the idealized content of a form of practical reason. This idealized content can be elucidated and philosophically articulated; in fact, the task of a philosophical theory of democracy would consist in the clarification and articulation of the form of practical rationality represented by democratic rule.[2]

The methodology of "philosophical reconstruction" differs from "ethnocentric liberalism" (Richard Rorty) as well as from more a prioristic forms of Kantianism.[3] As distinguished from certain kinds of Kantianism, I would like to acknowledge the historical and sociological specificity of the project of democracy while, against ethnocentric liberalism, I would like to insist that the practical rationality embodied in democratic institutions has a culture-transcending validity claim. This form of practical reason has become the collective and anonymous property of cultures, institutions, and traditions as a result of the experiments and experiences, both ancient and modern, with democratic rule over the course of human history.[4] The insights and perhaps illusions resulting from these experiments and experiences are sedimented in diverse constitutions, institutional arrangements, and procedural specifics. When one thinks through the form of practical rationality at the core of democratic rule, Hegel's concept of "objective Spirit" (*objektiver Geist*) appears to me particularly appropriate.[5] To make this concept useful today we have to think of it without recourse to the metaphorical presence of a supersubject; we have to desubstantialize the model of a thinking and acting supersubject that still governs Hegelian philosophy. Without this metaphor of the subject implicitly governing it, the term "objective spirit" would refer to those *anonymous yet intelligible* collective rules, procedures, and practices that form a way of life. It is the rationality intrinsic to these anonymous yet intelligible rules, procedures, and practices that any attempt aiming at the reconstruction of the logic of democracies must focus upon.

A Deliberative Model of Democracy

According to the deliberative model of democracy, it is a necessary condition for attaining legitimacy and rationality with regard to collective decision making processes in a polity, that the institutions of this polity are so arranged that what is considered in the common interest of all results from processes of collective deliberation conducted rationally and fairly among free and equal individuals.[6] The more collective decision-making processes approximate this model the more increases the presumption of their legitimacy and rationality. Why?

The basis of legitimacy in democratic institutions is to be traced back to the presumption that the instances which claim obligatory power for themselves do so because their decisions represent an impartial standpoint said to be equally in the interests of all. This presumption can be fulfilled only if such decisions are in principle open to appropriate public processes of deliberation by free and equal citizens.

The discourse model of ethics formulates the most *general principles* and *moral intuitions* behind the validity claims of a deliberative model of democracy.[7] The basic idea behind this model is that only those norms (i.e., general rules of action and institutional arrangements) can be said to be valid (i.e., morally binding), which would be agreed to by all those affected by their consequences, if such agreement were reached as a consequence of a process of deliberation that had the following features: 1) participation in such deliberation is governed by the norms of equality and symmetry; all have the same chances to initiate speech acts, to question, to interrogate, and to open debate; 2) all have the right to question the assigned topics of conversation; and 3) all have the right to initiate reflexive arguments about the very rules of the discourse procedure and the way in which they are applied or carried out. There are no prima facie rules limiting the agenda of the conversation, or the identity of the participants, as long as each excluded person or group can justifiably show that they are relevantly affected by the proposed norm under question. In certain circumstances this would mean that citizens of a democratic community would have to enter into a practical discourse with noncitizens who may be residing in their countries, at their borders, or in neighboring communities if there are matters that affect them all. Ecology and environmental issues in general are a perfect example of such instances when the boundaries of discourses keep expanding because the consequences of our actions expand and affect increasingly more people.

The procedural specifics of those special argumentation situations called "practical discourses" are not automatically transferable to a macroinstitutional level, nor is it necessary that they should be so transferable. A theory of democracy, as opposed to a general moral theory, would have to be concerned with the question of institutional specifications and practical feasibility. Nonetheless, the procedural constraints of the discourse model can act as test cases for critically evaluating the criteria of membership and the rules for agenda setting, and for the structuring of public discussions within and among institutions.

In closely tying the normative foundations of democratic legitimacy to a general moral theory based on a discursive model of validity, I depart from several other influential models of democratic theory. These are: Hannah Arendt's theory of political action in the public sphere; Benjamin Barber's model of "strong democracy," and antifoundationalist, poststructuralist models of democracy recently developed by William Connolly, Chantal Mouffe, and Ernesto Laclau.[8] Here I will briefly articulate the central premises around which my deliberative model differs from these other modes of democratic theorizing: Though hardly conceivable without strong norms of moral equality, freedom, and respect, Hannah Arendt's political philosophy is ultimately rooted in her "phenomenological essentialism," and cannot clarify the normative foundations of democratic politics. Benjamin Barber's model of strong democracy is, like Hannah Arendt's, based on an opposition between moral theory and political philosophy that is conceptually overdrawn and politically unrealistic. Finally, antifoundationalist theories of democracy are circular in that they either posit or simply take for granted precisely those moral and political norms of citizens' equality, freedom, and democratic legitimacy for the justification of which what are dubbed "foundationalist" models were developed in the first place.

According to the deliberative model, procedures of deliberation generate legitimacy as well as assure some degree of practical rationality.[9] But what are the claims to practical rationality of such deliberative democratic processes? Deliberative processes are essential to the rationality of collective decision-making processes for three reasons. First, as Bernard Manin has observed in an excellent article "On Legitimacy and Deliberation," deliberative processes are also processes that impart information.[10] New information is imparted because 1) no single individual can anticipate and foresee all the variety of perspectives through which matters of ethics and politics would be perceived by different individuals; and 2) no single individual can possess all the information deemed relevant to a certain decision affecting all.[11] Deliberation is a procedure for being informed.

Furthermore, much political theory under the influence of economic models of reasoning in particular proceeds from a methodological fiction: this is the methodological fiction of an individual with an ordered set of coherent preferences. This fiction does not have much relevance in the political world. On complex social and political issues, more often than not, individuals may have views and wishes but no ordered set of preferences, since the latter would imply that they would be enlightened not only about the preferences but about the consequences and relative merits of each of their preferred choices in advance. It is actually the deliberative process itself that is likely to produce such an outcome by leading the individual to further critical reflection on his already held views and opinions; it is incoherent to assume that individuals can start a process of public deliberation with a level of conceptual clarity about their choices and preferences that can actually result only from a successful process of deliberation. Likewise, the formation of coherent preferences cannot precede deliberation; it can only succeed it. Very often individuals' wishes as well as views and opinions conflict with one another. In the course of deliberation and the exchange of views with others, individuals become more aware of such conflicts and feel compelled to undertake a coherent ordering.

More significantly, the very procedure of articulating a view in public imposes a certain reflexivity on individual preferences and opinions. When presenting their point of view and position to others, individuals must support them by articulating good reasons in a public context to their co-deliberators. This process of *articulating good reasons in public* forces the individual to think

of what would count as a good reason for all others involved. One is thus
forced to think from the standpoint of all involved for whose agreement one
is "wooing." Nobody can convince others in public of her point of view without being able to state why what appears good, plausible, just, and expedient
to her can also be considered so from the standpoint of all involved. Reasoning
from the standpoint of all involved not only forces a certain coherence upon
one's own views but also forces one to adopt a standpoint that Hannah Arendt,
following Kant, had called the "enlarged mentality."[12]

A deliberative model of democracy suggests a necessary but not sufficient
condition of practical rationality, because, as with any procedure, it can be
misinterpreted, misapplied, and abused. Procedures can neither dictate outcomes nor define the quality of the reasons advanced in argumentation nor
control the quality of the reasoning and rules of logic and inference used by
participants. Procedural models of rationality are underdetermined. Nonetheless, the discourse model makes some provisions against its own misuses and
abuses in that the reflexivity condition built into the model allows abuses and
misapplications at the first level to be challenged at a second, metalevel of
discourse. Likewise, the equal chance of all affected to initiate such discourse
of deliberation suggests that no outcome is prima facie fixed but can be revised
and subjected to reexamination. Such would be the normative justification of
majority rule as a decision procedure following from this model: in many
instances the majority rule is a fair and rational decision procedure, not because legitimacy resides in numbers but because if a majority of people are
convinced at one point on the basis of reasons formulated as closely as possible as a result of a process of discursive deliberation that conclusion A is
the right thing to do, then this conclusion can remain valid until challenged
by good reasons by some other group. It is not the sheer numbers that support the rationality of the conclusion, but the presumption that if a large number of people see certain matters a certain way as a result of following certain
kinds of rational procedures of deliberation and decision-making, then such
a conclusion has a presumptive claim to being rational until shown to be
otherwise. The simple practice of having a ruling and an opposition party in
democracies in fact incorporates this principle: we accept the will of the majority at the end of an electoral process that has been fairly and correctly
carried out, but even when we accept the legitimacy of the process we may
have grave doubts about the rationality of the outcome. The practice of there
being a parliamentary opposition says that the grounds on which the majority
party claims to govern can be examined, challenged, tested, criticized, and
rearticulated. Parliamentary procedures of opposition, debate, questioning,
and even impeachment proceedings, and investigatory commissions incorporate this rule of deliberative rationality that majoritarian decisions are temporarily agreed-upon conclusions, the claim to rationality and validity of which
can be publicly reexamined.

This deliberative model of democracy is proceduralist in that it emphasizes first and foremost certain institutional procedures and practices for attaining decisions on matters that would be binding on all. Three additional points are worthy of note with respect to such a conception of democracy: first, I proceed from the assumption of value pluralism. Disagreement about the highest goods of human existence and the proper conduct of a morally righteous life are a fundamental feature of our modern value-universe since the end of natural law cosmologies in the sixteenth and seventeenth centuries, and the eventual separation of church and state.[13] The challenge to democratic rationality is to arrive at acceptable formulations of the common good despite this inevitable value-pluralism. We cannot resolve conflicts among value systems and visions of the good by reestablishing a strong unified moral and religious code without forsaking fundamental liberties. Agreements in societies living with value-pluralism are to be sought for not at the level of substantive beliefs but at that of procedures, processes, and practices for attaining and revising beliefs. Proceduralism is a rational answer to persisting value conflicts at the substantive level.[14]

Second, the deliberative model of democracy proceeds not only from a conflict of values but also from a conflict of interests in social life. Social life necessitates both conflict of interests and cooperation. Democratic procedures have to convince, even under conditions when one's interests as an individual or as a group are negatively affected, that the conditions of mutual cooperation are still legitimate. Procedures can be regarded as methods for articulating, sifting through, and weighing conflicting interests. The more conflicts of interests there are the more it is important to have procedural solutions of conflict adjudication through which parties whose interests are negatively affected can find recourse to other methods of the articulation and representation of their grievances. Proceduralist models of democracy allow the articulation of conflicts of interests under conditions of social cooperation mutually acceptable to all.[15]

Finally, any proceduralist and deliberative model of democracy is prima facie open to the argument that no modern society can organize its affairs along the fiction of a mass assembly carrying out its deliberations in public and collectively. Here more than an issue of size is at stake. The argument that there may be an invisible limit to the size of a deliberative body that, when crossed, affects the nature of the reasoning process is undoubtedly true. Nonetheless the reason why a deliberative and proceduralist model of democracy does not need to operate with the fiction of a general deliberative assembly is that the procedural specifications of this model privilege a *plurality of modes of association* in which all affected can have the right to articulate their point of view. These can range from political parties, to citizens' initiatives, to social movements, to voluntary associations, to consciousness-raising groups, and the like. *It is through the interlocking net of these multiple forms of*

associations, networks, and organizations that an anonymous "public conversation"
results. It is central to the model of deliberative democracy that it privileges such a
public sphere of mutually interlocking and overlapping networks and associations of
deliberation, contestation, and argumentation. The fiction of a general deliberative assembly in which the united people expressed their will belongs to the
early history of democratic theory; today our guiding model has to be that of
a medium of loosely associated, multiple foci of opinion formation and dissemination which affect one another in free and spontaneous processes of
communication.[16]

Such a strong model of deliberative democracy is subject to three different
kinds of criticism: first, liberal theorists will express concern that such a strong
model would lead to the corrosion of individual liberties and may in fact
destabilize the rule of law. In his earlier work, Bruce Ackerman had formulated a theory of "conversational neutrality" to voice some of these concerns.[17]
Stephen Holmes has defended the plausibility of certain "gag rules" on public
conversation.[18] Second, feminist theorists are skeptical about this model, because they see it as privileging a certain mode of discourse at the cost of silencing others: this is the rationalist, male, univocal, hegemonic discourse of a
transparent polity that disregards the emotions, polyvocity, multiplicity, and
differences in the articulation of the voice of the public; third, institutionalists
and realists consider this discourse model to be hopelessly naive, maybe even
dangerous, in its seemingly plebiscitary and anti-institutional implications. I
would briefly like to consider these objections.

Liberal Misgivings about Deliberative Democracy

The contrast between deliberative democracy, as outlined in the preceding,
and the liberal conception of public dialogue can be well captured from the
standpoint of John Rawls's idea of "public reason."[19] Rawls specifies this principle as follows: "In a democratic society public reason is the reason of equal
citizens who, as a collective body, exercise final political and coercive power
over one another in enacting laws and in amending the constitution. The first
point is that the limits imposed by public reason do not apply to all political
questions but only to those involving what we may call 'constitutional essentials' and questions of basic justice. . . . This means that political values alone
are to settle such fundamental questions as: who has the right to vote, or what
religions are to be tolerated, or who is to be assured fair equality of opportunity, or to hold property."[20]

Rawls's idea of public reason and the deliberative model of democracy share
certain fundamental premises: both theories view the legitimation of political
power and the examination of the justice of institutions to be a public process,
open to all citizens to partake in. The idea that the justice of institutions be "in

the public's eye," so to speak, for the public to scrutinize, examine, and reflect upon is fundamental. From the standpoint of a deliberative model of democracy as well this is crucial. Note, however, that there are three significant ways in which the Rawlsian idea of public reason differs from the model of public deliberation proposed earlier. Some of these differences are of a sociological nature; others indicate significant philosophical divergences.

First, unlike the deliberative model, which insists upon the openness of the agenda of public debate, Rawls restricts the exercise of public reason to deliberation about a specific subject matter. These are issues involving "constitutional essentials" and questions of basic justice.[21] Rawls's model of public reason proceeds from a *restricted agenda*.

Second, public reason is best viewed not as a *process* of reasoning among citizens but as a regulative *principle* imposing limits upon how individuals, institutions, and agencies *ought to reason about public matters*. The limits of public reason are set by a "political conception of liberalism." In Rawls's words: "The point of the ideal of public reason is that citizens are to conduct their fundamental discussions within the framework of what each regards as a political conception of justice based on values that the others can reasonably be expected to endorse and each is, in good faith, prepared to defend that conception so understood. This means that each of us must have, and be ready to explain, a criterion of what principles and guidelines we think other citizens (who are also free and equal) may reasonably be expected to endorse along with us."[22] Rawls cites his own elaboration of the political values of liberalism as an example of such criteria, while admitting that there will be divergence as to the "most appropriate political conception."[23]

Third, for Rawls the social spaces within which public reason is exercised are also restricted. The limits of public reason do not apply to personal deliberations and reflections about political questions or "to the reasoning about them by members of associations such as churches and universities, all of which is a vital part of the background culture."[24] The reasoning of corporate bodies and associations is "public" with respect to its members, "but nonpublic with respect to political society and to citizens generally. Nonpublic reasons comprise the many reasons of civil society and belong to what I have called the 'background culture,' in contrast with the public political culture."[25] The public sphere, for Rawls then, is not located *in civil society but in the state and its organizations, including first and foremost the legal sphere and its institutions*.

Although this characterization is adequate for articulating the contrast between Rawls's idea of public reason and the model of deliberative democracy, I think Rawls himself cannot sustain the distinction between "civil society" and the restricted conception of the public, and this in two ways: first, in a constitutional democracy many, if not all, associations and organizations are also "public" bodies, for to become incorporated and recognized as a corporate body, they have to comply with the same constitutional essentials and the rule of law as do all other more obviously public institutions. Take the case of country clubs that discriminate against blacks, Jews, Hispanics, and so on. To be recognized as a legally incorporated entity under the due process of the law, such country clubs in recent years have had to change their charters. The constitutional-democratic state and the institutions of civil society are therefore not as sharply separable as some of Rawls's formulations suggest. All clubs, associations, and organizations within civil society have charters that can be subject to public as well as legal scrutiny.

Second, institutions, individuals, and movements in civil society attempt to influence the public-political process and in doing so cross the boundaries between public and more private-civil associations. For Rawls this is the case with citizens who engage in political advocacy in the public forum and with members of political parties and with candidates and individuals supporting them.[26] To say that when in civil society these individuals and associations are governed by one kind of reason, a nonpublic one, but that they have to respect the limits of public reason once they enter the political arena is inadequate, for *civil society is also public*. Civil society and its associations are not public in the sense of always allowing universal access to all, but they are public in the sense of being part of that anonymous public conversation in a democracy. A deliberative model of democracy is much more interested than Rawls in what he calls "background cultural conditions," precisely because politics and political reason are always seen to emerge out of a cultural and social context. Public reason can certainly distance itself from this context and evaluate it critically, but it can never completely render transparent all the background condition that gives rise to it. This is the kernel of truth in postmodernist critiques of Kantian rationalism, which point out that reason is always situated in a context that it can never render completely comprehensible to discursive analysis.

In these three respects, the Rawlsian model diverges from the deliberative model: the deliberative model does not restrict the agenda of public conversation; in fact it encourages discourse about the lines separating the public from the private;[27] second, the deliberative model locates the public sphere in civil society,[28] and is much more interested in the ways in which political processes and the "background culture" interact. Finally, while the Rawlsian model focuses upon "final and coercive political power," the deliberative model focuses upon noncoercive and nonfinal processes of opinion formation in an unrestricted public sphere.[29]

Although there is little doubt that the Rawlsian principle of public reason expresses a governing limit upon the coercive power and public accountability of the major institutions of a liberal-democratic society, consider also what is missing from it. All contestatory, rhetorical, affective, impassioned elements of public discourse, with all their excesses and virtues, are absent from this view.

Public reason is not freely wielded public reasoning, with all the infuriating ideological and rhetorical mess that this may involve.[30] To this conception of contestatory public speech[31] or shared reasoning, the liberal theorist will respond that lofty and ennobling as its vision may be, this view of the political leaves the floodgates open for the whim of majoritarian decisions. What if less than noble majorities challenge the principles of political liberalism and the lines between the right and the good in such ways as to lead to religious fanaticism, persecution of unpopular minorities, intrusion of the state into the domain of private life, or even the political surveillance by children of parents, by spouses of each other, all in the name of some shared good?

Thus it is not surprising that for Rawls the prime exemplar of the exercise of public reason is not the anonymous public but very often is and "ought to be" the Supreme Court: "Public reason is well suited to be the court's reason in exercising its role as the highest judicial interpreter but not as the final interpreter of the higher law; and second, that the Supreme Court is the branch of government that serves as the exemplar of public reason."[32]

The liberal concern about the corrosive effect of unbridled majoritarian politics upon civil and political liberties is, I believe, incontrovertible. Nonetheless, the deliberative model of democracy can offer certain conceptual as well as institutional solutions to soften, and perhaps to transcend, the old dichotomy between the liberal emphasis on individual rights and liberties—what Rawls would call "constitutional essentials"—and democratic theory's emphasis on collective deliberation and will-formation. I would like to single out two sets of issues around which further exchange between deliberative democracy advocates and liberal theorists is necessary. This brief discussion should also indicate why I see the deliberative democracy model as transcending the stark opposition between liberal and democratic theory.

Basic Rights and Deliberative Democracy

Deliberative democracy models often seem subject to the argument that they do not protect individuals' basic rights and liberties sufficiently.[33] This objection is rooted in two assumptions: first, insofar as deliberative models appear to make a high degree of consensus or unanimity on public issues a value, it is fair to suspect that such unanimity could only be attained at the cost of silencing dissent and curtailing minority viewpoints. Second, what protection does a deliberative model allow against the tyranny of democratic majorities from imposing its choices and norms upon the minority?

I believe that these objections are fair when raised against most versions of radical participatory democratic theories that also prioritize political deliberation. I think it is fair to ask whether the radical democratic theories of Hannah Arendt, Benjamin Barber, or Mouffe and Laclau allow for a coherent theory of rights such as would protect both basic rights and liberties for all, and defend minority rights against the tyranny of the majority. But such objections are not applicable to the model of deliberative democracy developed here.

Precisely because I share with the Kantian liberal tradition the assumption that moral respect for the autonomous personality is a fundamental norm of morality and democracy, the deliberative model of democracy presupposes a discourse theory of ethics to supply it with the most general moral principles upon which rights claims would be based.[34] Insofar as a discourse theory of ethics considers participants to be equal and free beings, equally entitled to take part in those discourse which determine the norms that are to affect their lives, it proceeds from a view of persons as beings entitled to certain "moral rights." I have named this moral right the entitlement to *universal moral respect*, and have attempted in *Situating the Self* to give a nonfoundationalist but principled justification for the recognition of this norm.[35] I further maintain that within a discourse theory each individual has the same symmetrical rights to various speech acts, to initiate new topics, to ask for reflection about the presuppositions of the conversations, and so on. I call this the principle of *egalitarian reciprocity*. In my view the norms of universal moral respect and egalitarian reciprocity are moral rights in that they are entitlements that accrue to individuals insofar as we view them as moral persons.

The step that would lead from a recognition of these two moral rights to the formulation of a principle of basic rights and liberties is certainly not very wide.[36] Basically it would involve a hypothetical answer to the question, If it is plausible for individuals to view one another as beings entitled to universal moral respect and egalitarian reciprocity, which most general principles of basic rights and liberties would such individuals also be likely to accept as determining the conditions of their collective existence?[37]

Although the discourse theory shares this kind of hypothetical and counter-factual moral reasoning procedure with Kant and Rawls, it would be different from a Kantian deduction of the concept of right and from a Rawlsian construction of the "original position," in that it would privilege a discourse model of practical debate as being the appropriate forum for determining rights claims. But are we not thereby landing in a vicious circle, that is, discourses, even to get started, presuppose the recognition of one another's moral rights among discourse participants; on the other hand, such rights are said to be specified as a result of the discursive situation.

I have indicated elsewhere that this is not a vicious circle but rather the hermeneutic circle that characterizes all reasoning about morals and politics.[38] We never begin our deliberations concerning these matters at a "moral ground zero." Rather, in moral theory as in everyday morality, in political theory as in everyday political discourse, we are always situated within a horizon of pre-suppositions, assumptions, and power relations, the totality of which can never become wholly transparent to us. This much we must have learned from all the criticisms of rationalism in the last three centuries. Discourse ethics in this sense presupposes the reciprocal moral recognition of one another's claims to be participants in the moral-political dialogue. I am still enough of a Hegelian to maintain, however, that such reciprocal recognition of one another's rights to moral personality is a result of a world-historical process that involves struggle, battle, and resistance, as well as defeat, carried out by social classes, genders, groups, and nations.

What is distinctive about the discourse model is that although it presupposes that participants must recognize one another's entitlement to moral respect and reciprocity in some sense, the determination of the precise content and extent of these principles would be a consequence of discourses themselves.[39] Insofar as the precise meaning and entailment of the norms of universal moral respect and egalitarian reciprocity would be subject to discursive validation, we can speak here of a procedure of "recursive validation."[40] The methodological procedure of recursive validation rules out the two consequences most feared by liberals vis-à-vis the model of deliberative democracy—namely, too strong a formulation of the conditions of consent, and the tyranny of the majority. The norms of universal moral respect and egalitarian reciprocity allow minorities and dissenters both the right to withhold their assent and the right to challenge the rules as well as the agenda of public debate. For what distinguishes discourses from compromises and other agreements reached under conditions of coercion is that only the *freely given assent of all concerned* can count as a condition of having reached agreement in the discourse situation.[41]

Deliberative Democracy and Constitutionalism

Upon reflection, we can see that institutionally as well, complex constitutional democracies, and particularly those in which a *public sphere* of opinion formation and deliberation has been developed, engage in such recursive validation continually. Basic human civil and political rights, as guaranteed by the Bill of Rights to the U.S. Constitution and as embodied in the constitution of most democratic governments, are never really "off the agenda" of public discussion and debate. They are simply constitutive and regulative institutional norms of debate in democratic societies that cannot be transformed and abrogated by simple majority decisions. The language of keeping these rights off the agenda mischaracterizes the nature of democratic debate in our kinds of societies: although we cannot change these rights without extremely elaborate political and juridical procedures, we are always disputing their meaning, their extent, and their jurisdiction. Democratic debate is like a ball game where there is

no umpire to interpret the rules of the game and their application defini-
tively. Rather, in the game of democracy the rules of the game no less than
their interpretation and even the position of the umpire are essentially contestable. Contestation means neither the complete abrogation of these rules
nor silence about them. When basic rights and liberties are violated the game
of democracy is suspended and becomes either martial rule, civil war, or dictatorship; when democratic politics is in full session, the debate about the meaning of these rights, what they do or do not entitle us to, their scope and en-
forcement, is what politics is all about. One cannot challenge the specific
interpretation of basic rights and liberties in a democracy without taking these
absolutely seriously.

The deliberative theory of democracy transcends the traditional opposition
of majoritarian politics vs. liberal guarantees of basic rights and liberties to the
extent that the normative conditions of discourses, like basic rights and liberties, are to be viewed as rules of the game that can be contested within the
game but only insofar as one first accepts to abide by them and play the game
at all. This formulation seems to me to correspond to the reality of democratic
debate and public speech in real democracies much more accurately than the
liberal model of deliberation upon constitutional essentials or the reasonings
of the Supreme Court. Crucial to the deliberative model of democracy is
the idea of a "public sphere" of opinion-formation, debate, deliberation, and
contestation among citizens, groups, movements, and organizations in a
polity. When this concept of a public sphere is introduced as the concrete
embodiment of discursive democracy in practice, it also becomes possible to
think of the issue of conversational constraints in a more nuanced way. While
the deliberative model of democracy shares with liberalism a concern for
the protection of the rights to autonomy of equal citizens, the conceptual
method of discursive validation and the institutional reality of a differentiated
public sphere of deliberation and contestation provide plausible beginning
points for a mediation of the stark opposition between liberalism and deliberative democracy.

Bruce Ackerman's conception of dualist democracy is based upon a similar
strategy of overcoming the opposition between the standpoint of foundationalist rights-liberals on the one hand and monist majoritarian democrats on the
other: "The basic mediating device is the dualist's two-track system of democratic lawmaking. It allows an important place for the foundationalist's view
of 'rights as trumps' without violating the monist's deeper commitment to the
primacy of democracy."[42] In a constitutional democracy the question as to
which aspects of the higher law are entrenched against revision by the people
as opposed to which aspects may be repealed is itself always open and contestable. Conceptually as well as sociologically, models of deliberative and dualistic democracy focus on this process of "recursive" and "hermeneutic" interdependence between constitution-making and democratic politics.[43]

Feminist Suspicions toward Deliberative Democracy

While liberals criticize the model of deliberative democracy for possibly over-extending itself and corroding the sphere of individual privacy, feminist theorists criticize this model for not extending itself broadly enough to be truly inclusive. In an illuminating article entitled "Impartiality and the Civic Public," Iris Young, for example, has argued:

> The distinction between public and private as it appears in modern political theory expresses a will for homogeneity that necessitates the exclusion of many persons and groups, particularly women and radicalized groups culturally identified with the body, wildness and rationality. In conformity with the modern idea of normative reason, the idea of the public in modern political theory and practice designates a sphere of human existence in which citizens express their rationality and universality, abstracted from their particular situations and need, and opposed to feeling. . . . Examination of the exclusionary and homogeneous ideal in modern political theory, however, shows that we cannot envision such renewal of public life as a recovery of Enlightenment ideals. Instead, we need to transform the distinction between public and private that does not correlate with an opposition between reason and affectivity and desire, or universal and particular.[44]

Iris Young's cogent and penetrating feminist critique of the ideal of the impartial public applies to the model of deliberative democracy suggested in the preceding only in certain respects. Certainly, the model of a general deliberative assembly that governed our conceptions of the public sphere well into the twentieth century was historically, socially, and culturally a space for male bodies. I mean this not only in the sense that only men were active citizens, entitled to hold office and appear in public, but also in the sense that the institutional iconography of early democratic theory privileged the male mode of self-representation.[45]

Yet here we must distinguish between the *institutional* and the *conceptual* critiques. There is a certain ambivalence in the feminist critique of such models of the public sphere and deliberative democracy. On the one hand, the critique appears to take democratic institutions at their principled best and to criticize their biased and restrictive implementations in practice; on the other hand, the feminist critique appears to aim at a rejection of the ideals of free public reason and impartiality altogether. As Joan Landes puts it, the democratic public sphere appears to be essentially and not just accidentally "masculinist."[46] A normative theory of deliberative democracy requires a strong concept of the public sphere as its institutional correlate. The public sphere replaces the model of the general deliberative assembly found in early democratic theory. In this context, it is important for feminist theorists to specify the level of their conceptual objection, and to differentiate among institutional and normative presuppositions.[47]

Iris Young does not reject the ideal of a public sphere, only its Enlightenment variety. She proposes to replace the ideal of the "civil public" with that of a heterogeneous public. In her recent work she has advocated a number of institutional measures that would guarantee and solidify group representation in such a public sphere.[48] Yet wanting to retain the public sphere and according it a place in democratic theory is not compatible with the more radical critique of the ideal of impartial reason that Young also develops in some of her essays.

In her essay "Communication and the Other: Beyond Deliberative Democracy," in this volume, Iris Young distinguishes between "deliberative" and "communicative" democracy on the grounds that most theories of deliberative democracy offer too narrow a conception of the democratic process because they continue to privilege an ideal of "a common good in which [the discussion participants] are all supposed to leave behind their particular experience and interests" (126).

By contrast, Young advocates a theory of communicative democracy according to which individuals would attend to one another's differences in class, gender, race, religion, and so on. Each social position has a partial perspective on the public that it does not abandon; but through the communicative process participants transcend and transform their initial situated knowledges (127). Instead of critical argumentation, such processes of communicative confrontation privilege modalities of communication like "greeting, rhetoric, and storytelling" (120).

I think this distinction between deliberative and communicative democracy is more apparent than real. To sustain her critique of the ideals of impartiality and objectivity, which she associates with the deliberative model, Young must be able to distinguish the kind of *transformation* and *transcendence* of partial perspectives that occurs in communicative democracy from the *mutual agreement* to be reached in processes of deliberative democracy. Yet how can we distinguish between the emergence of common opinion among members of one group, if we do not apply to such processes of communication or deliberation some standards of fairness and impartiality in order to judge the manner in which opinions were allowed to be brought forth, groups were given chances to express their points of view, and the like? The model of communicative democracy, far from dispensing with the need for standards of impartiality and fairness, requires them to make sense of its own formulations. Without some such standards, Young could not differentiate the genuine transformation of partial and situated perspectives from mere agreements of convenience or apparent unanimity reached under conditions of duress.

With respect to modes of communication like "greeting, rhetoric, and storytelling," I would say that each of these modes may have their place within the *informally structured process of everyday communication among individuals who share a cultural and historical life world.* However, it is neither necessary for the democratic theorist to try to formalize and institutionalize these aspects of communicative everyday competence, nor is it plausible—and this is the more important objection—to build an opposition between them and critical argumentation. Greeting, storytelling, and rhetoric, although they may be aspects of informal communication in our everyday life, cannot become the public language of institutions and legislatures in a democracy for the following reason: to attain legitimacy, democratic institutions require the articulation of the bases of their actions and policies in discursive language that appeals to commonly shared and accepted public reasons. In constitutional democracies such public reasons take the form of general statements consonant with the rule of law. The rule of law has a certain rhetorical structure of its own: it is general, applies to all members of a specified reference group on the basis of legitimate reasons. Young's attempt to transform the language of the rule of law into a more partial, affective, and situated mode of communication would have the consequence of inducing arbitrariness, for who can tell how far the power of a greeting can reach? It would further create capriciousness—what about those who simply cannot understand my story? It would limit rather than enhance social justice because rhetoric moves people and achieves results without having to render an account of the bases upon which it induces people to engage in certain courses of action rather than others. In short, some moral ideal of impartiality is a regulative principle that should govern not only our *deliberations* in public but also the *articulation* of reasons by public institutions. What is considered impartial has to be "in the best interests of all equally." Without such a normative principle, neither the ideal of the rule of law can be sustained nor deliberative reasoning toward a common good occur. Some Enlightenment ideals are part of any conception of democratic legitimacy and the public sphere. The point therefore is not a rejection of the Enlightenment in toto but a critical renegotiation of its legacy.

Expanding on the model of a heterogeneous, dispersed network of many publics, Nancy Fraser has suggested how, in fact, once the unitary model of the public sphere is abandoned, women's concerns, as well as those of other excluded groups, can be accommodated. Such a nonunitary and dispersed network of publics can accommodate women's desires for their own spaces, in their own terms. In such "subaltern counterpublics," to use Fraser's term,[49] the lines between the public and the private, for example, can be renegotiated, rethought, challenged, and reformulated. It is nonetheless a long step from the cultural and social rethinking and reformulation of such distinctions as between the public and the private to their implementation in legislation and governmental regulation. While sharing the concern of liberal theorists that the precipitous reformulation of such a divide may corrode individual liberties, Fraser rightly points out that there is a distinction between "opinion-

making" and "policy-making" public bodies, and that the same kinds of constraints may not apply to each alike.[50] Opinion-making publics, as found in
social movements, for example, can lead us to reconsider and rethink very
controversial issues about privacy, sexuality, and intimacy; but this does not
imply that the only or even most desirable consequence of such processes of
public deliberation should be general legislation. Thus when conceived as an
anonymous, plural, and multiple medium of communication and deliberation, the public sphere need not homogenize and repress difference. Heterogeneity, otherness, and difference can find expression in the multiple associations, networks, and citizens' forums, all of which constitute public life under
late capitalism.[51]

Institutionalist Distrust of Deliberative Democracy

The criticism most frequently leveled against normative models of democracy
is that of utopian irrelevance. "This may sound good in theory, but it is irrelevant to practice!" "Complex, modern societies," the objection continues, "with
their highly differentiated cultural, economic, social and artistic spheres of
life, can never be and will never be organized along the lines suggested by a
model of deliberative democracy." Let me deal with this line of objection in
several steps:

The deliberative model of democracy does not represent a counterfactual
thought experiment. As I suggested at the beginning, I understand such a
theory to be elucidating the already implicit principles and logic of existing
democratic practices. Among the practices that such a theory of democracy
can elucidate are the significance of deliberative bodies in democracies, the
rationale of parliamentary opposition, the need for a free and independent
media and sphere of public opinion, and the rationale for employing majority
rule as a decision procedure. For this reason, the deliberative theory of democracy is not a theory in search of practice; rather it is a theory that claims to
elucidate some aspects of the logic of existing democratic practices better
than others. Theorists of social complexity should really reframe the question:
the question is not whether discursive democracy can become the practice
of complex societies but whether complex societies are still capable of democratic rule.

Niklas Luhmann concludes an article entitled "Gesellschaftliche Komplexität und öffentliche Meinung" ("Social Complexity and Public Opinion")
with the argument that: "political systems of modern societies cannot be understood as a central instance, whose virtues or vices can be observed by the
people. Instead of a central instance, we have the continuous observation of
the observers, thus the self-referential closure of the system. It goes along with
this that the political code no longer depends upon the distinction between

power-holders vs. those upon whom power is exercised; rather this is coded on the side of power through the scheme of government/opposition. One has to reduce the concept of democracy to this central point."[52] Luhmann precedes this paragraph with the observation that this concept of politics "compels one certainly painfully to give up any expectations of rationality and any hopes of a revitalization of a civic republican 'life.'"[53]

When societal complexity would compel one to adopt this curiously science-fiction language of the observation of the observed in the place of the language of democratic citizenship and participation, then indeed complexity and democracy are not compatible. However, I not only have doubts whether this social framework is appropriate for thinking of the complexity of modern societies, empirically as well, the presentation of the political system as a self-immunized closed circuit, in which the government and the opposition merely observe each other in reflector mirrors, is simply untrue. Beginning with the 1970s and well into the 1980s, all over the United States and Europe, one had observed the rise and decline of new social movements, great citizens' coalitions, like the Freeze and antinuclear movements, as well as radical changes of course from welfarist economics to free market ideologies and possibly a swing back to welfarism in the 1990s. It is hard to see what empirical value Luhmann's thesis of the "self-immunization of the political system" could have in view of fairly significant electoral swings and transitions in most capitalist democracies.

Normatively as well, since its inception with the Greeks the question of the most adequate socioeconomic order most compatible with democratic rule has been intensely debated. Rousseau's own wisdom on the matter was that only a society in which no one was poor enough to have to sell himself and no one rich enough to buy another could be democratic.[54] Since the nineteenth century, the question of the compatibility between democracy and capitalism has been on the agenda. For this reason the relationship between deliberative democracy and social complexity needs to be posed otherwise: what are the forms of association and modes of organization, at the economic, social, cultural spheres, that bear an "elective affinity" with the principle of deliberative democracy at the political sphere?

In conclusion, I want to summarize three recent attempts that take this question seriously and investigate the *institutional possibilities* of realizing a democracy centered around a procedure of free, public deliberation. In "The Market and the Forum: Three Varieties of Political Theory," Jon Elster discusses the relevance of public deliberative models to political life. Arguing against narrowly designed market preference models, Elster observes: "But the task of politics is not only to eliminate inefficiency, but also to create justice—a goal to which the aggregation of prepolitical preferences is a quite incongruous means."[55] While not agreeing with all aspects of the discourse model, particularly in its strong consensus-oriented version, which Habermas espouses, Elster also points out, "I am not arguing against the need for public discussion, only for the need to take the question of institutional and constitutional design very seriously."[56] For Elster this translates into the question of the proper place of politics, situated as it is, between the market on the one hand and the forum on the other.

Writing from a perspective largely sympathetic to the discourse model of democracy, Claus Offe recently has echoed Elster's question with a call for concrete thinking on "associative designs": "Not only the procedures of an open, fair, and argumentative will- and decision-formation that are laid down by *constitutions* and not only the capacity for postconventional moral judgment-formation that is constituted in socialization processes, but also the socio-structural and institutional conditions of collective action within civil society—its pattern of the division of labor and its 'associative design' must 'meet halfway' the formation of certain moral capacities."[57] For Offe, unlike for Elster, these "associative designs" have their proper place not primarily at the legal-constitutional level but rather in the associative realm of civil society, of which the public sphere is a central domain.

To date the most courageous attempt to translate the normative theory of deliberative democracy into institutional-political reality has been by John S. Dryzek in his book *Discursive Democracy: Politics, Policy and Political Science*.[58] Dryzek defines a "discursive design" as "a social institution around which the expectations of a number of actors converge. It therefore has a place in their conscious awareness as a site for recurrent communicative interaction among them. Individuals should participate as citizens, not as representatives of the state or any other corporate and hierarchical body. No concerned individuals should be excluded. . . . The focus of deliberations should include, but not be limited to, the individual or collective needs and interests of the individuals involved. . . . Within discursive design, there should be no hierarchy of formal rules, though debate may be governed by informal canons of discourse. A decision rule of consensus should obtain. Finally, all the features I have enumerated should be redeemable within the discursive design itself. Participants should be free to reflectively and discursively override any or all of them."[59]

There is a remarkable convergence between the procedures for deliberative democracy suggested above and Dryzek's rules of "discursive design." More important, Dryzek is concerned to show that incipient forms of discursive design already obtain in "alternative dispute resolution procedures generally"; in regulatory negotiation; in policy dialogue, and "problem-solving" workshops in international conflict resolution.[60] His aim is to establish that as populations grow, natural resources are depleted, and individuals interact with complex numbers of others in unpredictable ways, "discursive action facilitates the provision of public goods in a decentralized and noncoercive manner, for public goods and the condition of common resources are a kind of generalizable interests."[61] Particularly, citizens' environmental groups are interesting examples in which the practice of discursive design enables efficiency and success through voluntary compliance, consciousness raising, and decentralized problem solving. Thus reversing the argument of the incompatibility of social complexity and deliberative democracy, Dryzek maintains that "discursive design can contribute to the solution of complex social problems" more than the three methods of analytical problem disaggregation, systems modeling, and structured integration.[62] Recent literature on democratic institutionalization suggests then that the model of deliberative democracy, far from being irrelevant to contemporary, complex societies, has inspired a number of social and political theorists to envisage new institutional designs within the context of such societies.

My goal in this essay has been to outline a deliberative model of democracy that incorporates features of practical rationality. Central to practical rationality is the possibility of free public deliberation about matters of mutual concern to all. The discourse model of ethics and politics suggests a procedure for such free public deliberation among all concerned. Such processes of public deliberation have a claim to rationality because they increase and make available necessary information, because they allow the expression of arguments in the light of which opinions and beliefs need to be revised, and because they lead to the formation of conclusions that can be challenged publicly for good reasons. Furthermore, such procedures allow self-referential critique of their own uses and abuses. The chief institutional correlate of such a model of deliberative democracy is a multiple, anonymous, heterogeneous network of many publics and public conversations. In other domains of social life as well, the model of deliberative democracy based on the centrality of public deliberation can inspire the proliferation of many institutional designs.

Notes

1. See John Rawls, "Kantian Constructivism in Moral Theory," *Journal of Philosophy* 77, no. 9 (1980): 515–72, a revised and enlarged version of which is included in *Political Liberalism* (New York: Columbia University Press, 1993), 89–131; Jürgen Habermas, *Moral Consciousness and Communicative Action*, trans. Christian Lenhardt and Shierry Weber Nicholsen (Cambridge, Mass.: MIT Press, 1990), and in particular the essay "Discourse Ethics: Notes on a Program of Philosophical Justification," 76ff.

2. In a helpful survey article entitled "Freedom, Consensus, and Equality in Collective Decision Making," *Ethics* 101, no. 1 (October 1990): 151ff., Thomas Christiano examines different approaches to the philosophical foundations of democracy.

3. It is well known that nearly a decade ago now, John Rawls retracted the Kantian strategy of normative justification followed in his *Theory of Justice* in favor of a more historicist, and social and politically situated concept of an "overlapping consensus." The two principles of justice were valid, he claimed, not sub specie aeternitatis but

because they articulated some deeply shared convictions in liberal democracies of the West about the foundations of their forms of government. These deeply held convictions would constitute, when properly sifted through, clarified, and articulated, the bases of an "overlapping consensus" in such societies. See John Rawls, "Justice as Fairness: Political Not Metaphysical," *Philosophy and Public Affairs* 14 (1985): 223–51; and "The Idea of an Overlapping Consensus," *Oxford Journal of Legal Studies* 7 (1987): 1–25. This shift from a Kantian strategy of justification to a more historicist mode has been celebrated by some. Richard Rorty has seen in these recent developments of Rawls's work a confirmation for his own brand of "ethnocentric liberalism." See Richard Rorty, "The Priority of Democracy to Philosophy," in *Objectivism, Relativism, and Truth* (New York: Cambridge University Press, 1991), 175–96. For a lucid account of these developments in Rawls's position and a critical examination of the idea of an "overlapping consensus," see Kenneth Baynes, "Constructivism and Practical Reason in Rawls," in *Analyse und Kritik. Zeitschrift für Sozialwissenschaften* 14 (June 1992): 18–32.

4. See M. I. Finley's still-classic essays in *Democracy: Ancient and Modern* (New Brunswick, N.J.: Rutgers University Press, 1985).

5. The most brilliant example of Hegel's methodology remains the 1821 *Philosophy of Right*, trans. T. M. Knox (New York: Oxford University Press, 1973). The kind of anonymous collective rationality I have in mind has been developed by Karl Popper in the domain of epistemology. See Karl R. Popper, *Objective Knowledge: An Evolutionary Approach* (Oxford: Clarendon, 1972).

6. My formulation is wholly akin to that proposed by Joshua Cohen, "Deliberation and Democratic Legitimacy," in *The Good Polity: Normative Analysis of the State*, ed. Alan Hamlin and Philip Pettit (London: Blackwell, 1989), 17–34; see also Joshua Cohen, "Procedure and Substance in Deliberative Democracy," in this volume.

7. I have outlined my understanding of this project as well as indicating the manner in which my interpretation of the general program of discourse ethics differs from that of Habermas and Apel in *Situating the Self* (New York: Routledge, 1992). This article presupposes the general argument set forth in that book in chapters 1, 2, and 3 in particular, and documents my effort to apply the principles of discourse ethics to political-institutional life. Independently of the project of discourse ethics but in fascinating affinity to it, in recent years there has also been a revival of deliberative models of democracy among political theorists and legal philosophers. See in particular Frank I. Michelman, "Law's Republic," *Yale Law Journal* 93 (1984): 1013ff.; and Cass R. Sunstein, "Beyond the Republican Revival," *Yale Law Journal* 97 (1988): 1539.

8. See Hannah Arendt, *On Revolution* (New York: Viking, 1963); Benjamin Barber, *Strong Democracy* (Berkeley: University of California Press, 1984); Chantal Mouffe and Ernesto Laclau, *Hegemony and Socialist Strategy: Towards a Radical Democratic Politics*, trans. Winston Moore and Paul Commack (London: Verso, 1985); Chantal Mouffe, "Feminism, Citizenship, and Radical Democratic Politics," in *Feminists Theorize the Political*, ed. Judith Butler and Joan W. Scott (New York: Routledge, 1992), 369–85; and William E. Connolly, *Identity\Difference: Democratic Negotiations of Political Paradox* (Ithaca: Cornell University Press, 1991). I explore this criticism of Hannah Arendt's theory in particular in my book *The Reluctant Modernism of Hannah Arendt* (Newbury Park, Calif.: Sage, 1996).

9. In some contemporary models of deliberative democracy, a distinction between "constitutional" (high) politics and "ordinary" (low) politics dominates. The claim is

that deliberative politics more properly characterizes constitution-making processes, whereas mundane, day-to-day politics may be governed by nondeliberative and narrowly instrumental, self-regarding pursuits. See David Gauthier, "Constituting Democracy," in *The Idea of Democracy*, ed. David Copp et al. (Cambridge: Cambridge University Press, 1993), 314–15; and David M. Estlund's very instructive discussion, "Who's Afraid of Deliberative Democracy? On the Strategic/Deliberative Dichotomy in Recent Constitutional Jurisprudence," *Texas Law Review* 71, no. 7 (June 1993): 1437–77. Although I believe that a distinction between "constitution-making" and "ordinary" politics is extremely useful and unavoidable for democratic theory, I think that it can be and has been overdrawn. The main motivation for overdrawing this distinction seems to be traditional liberal fears about unbridled majoritarian decisions and distrust in the rationality of political judgment as exercised by ordinary people. The deliberative model of democracy that I am advocating seeks to bridge the gap between high and low politics by raising the quality of ordinary people's everyday deliberations. This does not mean that constitutional issues are always and at all times open for reconsideration. Not at all; but it does suggest that ordinary politics cannot but be informed by such constitutional issues and principles—as examples take debates ranging from prayer in public schools to violence in the media to pornography and abortion. My assumption is that the more such ordinary political deliberation approximates the model suggested above, the more the likelihood increases that it will be informed by constitutional principles in the "right way." For further discussion see also the "Deliberative Democracy and Constitutionalism" section that follows.

10. Bernard Manin, "On Legitimacy and Political Deliberation," *Political Theory* 15, no. 3 (August 1987): 338–68.

11. In a recent article, "The Voice of the People," Sidney Verba discusses citizens' communications to their representatives and other governmental offices via letters, calls, and increasingly faxes and e-mail. (677ff.) Reflecting upon the phenomenal increase of such direct communication (about a fifth to a quarter of the public in the U.S.A. report contacting an official—"depending on the way the question is framed" [679]), Verba expresses the hope that "perhaps citizen-initiated messages, especially when enhanced by new technology, can become part of a public discourse" (685). See Sidney Verba, "The Voice of the People," 1993 James Madison Award Lecture, *PS: Political Science and Politics* 26, no. 4 (December 1993): 677–86.

12. Hannah Arendt, "The Crisis in Culture," in *Between Past and Future: Six Exercises in Political Thought* (New York: Meridian, 1961), 220–21.

13. Charles Larmore has provided an eloquent statement of this view in recent years. See *Patterns of Moral Complexity* (Cambridge: Cambridge University Press, 1987), 119ff.; and "Political Liberalism," *Political Theory* 18, no. 3 (August 1990): 342ff.

14. I would like to attempt to answer here a very important objection raised by Donald Moon. How plausible is it to distinguish value disagreements concerning *substantive* moral, religious, or philosophical doctrines from *procedural* agreement about processes for adjudicating and revising beliefs in a public context? Very often, such substantive beliefs will not permit one to distinguish so sharply between content and form, substance and procedure. As examples of cases when value systems do not permit a sharp distinction between substance and procedure we can think of religious sects living within the boundaries of the liberal-democratic constitutional state such as certain Orthodox Jewish sects in Israel who refuse to recognize the secular authority of the

State of Israel; Orthodox Moslems living in some European states, like Germany and France for example, who experience conflict between their views of the proper education and place of women and the views of the liberal-democratic state; or Christian scientists in the United States who want to provide medical treatment to their children consonant with their own beliefs and who come into conflict with local and federal authorities. In each of these cases clashes can and do arise that prima facie cannot be solved by resorting to a simple substance/form distinction. To deal properly with the issues raised by such examples and in particular to explore the ways in which a deliberative model of democracy based upon discourse ethics may or may not presuppose too strong a model of agreement clearly goes beyond the scope of this article. However, I do think that in the face of all these cases as well a form of deliberative proceduralism is the most viable normative answer.

Insofar as these groups live within the jurisdiction of the liberal-constitutional and democratic state they have accepted certain "constitutional minimums." Debates usually arise not around these constitutional minimal rights, which are guaranteed to all citizens and residents (in varying degrees) under the rule of law, but around whether certain cultural and religious practices do or do not contradict these constitutional minimums or whether they can be considered matters of the religious and cultural autonomy of a group. Is the duty to serve in the Israeli army a constitutional obligation to which there can be no exceptions on religious grounds? Can Orthodox Muslim families choose not to send their daughters to public schools? And when they do send them to public schools, should these children be allowed to wear head scarves or should they be obliged to wear school uniforms? Can a Christian Scientist family refuse medical treatment to a child suffering from an infectious disease that requires standard medication? Should the state protect the rights of the child against the judgment of the family in this case? I am inclined to think that vis-à-vis such issues there is no single answer applicable to each case but more or less a gradation of moral and political principles and intuitions. The possibility not to serve in the army on the basis of religious beliefs is a right of conscientious objection recognized by many modern states, which can be made consonant with the principle of the separation of church and state. On the other hand, to deny a child the fundamentals of a secular education in our world or the best treatment that medical science can offer violate the respect and equality we owe that child as a future citizen of our polity. Yet whether Muslim girls can wear their head scarves (the chador) to French schools or whether Sikh soldiers can wear their turbans in the Canadian Royal Police strikes me as being a qualitatively different matter from the provision of either education or health care. A more pluralistic conception of the public sphere and of civic identity than that displayed by the French public and authorities in the debate around the chador is perfectly compatible with, and in fact required by, the model of deliberative democracy and public dialogue developed in this essay.

15. See Jane Mansbridge's article "Using Power/Fighting Power: The Polity," in this volume, for an exploration of the dilemmas of deliberative democracy models in the face of persistent and ineliminable conflicts of interests and wills in public life, and the problems involved in the use of coercion.

16. For a recent statement of the transformation of the concept of the public sphere from a centralized to a decentered model, see Jürgen Habermas, "Ist der Herzschlag der Revolution zum Stillstand gekommen? Volkssouveränität als Verfahren. Ein normativer

Begriff der Öffentlichkeit?" in *Die Ideen von 1789*, ed. Forum für Philosophie Bad Homburg (Frankfurt: Suhrkamp, 1989), 7ff.

17. Bruce Ackerman, *Social Justice in the Liberal State* (New Haven: Yale University Press, 1980) and "Why Dialogue?" *Journal of Philosophy* 86 (January 1989). I have dealt with Bruce Ackerman's model of liberal conversation in several articles. See Benhabib, "Liberal Dialogue vs. a Critical Model of Discursive Legitimacy" and "Models of Public Space: Hannah Arendt, the Liberal Tradition and Jürgen Habermas," in *Situating the Self*.

18. Cf. Stephen Holmes, "Gag Rules or the Politics of Omission," in *Constitutionalism and Democracy*, ed. Jon Elster and R. Slagstad (Cambridge: Cambridge University Press, 1988), 19–58; and John Rawls, "The Idea of an Overlapping Consensus."

19. In addition to John Rawls's *Political Liberalism*, see also the manuscript "On the Idea of Free Public Reason," a lecture delivered at the "Liberalism and the Moral Life" conference at CUNY in April 1988, and "The Idea of an Overlapping Consensus," for the development of Rawls's views on the matter. A great deal more needs to be said about the contrast of these two projects than I can undertake in this section, but see also Thomas McCarthy, "Kantian Constructivism and Reconstructivism: Rawls and Habermas in Dialogue," *Ethics* 105, no.1 (October 1994): 44–64.

20. Rawls, *Political Liberalism*, 214.

21. Ibid., 223ff. In his comments on an earlier version of this essay delivered in the Political Theory Colloquium of the department of government at Harvard, in spring of 1994, Stephen Macedo misconstrued these remarks to mean that I was attributing to Rawls some kind of infringement or limitation upon First Amendment rights of free speech and expression. This is a misunderstanding of the phrase "restricted agenda." Obviously Rawls's theory does not place restrictions upon the exercise of the most extensive basic liberty of free speech compatible with the like liberty of all; the lexical ordering of the two principles of justice means that the principle of basic rights and liberties cannot be simply abrogated. My phrase "restrictive agenda" refers to what Rawls's conception of public reason considers as being the *proper domain* or *subject matter* of public reason. This is less a question of free speech rights and limitations upon them than a question of one's social theory of civil society and democratic politics.

22. Rawls, *Political Liberalism*, 226.

23. Ibid., 227.

24. Ibid., 215.

25. Ibid., 220.

26. Ibid., 215.

27. I have dealt with this issue in "Models of Public Sphere," 89–121; see also the "Institutionalist Distrust of Deliberative Democracy" section that follows.

28. For a broad statement of the theoretical and political significance of the project of civil society to contemporary democracy, see Jean Cohen and Andrew Arato, *Civil Society and Political Theory* (Cambridge, Mass.: MIT Press, 1992).

29. The question of coercion would have to be dealt with in the context of the institutionalization of deliberative processes. It is within this framework as well that issues of closure, decision-making prerogatives, and jurisdictions would have to be articulated. See the section "Institutionalist Distrust of Deliberative Democracy" in this essay for some thoughts on this.

30. Benjamin Barber, *The Conquest of Politics: Liberal Philosophy in Democratic Times* (Princeton: Princeton University Press, 1988), 151. Certainly, one cannot focus only

on the speeches of Abraham Lincoln, Adlai Stevenson, and Jesse Jackson to the exclusion of the less ennobling outbursts of a Richard Nixon, Fidel Castro, or Nikita Kruschev. What Barber's observation captures nonetheless is the open-ended, contestatory, affective dimension of the political through which free public reason can assume the character of "shared reasoning." What Barber fails to emphasize are the institutional and other procedural conditions within the framework of which such conversations have to occur.

31. I owe this phrase to Nancy Fraser, who introduces it in the context of her discussion of discourses in the welfare state; cf. Nancy Fraser, *Unruly Practices: Power, Discourse and Gender in Contemporary Social Theory* (Cambridge: Polity Press, 1989), 144ff.

32. Rawls, *Political Liberalism*, 231. Rawls draws the distinction between the court as the "highest" judicial interpreter of the constitution as opposed to the "final" interpreter of the higher law, because, following Bruce Ackerman, he wants to retain a principle of popular sovereignty, respecting the will of "We the People."

33. For a further exploration of these themes see the article by Josh Cohen, "Procedure and Substance in Deliberative Democracy," in this volume.

34. This issue has been recently well formulated by Kenneth Baynes in "The Liberal/Communitarian Controversy and Communicative Ethics," *Philosophy and Social Criticism* 14, nos. 3–4 (1988): 305 (my emphasis).

35. See *Situating the Self*, 29ff.

36. Jürgen Habermas has embarked on this task in his new book, *Faktizität und Geltung* (Frankfurt: Suhrkamp, 1992), chap. 3.

37. In her contribution to this volume, "Diversity and Democracy: Representing Differences," Carol Gould objects that discourse-ethical theory cannot justify fundamental human rights. I would counter her criticisms by further exploring the implications of the counterfactual suggested above for a theory of rights.

38. In *Situating the Self*, 30ff.

39. Perhaps an example may clarify this procedure further: let us take the cases of Great Britain, the United States of America, and Israel as three models of liberal-democratic societies whose political and legal order is based upon some form of recognition of the norm of moral respect for persons. Certainly all three societies enjoy a system of parliamentary democracy in which, through legislatively or constitutionally determined periodic elections, public officials are brought to and removed from office. In all three societies individuals enjoy certain rights and liberties that are upheld by the political system and protected by the courts. However, these societies have radically divergent and at times incompatible views of what constitutes the legitimate exercise of the right of free speech. Whereas in the United States considerations of public propriety, fair trial, or national security would hardly serve as routine grounds on the basis of which to curtail First Amendment rights, in Great Britain and Israel they are commonly invoked. In Great Britain the media's access to court hearings and trials is restricted, while in Israel even the publication of certain scholarly articles can be subjected to the prohibition of the military censor if they are deemed to contain "security-sensitive information."

The relevance of this example to the theoretical principle of discursive validation is the following: just as differences in the extent and application of the fundamental right of free speech would not lead us to deny that Great Britain and Israel are democratic societies just as the United States is, so too a number of more specific interpretations of the norms of universal moral respect and egalitarian reciprocity are compatible with democratic political dialogue. What results from a deliberative theory of democracy based upon the discourse model is not a catalog of unabridgeable basic rights and liberties but two most general moral norms that are compatible, within certain well-defined limits, with a variety of legal and political arrangements.

40. See Kenneth Baynes, *The Normative Grounds of Political Criticism: Kant, Rawls, Habermas* (Albany: SUNY Press, 1992), 1ff.

41. In his interesting criticism of some of my earlier formulations concerning discourse ethics in *Critique, Norm, and Utopia* (New York: Columbia University Press, 1986), Donald Moon charges that practical discourse could be potentially "coercive, leading to institutional forms that involve domination or imposition. It is hard to see how any form of 'discourse' could achieve a consensus that is genuinely free and uncoerced unless participants enjoy some rights of privacy and personal integrity, unless they can resist the demand for self-disclosure." Donald Moon, *Constructing Community: Moral Pluralism and Tragic Conflicts* (Princeton: Princeton University Press, 1993), 95. Given the norms of universal moral respect and egalitarian reciprocity presupposed by discourses, and given the strong emphasis on voluntarily given assent, based upon one's evaluation of certain kinds of validity claims, I fail to see how discourses could violate individual privacy or force self-disclosure. I maintain, however, that discourses can challenge the line between the public and the private spheres, in the sense that citizens in a polity may make into a public issue some areas of concern that were hitherto considered private matters, such as domestic violence, or, conversely, may plead for the privacy of certain kinds of information, such as buying and consumption patterns or other kinds of personal facts contained in data banks, for example. What moral and political theory should not do is freeze the historical and essentially contestable outcomes of democratic discourses into some immutable catalog of rights; rather moral and political theory should provide us with general principles to guide our moral intuitions and concrete deliberations when we are confronted with such controversial cases as domestic violence, child abuse, and marital rape, or using the sex of an unborn baby as a basis for aborting that fetus.

42. Bruce Ackerman, *We the People*, vol. 1: *Foundations* (Cambridge, Mass.: Harvard University Press, 1991), 12.

43. Some questions of democratic legitimacy and antifoundationalism as they apply to the Supreme Court's dilemma in a democracy have been most fruitfully explored by Morton J. Horwitz in "The Constitution of Change: Legal Fundamentality without Fundamentalism," *Harvard Law Review* 107 (1993): 32–117.

44. Iris Young, "Impartiality and the Civic Public," in *Feminism as Critique*, ed. Seyla Benhabib and Drucilla Cornell (London: Polity Press), 73.

45. For historical analyses, see Joan B. Landes, *Women and the Public Sphere in the Age of the French Revolution* (Ithaca: Cornell University Press, 1988); and Linda Kerber, *Women of the Republic: Intellect and Ideology in Revolutionary America* (New York: Norton, 1986).

46. Landes's illuminating early work *Women and the Public Sphere in the Age of the French Revolution* was marred by one conceptual issue. Particularly in her critique of Habermas's work on the public sphere, Landes conflated the Habermasian model of the public sphere that was part of civil society with the Rousseauian-republican model based upon an opposition to civil society. Much of her criticism of the "masculinism"

of the public sphere applies only to this republican, civic-virtue version that has little to do with the Enlightenment conception of the public sphere, which Habermas defines as "private individuals using their reason about public matters." Clearly the concept of the public sphere developed in this essay emerges out of this second tradition. See Keith Baker's illuminating discussion of this issue in "Defining the Public Sphere in Eighteenth-Century France: Variations on a Theme by Habermas," in *Habermas and the Public Sphere*, ed. Craig Calhoun (Cambridge, Mass.: MIT Press, 1992), 181–212.

47. A provocative but inadequate critique of the public sphere concept has been given by Dana Villa who minimizes the role and significance of this concept in securing legitimation in democratic theory while focusing on its agonistic and performative dimensions. See "Postmodernism and the Public Sphere," *American Political Science Review* 86, no. 3 (September 1992): 712–25.

48. Iris Marion Young, *Justice and the Politics of Difference* (Princeton: Princeton University Press, 1990).

49. Nancy Fraser, "Rethinking the Public Sphere: A Contribution to the Critique of Actually Existing Democracy," in Calhoun, ed., *Habermas and the Public Sphere*, 123.

50. Ibid., 132ff.

51. Ibid., 108ff.

52. Niklas Luhmann, "Gesellschaftliche Komplexität und öffentliche Meinung," in *Soziologische Aufklärung*, vol. 5 (Opladen: Westdeutscher Verlag, 1990), 182.

53. Ibid., 182.

54. See Jean-Jacques Rousseau, *On the Social Contract* (1762), chap. 11. I am using the translation by Donald A. Cress (Indianapolis: Hackett, 1987), 46.

55. Jon Elster, "The Market and the Forum: Three Varieties of Political Theory," in *Foundations of Social Choice Theory*, ed. Jon Elster and Aanund Hylland (New York: Cambridge University Press, 1989), 111.

56. Ibid., 117.

57. Claus Offe, "Fessel und Bremse. Moralische und institutionelle Aspekte 'intelligenter Selbstbeschränkung,'" in *Zwischenbetrachtungen im Prozess der Aufklärung*, ed. Axel Honneth, Thomas McCarthy, Claus Offe, and Albrecht Wellmer (Frankfurt: Suhrkamp, 1986), 761; translated into English as "Bindings, Shackles, Brakes: On Self-Limitation Strategies," in *Cultural-Political Interventions in the Unfinished Project of Enlightenment*, ed. Axel Honneth, Thomas McCarthy, Claus Offe, and Albrecht Wellmer (Cambridge, Mass.: MIT Press, 1992), 80. The English translation is not altogether accurate; I have altered it slightly.

58. John Dryzek, *Discursive Democracy: Politics, Policy and Political Science* (New York: Cambridge University Press, 1990).

59. Ibid., 43.

60. Ibid., 44.

61. Ibid., 55.

62. Ibid., 57.

Five

Procedure and Substance in Deliberative Democracy

JOSHUA COHEN

Substance, Procedure, and Pluralism

The fundamental idea of democratic legitimacy is that the authorization to exercise state power must arise from the collective decisions of the members of a society who are governed by that power.[1] More precisely—and stated with attention to democracy's institutional character—it arises from the discussions and decisions of members, as made within and expressed through social and political institutions designed to acknowledge their collective authority. That is an abstract statement of the concept of democracy, and deliberately so. Democracy comes in many forms, and more determinate conceptions of it depend on an account of membership in the people and, correspondingly, what it takes for a decision to be *collective*—made by citizens "as a body."

Take a political community in which adherence to a comprehensive moral or religious doctrine,[2] perhaps rooted in national tradition, is a condition of full membership. Authorization, then, will require congruence with that view, and only decisions exhibiting such congruence can properly be deemed "collective." For that reason, the test for democratic legitimacy will be, in part, substantive—dependent on the content of outcomes, not simply on the processes through which they are reached.

What happens, though, when the idea of collective authorization is set against a different background: where there is no shared comprehensive moral or religious view, members are understood as free and equal, and the national project, such as it is, embraces a commitment to expressing that freedom and

I would like to thank John Rawls, Charles Sabel, T. M. Scanlon, Cass Sunstein, and Iris Marion Young for illuminating comments on earlier drafts of this essay. The "Deliberative Democracy" section draws on my "Deliberation and Democratic Legitimacy," in Alan Hamlin and Phillip Petit, eds., *The Good Polity* (Oxford: Blackwell, 1989), 17–34. The "Three Principles" section draws on my review of Robert Dahl's *Democracy and Its Critics* (New Haven: Yale University Press, 1989) in *Journal of Politics* 53, no. 1 (1991): 221–25, and on my "Pluralism and Proceduralism," *Chicago-Kent Law Review* 69, no. 3 (1994): 589–618. The "Realizing Democracy" section draws on Joshua Cohen and Joel Rogers, *Democracy and Association* (London: Verso, 1995).

equality in the design of institutions and collective choices?[3] Does this shift in background drive us to an entirely procedural view of democracy and collective decision? I think not. But before explaining why, I want to say something about the interest of the question, and terms in which it is stated.

My question about the effects of a shift in background is prompted by the aim of formulating a conception of democracy suited to the kind of human difference captured in the "fact of reasonable pluralism"[4]—the fact that there are distinct, incompatible understandings of value, each one reasonable, to which people are drawn under favorable conditions for the exercise of their practical reason. The good-faith exercise of practical reason, by people who are reasonable in being concerned to live with others on terms that those others can accept, does not lead to convergence on one particular philosophy of life.

The claim about reasonable pluralism is suggested by persistent disagreement about, for example, the values of choice and self-determination, happiness and welfare, and self-actualization; disputes about the relative merits of contemplative and practical lives and the importance of personal and political engagement; and disagreements about the religious and philosophical backgrounds of these evaluative views. Apart from the sheer fact of disagreement, there is, moreover, no apparent tendency to convergence generated by the exercise of practical reason; furthermore, we have no *theory* of the operations of practical reason that would lead us to predict convergence on comprehensive moralities; nor can I think of any marginally attractive social or political mechanisms that might generate such agreement.

This fact of reasonable pluralism gives shape to the conception of citizens as free and equal that constitutes part of the conception of democracy I want to explore here. To say that citizens are free is to say, inter alia, that no comprehensive moral or religious view provides a defining condition of membership or the foundation of the authorization to exercise political power. To say that they are equal is to say that each is recognized as having the capacities required for participating in discussion aimed at authorizing the exercise of power.

What, then, are the implications of reasonable pluralism for a conception of democracy? It is natural to suppose that by excluding a comprehensive consensus on values the fact of reasonable pluralism leads to a procedural conception of democracy. According to such a conception, the democratic pedigree that lies at the source of legitimacy can be settled by looking exclusively to the processes through which collective decisions are made and to values associated with fair processes: for example, values of openness, equal chances to present alternatives, full and impartial consideration of those alternatives. The fact of reasonable pluralism appears to require a procedural conception because it deprives us of a background of shared moral or religious premises that could give determinate content to the idea of popular authorization or constrain the substance of genuinely collective choices. Without that background, we are left, it may seem, with no basis for agreement on anything more than fair procedures—and perhaps not even that.

I think this conclusion is not right, and will sketch a view that combines an assumption of reasonable pluralism with a more substantive conception of democracy. Moreover, I will argue that this combination is a natural result of a particular way of thinking about democracy—a "deliberative" understanding of the collective decisions that constitute democratic governance. Before discussing the deliberative conception, though, I need first to fix the concerns about procedure and substance more precisely, distinguish a deliberative from an aggregative conception of democracy, and show how aggregative conceptions lead to proceduralism.

Liberties, Ancient and Modern

Consider a familiar dilemma associated with the idea of tracing legitimacy to popular authorization.[5] On the one hand, democracy may seem too much a matter of procedure to provide a basis for an account of legitimacy; some democratic collective choices are too execrable to be legitimate, however attractive the procedures that generate them. On the other hand, the idea of democracy appears to exclude any competing basis of legitimacy. Democracy appears to be the form of collective choice mandated by the fundamental idea that citizens are to be treated as equals. So democracy is commonly thought to be the way we must decide how other political values are to be ordered, not simply one political value to be combined with others.

This dilemma is familiar from discussions of democracy and the "liberties of the moderns"—religious liberty, liberty of conscience more generally, liberty of thought and expression, rights of person and personal property. Lacking any evident connection to conditions of democratic procedure, such liberties are commonly understood as constraints on democratic process. Not so with political liberties. A constitution disabling government from restricting political participation or regulating the content of political speech can be interpreted as safeguarding, rather than constraining, democratic process. Assurances of such political liberties help to preserve the connection between popular authorization and political outcome—to preserve the continuing authority of the people, and not simply the majority of them.[6] These liberties—the liberties of the ancients—are constitutive elements of democratic process.

Things are different when it comes to abridgments of religious liberty, or restrictions on expression whose content can be construed as political only on a uselessly capacious construal of "political." In these cases, disabling provisions in a constitution appear simply to limit democracy, not to be among its preconditions, either implicit or explicit.

The liberties of the moderns appear, then, to be founded on values entirely independent from the values of democracy. And that appearance may prompt one of two undesirable conclusions. The first is that the political liberties are merely instrumental, of value just insofar as they protect the liberties of the moderns; when they fail to ensure such protection, an authority external to the people ought to do so. Here, a conflict between democracy and other political values is easily translated into a conflict between democratic and nondemocratic procedures of political decision-making.[7]

A second view holds that the liberties of the moderns have no standing deeper than contingent popular consensus. Although abridgments of nonpolitical liberties that emerge from a fair democratic process may be unjust, then, they face no problems of democratic legitimacy.[8]

We are pushed into this dilemma by a particular understanding of democracy, which I will call "aggregative"—as distinct from deliberative.[9] According to an aggregative conception, democracy institutionalizes a principle requiring equal consideration for the interests of each member; or, more precisely, equal consideration along with a "presumption of personal autonomy"—the understanding that adult members are the best judges and most vigilant defenders of their own interests.[10] To criticize processes as undemocratic, then, is to claim that those processes failed to give equal consideration to the interests of each member. The natural method for giving such consideration is to establish a scheme of collective choice—majority or plurality rule, or group bargaining—that gives equal weight to the interests of citizens in part by enabling them to present and advance their interests. And that requires a framework of rights of participation, association, and expression.

Arguably, the aggregative view can be extended beyond such straightforwardly procedural rights to some concerns about outcomes. For it might be said that collective choices that depend on discriminatory views—on hostility or stereotyping—do not give equal weight to the interests of each who is governed by them. And when we face outcomes that disadvantage people who are the likely targets of such views, we have strong evidence of a failure of the process to give equal consideration to the interests of each.[11]

This procedural reinterpretation of important political values can, however, go only so far. Religious liberty, for example, has no apparent procedural basis. To be sure, abridgments of freedom of worship are sometimes troubling because they result from discriminatory (anti-Catholic, anti-Semitic) attitudes. When they do, protections of religious liberties will emerge from the requirement of equal consideration. But the failure to give appropriate weight to religious convictions need not reflect hatred, discrimination, or stereotyping of the person—nor must it depend on any other of the conventional ways of demeaning a person or failing to treat her as an equal. The problem may have a different source: it may trace to a failure to take seriously the stringency or weight of the demands placed on the person by her reasonable moral or religious convictions—not the intensity with which she holds those convictions—which does figure in aggregative views—but the stringency or weight of the demands imposed by the convictions, given their content.[12] It is precisely this stringency that compels reasons of especially great magnitude for overriding those demands. But such considerations about the relative stringency of demands are absent from the aggregative conception; so, therefore, is the need to find reasons of great weight before overriding those demands. That is a fundamental deficiency, and lies at the source of the dilemma I sketched earlier.

A deliberative conception of democracy does not face the same troubles about reconciling democracy with nonpolitical liberties and other substantive, nonprocedural requirements. While accepting the fact of reasonable pluralism, it is attentive to the stringency of demands to which agents are subject, and therefore does not present its conception of democracy or collective decision in an exclusively procedural way. To make this case, I will first sketch the main ideas of a deliberative view; then I will show how, on the deliberative conception, we can accommodate the fact of reasonable pluralism without endorsing a wholly procedural conception of democracy. In particular, I will show how the liberties of the moderns and other substantive conditions are themselves elements in an institutional ideal of deliberative democracy.

Deliberative Democracy

The deliberative conception of democracy is organized around an ideal of political justification. According to this ideal, justification of the exercise of collective political power is to proceed on the basis of a free public reasoning among equals. A deliberative democracy institutionalizes this ideal. Not simply a form of politics, democracy, on the deliberative view, is a framework of social and institutional conditions that facilitates free discussion among equal citizens—by providing favorable conditions for participation, association, and expression—and ties the authorization to exercise public power (and the exercise itself) to such discussion—by establishing a framework ensuring the responsiveness and accountability of political power to it through regular competitive elections, conditions of publicity, legislative oversight, and so on.[13]

I will come back later to the conditions for institutionalizing deliberation in greater detail. First, though, I want to say more about the idea of deliberative justification itself.

A deliberative conception puts public reasoning at the center of political justification. I say "public reasoning" rather than "public discussion" because a deliberative view cannot be distinguished simply by its emphasis on discussion rather than bargaining or voting. Any view of democracy—indeed any view of intelligent political decision-making—will see discussion as important, if only because of its essential role in pooling information against a background of asymmetries in its distribution. Nor is it marked by the assumption that political discussion *aims* to change the preferences of other citizens. Though a deliberative view must assume that citizens are prepared to be moved by reasons that may conflict with their antecedent preferences and interests, and that being so moved may change those antecedent preferences and interests,[14] it does not suppose that political deliberation takes as its goal the alteration of preferences. Nor is it distinguished by its endorsement of an epistemic conception of voting, according to which votes are interpreted as expressions of beliefs about the correct answer to a political question, rather than as preferences about what policy is to be implemented.[15]

The conception of justification that provides the core of the ideal of deliberative democracy can be captured in an ideal procedure of political deliberation. In such a procedure participants regard one another as equals; they aim to defend and criticize institutions and programs in terms of considerations that others have reason to accept, given the fact of reasonable pluralism and the assumption that those others are reasonable; and they are prepared to cooperate in accordance with the results of such discussion, treating those results as authoritative.

Which considerations count as reasons? A suitable answer will take the form not of a generic account of reasons but of a statement of which considerations count in favor of proposals in a deliberative setting suited to free association among equals, where that setting is assumed to include an acknowledgment of reasonable pluralism. This background is reflected in the kinds of reasons that will be acceptable. In an idealized deliberative setting, it will not do simply to advance reasons that one takes to be true or compelling: such considerations may be rejected by others who are themselves reasonable. One must instead find reasons that are compelling to others, acknowledging those others as equals, aware that they have alternative reasonable commitments, and knowing something about the kinds of commitments that they are likely to have—for example, that they may have moral or religious commitments that impose what they take to be overriding obligations. If a consideration does not meet these tests, that will suffice for rejecting it as a reason. If it does, then it counts as an acceptable political reason.

To be sure, the precise characterization of the acceptable reasons, and of their appropriate weight, will vary across views. For that reason, even an ideal deliberative procedure will not, in general, produce consensus. But even if there is disagreement, and the decision is made by majority rule, participants may appeal to considerations that are quite generally recognized as having considerable weight, and as a suitable basis for collective choice, even among people who disagree about the right result: when participants confine their argument to such reasons, majority support itself will commonly count as reason for accepting the decision as legitimate.

To underscore this point about the importance of background context in the account of acceptable political reasons, I want to highlight a difference between the idea of reasonable acceptance at work here, and the idea of reasonable rejection in Scanlon's contractualism.[16] Scanlon characterizes the wrongness of conduct in terms of the idea of a rule "which no one could reasonably reject," and he advances this characterization as part of a general account of the subject matter of morality and the nature of moral motivation. So his account of reasonableness—of reasonable grounds for rejecting principles—is required to work quite generally, even in settings with no ongoing cooperation, institutional ties, or background of equal standing as citizens.

My concern is not with reasons generally, or morality generally, or with political deliberation generally, or with the reasons that are suited to democratic discussion quite generally, but with a view about the implications of democracy given a specific background. And that background constrains what can count as an acceptable reason within a process of deliberation. For if one accepts the democratic process, agreeing that adults are, more or less without exception, to have access to it, then one cannot accept as a reason within that process that some are worth less than others or that the interests of one group are to count for less than those of others. And these constraints on reasons will limit the substantive outcomes of the process; they supplement the limits set by the generic idea of a fair procedure of reason-giving.

I am not here raising an objection to Scanlon's view. He has a different topic—morality generally, as distinct from democratic legitimacy. Instead, I am urging that this difference in background makes a difference to the kinds of reasons that are suited to the two cases.

To conclude these general remarks about the deliberative view, I want to emphasize that its virtues are allied closely with its conception of binding collective choice, in particular with the role in that conception of the idea of reasons acceptable to others who are governed by those choices, and who themselves have reasonable views. By requiring reasons acceptable to others, the deliberative view suggests an especially compelling picture of the possible relations among people within a democratic order.

To see the character of those relations, notice first that the deliberative conception offers a more forceful rendering than the aggregative view of the fundamental democratic idea—the idea that decisions about the exercise of state power are *collective*. It requires that we offer considerations that others (whose conduct will be governed by the decisions) can accept, not simply that we count their interests in deciding what to do, while keeping our fingers crossed that those interests are outweighed. Thus the idea of popular authorization is reflected not only in the processes of decision-making but in the form—and, we will see later, the content—of political reason itself.

This point about the force of the deliberative view and its conception of collective decisions can be stated in terms of the idea of political community. If political community depends on sharing a comprehensive moral or religious view, or a substantive national identity defined in terms of such a view, then reasonable pluralism ruins the possibility of political community. But an alternative conception of political community connects the deliberative view to the value of community. In particular, by requiring justification on terms acceptable to others, deliberative democracy provides for a form of political autonomy: that all who are governed by collective decisions—who are expected to govern their own conduct by those decisions—must find the bases of those decisions acceptable. And in this assurance of political autonomy, deliberative democracy achieves one important element of the ideal of community. Not because collective decisions crystallize a shared ethical outlook that informs all social life, nor because the collective good takes precedence over the liberties of members, but because the requirement of providing acceptable reasons for the exercise of political power to those who are governed by it—a requirement absent from the aggregative view—expresses the equal membership of all in the sovereign body responsible for authorizing the exercise of that power.

To explain the deliberative ideal more fully, I want now to explore some of its implications: the conditions that need to be met by social and political arrangements that, within the setting of a modern state, institutionalize deliberative justification. What conditions will such arrangements need to satisfy, if they are to sustain the claim that they establish the conditions for free reasoning among equals, and root the authorization to exercise state power in those conditions?

As a partial answer, I will indicate why deliberative democracy needs to ensure the liberties of the moderns. Then I will connect the deliberative view to conceptions of the common good and political equality.

Three Principles

The aggregative conception of democracy promises the protections required for a fair process of binding collective choice, including protections against discrimination that would undermine the claim of the process to ensure equal consideration. I said earlier that the deliberative view will provide a basis for wider guarantees of basic liberties. It is time to make good on that claim. The main idea is that the deliberative conception requires more than that the interests of others be given equal consideration; it demands, too, that we find politically acceptable reasons—reasons that are acceptable to others, given a background of differences of conscientious conviction. I will call this requirement the "principle of deliberative inclusion."

Consider, for example, the case of religious liberty. Religious views set demands of an especially high order—perhaps transcendent obligations—on their adherents; moreover, if we see these requirements from the believer's point of view, then we cannot think of them as self-imposed. Instead, the requirements are fixed by the content of the convictions, which the agent takes to be true. Reasonable adherents, then, cannot accept, as sufficient reasons in support of a law or system of policy, considerations that would preclude their compliance with those demands. What, then, about people who do not share those views? (I will describe the issue from the point of view of citizens who have fundamental moral convictions but no religious convictions. Broadly parallel remarks could be made from the standpoint of citizens with different religious convictions.) They might regard all religious views that impose such stringent demands, whatever their content and foundation, as unreasonable. I see no rationale for this view. Or they might treat the religious demands as intense preferences, to be given equal consideration along with other preferences of equal intensity. This reductive response indicates an unwillingness to see the special role of religious convictions from the point of view of the person who has them, an unwillingness to see how the religious view, in virtue of its content, states or implies that the requirements provide especially compelling reasons.

Alternatively, they might take seriously that the demands impose what the adherent reasonably regards as fundamental obligations, accept the requirement of finding reasons that might override these obligations, and acknowledge that such reasons cannot normally be found. The result is religious liberty, understood to include freedom of conscience and worship. It emerges as the product of the demanding character of religious requirements—which are seen, from the point of view of those who are subject to them, as matters of fundamental obligation—together with the requirement of finding reasons that those who are subject to those requirements can reasonably be expected to acknowledge, and the fact that citizens who are not religious have fundamental convictions that they take to impose especially compelling obligations.

Suppose, then, that we prevent others from fulfilling such demands for reasons that they are compelled—by the lights of a view that commands their conviction—to regard as insufficient. This is to deny them standing as equal citizens—full membership in the people whose collective actions authorize the exercise of power. And that, according to the deliberative conception, is a failure of democracy. We have failed to provide a justification for the exercise of power by reference to considerations that all who are subject to that power, and prepared to cooperate on reasonable terms, can accept. There are many ways to exclude individuals and groups from the people, but this surely is one.

These points about religious liberty—essentially about its free exercise—do not say anything about how to handle claims for religious exemption from general obligations with a strong secular justification (including obligations to educate children); or whether special provision is to be made for specifically religious convictions, as distinct from conscientious ethical convictions with no religious roots.[17] My aim here is not to resolve or even address these issues: any view that recognizes rights of free exercise will need to face those hard questions. My aim is only to show that a deliberative conception of democracy is not barred—by its structure—from acknowledging a fundamental role for rights of religious liberty; indeed it must provide a place for such rights.[18]

Finally, I emphasize that the point of guarantees of religious liberty, which fall under the requirement of deliberative inclusion, is not narrowly political: it is not to enable people to participate in politics—or to participate without fear—nor is the aim to improve public discussion by adding more diverse voices to it.[19] The idea instead is that abridgments of such liberties would constitute denials to citizens of standing as equal members of sovereign people, by imposing in ways that deny the force of reasons that are, by the lights of their own views, compelling. The reasons for abridgment are unacceptably exclusionary because they are unsuited to the ideal of guiding the exercise of power by a process of reason-giving suited to a system of free and equal citizens.

The principle of deliberative inclusion extends naturally from religious liberty to a wide guarantee of expressive liberty.[20] In this respect, it contrasts with a more familiar strand of free speech theory that traces the foundations of stringent guarantees of expressive liberty to the need to assure a democratic framework of collective choice, but guarantees stringent protection only for political speech.[21] This limit is in tension with the requirement of deliberative inclusion.

Confining stringent protection to political speech seems natural, once one has decided to found rights to free expression on the importance of requiring government accountability and responsiveness to citizens as a body. But as my remarks on the religion case suggest, a deliberative conception of democracy cannot accept such a limit. To be sure, the idea of discussion aimed at reaching reasonable agreement is fundamental to the deliberative view. But it does not follow that the protection of expression is to be confined to speech that contributes to such discussion.

Consider expression that is not part of any process of discussion or persuasion—that is not "intended and received as a contribution to public deliberation about some issue"[22]—but that nevertheless reflects what a citizen takes, for quite understandable reasons, to be compelling reasons for expression.[23] This might be so in cases of bearing witness, with no expectation or intention of persuading others, or giving professional advice, with no expectation or intention of shaping broader processes of collective decision-making. The deliberative view extends stringent protection to such expression, as a way to acknowledge the weight of those reasons. Given the background of reasonable pluralism, the failure to do so—to give due weight to an expressive interest that does not serve as input to political discussion—will constitute a denial of equal standing, and decisions that fail to ensure those stringent protections are not suitably collective.

The tradition that traces protections of expressive liberty to democratic ideals and then restricts stringent protection to contributions to debate in the public forum conflates the general strategy of providing a case for freedom of expression rooted in the idea of democracy with one element of that strategy: the need to protect *inputs* to a process of discussion. But as with religious liberty, so, too, with expressive liberty: the deliberative view also ties protections to acceptable *outcomes* of a deliberative process, outcomes, that is, that can be justified given the requirement on finding reasons acceptable to others under conditions of reasonable pluralism.

Earlier I suggested a connection between the deliberative conception and the value of community. That suggestion may now seem strained in light of the connections between the requirement of acceptable reasons and the protection of nonpolitical liberties. For such liberties are commonly represented as—for better or worse—the solvent of community.

But the deliberative view suggests a need for caution about that representation. Given conditions of reasonable pluralism, the protection of the liberties of the moderns is not a solvent of community. Reasonable pluralism itself may be such a solvent: at least if we define community in terms of a shared comprehensive moral or religious view. But once we assume reasonable pluralism, the protection of the liberties of the moderns turns out to be a necessary though insufficient condition for the only plausible form of political community. As the phrase "principle of exclusion" indicates, those liberties express the equal standing of citizens as members of the collective body whose authorization is required for the legitimate exercise of public power.

Turning now to the common good: aggregative views of democracy are conventionally skeptical about conceptions of the common good. Robert Dahl, for example, has suggested that in pluralistic societies conceptions of the common good are either too indeterminate to provide guidance, determinate but unacceptable because they lead us to "appalling results" in conditions that "are by no means improbable,"[24] or determinate and acceptable because purely procedural—because they define the common good as a democratic process.[25] On the deliberative conception, this skeptical outlook is unwarranted, yet another reflection of the absence of constraints beyond the requirement of fair aggregation.

A deliberative account of the principle of the common good begins by observing that citizens have good reason to reject a system of public policy that fails to advance their interests at all. (I say a "system of policy" because I do not wish to exclude the possibility that particular laws, regulations, or policies that are not attentive to the interests of some citizens may be justifiable as part

of an overall package of laws and policies that is.[26]) This minimal constraint—
of advancing the interests of each—comes out of the generic conception of a
deliberative process, and suffices to establish a pareto-efficiency requirement,
as one element of a conception of democracy.

But as I have emphasized, the deliberation that plays a role in the conception of deliberative democracy is not simply a matter of reason-giving, generically understood. The background conception of citizens as equals sets limits
on permissible reasons that can figure within the deliberative process. For
suppose one accepts the democratic process of binding collective choice,
agreeing that adults are, more or less without exception, to have access to it.
One can then reject, as a reason within that process, that some are worth less
than others or that the interests of one group are to count for less than the
interests of others. That constraint on reasons will, in turn, limit the outcomes
of the process, adding to the conditions set by the generic idea of deliberation.
In particular, it provides a case for a public understanding about the distribution of resources that severs the fate of citizens from the differences of social
position, natural endowment, and good fortune that distinguish citizens.

John Rawls's difference principle provides one illustration of such an understanding.[27] Treating equality as a baseline, it requires that inequalities established or sanctioned by state action must work to the maximal advantage
of the least advantaged. That baseline is a natural expression of the constraints
on reasons that emerge from the background equal standing of citizens: it will
not count as a reason for a system of policy that that system benefits the
members of a particular group singled out by social class, or native talent, or
by any of the other features that distinguish among equal citizens. I do not
wish to suggest here that Rawls's difference principle is the uniquely acceptable conception of the common good. But there is an especially strong case
for it, both because it accepts the presumption of equality that emerges
from the special constraints on reasons within the deliberative democratic
view and because it insists, roughly speaking, that no one be left less well off
than anyone needs to be—which is itself a natural expression of the deliberative conception.

I want finally to connect the deliberative view with rights of participation—
the liberties of the ancients. More particularly, I want to show how the deliberative view accommodates a "principle of participation."[28] According to that
principle, democratic collective choice—institutionalizing the tie between deliberative justification and the exercise of public power—must ensure equal
rights of participation, including rights of voting, association, and political
expression, with a strong presumption against restrictions on the content or
viewpoint of expression; rights to hold office; a strong presumption in favor of
equally weighted votes; and a more general requirement of equal opportunities for effective influence.[29] This last requirement condemns inequalities in

opportunities for office-holding and political influence that result from the design of arrangements of collective decision-making.[30]

Notice first that the mere fact that decisions are to be made in a generically deliberative way does not go very far toward establishing a case for the principle of participation.[31] Perhaps an ideal deliberative procedure is best institutionalized by ensuring well-conducted political debate among elites, thus enabling people to make informed choices among them and the views they represent, without any special provision for more substantive political equality, understood as requiring equally weighted votes and equal opportunities for effective influence.[32] How, then, does the deliberative view connect to concerns about participation and political equality?

Three considerations are important.

First, given the principles of deliberative inclusion and of the common good, the deliberative view can avail itself of conventional instrumental reasons in support of equal political rights. Such rights provide the means for protecting other basic rights and for advancing interests in ways that might plausibly promote the common good. Moreover, absent assurances of effective influence, such promotion seems an unlikely result. And it would be especially unlikely if inequalities in effectiveness corresponded to underlying social or economic inequalities in the society.[33]

In making this instrumental case, I may appear to be shifting to a bargaining conception of politics, with assurances of equal power working to ensure a political equilibrium with fair outcomes. But that gets the instrumental rationale and the mechanism wrong. The idea instead is that ensuring that all citizens have effective political rights serves as a reminder that citizens are to be treated as equals in political deliberation, and, by reducing inequalities of power, reduces the incentives to shift from deliberative politics to a politics of bargaining.

A second consideration is that many of the conventional, historical justifications for exclusions from or inequalities of political rights—justifications based on race and gender, for example—will not provide acceptable reasons in public deliberation. This consideration will not exclude all reasons for inequality—for example, if votes are of unequal weight because the political system relies—as in the case of the U.S. Senate—on a scheme of territorial representation in which districts correspond to political subdivisions. But it establishes a further presumption in favor of the principle of participation.

Finally, considerations analogous to those we met with in the case of religion and expression strengthen the case for equal political rights, with assurances of equal opportunities for effective influence. A characteristic feature of moral and religious convictions is that they give us strong reasons for seeking to shape our political-social environment. The comprehensive views underlying those reasons range from Aristotelian views about the central role of civic engagement in a good life, to Rousseauean claims about the connection between personal autonomy and participation, to views, founded on religious convictions, about the commanding personal responsibility to ensure social justice and the corresponding personal sin of failing in that responsibility. It is common ground, however, that citizens have substantial, sometimes compelling reasons for addressing public affairs. Because they do, the failure to acknowledge the weight of those reasons for the agent and to acknowledge the claims to opportunities for effective influence that emerge from them reflects a failure to endorse the background idea of citizens as equals.

Realizing Democracy

The deliberative conception of democracy captures the role of "undemocratic" as a term of criticism applying to results as well as processes: it provides common roots for the "by the people" and "for the people" aspects of the ideal of democracy. But this incorporation of important substantive requirements into the conception of democracy gives rise to a problem of its own. The concern is that if we offer an interpretation of democracy that treats all good things as ingredient in the idea of democracy—requirements of political equality, considerations of the common good, and the liberties of the moderns—then we may appear to integrate procedural and substantive values at the cost of practical guidance. What are we to do when the many elements of deliberative democracy come into conflict? Common foundations in deliberative democracy do not provide any insurance against conflict in practice. For example, the liberties mandated by the requirement of deliberative inclusion may conflict with the equal political liberties that fall under the requirement of participation. Why does it help to have all these elements ingredient within the ideal of democracy, given conflicts among them?

The answer is that by underscoring common foundations we highlight the need to find ways to accommodate the different requirements, so far as accommodation is possible. That may be more often than we are inclined to think, though how often is a function of politics. To make this point less telegraphic, I will sketch some examples. I want to focus the discussion on two cases in which the various requirements arguably conflict, and see what might be said about their reconciliation in these cases.

My first case is campaign finance. The central problem arises from a familiar dilemma: on the one hand, restrictions on political expenditures by candidates, parties, individual citizens, and organizations appear to burden expressive liberty, particularly given a background expectation that such expenditures are permissible; arguably, burdens also result from very stringent limits on contributions to political campaigns. Moreover, restrictions on candidate and party expenditures, even when they are accepted as a condition for receiving public financing, may reinforce incumbency advantages, resulting in a less competitive electoral system, less capable of holding elected officials account-able and so of ensuring public authorization of the exercise of power.[34] On the other hand, a regime of unrestricted expenditures is a regime in which politi-cal influence—chances to hold office and to effect the outcomes of political contests—reflect economic position, and that means inequalities in opportu-nities for effective influence.[35]

Thus the familiar conflict about restrictions on political spending. Some reject restrictions, even if they are content-neutral and motivated by a sincere desire to ensure greater equality of political influence. In an infamous sentence in the majority opinion in *Buckley v. Valeo*, the Supreme Court said that "the concept that government may restrict the speech of some elements of our society in order to enhance the relative voice of others is wholly foreign to the First Amendment";[36] as a result, they were unwilling to find any basis beyond concerns about *quid pro quo* corruption for regulating political spending.[37] Others, concerned to insist on the importance of fair political equality, argue that limits are essential.

The first idea—that it is impermissible to restrict the voice of some in order to enhance the relative voice of others—seems bizarre. My earlier account of the bases of rights of expression and political participation suggested a com-mon foundation for both; so there is no basis for the subordinate role of polit-ical equality. Moreover, once we have accepted a presumption in favor of equally weighted votes—one person/one vote—we are already committed to precisely such restrictions and enhancements.[38]

Still, focusing on the permissibility of restrictions may be putting the em-phasis in the wrong place. Given the bases of rights of expression in the princi-ples of participation and deliberative inclusion, it would be desirable to pro-mote equality of opportunity for effective influence through less restrictive means than expenditure limits, should such means be available.[39] And the natural route to such reconciliation is to establish a scheme of public financ-ing. The idea of such a system is to rely principally on "floors" rather than "ceilings"—subsidies rather than limits—to remedy violations of the principle of participation.[40] By establishing floors, a suitable scheme of public financing helps to make office-holding more widely available; by reducing dependence of parties and candidates on private resources, it assures greater equality of opportunity for influence.[41] The effectiveness of floors in providing such as-surance may depend on making the availability of support conditional on accepting spending limits. But limits of this kind may be unnecessary, given a regime with substantial public financing.

Of course a wide range of public financing schemes are possible: support can be provided to candidates or parties[42] or individual voters (as citizen vouchers[43]) or, in the case of initiatives and referenda, to nonparty organiza-tions; funds can be made available for electoral activity or for more general party support; and support can be provided in the form of free media access.

And in deciding among such schemes, it is important to consider their effects on deliberation as well as opportunities for effective influence. Citizen vouchers are especially promising, I think. But I do not propose to go into such details here. The point is to state the main principles, emphasize the importance of finding some accommodation of them in view of their common basis in the value of democracy, and indicate that the strategy of accommodation is, roughly stated, a strategy of empowerment, not of restriction.

My second case concerns possible tensions between a deliberative politics and the principles of participation and the common good—and the role of a strategy of "associative democracy" in blunting those tensions.[44] The problem here is less straightforward, as is the proposed solution. So I first need to set some background.[45]

Begin, then, with two familiar premises. First, any well-functioning democratic order satisfying the principles of participation and the common good requires a social base. Beyond the world of voters and parties, secondary associations—organized groups intermediate between market and state—are needed both to represent otherwise underrepresented interests (as in the case of trade unions or other independent worker organizations) and to add to public competence in advancing the common good (think of the role played by unions and employer associations in establishing standards on worker training in any well-functioning training system). Representing underrepresented interests helps to ensure political equality; adding to public competence helps to promote the common good.

Second, the right kinds of association do not naturally arise, either for the purposes of addressing problems of underrepresentation or for more functional tasks: there is, for example, no natural tendency for an emergence of secondary associations to correct for inequalities of political opportunity due to underlying economic inequalities or to ensure the regulatory competence needed to advance the common good.

Now put together the need for a favorable associative environment with the fact that such an environment is not naturally provided. This conjunction suggests a strategy for addressing the associative deficit: a strategy of associative democracy that would use public powers to encourage the development of the right kinds of secondary association. For example, where manifest inequalities in political representation exist, the associative strategy recommends promoting the organized representation of presently excluded interests. Where associations have greater competence than public authorities for advancing the common good, it would recommend encouraging a more direct and formal governance role for groups. So trade unions and employer associations that took on responsibility for the joint development of training curricula, for example, might be encouraged by public grants contingent on their assumption of such responsibilities.

But here we arrive at the tension. In seeking to meet the principles of participation and the common good by fostering governance roles for groups we may heighten the role of group affiliation in defining political identity. And that may encourage a factionalized politics of group bargaining—albeit under more fair conditions—rather than a more deliberative politics.[46]

Standard responses to this problem are to encourage greater insulation of the state from groups, or to give up on egalitarian political values because no agent has the capacity to advance them. The idea of associative democracy suggests a different line of response. It begins by rejecting the implicit assumption that solidarities formed outside formal political arenas must be narrowly focused on particular groups, and proposes some institutional invention guided by that rejection. To explain the bases for rejecting that assumption and the relevant kinds of invention, I will make some very sketchy remarks about the idea of a deliberate use of associations in regulation.

Generally speaking, the idea of a regulatory role for associations reflects a sense of the limited capacity of the state to regulate for the common good. Those limits appear in four kinds of cases:

1) Where government has the competence to set specific regulatory terms, but the objects of regulation are sufficiently numerous, dispersed, or diverse to preclude serious government *monitoring* of compliance. Many workplace regulations—on appropriate wages and hours, compensation, and especially the appropriate organization of work, pertaining for example to occupational health and safety—provide instances of this monitoring problem.

2) Where government has the competence to set general standards of performance, but the objects of regulation are sufficiently diverse or unstable to preclude government specification of the most appropriate *means* of achieving them at particular regulated sites. Much environmental regulation is of this kind.

3) Where government may (or may not) be able to enforce standards once set, but cannot set appropriate *ends* itself.[47] Often, an appropriate standard can be determined only by those with local knowledge not readily available to government, or can be specified only as the outcome or in the context of prolonged cooperation among nongovernment actors. Industry standards on product or process uniformity and performance are often of this kind, as are standards on training. The appropriate norm shifts constantly; the content of the norm derives from cooperation in the process of establishing it.[48]

4) Where problems are substantially the product of multiple causes and connected with other problems, crossing conventional policy domains and processes. In such cases, the appropriate strategy requires *coordination* across those domains as well as cooperation from private actors within them. Urban poverty, local economic development, and effective social service delivery are among the familiar problems in this class. None can be solved without cooper-

ation across quite different institutions and groups—lending institutions, health care providers, technology diffusers, education and training establishments, housing authorities, community development corporations, neighborhood associations—operating wholly or substantially outside the state itself. These and other parties involved in the problem and its proposed solution, however, typically have distinct if not competing agendas, and different identities and interests.

To address such problems, the associative approach recommends explicitly relying on the distinctive capacity of associations to gather local information, monitor compliance, and promote cooperation among private actors. When problems are more or less *functionally specific*—corresponding roughly to the first three classes of cases described earlier, associative governance is not uncommon. As a general matter, it is best developed in the areas of workplace regulation and training, and relies on institutions controlled by the traditional "social partners" of labor and capital. The use of plant committees to enforce occupational safety and health regulations, for example, or groupings of trade unions and employers to facilitate technology diffusion, or employer and union associations to set standards on training, are all familiar. The lessons of practice in these areas might be more explicitly generalized to include nontraditional parties.

As the scope of associative efforts moves beyond functionally specific problems to issues that are decidedly more sprawling and open-ended—as in the urban poverty or regional economic development examples—models are less clear. Here the associative strategy recommends the construction of new arenas for public deliberation that lie outside conventional political arenas,[49] and whose aim is to establish the desired coordination.

Notice, however, that both the inclusion of nontraditional stakeholders and the development of deliberative arenas suggest a new possibility: that of constructing new bases of social solidarity *through* a process of defining and addressing common concerns. It is one thing for a well-funded union to be asked to participate in the design of training standards of obvious concern to it as well as the broader society. It is quite another for a nascent or underfunded community environmental organization to gain significant resources (and thus greater organizational life) if it assists in designing an environmental early warning system that is expected to take notice of emerging environmental problems before they become unmanageable. In this case, support is tied to public service. Or for a neighborhood association and economic development corporation in a poor community to receive assistance conditional on their jointly organizing a training program for parents and a child care program for trainees as part of a broader job-training effort: once more, participation and support are tied to a project of public advantage.

The solidarities characteristic of such efforts will be the bonds of people with common concerns—say, a concern to address persistent urban poverty—who treat one another as equal partners in addressing those shared concerns.[50] In short, these efforts—which could have very wide scope—have the potential to create new "deliberative arenas" outside formal politics that might work as "schools of deliberative democracy" in a special way. Deliberative arenas established for such coordination bring together people with shared concrete concerns, very different identities, and considerable uncertainty about how to address their common aims. Successful cooperation within them, fostered by the antecedent common concerns of participants, should encourage a willingness to treat others with respect as equals, precisely because discussion in these arenas requires fashioning arguments acceptable to those others. Assuming fair conditions of discussion and an expectation that the results of deliberation will regulate subsequent action, the participants would tend to be more other-regarding in their outlook. The structure of discussion, aimed at solving problems rather than pressuring the state for solutions, would encourage people to find terms to which others can agree. And that would plausibly drive argument and proposed action in directions that respect and advance more general interests. Moreover, pursuing discussion in the context of enduring differences among participants would incline parties to be more reflective in their definition of problems and proposed strategies for solution; it would tend to free discussion from the preconceptions that commonly limit the consideration of options within more narrowly defined groups.

If this is right, then a social world in which solidarities are formed in part by reference to such arenas is different from a social world whose associational life is narrower and factionalized. And that means that it may be possible to use the associative strategy to advance the principles of participation and the common good without thereby encouraging particularistic group identities that turn politics from deliberation to bargaining.

Conclusion

The fact of reasonable pluralism does not, I have argued, mandate a procedural account of democracy and collective choice. Conjoined with a deliberative conception of justification, it is compatible with a substantive account of democracy, whose substance—captured in principles of deliberative inclusion, the common good, and participation—includes values of equality and liberty. Moreover, such a deliberative conception offers an attractive rendering of the idea of collective choice, tying that idea to a view of political community. Finally, we are not without resources for addressing possible tensions between and among the values of liberty, equality, and community built into the deliberative conception. But whether or not those resources are exploited is, of course, a matter of politics.

Notes

1. "Governed by" rather than "affected by." Democracy is about justifying authority, not about justifying influence. See Michael Walzer, *Spheres of Justice* (New York: Basic Books, 1983); and Christopher McMahon, *Authority and Democracy* (Princeton: Princeton University Press, 1994). Alternatively stated, authorization must come from the popular will, where "popular will" is understood as indicating the ultimate authority and responsibility of citizens as a body, not as implying a collective ranking of alternatives that preexists institutions and seeks authentic expression through them. See William Riker, *Liberalism against Populism* (San Francisco: W. H. Freeman, 1992).

2. On the notion of a comprehensive doctrine, see John Rawls, *Political Liberalism* (New York: Columbia University Press, 1993), 13.

3. American national identity is commonly tied to such a conception, as in Lincoln's claim that the nation was conceived in liberty and dedicated to the proposition that all men are created equal. Some regard this abstract national self-definition as exceptionally American. Considering the conflictual conditions under which modern nationalism evolved, I doubt that this claim can be sustained without substantial qualification. Claims about the content of national identity—like all claims about group identity—are endlessly contested: they are as much moves in social and political conflicts aimed at establishing the authority of a particular nationalist understanding as they are intellectual discoveries. For every person who will claim that the conception of people as free and equal is foreign to their particular national identity, we can always find someone who shares the national self-definition and will deny that foreignness.

4. For discussion of this fact, see Joshua Cohen, "Moral Pluralism and Political Consensus," in *The Idea of Democracy*, ed. David Copp, Jean Hampton, and John Roemer (Cambridge: Cambridge University Press, 1993), 270–91; John Rawls, *Political Liberalism*; and Joshua Cohen, "A More Democratic Liberalism," *Michigan Law Review* 92, no. 6 (May 1994): 1502–46.

5. By "tracing legitimacy to popular authorization," I mean treating such authorization as a sufficient condition for the exercise of political power.

6. See John Hart Ely, *Democracy and Distrust* (Cambridge, Mass.: Harvard University Press, 1980); and Robert Dahl, *Democracy and Its Critics* (New Haven: Yale University Press, 1989).

7. See Dahl's concerns about judicial review in *Democracy and Its Critics*, 183.

8. It is of course open to a democratic pluralist to hold that such infringements are unjust and that the people ought not to reject them.

9. On the distinction between aggregative and deliberative views, and its bearing on the possibility of reconciling commitments to values of liberty and equality within a conception of democracy, see my review of Dahl's *Democracy and Its Critics*. For discussion of the related distinction between strategic and deliberative conceptions, see David Estlund, "Who's Afraid of Deliberative Democracy? On the Strategic/Deliberative Dichotomy in Recent Constitutional Jurisprudence," *Texas Law Review* 7, no. 7 (June 1993): 1437–77. Estlund identifies strategic theories with views that make use of the idea of utility-maximization. I think that the crucial issue is whether a conception of democracy emphasizes the idea of providing reasons acceptable to others.

10. In *Democracy and Its Critics*, chaps. 6–8, Robert Dahl derives conditions on democratic procedure from a principle of equal consideration and a presumption of personal autonomy.

11. When, for example, legislation relies on racial classifications—or at least on malign racial classification—we have reason to suspect that discriminatory preferences prompted the legislation. And if they did, then the procedural-democratic pedigree of the regulation is arguably corrupt. See Ely, *Democracy and Distrust*, chap. 6; and Ronald Dworkin, *Law's Empire* (Cambridge, Mass.: Harvard University Press, 1986), chap. 10. For a less social-psychological view of unacceptable procedural pedigree, see Bruce Ackerman, "Beyond Carolene Products," *Harvard Law Review* 98 (1985): 713–46. Unfortunately, the Supreme Court has recently endorsed the view that "malign racial classification" is a pleonasm, and "benign racial classification" a contradiction in terms. See *Richmond v. Croson*, 488 U.S. 469 (1989); *Shaw v. Reno*, 113 S. Ct. 2816 (1993); and *Miller v. Johnson*, slip op. (1995). For an alternative view, see *Metro Broadcasting v. FCC*, 497 U.S. 547 (1990).

12. The distinction between rights required to prevent discrimination and rights required to protect fundamental interests plays a central role in equal protection doctrine. See Laurence Tribe, *American Constitutional Law* (Mineola, N.Y.: Foundation Press, 1988), chap. 16. On the importance of paying attention to the content of views in an account of free exercise, see Ronald Dworkin, *Life's Dominion* (New York: Knopf, 1993), 162–66.

13. On the role of the idea of democracy as more than a political idea, see Gordon Wood, *The Radicalism of the American Revolution* (New York: Knopf, 1992), esp. 232.

14. See Cohen, "Deliberation and Democratic Legitimacy," 24.

15. On the idea of an epistemic conception, see Jules Coleman and John Ferejohn, "Democracy and Social Choice," *Ethics* 97 (October 1986): 6–25; and Joshua Cohen, "An Epistemic Conception of Democracy," *Ethics* 97 (October 1986): 26–38.

16. T. M. Scanlon, "Contractualism and Utilitarianism," in Amartya Sen and Bernard Williams, eds., *Utilitarianism and Beyond* (Cambridge: Cambridge University Press, 1982). The point of contrast in the text is prompted by Scanlon's discussion of the role of maximin reasoning in moral contractualism in "What Do We Owe Each Other?" (unpublished typescript, July 1994), chap. 5, 47–54.

17. On this last point: the key to the case for religious liberty is that the content of a view assigns stringent obligations to a person who holds it. But specifically *religious* content is not essential.

18. This account of religious liberty may seem to rest on the idea of a natural right to religious liberty—to say, in effect, that reasons will count as acceptable in a deliberative process only if they accept this right. If the idea of a natural right to religious liberty simply comes to the claim that there is a right that can be abridged only on pain of illegitimacy, then the deliberative view includes natural rights. But natural rights views have claimed more than this: they offer an explanation of the basis of fundamental rights in human nature, or natural law, or a prepolitical normative order to which political society must conform. The idea of democratic legitimacy does not depend on that explanation—though it asserts nothing inconsistent with it. It suffices that religious liberties have an explanation tied to the idea of democratic legitimacy. For the purposes of political argument, nothing more needs to be said, positively or negatively.

19. Roberto Unger argues that a system of immunity rights is one component of a democratic order, because "freedom as participation presupposes freedom as immunity." Rejecting the view of "critics of traditional democratic theory" who hold that "participatory opportunities [are] a more than satisfactory substitute for immunity guarantees," Unger sees immunity rights as necessary if a citizen is to have the "safety that encourages him to participate actively and independently in collective decision-making." In *False Necessity* (Cambridge: Cambridge University Press, 1987), 525. I agree with Unger's observations, but I think that a conception of democracy can make a less instrumental place for certain liberties, even when those liberties are not procedural.

20. This discussion draws on my "Freedom of Expression," *Philosophy and Public Affairs* 22 (Summer 1993): 207–63.

21. See Alexander Meiklejohn, *Free Speech and Its Relation to Self-Government* (New York: Harper and Row, 1948); and Cass R. Sunstein, *Democracy and the Problem of Free Speech* (New York: Free Press, 1993). Also, Robert Bork, "Neutral Principles and Some First Amendment Problems," *Indiana Law Journal* 47, no. 1 (Fall 1971): 1–35; Ely, *Democracy and Distrust*; and Owen Fiss, "Why The State?" *Harvard Law Review* 100 (1987): 781–94.

22. This is Sunstein's account of political speech in *Democracy and the Problem of Free Speech*, 130.

23. I do not mean to suggest that stringent protection ought to be confined to expression animated by such compelling reasons. The conventional democratic defense of rights of expression also provides a basis for stringent protection. My aim is to supplement that rationale.

24. *Democracy and Its Critics*, 283.

25. Ibid., 306–8.

26. The vices of a sales tax, for example, depend on the nature and level of exemptions, the presence (or not) of tax credits, and the nature of the policies that the revenue pays for.

27. See John Rawls, *A Theory of Justice* (Cambridge, Mass.: Harvard University Press, 1971), 513. For discussion of the connections between the difference principle and an ideal of democracy, see Joshua Cohen, "Democratic Equality," *Ethics* 99 (July 1989): 736–43. Another view that might be used to illustrate the points in the text is Dworkin's equality of resources. See Ronald Dworkin, "What is Equality? Part 2: Equality of Resources," *Philosophy and Public Affairs* 10 (1981): 283–345.

28. See Rawls, *A Theory of Justice*, 36–37.

29. On the requirement of opportunities for effective influence, see Rawls, *Political Liberalism*, 327–30. For a discussion of the constitutional dimension of the problem, see *Davis v. Bandemer* 478 U.S. 109, 132 (1986). The Court here acknowledges equal protection troubles when the "electoral system is arranged in a manner that will consistently degrade a voter's or group of voters' influence on political process as a whole." Low-Beer distinguishes a requirement of equally weighted votes, at stake in apportionment issues, from equally meaningful votes, at stake in gerrymandering cases. The value threatened by gerrymandering is better understood, I believe, as political influence more generally, not simply voting strength. See John Low-Beer, "The Constitutional Imperative of Proportional Representation," *Yale Law Journal* 94 (1984).

30. Among the concerns that fall under this requirement are vote dilution due to racial and political gerrymandering, and unequal influence due to campaign finance arrangements, restrictive rules on ballot access, and regulations of political parties.

31. Historically, the deliberative conception of politics was associated with highly exclusivist forms of parliamentarism; moreover, according to one influential line of thought, mass democracy destroyed the possibility of deliberative political decision-making. According to Carl Schmitt, "The belief in parliamentarism, in government by discussion, belongs to the intellectual world of liberalism. It does not belong to democracy." Moreover, "the development of modern mass democracy has made argumentative public discussion an empty formality." See *The Crisis of Parliamentary Democracy*, trans. Ellen Kennedy (Cambridge, Mass.: MIT Press, 1985), 6, 8.

32. Thus Beitz's account of political equality connects the interests in recognition and equitable treatment with assurances of equally weighted votes and fair access. What he calls the "deliberative interest," by contrast, simply requires well-conducted political debate. See *Political Equality* (Princeton: Princeton University Press, 1989).

33. See the discussion of the interest in equitable treatment in Beitz, *Political Equality*, 110–14. This interest plays an important role in the apportionment cases decided by the Supreme Court in the early 1960s. "No right is more precious in a free country than that of having a voice in the election of those who make the laws under which, as good citizens, we must live. *Other rights, even the most basic, are illusory if the right to vote is undermined.*" *Gray v. Sanders*, cited in *Reynolds v. Sims* 377 U.S. 533, at 558 (1964). Or again: "Especially since the right to exercise the franchise in a free and unimpaired manner is *preservative of other basic civil and political rights*, any alleged infringement of the right of citizens to vote must be carefully and meticulously scrutinized." *Reynolds v. Sims*, at 562.

34. This may seem puzzling. Making the safe assumption that incumbents have advantages in raising funds, it might seem clear that challengers would fare better under a system of spending restrictions. But, according to one influential line of argument, background incumbency advantages make challengers *more dependent* on money. Thus a challenger is better off running with $300,000 against an incumbent with $500,000 than running with $250,000 against an incumbent with $250,000. See Gary Jacobson, "Enough Is Too Much: Money and Competition in House Elections," in *Elections in America*, ed. Kay Lehman Schlozman (Boston: Allen and Unwin, 1987), 173–95. For criticisms of Jacobson's view, see Donald Philip Green and Jonathan S. Krasno, "Salvation for the Spendthrift Incumbent: Reestimating the Effects of Campaign Spending in House Elections," *American Journal of Political Science* 32, no. 4 (November 1988): 884–907.

35. I say a "regime" of unrestricted expenditures because the choice among systems of financing is a choice among alternative schemes of permissions and restrictions, not a choice between regulation and nonregulation.

36. 424 U.S. 1 (1976), 48–49.

37. *Buckley*, at 26–27.

38. See *Gray v. Sanders*, 372 U.S. 368 (1963); *Wesberry v. Sanders*, 376 U.S. 1 (1964); and *Reynolds v. Sims*, 377 U.S. 533 (1964). The tension between the apportionment decisions and Buckley is noted in Rawls, *Political Liberalism*, 361; and David A. Strauss, "Corruption, Equality, and Campaign Finance Reform," *Columbia Law Review*

94, no. 4 (May 1994): 1382–83. The Court itself has retreated from the *Buckley* position, acknowledging possibilities of corruption involving unfair influence without *quid pro quo*, and the permissibility of regulating expenditures—at least in the case of for-profit corporations—in order to avoid such corruption. See *Austin v. Michigan Chamber of Commerce*, 494 U.S. 652, 660 (1990).

39. A problem with relying principally on spending restrictions is the capacity of contributors and candidates to maneuver around restrictions. See Frank Sorauf, *Inside Campaign Finance: Myths and Realities* (New Haven: Yale University Press, 1992). Increase the level of public subsidy, and you reduce the incentives to such maneuvering.

40. The United States is one of four OECD countries with contribution limits. All the other political systems rely more substantially than the United States on public financing; the Scandinavian countries have no contribution or expenditure limits and rely entirely on public funding. See Ellen S. Miller and Joel Rogers, *The World of Campaign Finance* (Madison and Washington, D.C.: Center for a New Democracy and Center for Responsive Politics, 1992).

41. For a description of a scheme of public financing animated by concerns about equality and deliberation, see Jamin Raskin and John Bonifaz, "The Constitutional Imperative and Practical Superiority of Democratically Financed Elections," *Columbia Law Review* 94, no. 4 (May 1994): 1160–1203.

42. For an interesting public financing proposal, built around support for parties that would be distributed by congressional leadership, see Daniel Hays Lowenstein, "The Root of All Evil Is Deeply Rooted," *Hofstra Law Review* 18, no. 2 (Fall 1989): 351–55.

43. On voucher systems, see Bruce Ackerman, "Crediting the Voters: A New Beginning for Campaign Finance," *American Prospect* (Spring 1993); and Edward Foley, "Equal Dollars per Voter: A Constitutional Principle of Campaign Finance," *Columbia Law Review* 94, no. 4 (May 1994): 1204–57.

44. A broadly parallel concern arises in connection with the role of race-conscious measures in drawing lines around electoral districts. Given a background of racial bloc voting, the principle of participation may suggest a need for race-conscious districting to ensure opportunities for effective influence. But race-conscious districting arguably works against deliberative politics. According to Lani Guinier, cumulative voting would address this tension. Like other forms of proportional representation, cumulative voting combines increased chances of effective minority influence with voluntary constituencies that may encourage deliberation. See her "Second Proms and Second Primaries: The Limits of Majority Rule," *Boston Review* 17, no. 5 (September–October 1992): 32–34; and *The Tyranny of the Majority* (New York: Basic Books, 1994).

45. This section of the paper draws on Joshua Cohen and Joel Rogers, "Solidarity, Democracy, Association," in Wolfgang Streeck, ed., *Staat und Verbände*, special issue of *Politischen Vierteljahresschrift* (Wiesbaden: Westdeutscher Verlag, 1994), 136–59.

46. This concern emerges naturally from criticisms of modern pluralism. See, for example, Theodore Lowi, *The End of Liberalism: The Second Republic of the United States*, 2d ed. (New York: Norton, 1979). For discussion of associative democracy as a response to the problem of faction, see Joshua Cohen and Joel Rogers, "Secondary Associations in Democratic Governance," *Politics and Society* 20 (December 1992): 393–472.

47. Or it can set them only in very abstract terms, for example, as requirements of "reasonableness" or "due care."

48. For discussion of the problem of shifting standards as it applies to the more general problem of measures of business performance, see Charles Sabel, "A Measure of Federalism: Assessing Manufacturing Technology Centers," forthcoming in *Research Policy* (1996).

49. Though to the extent that they receive public support, they are to be subject to constitutional constraints, in particular guarantees of equal protection.

50. This claim depends, of course, on the background assumption of a democratic state protecting basic liberties and ensuring equal protection.

Six

Communication and the Other: Beyond Deliberative Democracy

IRIS MARION YOUNG

A NUMBER of political and legal theorists in recent years have promoted a concept of deliberative democracy as an alternative to an interest-based theory of democracy. In this essay I endorse such a discussion-based ideal of democracy. I find two problems, however, with the way this ideal is usually articulated. First, by restricting their concept of democratic discussion narrowly to critical argument, most theorists of deliberative democracy assume a culturally biased conception of discussion that tends to silence or devalue some people or groups. Deliberative theorists, moreover, tend inappropriately to assume that processes of discussion that aim to reach understanding must either begin with shared understandings or take a common good as their goal.

After exploring these shortcomings of the ideal of deliberative democracy as usually formulated, I propose some revisions to this approach to democratic theory, which I call communicative democracy.[1] First, I propose that we understand differences of culture, social perspective, or particularist commitment as resources to draw on for reaching understanding in democratic discussion rather than as divisions that must be overcome. Second, I propose an expanded conception of democratic communication. Greeting, rhetoric, and storytelling are forms of communication that in addition to argument contribute to political discussion.

The Model of Deliberative Democracy

Theorists of deliberative democracy usually contrast their view with what I shall call the interest-based model of democracy.[2] Interest-based conceptions of democracy consider democracy primarily as a process of expressing one's preferences and demands, and registering them in a vote. The goal of democratic decision-making is to decide what leaders, rules, and policies will best serve the greatest number of people, where each person defines his or her own interests. In the process of democratic decision-making, individuals and interest groups determine and vote for policies that will best serve their own perceived interests, including in their calculations the knowledge that the others in the polity do the same. Democratic decisions are the outcome of successful completion of ideas and coalitions for self-interested votes.

Deliberative critics of the interest-based model of democracy object to what they perceive as its irrationality and its privatized understanding of the political process. In this model, citizens never need to leave their own private and parochial pursuits and recognize their fellows in a public setting to address one another about their collective, as distinct from individual, needs and goals. Each citizen may reason about the best means for achieving his or her own privately defined ends, but the aggregate outcome has no necessary rationality and itself has not been arrived at by a process of reasoning.[3] People need not leave their own subjective point of view to take a more objective or general view of political issues. Thus the interest-based model of democracy also presumes that people cannot make claims on others about justice or the public good and defend those claims with reasons.[4]

By contrast, the model of deliberative democracy conceives of democracy as a process that creates a public, citizens coming together to talk about collective problems, goals, ideals, and actions. Democratic processes are oriented around discussing this common good rather than competing for the promotion of the private good of each. Instead of reasoning from the point of view of the private utility maximizer, through public deliberation citizens transform their preferences according to public-minded ends, and reason together about the nature of those ends and the best means to realize them. In free and open dialogue others test and challenge these assertions and reasons. Participants are careful to sort out good reasons from bad reasons, valid arguments from invalid. The interlocutors properly discount bad reasons and speeches that are not well argued, and they ignore or discount rhetorical flourishes and emotional outbursts. Putting forward and criticizing claims and arguments, participants in deliberation do not rest until the "force of the better argument" compels them all to accept a conclusion.

I agree with these critics of an interest-based model of democracy that it is better to have a conception of democracy that understands politics as the meeting of people to decide public ends and policies in a rational way. Though the interest-based model of democracy corresponds most to current practice and attitudes in contemporary Western democracies, norms of public reason sometimes do appear in the actual processes of liberal democracies as we know them. Such deliberative democracy appears most often in our current experience in the decision-making structures of voluntary associations outside the state. But processes of state policy formation in legislatures or public hearings sometimes exhibit features of the deliberative model. To the degree that contemporary democracies discourage deliberation and encourage a privatized consumer orientation toward politics on the part of citizens, they ought to be reformed to create more opportunities for deliberation. In what follows, however, I raise two criticisms of the model of deliberative democracy as usually articulated. Its tendency to restrict democratic discussion to argument carries implicit cultural biases that can lead to exclusions in practice. Its assumption that unity is either a starting point or goal of democratic discussion, moreover, may also have exclusionary consequences.

Exclusionary Implications of the Deliberative Model

A primary virtue of a deliberative model of democracy, I have argued thus far, is that it promotes a conception of reason over power in politics. Policies ought to be adopted not because the most powerful interests win but because the citizens or their representatives together determine their rightness after hearing and criticizing reasons. While there are some elitist tendencies in traditional republicanism, most contemporary deliberative theorists believe that a deliberative democracy is potentially more inclusive and egalitarian than an interest-based democracy.[5] Whereas an interest-based democracy does not preclude money and numbers from influencing decisions, for example, deliberative theorists usually assert that democracy requires an equal voice for all citizens to press their claims, regardless of social position or power.

Joshua Cohen gives a clear picture of the conditions of an ideal of deliberative democracy.[6] His formulation is close to Habermas's ideal of discourse that aims to reach understanding, which John Dryzek relies on as a basis for his conception of discursive democracy.[7] In the ideal of deliberative democracy, participants come to a political problem with an open mind about its solution; they are not bound by the authority of prior norms or requirements. The process of political discussion consists in reasoned argument. Participants put forward proposals and criticize them, and each assents to a conclusion only because of the "force of the better argument." For such assent to be rational, participants must be free and equal. Each must have the equal opportunity to make proposals and criticize, and their speaking situation must be free from domination. No one can be in a position to threaten or coerce others to accept or reject certain proposals. The goal of deliberation is to arrive at consensus; even when this is not possible and participants resort to voting, their result is a collective judgment rather than the aggregate of private preferences.

Deliberative theorists tend to assume that bracketing political and economic power is sufficient to make speakers equal. This assumption fails to notice that the social power that can prevent people from being equal speakers derives not only from economic dependence or political domination but also from an internalized sense of the right one has to speak or not to speak, and from the devaluation of some people's style of speech and the elevation of others. The deliberative ideal tends to assume that when we eliminate the influence of economic and political power, people's ways of speaking and understanding will be the same; but this will be true only if we also eliminate their cultural differences and different social positions. The model of deliberative democracy, that is, tends to assume that deliberation is both culturally neutral and universal. A theory of communicative democracy that attends to social difference, to the way that power sometimes enters speech itself, recognizes the cultural specificity of deliberative practices, and proposes a more inclusive model of communication.

The deliberative model of communication derives from specific institutional contexts of the modern West—scientific debate, modern parliaments, and courts (each with progenitors in ancient Greek and Roman philosophy and politics, and in the medieval academy). These were some of the aspiring institutions of the bourgeois revolution that succeeded in becoming ruling institutions. Their institutional forms, rules, and rhetorical and cultural styles have defined the meaning of reason itself in the modern world. As ruling institutions, however, they have been elitist and exclusive, and these exclusions mark their very conceptions of reason and deliberation, both in the institutions and in the rhetorical styles they represent. Since their Enlightenment beginnings they have been male-dominated institutions, and in class- and race-differentiated societies they have been white- and upper class–dominated. Despite the claim of deliberative forms of orderly meetings to express pure universal reason, the norms of deliberation are culturally specific and often operate as forms of power that silence or devalue the speech of some people.

Parliamentary debates or arguments in court are not simply free and open public forums in which all people actually have the right to express claims and give reasons according to their own understanding. Instead of defining discussion as the open reciprocal recognition of the point of view of everyone, these institutions style deliberation as agonistic. Deliberation is competition. Parties to dispute aim to win the argument, not to achieve mutual understanding. Consenting because of the "force of the better argument" means being unable to think of further counterargument, that is, to concede defeat.[8] The agonistic norms of deliberation reveal ways that power reenters this arena, even though deliberative theorists may claim to have bracketed it.

Restricting practices of democratic discussion to moves in a contest where some win and others lose privileges those who like contests and know the rules of the game. Speech that is assertive and confrontational is here more valued than speech that is tentative, exploratory, or conciliatory. In most actual situations of discussion, this privileges male speaking styles over female. A growing literature claims to show that girls and women tend to speak less than boys and men in speaking situations that value assertiveness and argument competition. When women do speak in such situations, moreover, they tend to give information and ask questions rather than state opinions or initiate controversy.[9]

In many formal situations the better-educated white middle-class people, moreover, often act as though they have a right to speak and that their words carry authority, whereas those of other groups often feel intimidated by the argument requirements and the formality and rules of parliamentary procedure, so they do not speak, or speak only a way that those in charge find "disruptive." Norms of assertiveness, combativeness, and speaking by the contest rules are powerful silencers or evaluators of speech in many actual speaking situations where culturally differentiated and socially unequal groups live together. The dominant groups, moreover, often fail entirely to notice this devaluation and silencing, while the less privileged often feel put down or frustrated, either losing confidence in themselves or becoming angry.

The norms of deliberation also privilege speech that is formal and general. Speech that proceeds from premise to conclusion in an orderly fashion that clearly lays out its inference structure is better than other speech. It is also better to assert one's position in terms of generalities and principles that apply to particular instances. These norms of "articulateness," however, must be learned; they are culturally specific, and in actual speaking situations in our society exhibiting such speaking styles is a sign of social privilege. Deliberation thus does not open itself equally to all ways of making claims and giving reasons. In formal situations of discussion and debate, such as classrooms, courtrooms, and city council chambers, many people feel they must apologize for their halting and circuitous speech.

The norms of deliberation, finally, privilege speech that is dispassionate and disembodied. They tend to presuppose an opposition between mind and body, reason and emotion. They tend falsely to identify objectivity with calm and absence of emotional expression. Thus expressions of anger, hurt, and passionate concern discount the claims and reasons they accompany. Similarly, the entrance of the body into speech—in wide gestures, movements of nervousness or body expressions of emotion—are signs of weakness that cancel out one's assertions or reveal one's lack of objectivity and control. Deliberative norms tend to privilege "literal" language over figurative language such as hyperbole, metaphor, and so on.

Once again, in our society these differences of speech privilege correlate with other differences of social privilege. The speech culture of white middle-class men tends to be more controlled, without significant gesture and expression of emotion. The speech culture of women and racial minorities, on the other, tends to be more excited and embodied, more valuing the expression of emotion, the use of figurative language, modulation in tone of voice, and wide gesture.[10]

I conclude from these considerations that this discussion-based theory of democracy must have a broader idea of the forms and styles of speaking that political discussion involves than deliberative theorists usually imagine. I prefer to call such a broadened theory communicative, rather than deliberative, democracy, to indicate an equal privileging of any forms of communicative interaction where people aim to reach understanding. While argument is a necessary element in such effort to discuss with and persuade one another about political issues, argument is not the only mode of political communication, and argument can be expressed in a plurality of ways, interspersed with or alongside other communicative forms.

Deliberative Model Assumes Unity

Unlike the interest-based conception of democracy, communicative democracy emphasizes that people's ideas about political questions often change when they interact with other people's ideas and experiences. If in a public discussion about collective action or public policy people simply say what they want, without any claims of justice or rightness, they will not be taken seriously. Instead, they must appeal to others by presenting proposals they claim are just or good and that others ought to accept. In this process people's own initial preferences are transformed from subjective desires to objective claims and the content of these preferences must also often change to make them publicly speakable, as claims of entitlement or what is right. People's ideas about the solution to collective problems are also sometimes transformed by listening to and learning about the point of view of others.

Deliberative theorists commonly write about this process of moving from subjective self-regarding preferences to more objective or general opinions about the solution to collective problems as a process of discovering or constructing unity among them. I see two approaches that deliberative theorists take in discussing such unity. Some take unity to be a prior condition of deliberation. Michael Walzer, for example, argues that effective social criticism locates and appeals to a community's prior "shared understandings."[11] Sometimes Jürgen Habermas writes as though reaching understanding through discourse about norms depends on restoring a disrupted consensus.[12]

There are at least two problems with this way of constructing the process of discussion. First, in contemporary pluralist societies we cannot assume that there are sufficient shared understandings to appeal to in many situations of conflict and solving collective problems. Second, the assumption of prior unity obviates the need for the self-transcendence, which I cited earlier as an important component of a communicative model of democracy. If discussion succeeds primarily when it appeals to what the discussants all share, then none need revise their opinions or viewpoints in order to take account of perspectives and experiences beyond them. Even if they need the others to see what they all share, each finds in the other only a mirror for him- or herself.

Recognizing such problems, some theorists of discussion-based democracy conceptualize unity not as a starting point but as a goal of political dialogue.

On this view, participants transcend their subjective, self-regarding perspective on political issues by putting aside their particular interests and seeking the good of the whole. Participants in a communicative democratic interchange often begin with differences of culture, perspective, interest, but the goal of discussion is to locate or create common interests that all can share. To arrive at the common good it may be necessary to work through differences, but difference itself is something to be transcended, because it is partial and divisive.[13]

The problem with this conception of the unity of democratic discussion is that it may harbor another mechanism of exclusion. Assuming a discussion situation in which participants are differentiated by group-based culture and social position, and where some groups have greater symbolic or material privilege than others, appeals to a "common good" are likely to perpetuate such privilege. As I argued in the previous section, even communication situations that bracket the direct influence of economic or political inequality nevertheless can privilege certain cultural styles and values. When discussion participants aim at unity, the appeal to a common good in which they are all supposed to leave behind their particular experience and interests, the perspectives of the privileged are likely to dominate the definition of that common good. The less privileged are asked to put aside the expression of their experience, which may require a different idiom, or their claims of entitlement or interest must be put aside for the sake of a common good whose definition is biased against them.[14]

Considering Difference a Resource

There is no reason or structure for differently situated groups to engage in democratic discussion if they do not live together in a polity. In this sense some unity is of course a condition of democratic communication. But the unity of a single polity is a much weaker unity, I suggest, than deliberative theorists usually assume. The unity that motivates politics is the facticity of people being thrown together, finding themselves in geographical proximity and economic interdependence such that activities and pursuits of some affect the ability of others to conduct their activities. A polity consists of people who live together, who are stuck with one another.

If a polity is to be a communicative democracy, even more unity is necessary. Its members must have a commitment to equal respect for one another, in the simple formal sense of willingness to say that all have a right to express their opinions and points of view, and all ought to listen. The members of the polity, furthermore, must agree on procedural rules of fair discussion and decision-making. These three conditions—significant interdependence, formally equal respect, and agreed-on procedures—are all the unity necessary for communicative democracy. They are much thinner conditions than those of shared understandings or the goals of finding common goods. Within the context of this minimal unity that characterizes communicative democracy, a richer understanding of processes of democratic discussion results if we assume that differences of social position and identity perspective function as a resource for public reason rather than as divisions that public reason transcends.

I have already argued that one of the problems with assuming unity as a starting point or goal of deliberative democracy is that such a conception cannot account well for the transformation the communicative process should often produce in the opinions of the participants. If we are all really looking for what we have in common—whether as a prior condition or as a result— then we are not transforming our point of view. We only come to see ourselves mirrored in others. If we assume, on the other hand, that communicative interaction means encountering differences of meaning, social position, or need that I do not share and identify with, then we can better describe how that interaction transforms my preferences. Different social positions encounter one another with the awareness of their difference. This does not mean that we believe we have no similarities; difference is not total otherness. But it means that each position is aware that it does not comprehend the perspective of the others differently located, in the sense that it cannot be assimilated into one's own. There is thus something to be learned from the other perspectives as they communicate their meanings and perspectives, precisely because the perspectives are beyond one another and not reducible to a common good. This process of mutual expression of experience and points of view that transcend the initial understanding of each accounts for a transformation in their opinions.

Communication among perspectives that transcend one another preserves the plurality that Hannah Arendt understood as a condition of publicity. The plural standpoints in the public enable each participant to understand more of what the society means or what the possible consequences of a policy will be by each situating his or her own experience and interest in a wider context of understanding something in other social locations. By "understand" I mean something somewhat different from what some deliberative theorists mean. Frequently in communicative contexts when people say they have come to an understanding or they understand one another, they think that this implies a mutual identification. People have reached understanding, in this conception, when they have transcended what differentiates and divides them and now have the same meaning or beliefs or principles.

If communicative democracy is better conceived as speaking across differences of culture, social position, and need, which are preserved in the process, however, then understanding one another and reaching understanding does not imply this identification. Understanding another social location can here mean that there has been successful expression of experience and perspective, so that other social positions learn, and part of what they understand is that there remains more behind that experience and perspective that transcends their own subjectivity.[15]

Preserving and listening across such differences of position and perspective causes the transformation in preference that deliberative theorists recommend. This transformation occurs in three ways. 1) Confrontation with different perspective, interests, and cultural meanings teaches me the partiality of my own, reveals to me my own experience as perspectival. 2) Knowledge that I am in a situation of collective problem solving with others who have different perspectives on the problems and different cultures and values from my own, and that they have the right to challenge my claims and arguments, forces me to transform my expressions of self-interest and desire into appeals to justice. Proposals for collective policies need not be expressed as general interest, an interest all can share; they may be claims about an obligation on the part of the public to recognize and provide for some unique needs of uniquely situated persons. Nevertheless the plural public perspectives require such expressed claims to appeal across difference, to presume a lack of understanding to be bridged, thus transforming the experience itself. 3) Expressing, questioning, and challenging differently situated knowledge, finally, adds to the social knowledge of all the participants. While not abandoning their own perspective, through listening across difference each position can come to understand something about the ways proposals and claims affect others differently situated. By internalizing this mediated understanding of plural positions to some extent, participants gain a wider picture of the social processes in which their own partial experience is embedded. This greater social objectivity increases their wisdom for arriving at just solutions to collective problems.

The Breadth of Communicative Democracy

In Plato's *Gorgias*, Socrates discusses the virtues and vices of rhetoric with students of the famous rhetorician, and with Gorgias himself. Socrates pushes his interlocutors to seek a distinction between the art of argument that reveals truth, on the one hand, and mere knack of persuasion that only produces appearances, on the other. Rhetoric is a mere knack of knowing how to please and flatter an audience, the dialogue suggests, in contrast to the critical thinking of philosophy, which sometimes displeases and discomforts the audience in order to lead them to shed comfortable falsehoods. As the dialogue proceeds it becomes clear, however, that Socrates and his interlocutors cannot sustain such a distinction between truth and rhetoric; argument also persuades, and the best one can say is that there is a difference between good rhetoric and bad rhetoric. Through the events of the dialogue Plato also illustrates the untenability of the distinction. Socrates engages in flattery in order to motivate his interlocutors to continue the discussion. He uses countless rhetorical tricks, from humor to irony to ridicule to self-effacement. Here as in nearly every other of Plato's dialogues, Socrates recites a myth, a poetic story that passes over argument to pull on intuition.

Following recent feminist accounts of dialogical reason,[16] as well as male African-American and Latino articulations of cultural biases in dominant conceptions of deliberation,[17] I propose three elements that a broader conception of communicative democracy requires in addition to critical argument: greeting, rhetoric, and storytelling. Because they recognize the embodiment and particularity of interlocutors, these three modes of communication help establish and maintain the plurality that I have argued, following Arendt, is necessary to the meaning and existence of publicity. Where such a public contains group-based cultural, social perspectival, and valuative differences, moreover, these communicative forms supplement argument by providing ways of speaking across difference in the absence of significant shared understandings.

Greeting. With the term "greeting" I wish to present the virtuous form of the communication mode that the *Gorgias* presents as the vice of flattery. A logical and motivational condition for dialogue that aims to reach understanding is that the parties in the dialogue recognize one another in their particularity. I call this moment of communication "greeting" to evoke the everyday pragmatic mode in which we experience such acknowledgment. Here is speech necessary to communication that does not *say* anything—it makes no assertion and has no specific content:[18] "Good morning," "How are you," "Welcome," "See you later," "Take care." In the category of greeting I also include such expressions of leave taking, as well as the forms of speech that often lubricate ongoing discussion with mild forms of flattery, stroking of egos, and deference.

Especially when parties to dialogue differ in many ways, either in their culture and values or in the interests and aims they bring to discussion, their effort to resolve conflict or come to agreement on a course of action cannot begin without preliminaries in which the parties establish trust or respect. These preliminaries often consist in various forms of flattery; introductory speeches that name the others with honorific titles, acknowledge the greatness of their achievements and ideals, and so on.[19]

Communicative interaction in which participants aim at reaching understanding is often peppered with gestures of politeness and deference, the absence of which is felt as coldness, indifference, insult. Discussion is also wrapped in nonlinguistic gestures that bring people together warmly, seeing conditions for amicability: smiles, handshakes, hugs, the giving and taking of food and drink.[20] In this respect bodies, and care for bodies, must enter an ideal of communicative democracy. Theorists of deliberative democracy,

however, seem to have no place for care-taking, deferential, polite acknowledgment of the Otherness of others. Since much democratic discussion will be
fraught with disagreement, anger, conflict, counterargument, and criticism,
intermittent gestures of flattery, greeting, deference, and conciliatory caring
keep commitment to the discussion at times of anger and disagreement.

Rhetoric. Deliberative theorists typically aim to fulfill the Platonic attempt to
distinguish rational speech from mere rhetoric, and in so doing they usually
denigrate emotion and figurative language. Rational speech, on this view, the
speech to which deliberative democracy should be confined, consists in
making assertions and giving sober reasons for them, with the logical connections among them clearly spelled out. Thus Thomas Spragens, for example,
invokes Hitler's disdain for the rationality of the masses as a warning against
rhetorical speech that aims to move the masses with hot passion. A rational
democracy, he claims, will engage the mind rather than ignite the passions.[21]
As James Bohman points out, Habermas also tries to distinguish rational
speech from rhetoric by distinguishing between illocutionary and perlocu-
tionary speech acts.[22] But the opposition between rational discourse and rhetoric, in my view, denigrates both the situatedness of communication and its
necessary link to desire.

In a discussion situation in which different people with different aims, values, and interests seek to solve collective problems justly, it is not enough to
make assertions and give reasons. One must also be heard. As Benjamin Barber
points out, democratic theorists value speaking, but they less often discuss
listening.[23] Rhetoric names the forms and styles of speaking that reflexively
attend to the audience in speech. While there are many aspects to this styling
of speech for its listeners, I will focus on the two I mentioned earlier: situatedness and the link to desire.

Rhetoric announces the situatedness of communication. With rhetorical
figures a speech constructs the speaker's position in relation to those of the
audience. Through rhetoric the speaker appeals to the particular attributes or
experience of the audience, and his or her own particular location in relation
to them. Rhetoric also constructs the occasion of the speech—today we com-
memorate, or we have just had an urgent phone call, or there is an ongoing
policy discussion we are having. Rhetoric constructs speaker, audience, and
occasion by invoking or creating specific meanings, connotations, and symbols, and it serves this connecting function whether the speaker and audience
share meanings or not.

Socrates faults the rhetorician for aiming to please the audience rather
than telling them hard truths. But Plato shows in Socrates' person that there
is an important erotic dimension in communication that aims to reach understanding, that persuasion is partly seduction. One function of rhetoric is to
get and keep attention. The most elegant and truthful arguments may fail to
evoke assent if they are boring. Humor, wordplay, images, and figures of

speech embody and color the arguments, making the discussion pull on thought through desire.

Storytelling. In a communicative democracy participants in discussion aim at reaching understandings about solutions to their collective problems. Although there is hardly a speaking situation in which participants have no shared meanings, disagreements, divergent understandings, and varying perspectives are also usually present. In situations of conflict that discussion aims to address, groups often begin with misunderstandings or a sense of complete lack of understanding of who their interlocutors are, and a sense that their own needs, desires, and motives are not understood. This is especially so where class or culture separates the parties. Doing justice under such circumstances of differences requires recognizing the particularity of individuals and groups as much as seeking general interests. Narrative fosters understanding across such difference without making those who are different symmetrical, in at least three ways.

First, narrative reveals the particular experiences of those in social locations, experiences that cannot be shared by those situated differently but that they must understand in order to do justice to the others. Imagine that wheelchair-bound people at a university make claims upon university resources to remove what they see as impediments to their full participation, and to give them positive aid in ways they claim will equalize their ability to compete with able-bodied students for academic status. A primary way they make their case will be through telling stories of their physical, temporal, social, and emotional obstacles. It would be a mistake to say that once they hear these stories the others understand the situation of the wheelchair-bound to the extent that they can adopt their point of view. On the contrary, the storytelling provides enough understanding of the situation of the wheelchair-bound by those who can walk for them to understand that they cannot share the experience.

Narrative exhibits subjective experience to other subjects. The narrative can evoke sympathy while maintaining distance because the narrative also carries an inexhaustible latent shadow, the transcendence of the Other, that there is always more to be told.

Second, narrative reveals a source of values, culture, and meaning. When an argument proceeds from premise to conclusion, it is only as persuasive as the acceptance of its premises among deliberators. Few institutions bring people together to face collective problems, moreover, where the people affected, however divided and diverse, can share no premises. Pluralist polities, however, often face serious divergences in value premises, cultural practices and meanings, and these disparities bring conflict, insensitivity, insult, and misunderstanding. Under these circumstances, narrative can serve to explain to outsiders what practices, places, or symbols mean to the people who hold them. Values, unlike norms, often cannot be justified through argument. But neither are they arbitrary. Their basis often emerges from the situated history of a people. Through narrative the outsiders may come to understand why the insiders value what they value and why they have the priorities they have.

How do the Lakota convey to others in South Dakota why the Black Hills mean so much to them, and why they believe they have special moral warrant to demand a stop to forestry in the Black Hills? Through stories—myths in which the Black Hills figure as primary characters, stories of Lakota individuals and groups in relation to those mountains. Values appear as a result of a history, by which a group relate "where they are coming from."

Finally, narrative not only exhibits experience and values from the point of view of the subjects that have and hold them. It also reveals a total social knowledge from the point of view of that social position. Each social perspective has an account not only of its own life and history but of every other position that affects its experience. Thus listeners can learn about how their own position, actions, and values appear to others from the stories they tell. Narrative thus exhibits the situated knowledge available of the collective from each perspective, and the combination of narratives from different perspectives produces the collective social wisdom not available from any one position.

There are two general conclusions to draw from this account of the role of narrative communication in which people aim to solve collective problems through discussion. First, narrative can often play an important role in argument in democratic discussion. Where arguments about policy or action depend on appeals to need or entitlement, narrative provides an important way to demonstrate need or entitlement. Narrative also contributes to political argument by the social knowledge it offers of how social segments view one another's actions and what are the likely effects of policies and actions on people in different social locations.[24]

As Lynn Sanders argues, storytelling complements arguments in a communicative democracy because it tends to be more egalitarian than typical deliberative processes.[25] I discussed earlier how deliberation can privilege the dispassionate, the educated, or those who feel they have a right to assert. Because everyone has stories to tell, with different styles and meanings, and because each can tell her story with equal authority, the stories have equal value in the communicative situation.[26]

I thus propose in this essay an ideal of communicative rather than deliberative democracy. The ideal of communicative democracy includes more than deliberative democracy, because it recognizes that when political dialogue aims at solving collective problems, it justly requires a plurality of perspectives, speaking styles, and ways of expressing the particularity of social situation as well as the general applicability of principles. A theory of democratic discussion useful to the contemporary world must explain the possibility of communication across wide differences of culture and social position.

Such a theory of democracy needs a broad and plural conception of communication that includes both the expression and the extension of shared understandings, where they exist, and the offering and acknowledgment of unshared meanings.

Notes

1. I have begun to develop this idea of communicative democracy in another essay, "Justice and Communicative Democracy," in Roger S. Gottlieb, ed., *Radical Philosophy: Tradition, Counter-Tradition, Politics* (Philadelphia: Temple University Press, 1993), 23–42.

2. Among the writers whom I include as theorists of deliberative democracy are Joshua Cohen, "Deliberation and Democratic Legitimacy," in Alan Hamlin and Philip Pettit, *The Good Polity* (London: Blackwell, 1989), 17–34; Thomas Spragens, *Reason and Democracy* (Durham, N.C.: Duke University Press, 1990); Benjamin Barber, *Strong Democracy* (Berkeley and Los Angeles: University of California Press, 1984), though Barber is not as susceptible to one of the critiques I offer as the other; Cass R. Sunstein, "Beyond the Republican Revival," *Yale Law Journal* 97 (1988): 1539–90; Frank Michelman, "Traces of Self-Government," *Harvard Law Review* 100 (1986): 4–77; Jane Mansbridge, "A Deliberative Theory of Interest Representation," in Mark P. Patracca, ed., *The Politics of Interests: Interest Groups Transformed* (Boulder, Colo., Westview Press, 1992); John Dryzek, *Discursive Democracy* (Cambridge: Cambridge University Press, 1990); James Bohman, "Democracy and Cultural Pluralism," *Political Theory* 23, no. 2 (1995): 253–79; and James Fishkin, *Deliberative Democracy* (New Haven: Yale University Press, 1991). I also assume Habermas's theory of communicative action as a basis for a theory of deliberative democracy, and some of my criticism is directed at his theory. Later I will refer to some of Michael Walzer's writing as falling within this general approach to democratic theory.

3. Spragens and Bohman both point to the potential irrationality of an interest-based conception of democracy. See also Jack Knight and James Johnson, "Aggregation and Deliberation: On the Possibility of Democratic Legitimacy," *Political Theory* 22, no. 2 (May 1994): 277–98.

4. See John Burke for a particularly bold assertion of the impossibility of moral claims in public life. *Bureaucratic Responsibility* (Baltimore: Johns Hopkins University Press, 1989).

5. James Fishkin is something of an exception here. He argues that there is a tradeoff between political equality and participation. Giving every citizen an equal influence over outcomes, he suggests, precludes deliberation, because in a large-scale democracy this means one person/one vote in aggregated elections and referenda. See *Deliberative Democracy*.

6. Cohen, "Deliberation and Democratic Legitimacy," 22–23.

7. Habermas, *A Theory of Communicative Action*, vol. 1: *Reason and the Rationalization of Society* (Boston: Beacon Press, 1981); Dryzek, *Discursive Democracy*, chaps. 1 and 2.

8. A passage from Habermas's exposition of the function of moral argument shows this unquestioned acceptance of the model of dialogue as competition: "What happens

in argumentation is that the success orientation of competitors is assimilated into a form of communication in which action oriented toward reaching understanding is continued by other means. In argumentation, proponents and opponents engage in *competition with arguments* in order to convince one another, that is, in order to reach a consensus. This dialectical role structure makes forms of disputation available for a comparative search for truth. Argumentation can exploit the conflict between success-oriented competitors for the purpose of achieving consensus so long as the arguments are not reduced to mere means of influencing one another." *Moral Consciousness and Communicative Action*, trans. Christian Lenhardt and Shierry Weber Nicholsen (Cambridge, Mass.: MIT Press, 1991), 160.

9. See Lynn Sanders, "Against Deliberation," a paper presented at a meeting of the American Political Science Association, September 1992; she cites studies that show that in juries men talk considerably more than women and are leaders more often. Jane Mansbridge cites studies that show that female state legislators speak less than their male counterparts and that in public meetings women tend more to give information and ask questions, while men state opinions and engage in confrontation. Mansbridge, "Feminism and Democratic Community," in John W. Chapman and Ian Shapiro, eds., *Democratic Community*, Nomos no. 35 (New York: New York University Press, 1991).

10. Anthony Cortese argues that the model of moral reasoning presupposed by Kohlberg and Habermas is ethnocentric and culturally biased, and tends to locate Chicano speaking and reasoning styles lower in its scale; see *Ethnic Ethics* (Albany: SUNY Press, 1990). Charles Henry discusses the tendency of African-Americans more than whites to couple emotion and anger with argument, influencing African-American styles of public debate; see *Culture and African American Politics* (Bloomington: Indiana University Press, 1990).

11. Michael Walzer, *Interpretation and Social Criticism* (Cambridge, Mass.: Harvard University Press, 1987).

12. Habermas, *Moral Consciousness*, 67.

13. For one statement of this kind of position, see Benjamin Barber, *Strong Democracy*, 197–212.

14. Compare Lynn Sanders, "Against Deliberation"; I have developed an argument similar to this at greater length in chap. 4 of *Justice and the Politics of Difference* (Princeton: Princeton University Press, 1990).

15. I have developed more of such a conception of understanding across difference in another article, "Asymmetrical Reciprocity: On Moral Respect, Wonder and Enlarged Thought," forthcoming in *Constellations*.

16. Alison Jaggar, "Feminist Practical Dialogue," an unpublished typescript; and Patricia Hill Collins, *Black Feminist Thought* (New York: Routledge, 1990), especially chap. 8.

17. Cortese, *Ethnic Ethics*; and Henry, *Culture and African American Politics*.

18. I have arrived at this moment of communication by way of a reading of Emmanuel Levinas's distinction between the Saying and the Said in *Otherwise than Being, or Beyond Essence* (The Hague: Nijhoff, 1981).

19. Upendia Baxi criticizes those who might judge what he calls sycophancy in politics as a symptom of underdevelopment, and calls such a reaction ethnocentric. Sycophancy, or the mutual exchange of flattery and praise, he argues, is an important element in maintaining relationships. To the degree that Western public culture re-

duces such behavior, he suggests, it impoverishes communication. "What Is Wrong with Sycophancy? A Caveat on Overrationalized Notions of Political Communication," in Bhikhu Parekh and Thomas Pantham, *Political Discourse: Explorations in Indian and Western Thought* (Beverly Hills: Sage, 1987).

20. In "Feminist Practical Dialogue," Alison Jaggar remarks on the importance of such bodily care-taking for promoting the ends of democratic communication.

21. Spragens, *Reason and Democracy* (Durham, N.C.: Duke University Press, 1990), 128.

22. James Bohman, "Emancipation and Rhetoric: The Perlocutions and Illocutions of the Social Critic," *Philosophy and Rhetoric* 21, no. 3 (1988).

23. Barber, *Strong Democracy*, 175.

24. Compare Kathryn Abrams, "Hearing the Call of Stories," *California Law Review* 79, no. 4 (July 1991): 971–1052. Reviewing the use of narrative in feminist legal theory, Abrams argues that narrative serves important argumentative functions.

25. Sanders, "Against Deliberation."

26. Jane Braten, "From Communicative Rationality to Communicative Thinking: A Basis for Feminist Theory and Practice," in Johanna Meehan, ed., *Feminists Read Habermas* (New York: Routledge, 1995).

Part Two

EQUALITY, DIFFERENCE, AND
PUBLIC REPRESENTATION

Seven

Dealing with Difference: A Politics of Ideas, or a Politics of Presence?

ANNE PHILLIPS

IN THE postcommunist world of the 1980s and 1990s, liberalism and liberal democracy have achieved an impressive ascendancy, and can more plausibly present themselves as the only legitimate bases for equality, justice, or democracy. Critics, of course, remain, but the grounds of complaint have shifted considerably. For many years, the central arguments against liberalism fell into three broad categories: that the liberal emphasis on individual freedoms and rights reflected a self-protective and competitive egotism that refused any wider community; that the liberal focus on "merely" political equalities ignored or even encouraged gross inequalities in social and economic life; and that the liberal consolidation of representative democracy reduced the importance of more active citizen participation. None of these complaints has disappeared, but each has been reformulated in terms of diversity and difference. Feminist theorists, in particular, have identified liberalism with an abstract individualism that ignores its own gendered content, and many have criticized the homogenizing ideals of equality that require us to be or become the same.[1] Accusations of gender-blindness and race- or ethnicity-blindness have added weight to older complaints that liberalism is blind to class. At a moment when most political theorists have situated themselves more firmly in the liberal tradition, liberalism is extensively criticized for erasing diversity and difference.

Left at such a level of generality, the accusation is distinctly odd, for notions of diversity and difference have been central to liberalism from its inception and to liberal democracy throughout its formation. What gave the original impetus to liberalism was the perception that neither nature nor tradition guaranteed political order, and that the very equality of what we now see as male subjects increased the potential diversity and conflict. Hence the search for a contractual basis for political authority that would bind these different individuals into a coherent whole; and hence the concern with rights and

The work for this essay was made possible by a Social Science Research Fellowship from the Nuffield Foundation, 1992–93. A longer version of it is published in *Constellations* 1 (1994): 74–91.

autonomies that would allow them to pursue part of their lives under their own steam. In these and subsequent developments, difference remained politically significant and theoretically important: a driving force, indeed, in the separation of public from private affairs.

The defining characteristics of liberal democracy, as Robert Dahl among others has clarified,[2] are also grounded in the heterogeneity of the societies that gave it birth. It was the diversity of the citizenry as much as its absolute size that made the earlier (more consensual) practices of Athenian democracy so inappropriate to the modern world. Lacking any half-credible basis for seeing citizens as united in their goals, theorists of liberal democracy took issue with the homogenizing presumptions of a common good or common purpose, and made diversity a central organizing theme. John Stuart Mill's famous vacillations over democracy derived from a double sense of democracy as both impetus and threat to diversity: something that breaks the hold of any single notion of the good life, but can also encourage a deadening conformity. In more straightforwardly confident vein, George Kateb has presented constitutional and representative democracy as that system par excellence that encourages and disseminates diversity. The procedures of electoral competition do not merely chasten and circumscribe the powers of government. By promoting a more skeptical attitude toward the basis on which competing claims are resolved, they also cultivate "'a general tolerance of, and even affection for diversity: diversity in itself, and diversity as the source of regulated contest and competition."[3]

Difference is not something we have only just noticed. What we can more usefully say is that difference has been perceived in an overly cerebral fashion as differences in opinions and beliefs, and that the resulting emphasis on what I will call a politics of ideas has proved inadequate to the problems of political exclusion. The diversity most liberals have in mind is a diversity of beliefs, opinions, preferences, and goals, all of which may stem from the variety of experience, but are considered as in principle detachable from this. Even the notion of interests, which seems most thoroughly grounded in differential material conditions, lends itself to at least semidetachment. The preference for higher taxes on those with higher incomes may be stronger among those with little money, especially if they believe the proceeds will finance public provision of educational or health services that would be otherwise beyond their reach. But support for higher taxation and better public provision is not restricted to those who most directly benefit: political preferences are influenced by material circumstances without being reducible to these. The interests of pensioners or the long-term unemployed can then be championed by those who are neither retired nor out of work; the interests of geographical localities can be represented by people who no longer live in the area; the interests of mothers with young children can be represented by childless men.

One consequence for democracy is that what is to be represented then takes priority over who does the representation. Issues of political presence are largely discounted, for when difference is considered in terms of intellectual diversity, it does not much matter who represents the range of ideas. One person may easily stand in for another; there is no additional requirement for the representatives to "mirror" the characteristics of the person or people represented. What concerns us in the choice of representative is a congruity in political beliefs and ideals, combined perhaps with a superior ability to articulate and register opinions. The quality of the democracy is guaranteed by the extension of the suffrage to all adults, each of whom contributes his or her vote to the opinions that gain public weight. Stripped of any predemocratic authority, the role of the politician is to carry a message: the messages will vary, but it hardly matters if the messengers are the same. (Those who believe that men have a monopoly on the political skills of articulating policies and ideas will not be surprised that most messengers are men.)

In Hanna Pitkin's influential discussion of representation, she criticizes the mirror view as beginning and ending with who is present, setting to one side the far more important question of what the representatives actually do. "Think of the legislature as a pictorial representation or a representative sample of the nation," she argues, "and you will almost inevitably concentrate on its composition rather than its activities."[4] But looking back at her discussion from a distance of twenty-five years, what is notable is how she elides the mapping of ideas with the mapping of people, not really distinguishing between a representative sample that captures the range of ideas, the range of interests, or the range of socially significant groups. Her emphasis throughout is on the distinction between being and doing, and her arguments are as much directed against versions of proportional representation that would more precisely reflect the multiplicity of parties and opinion as against later preoccupations with representing excluded or marginalized groups. Questions of power and inequality do not figure largely in Pitkin's account. Such questions have become central to democratic debate today.

It is no part of my intention to disparage politics as a battleground for ideas. Much of the radicalizing impetus to democracy has centered around initiatives to make ideas more rather than less important, as in efforts to bind representatives more closely to the opinions they profess to hold, or in measures to reduce the backstage manipulations of pressure groups that disrupt the higher politics of ideas. But when the politics of ideas is taken in isolation from what I will call the politics of presence, it does not deal adequately with the experiences of those social groups who by virtue of their race or ethnicity or religion or gender have felt themselves excluded from the democratic process. Political exclusion is increasingly—I believe rightly—viewed in terms that can be met only by political presence, and much of this development has depended on a more complex understanding of the relationship between ideas and experience. The separation between who and what is to be repre-

sented, and the subordination of one to the other, relies on an understanding
of ideas and interests as relatively unproblematic. It is as if the field of politics
is already clearly demarcated, containing within it various clusters of preferences or ideas or concerns that exist independently of any process of formation. This is in stark contrast with the preoccupations that ran through the
early years of the contemporary women's movement, when women talked of
the difficulties in finding a voice, the way that dominant definitions of politics
blocked out alternatives, or hegemonic culture controlled what could or could
not be said. The emphasis then shifted from an objectively defined set of
interests (that just needed more vigorous pursuit) to a more exploratory notion of possibilities so far silenced and ideas one had to struggle to express. In
this later understanding of the processes that generate needs and concerns and
ideas, it is harder to sustain the primacy of ideas over political presence. If it
is simply a question of representing a given range of ideas and interests, it may
not much matter who does the work of representation. But if the range of ideas
has been curtailed by orthodoxies that rendered alternatives invisible, there
will be no satisfactory solution short of changing the people who represent
and develop the ideas.

Once raised, the issues of presence are unlikely to go away: these are questions that must be addressed if democracies are to deliver on political equality.
My concern in this essay is with what happens next and, in particular, with the
tensions that arise between ideas and political presence. In the caricatures of
those most resistant to a politics of presence, it is frequently misrepresented as
a kind of "groupthink": something that is necessarily separatist, necessarily
corrosive of any wider community, and falsely presuming not only that one
has to be a member of a particular group in order to understand or represent
that group's interests but that all members of the group in question will think
along similar lines.[5] The caricature misses its mark. Most contemporary theorists will shy away from the implications of an essential female subject, or an
authentic black subject, that can be represented by any one of its kind; far
more dominant today is the notion of multiple identities or multiple "subject
positions," each of which is subject to political transformation and change. An
attention to difference does not entail an essentialist understanding of identity; nor does it demand any wholesale rejection of the politics of competing
ideas. But then the very sophistication of contemporary theories of identity
can paralyze development; the very distance people have traveled from the
caricatures of their position can remove them from democracy as it currently
exists. In both the theoretical and the movement-centered literature that I now
go on to discuss, issues of difference have been construed within a robustly
democratic future that bears little relationship to contemporary political life.
One of the challenges of democracy is how to combine the insights from such
discussion with prescriptions that can be made relevant to representative democracy as practiced today.

Democracy as Public Contestation

As is evident through other contributions to this volume, much of the contemporary work on democracy and difference operates with notions of a more active and vigorous democracy that depends crucially on public debate. Rejecting both the false harmony that stamps out difference and the equally false essentialism that defines people through some single, authentic identity, many look to a democracy that maximizes citizen participation and requires us to engage and contest with one another. In a recent essay on feminism and democracy, Susan Mendus suggests that difference is the rationale for democracy, and that "whereas traditional democratic theory tends to construe difference as an obstacle to the attainment of a truly democratic state, feminist theory should alert us to the possibility that difference is rather what necessitates the pursuit of democracy."[6] In his work on multiculturalism, Charles Taylor calls for a politics of democratic empowerment as the way of dealing with demands for equal recognition without thereby entrenching people in fragmented identities.[7] In his discussion of the republican revival, Cass Sunstein argues for a deliberative democracy to which all citizens will have equal access, and where all perspectives can be equally addressed.[8]

All such arguments assume equality of access (without necessarily exploring the conditions that would deliver this result), and all differentiate themselves from merely majoritarian decision-making by anticipating some process of transformation and change. Where the classically liberal resolution of difference relies on a combination of private spaces and majority norms (these in turn established by majority vote), the democratic resolution of difference expects us to engage more directly with one another. We bring our differences to the public stage; we revise them through public debate. Major disagreements then surface between those who anticipate a full "resolution" in some newly achieved public consensus, and those who see differences as contingent but never as "difference" going away. The first position looks more utopian than the second, but both operate at a level of generality that barely touches on democracy as practiced today.

Consider William Connolly's arguments in *Identity\Difference*,[9] which are particularly interesting in that they say both what should happen and why it almost certainly will not. Here, a "robust" politics of democratic engagement is presented as something that neither evades nor confirms difference: a politics that enables people to disturb settled conventions and expose settled identities. All identities are formed through difference—you know who you are through your difference from some other—and all identities are simultaneously threatened by the difference(s) of the other. There is always a danger that identities will be dogmatized into some naturalistic or unchanging essence, and always a danger that difference will generate destructive resentments and fears. What keeps these at bay is a politics of mutual challenge and disruption in which we are constantly reminded of the contingent nature of our identities. This politics depends in turn on the successful permeation of a "culture of genealogy" that helps us to see our identities as ambiguous and contestable and contested. Democracy then appears as an exciting engagement with difference: the challenge of "the other"; the disruption of certainties; the recognition of ambiguities within one's self as well as one's differences with others.

All this is tremendously refreshing, and in no way relies on a future transcendence of difference. But just at the point where he has achieved the philosophical resolution, Connolly backs off from claiming any immediate relevance for today. The confidence that enables people to dispense with settled identities or to accept the contingencies of fate may not be available to those suffering from economic inequality and political exclusion. Indeed, in an environment characterized by systematic inequality, the appeals to a robust democracy in which no one shelters behind accusations of the other could "too readily be received as yet another attack on those already excluded from democratic politics."[10]

> One compelling attraction of democracy is that it enables anyone to engage in fundamental riddles of existence through participation in a public politics that periodically disturbs and denaturalizes elements governing the cultural unconscious. But these same characteristics can intensify the reactive demand to redogmatize conventional identities if a large minority of the society is already suffering under severe burden of material deprivation and effective exclusion from the good life offered to a majority.[11]

Robust democracy then becomes possible only when economic inequalities are substantially reduced. My problem with this is not that it begs the question of how we might achieve such a precondition (we all have difficulties answering this), but that so much of what currently drives a politics of identity and difference is precisely the sense of deprivation and exclusion that Connolly sees as making such a politics so dangerous. Again, this is a point Connolly makes himself, noting that against the background of U.S. neoconservatism, any politics of identity and difference tends to fuel "the energies of ressentiment and the dogmatization of identity."[12] The philosophical resolution of democracy and difference remains largely that.[13]

Democracy inside Social Movements

The second context in which these discussions take place is as interventions into specific movements that have formed around the politics of race, gender, sexuality, and ethnicity. All these movements have involved a critique of the phony essentialisms that disguised systematic difference and inequality;

nearly all of them, however, have also generated their own essentialisms that at some point or other claimed a unified female or lesbian or black or some other experience. Thus feminists took issue with the gender amnesia that transformed man "into a paradigm of humankind as such,"[14] but, in the further explorations of sexual difference, they often insisted on a primary distinction between men and women that obscured further differences between women. Lesbian feminists took issue with the hegemonic controls of a heterosexual norm but, in the search for an affirming identity, they often constructed "the" authentic lesbian who would not tolerate differences of sexual practice or political attitudes within the lesbian community.[15] Antiracists took issue with the mythologies of nation that had rendered black people invisible, but, in the subsequent racial dualism that focused so exclusively on differences between "black" and "white," they tended to obscure the cultural and religious pluralism that characterizes the many nonwhite minorities.[16]

The problems of essentialism have, as a consequence, figured largely in the internal politics and debates of these movements. Much contemporary attention is focused on the conditions that can articulate group difference without thereby "disciplining" group members into a single authentic identity; in the process, many have suggested limits to the very notion of "a" group. As Shane Phelan puts it in her discussion of lesbian feminism in the United States: "Politics that ignores our identities, that makes them 'private,' is useless; but nonnegotiable identities will enslave us whether they are imposed from within or without."[17] Speaking from the British context, Stuart Hall has suggested that we should pay more attention to the ways in which black experience is a diaspora experience, one in which the constructions of history and politics and culture are therefore fundamental, and not to be captured through notions of an essential black subject.[18] He talks here of "the end of innocence," "the recognition of the extraordinary diversity of subject positions, social experiences and cultural identities which compose the category 'black,'"[19] and the impossibility of grounding the black subject or black experience in the essentialisms of nature or any other such guarantee.

These arguments cut across the balder distinction between ideas and presence, for what is being identified are differences in experiences and identities within what has hitherto been seen as an all-embracing category or group. It is not simply that "black" people or women or lesbians will disagree among themselves as to the appropriate policies and ideas and goals (they will vote for different parties, for example) but that their very senses of what it means to be black or female or lesbian will necessarily vary. In the context of the political movements with which these arguments engage, there seem to be two important implications. One is that the diversity of "subject positions" should be reflected within the organizational structures that define who does or does not get into the conversation. There should be no privileging of some voices as more authentic than others, and no coercive imposition of a supposedly unified point of view. The other implication, however, is that there is no way of knowing in advance whether diversity has been successfully acknowledged. Any prior setting of the boundaries risks restoring some version of the authentic subject, for even if the boundaries are significantly pluralized, they still define in advance what are the appropriate or relevant differences. Thus Stuart Hall argues that it is no longer possible to represent "the black subject" without reference to class, gender, sexuality, ethnicity. But if this were taken as a series of guidelines about the different characteristics that must be covered within the membership of some campaigning organization, that would hardly be doing justice to his critique.

This is a problem that in some way or another besets every radical initiative, whether it is a matter of deciding whom to invite to address a meeting, who is to join an editorial board, or which groups are to participate in a campaign. We have become sufficiently attuned to the politics of presence to distrust the notion that anyone can "stand in" for anyone else, and sufficiently alert to the coercive powers of homogeneity to want to reflect diversity. But the critiques of essentialism deprive us of any simple mechanism for achieving the appropriate balance, and remind us that diversity is too great to be captured in any categorial list.

In the context of political movements, this is not such a serious difficulty. At their best, such movements already enjoy the kind of robust democracy that is proposed as an ideal for the polity as a whole: allowing for, indeed incapable of containing, the kind of contestation and mutual challenge that acknowledges difference and simultaneously disrupts it. The vehemence of debate indicates both a recurrent tendency toward essentialism and a continuous challenge to this: people are tough enough to resist prior classification and far too argumentative to accept someone else's definition of their selves. It is also worth noting that the fluidity of this politics lends itself more easily to a kind of learning through trial and error, for none of the consequences that people may derive from their current understandings of identity or difference is likely to be set in stone. The larger difficulties arise where we seek out more compromised intervention into democracies that are still pretty feeble.

Political Prescriptions for the Polity as a Whole

When we turn to the political prescriptions that might flow from a new understanding of democracy and difference, we are not dealing in far-off utopias: there is a range of policies already proposed or implemented; and change is neither distant nor unlikely. The problem, rather, is that because such prescriptions operate in a halfway house of remedial reform, they are less able to resolve the contradictory pressures between the politics of ideas and the politics of presence. The kinds of mechanisms I have in mind include the quota systems adopted by a number of European political parties to achieve gender parity in elected assemblies, the redrawing of boundaries around black-majority constituencies to raise the number of black politicians elected in the U.S., and the longer-established power-sharing practices of those European consociational democracies that have distributed executive power and economic resources between different religious and linguistic groups. In each of these instances, the initiatives operate within the framework of an existing (not very robust) democracy. Tensions that might more readily resolve themselves in a future ferment of activity and deliberation become more acute in what everyone knows is a compromised situation.

All the more immediate proposals for reform insist on deliberate intervention as necessary to break the link between social structures of inequality or exclusion and the political reflection of these in levels of participation and influence. All of them also agree in looking to specifically *political* mechanisms—rather than, or sometimes as well as, longer-term social transformation. They take issue therefore with the complacencies of a free market in politics, which sees political equality as sufficiently guaranteed by the procedures of one person/one vote; they also challenge the more standard radical alternative, which has focused attention on prior economic or social change. Whatever their differences on other issues, the traditions of revolutionary Marxism and welfare state social reform tended to agree on a broadly materialist analysis of the problems of political equality, seeing equal political access as something that depends on more fundamental changes in social, economic, and sometimes educational conditions. The current interest in achieving equal or proportionate presence reverses this, focusing instead on institutional mechanisms—its critics would say "political fixes"—that can achieve more immediate change.

The roots of this reversal lie partly in frustration with what has proved an unbelievably slow process of structural transformation (*first* eliminate the sexual division of labor . . . the racial ordering of income, education, and employment . . . the class patterning that determines children's futures—is it any wonder we search for shortcuts?). But political frustration is not new, and people do not normally change direction just because things take so long. The additional impetus comes from the kind of arguments already outlined, which suggest that the range of political ideas and preferences is seriously constrained by the characteristics of the people who convey them. In a more traditional base-superstructure model, we were advised to concentrate first on generating the social conditions for equal citizenship, then enjoy the political equalization that would flow from this. Such an approach, however, treats policy choices as more straightforward than they are, and fails to observe the way that strategies devised for equality reflect the limits of those currently in power.[20] Where policy initiatives are worked out *for* rather than *with* a politically excluded constituency, they rarely engage with all relevant concerns.

Again, it is only if we consider the field of politics as already clearly demarcated, with all possible options already in play, that we can put much confidence in such an approach.

I do not discount the criticism that regards institutional mechanisms for achieving equal or proportionate presence as a species of diversionary "political fixing," but we should not be required to choose between these and other urgent tasks of social and economic transformation. When political exclusion is such a marked feature of contemporary democratic life, it seems inappropriate to rely on distant prospects of a more robustly participatory democracy or structural changes in social and economic conditions. The very distance of such prospects puts a premium on political prescriptions that can be made relevant to representative democracy as currently practiced, and most of these will involve some form of affirmative action that can guarantee more equal representation in existing decision-making assemblies. Any specifically political mechanism, however, risks imposing a rigid definition of the identities that have to be included or the interests so far left out. The more complex understanding of multiple identities that change both over time and according to context is a potential casualty here, as is the continuing importance we would all want to attach to political disagreement and debate.

If we consider, for example, the mechanisms that might be appropriate in contemporary Britain to redress racial exclusions, one immediate problem is the diversity of nonwhite experience, and the major disagreements that have surfaced between taking race or ethnicity or religion as the basis of social identity and political exclusion. When we take race as the central indicator, this encourages a dualism of "black" or "white," a division of the universe that is often said to be closer to the political perceptions of Afro-Caribbeans than to the self-definitions of the significantly more numerous Asians. Tariq Modood, indeed, has argued that "the concept of Black is harmful to Asians and is a form of political identity that most Asians do not accept as their primary public identity."[21] But if we take ethnicity or religion instead, these are felt to be too closely associated with a politics of multiculturalism that has looked to the greater dissemination of knowledge about ethnic and religious minorities as the way of breaking down racial stereotypes, and has been thought insufficiently vigorous in its challenges to racism per se. Alternative ways of defining group identities or redressing group exclusions have become loaded with political significance, with an attention to cultural diversity being variously perceived as something that depoliticizes the antiracist struggle or is a crucial corrective to the simplicities of racial dualism.[22]

What, in this context, is an appropriate mechanism for dealing with political exclusion? Can Asians be represented by Afro-Caribbeans, Hindus by Muslims, black women by black men? Or do these groups have nothing more in common than their joint experience of being excluded from power? In their recent book on *Racialized Boundaries*, Floya Anthias and Nira Yuval-

Davies conclude that "the form of political representation which has grown out of identity politics and equal opportunities and which has attempted to represent social difference more genuinely, has created an impossible mission for itself,"[23] and that what is a positive diversity of overlapping identities becomes dangerously constrained in efforts toward proportional representation. But does this mean that nothing can be done—that given the risks, on the one hand, of an imposed and misleading uniformity, and the absurdities, on the other, of an endless search for sufficiently pluralized categories, we have to abandon the quest for specifically political mechanisms? Caucuses and quotas are the most obvious procedures for dealing with political exclusion, yet both of these depend on a prior categorization of the basis on which people have been kept out. Neither seems adequate to the complexity of political identities.

The politics that has developed in the U.S. around the strategy of black-majority, single-member constituencies might seem more straightforward, for it seems clear enough that it is race rather than ethnicity that has been at issue in the political exclusion of African-Americans, and racial bloc voting is plausibly described as "the single most salient feature of contemporary political life."[24] But even so, a political resolution that privileges race as the prime consideration can make it more difficult for people to articulate what are complex and multiple identities: can obscure tensions, for example, around gender and class, and block out major disagreements over policy preferences and political ideas. The implication that black representatives are representative merely by virtue of being black is inevitably problematic, even where "blackness" is a less contested category.

Those who consider the problems of political equality as adequately dealt with by provision for the equal right to vote will be happy to rest their case there, but criticism of the strategy of black electoral success has not been confined to these quarters. Equally powerful criticism comes from those who regard proportionate presence as a necessary but insufficient condition and are concerned that the focus on numbers alone can reduce political accountability, limit prospects for multiracial coalition, and undermine the urgency of policy debate.[25] There is, in other words, a strong sense of the tensions that can develop between a politics of presence and a politics of ideas. But instead of resolving this by opting for the second over the first, critics have looked to alternative patterns of representation that can make it possible to combine the two. Some of the most innovative work in this area comes from those pressing for a return to the more competitive politics of multimember constituencies but based on forms of proportional representation and cumulative voting that would maintain the scope for electing representatives from minority groups.[26] It is felt, in other words, that mechanisms *can* be devised that continue the gains in black political presence without forcing an either/or choice between the politics of presence and the politics of ideas.

European initiatives on gender parity can also be seen as successfully nego-
tiating the competing demands of ideas and presence—and here we enter
the realm of policies already in position rather than proposals in contested
debate. The favored strategy involves pressuring existing political parties to
introduce a more balanced ticket of both women and men in their candidates
for winnable seats, thus maintaining accountability through party policies
and programs while changing the gender composition of elected assemblies.
Often enough, the mechanism has been a straightforward quota, which has
contributed to a remarkable increase in the numbers of women elected in
the Nordic countries. Critics of such strategies usually rest their case on the
paucity of "experienced" women, the potential loss of "good" men to politics,
and the risk that the overall caliber of politicians (not too high in my opinion)
will fall. They do not dwell particularly on the essentialist presumptions of
"a" women's perspective, or the dangerous potential for women pressing only
narrowly sectional concerns. There are just too many women for them to
be considered as a unified or sectional group, and they are spread across
every class, or ethnic or religious dimension, and every conceivable political
persuasion. When it is applied to women, the politics of presence does not
seriously disrupt the politics of ideas; it is relatively easy to pursue both of
these together.

As both these examples indicate, the biggest mistake is to set up ideas as
the opposite of presence: to treat ideas as totally separate from the people
who carry them; or worry exclusively about the people without giving a
thought to their policies and ideas. It should be said, however, that this is not
such a frequent mistake as the caricatures suggest, and that those exploring
equal or proportionate representation rarely regard this as a substitute for
the politics of competing ideas. If anything, the most acute criticisms of the
politics of presence have come from those most committed to challenging
political exclusion, and the debate has long shifted beyond its either/or axis.
What is, perhaps, emerging is that the more satisfactory ways of redressing
group exclusion are those that are the less group-specific. This seems to be
the case in relation to gender quotas, if only because the category of woman is
so inclusive of other kinds of difference and division that it leaves open the
necessary space for a multiplicity of political identities. It also seems to be the
case in the proposals that have developed around the implementation of the
Voting Rights Act in the U.S., which have moved away from the more tightly
drawn voting districts that provide a "safe seat" for minority representatives,
toward a larger geographical constituency that can no longer pretend to contain only one voice.

Such developments acknowledge the danger in preemptive classifications
of people's political identities, and are well aware that essentialist definitions
of the groups who have been excluded can work to reduce political accountability and debate. They nonetheless take issue with the more traditional treat-

ment of diversity and difference as simply a matter of contested ideas. The overly cerebral understanding of difference has not engaged sufficiently with the problems of political presence, for it has encouraged an unacceptable level of complacency over the homogeneity of political elites. We can no longer pretend that the full range of ideas and preferences and alternatives has been adequately represented when those charged with the job of representation are all white or all male or all middle-class, or that democracies complete their task of political equality when they establish a free market in political ideas. One would not want to take up permanent residence in the halfway house of remedial reform, but mechanisms should be—and can be—devised that address the problems of group exclusion without fixing the boundaries or character of each group.

Notes

1. I summarize and discuss some of these arguments in *Engendering Democracy* (University Park: Pennsylvania State University Press, 1991). See also Jane Flax, "Beyond Equality: Gender, Justice and Difference," in Gisela Bock and Susan James, eds., *Beyond Equality and Difference* (London: Routledge, 1992).

2. Robert A. Dahl, *Democracy and Its Critics* (New Haven: Yale University Press, 1989).

3. George Kateb, "The Moral Distinctiveness of Representative Democracy," *Ethics* 91, no. 3 (1981): 361.

4. Hanna Fenichel Pitkin, *The Concept of Representation* (Berkeley and Los Angeles: University of California Press, 1967), 226.

5. All these points can be found in Cynthia V. Ward, "The Limits of 'Liberal Republicanism': Why Group-Based Remedies and Republican Citizenship Don't Mix," *Columbia Law Review* 91, no. 3 (1991). But in querying the notion that *only* the members of particular disadvantaged groups can understand or represent their interests, she might usefully turn this question around to ask whether such understanding or representation is possible without the presence of *any* members of the disadvantaged groups.

6. Susan Mendus, "Losing the Faith: Feminism and Democracy," in John Dunn, ed., *Democracy: The Unfinished Journey, 508 B.C. to A.D. 1993* (Oxford: Oxford University Press, 1992), 216.

7. Charles Taylor, *The Ethics of Authenticity* (Cambridge, Mass.: Harvard University Press, 1992); Charles Taylor, *Multiculturalism and "The Politics of Recognition,"* ed. Amy Gutmann (Princeton: Princeton University Press, 1992).

8. Cass R. Sunstein, "Beyond the Republican Revival," *Yale Law Journal* 97, no. 8 (1988).

9. William E. Connolly, *Identity\Difference: Democratic Negotiations of Political Paradox* (Ithaca: Cornell University Press, 1991).

10. Ibid., 197.

11. Ibid., 211.

12. Ibid., 213.

13. In a review of Connolly's book, Iris Young describes his prescriptions as "therapies." *Political Theory* 20, no. 3 (1992): 514.

14. Adriana Cavarero, "Equality and Sexual Difference: Amnesia in Political Thought," in Bock and James, *Beyond Equality and Difference*, 36.

15. Shane Phelan, *Identity Politics: Lesbian Feminism and the Limits of Community* (Philadelphia: Temple University Press, 1989). Phelan notes in particular the rows that broke out over sadomasochism, and whether this was an "acceptable" part of lesbian identity.

16. See the essays in Tariq Modood, *Not Easy Being British: Colour, Culture and Citizenship* (Stoke-on-Trent: Runnymede Trust and Trentham Books, 1992). The largest nonwhite group in Britain is Asians of Indian origin, many of whom have felt the racial dualism of antiracist politics rendered them invisible.

17. Phelan, *Identity Politics*, 170.

18. Stuart Hall, "New Ethnicities," in James Donald and Ali Rattansi, eds., *"Race," Culture and Difference* (London: Sage and Open University Press, 1992).

19. Hall, "New Ethnicities," 254.

20. Obvious examples include the postwar preoccupation with full employment as a condition for equal citizenship, where full employment was either unthinkingly equated with full employment for men or else extended formally to include women without any serious consideration of the structural changes that would then become necessary to reorder the relationship between paid and unpaid work. Will Kymlicka provides an alternative example in his discussion of the Trudeau reforms, which set out to promote more equal citizenship in Canada, but equated full and equal participation for the native Indian population with a color-blind constitution that would dismantle the system of segregated reserves. Though widely applauded by the country's media and even opposition parties, the proposals had to be withdrawn in the face of almost unanimous opposition from the Indians themselves. Kymlicka, *Liberalism, Community and Culture* (Oxford: Oxford University Press, 1989).

21. Modood, *Not Easy Being British*, 29.

22. For an excellent overview of these debates, and an attempt to push beyond them, see the essays in Donald and Rattansi, *"Race," Culture and Difference*.

23. Floya Anthias and Nira Yuval-Davies, *Racialized Boundaries: Race, Nation, Gender, Colour, Class and the Anti-Racist Struggle* (London: Routledge, 1992), 192.

24. S. Issacharoff, "Polarized Voting and the Political Process: The Transformation of Voting Rights Jurisprudence," *Michigan Law Review* 90, no. 7 (1992): 1855.

25. Bernard Grofman and Chandler Davidson, eds., *Controversies in Minority Voting: The Voting Rights Act in Perspective* (Washington D.C: Brookings Institution, 1992), provides a comprehensive range of the arguments that have developed around minority representation.

26. Lani Guinier, "The Triumph of Tokenism: The Voting Rights Act and the Theory of Black Electoral Success," *Michigan Law Review* 89, no. 5 (1991); and "No Two Seats: The Elusive Quest for Political Equality," *Virginia Law Review* 77, no. 8 (1991). I discuss this material at greater length in *The Politics of Presence* (Oxford: Oxford University Press, 1995).

Eight

Three Forms of Group-Differentiated Citizenship in Canada

WILL KYMLICKA

MUCH OF the Canadian political system is founded on the premise that, in the words of the Canadian Supreme Court, the "accommodation of difference is the essence of true equality."[1] While Canadian history contains its share of intolerance, prejudice, and oppression, it also contains many attempts to find new and creative mechanisms for accommodating difference. In this essay I will discuss some of these mechanisms, and the issues they raise.

As in all other liberal democracies, one of the major mechanisms for accommodating difference in Canada is the protection of the civil and political rights of individuals. Freedom of association, religion, speech, mobility, and political organization enable individuals to form and maintain the various groups and associations that constitute civil society, to adapt these groups to changing circumstances, and to promote their views and interests to the wider population. The protection afforded by these common rights of citizenship is sufficient for many of the legitimate forms of diversity in society.[2]

However, it is widely accepted in Canada that some forms of difference can be accommodated only through special legal or constitutional measures, above and beyond the common rights of citizenship. Some forms of group difference can be accommodated only if their members have what Iris Young calls "differentiated citizenship."[3] It is these special measures for accommodating difference that I will focus on in this essay.

Forms of Group Difference in Canada

Historically, the major challenge in Canada has been the accommodation of cultural difference. There are two forms of cultural pluralism in Canada that need to distinguished.

First, Canada is a *multination* state. Its historical development has involved the federation of three distinct peoples or nations (English, French, and Aboriginals).[4] These groups are "nations" in the sociological sense of being historical communities, institutionally complete, occupying a given territory or homeland, and sharing a distinct language and history. A "nation" in this sense is closely related to the idea of a "people" or a "culture." Since Canada contains more than one nation, it is not a nation-state but a multination state, and the Québécois[5] and Aboriginal communities form "national minorities."[6]

The original incorporation of these national minorities into the Canadian political community was largely involuntary. Indian homelands were overrun by French settlers, who were then conquered by the English. If a different balance of power had existed, it is possible that Aboriginals and French-Canadians would have retained their original sovereignty, rather than being incorporated into the larger Canadian federation. And it is still possible that Quebec will leave the federation. However, the historical preference of these national minorities has been not to secede but to renegotiate the terms of federation, so as to increase their autonomy within it.

Many of the pivotal moments in Canadian political history have centered on these attempts to renegotiate the terms of federation between English, French, and Aboriginals. The most recent effort at renegotiation ended in October 1992, when a proposal to amend the constitution (known the Charlottetown Accord) was defeated in a national referendum. This Accord (discussed in what follows) would have entrenched an "inherent right of self-government" for Aboriginals, and would have accorded Quebec a special status as "the only society with a majority French language and culture in Canada and in North America."[7]

In addition to being a multination state, Canada is also a *polyethnic* state. Canada, like the U.S., accepts large numbers of individuals and families from other cultures as immigrants. They are expected to integrate into the public institutions of either the French or English societies—for example, they must learn either French or English (Canada's two official languages) to acquire citizenship. Prior to the 1960s, they were also expected to shed their distinctive heritage and assimilate almost entirely to existing cultural norms.[8] However, in the 1970s the Canadian government rejected the assimilationist model of immigration and instead adopted a policy of polyethnicity that allows and indeed encourages immigrants to maintain various aspects of their ethnic heritage. Immigrants are free to maintain some of their old customs regarding food, dress, recreation, and religion, and to associate with one another to maintain these practices. This is no longer seen as unpatriotic or "un-Canadian."

But such groups are not "nations," and do not occupy homelands. Their distinctiveness is manifested primarily in their private lives, and does not affect their institutional integration—they still participate within either the French or English cultures, and speak one or the other of the official languages in public life. Because of extensive immigration of this sort, Canada has a number of "ethnic groups" as loosely aggregated subcultures within both the English- and French-speaking societies.

So Canada is both multinational (as a result of colonization, conquest, and confederation) and polyethnic (as a result of immigration).[9] Those labels are less popular than the term "multicultural." But that term can be confusing, precisely because it is ambiguous between multinational and polyethnic.[10]

It is important to note that national groups in Canada are not defined by race or descent. Since the early 1900s, there have been high rates of immigration into Canada, first from Europe, and now mostly from Asia and Africa (Quebec actively seeks francophone immigrants from the Caribbean and West Africa). There also high rates of intermarriage between the various national and ethnic groups. As a result, all three national groups are racially and ethnically mixed. In talking about French, English, and Aboriginal, therefore, I am talking not about racial groups but about multiracial and polyethnic cultural groups. It would be more accurate to talk of anglophone and francophone Canada rather than English Canada and French Canada, for the latter terms wrongly suggest that these groups are defined by ethnic descent rather than by integration into a common culture.[11]

Three Forms of Group-Differentiated Citizenship

There are at least three forms of differentiated citizenship in Canada intended to accommodate these ethnic and national differences: self-government rights, polyethnic rights, and special representation rights. I will say a few words about each.

Self-government rights. As I noted, Aboriginal peoples and the Québécois view themselves as "peoples" or "nations," and, as such, as having the inherent right of self-determination.[12] Both groups demand certain powers of self-government that they say were not relinquished by their (initially involuntary) federation into the larger Canadian state. They want to govern themselves in certain key matters, to ensure the full and free development of their cultures and the best interests of their people.

The main mechanism for recognizing the Québécois' claim to self-government is the system of federalism. Under the federal division of powers, Quebec has extensive jurisdiction over issues that are crucial to the survival of the French culture, including control over education, language, culture, and immigration. The other nine provinces also have these powers, but the major impetus behind the existing division of powers, and indeed behind the entire federal system, is the need to accommodate the Québécois. At the time of Confederation in 1867, most English Canadian leaders were in favor of a unitary state, like England, and only reluctantly agreed to a federal system to accommodate French Canadians. Similarly, while the Charlottetown Accord would have granted further powers to all ten provinces, the demand for this change came from Quebec. Most English Canadians have no desire for greater decentralization, and indeed this is one reason why the Charlottetown Accord was defeated in the national referendum. One of the questions facing Canada, therefore, is whether Canadians can find an acceptable form of "asymmetrical federalism," which grants Quebec powers not given to other provinces.[13]

Aboriginal self-government has been primarily tied to the system of Indian reserves, and the devolution of power from the federal government to the band councils that govern each reserve. Aboriginal bands have been acquiring increasing control over health, education, policing, criminal justice, and resource development. In the future, it is widely expected that they will become a constitutionally recognized third order of government within the federal system, with a collection of powers that is carved out of both federal and provincial jurisdictions, as was proposed in the Charlottetown Accord.[14] However, the administrative difficulties are forbidding—Indian bands differ enormously in the sorts of powers they desire and are capable of exercising. Moreover, they are territorially located within the provinces, and must therefore coordinate their self-government with provincial agencies. A second basic question, therefore, is whether Canadians can find a form of federalism that is flexible enough to accommodate a third order of government that lacks the symmetry and territorial contiguity of traditional federal units.

While the Charlottetown Accord, which would have increased the powers of both Quebec and Aboriginal communities, was defeated, it seems unlikely that the demand for increased self-government will go away. Self-government claims are not seen as a temporary measure. On the contrary, these rights are often described as "inherent," and therefore permanent (which is one reason why national minorities seek to have them entrenched at the constitutional level).

Polyethnic rights. Many ethnic groups and religious minorities have demanded various forms of public support and legal recognition of their cultural practices—from the funding of bilingual education and ethnic studies in schools to exemptions from laws that disadvantage them, given their religious practices. For example, Jews and Muslims have sought exemption from Sunday closing legislation; Sikhs have sought exemption from motorcycle helmet laws and from the official dress codes of police forces.[15]

These measures are intended to help ethnic groups and religious minorities express their cultural particularity and pride without it hampering their success in the economic and political institutions of the dominant society. A general commitment to such measures is reflected in section 27 of the Canadian Charter of Rights and Freedoms, which says that "this Charter shall be interpreted in a manner consistent with the preservation and enhancement of the multicultural heritage of Canadians." Like self-government rights, these rights are not seen as temporary, because the cultural differences they protect are not something we seek to eliminate. But unlike self-government rights, polyethnic rights are usually intended to promote integration into the larger society, not self-government.[16]

Special representation rights. While the traditional concern of national minorities and ethnic groups has been with either self-government or polyethnic rights, there has been increasing interest by these groups, as well as by other nonethnic social groups, in the idea of special representation rights.

Many Canadians believe the political process is "unrepresentative," in the sense that it fails to reflect the diversity of the population. This was illustrated most vividly during the constitutional negotiations leading up to the Charlottetown Accord, in which the fundamental terms of Canadian political life were negotiated by eleven middle-class, able-bodied, white men (the prime minister, and the premiers of the ten provinces). A more representative process, it was said, would have included women, members of ethnic and racial minorities, and people who are poor or disabled.

This has led to increasing interest in the idea that a certain number of seats in the Senate should be reserved for the members of disadvantaged or marginalized groups. During the debate over the Charlottetown Accord, for example, the National Action Committee on the Status of Women (the most powerful feminist lobby group in Canada) recommended that 50 percent of Senate seats should be reserved for women, and that proportionate representation of ethnic minorities also be guaranteed; others recommended that seats be reserved for the members of official language minorities, or for Aboriginals.[17]

The recent demands for special representation by women and other disadvantaged groups are largely an extension of long-standing demands for increased Senate representation by disadvantaged *regions*. Canada currently has an unelected Senate, which is widely viewed as illegitimate and ineffective. Many Canadians would like to simply abolish the Senate. But the outlying and less populated regions of English Canada—that is, the Maritime and Western provinces—want to reform the Senate and use it as a forum for increased regional representation at the federal level. They have demanded an American-style Senate, in which each province would elect an equal number of Senators regardless of its population. This is intended to ensure "effective representation" for smaller provinces that might be neglected in the House of Commons, where the majority of Members of Parliament come from the two most populated provinces in Central Canada (Ontario and Quebec).

Some Canadians have begun to believe that if disadvantaged or marginalized regions need special representation, then so surely do disadvantaged or marginalized groups, such as women or the poor. Historical evidence suggests that these groups, even more than smaller provinces, are likely to be underrepresented in Parliament, and ignored in political decision-making.

In the end, the Charlottetown Accord rejected most proposals for the guaranteed representation of social groups, and instead focused on increased regional representation. The one exception was a proposal for guaranteed Aboriginal seats. However, the Accord allowed each province to decide how its Senators would be elected, and three of the ten provincial premiers said that they would pass provincial legislation requiring that 50 percent of the Senate seats from their province be reserved for women.

Group representation rights are often defended as a response to some systemic barrier in the political process that makes it impossible for the group's views and interests to be effectively represented. For example, Iris Young, writing in the American context, argues that special representation rights should be extended to "oppressed groups" because they are at a disadvantage in the political process, and "the solution lies at least in part in providing institutionalized means for the explicit recognition and representation of oppressed groups."[18]

Insofar as these rights are defended as a response to oppression or systemic disadvantage, they are most plausibly seen as a temporary measure on the way to a society where the need for special representation no longer exists—a form of political "affirmative action." Society should seek to remove the oppression and disadvantage, thereby eliminating the need for these rights.

However, the issue of special representation rights is complicated in Canada, because special representation is sometimes defended not on grounds of oppression but as a corollary of self-government for national minorities. The right to self-government in certain areas seems to entail the right to guaranteed representation on any bodies that can intrude on those areas. Hence, it is argued, a corollary of self-government is that the national minority be guaranteed representation on any body that can interpret or modify its powers of self-government (e.g., the Supreme Court)[19] or that can make decisions in areas of concurrent or conflicting jurisdiction.

On the other hand, of course, insofar as self-government reduces the jurisdiction of the federal government over the national minority, self-government seems to entail that the group should have *reduced* influence (at least on certain issues) at the federal level. For example, if self-government for the Québécois leads to the asymmetrical transfer of powers from Ottawa to Quebec, so that the federal government would be passing laws that would not apply to Quebec, it seems only fair that Quebecers not have a vote on such legislation (particularly if they could cast the deciding vote).[20]

To oversimplify, self-government entails guaranteed representation on *intergovernmental* bodies, which negotiate, interpret, and modify the division of powers, but entails reduced representation on *federal* bodies that legislate in areas of purely federal jurisdiction. Since the claims of self-government are seen as permanent, so too are the guarantees of representation that flow from that self-government (unlike representation rights based on oppression).

These are the three forms of differentiated citizenship in Canada.[21] Many liberals, particularly in the postwar era, have opposed these policies as inconsistent with liberal democratic principles of freedom and equality. I think this opposition is mistaken. I cannot respond here to all the possible objections to these policies,[22] but I will focus on two standard objections—the conflict between group rights and individual rights, and the bases of social unity.

Individual and Group Rights

Recognizing groups in the constitution is often perceived as an issue of "collective rights," and many liberals fear that collective rights are, by definition, inimical to individual rights. This view has been popularized in Canada by former prime minister Pierre Trudeau, who explained his opposition to collective rights for Quebec by saying that he believed in "the primacy of the individual."[23]

However, we need to distinguish two kinds of collective rights that a group might claim. The first involves the right of a group against its own members; the second involves the right of a group against the larger society. Both kinds of collective rights can be seen as protecting the stability of national, ethnic, or religious groups. However, they respond to different sources of instability. The first kind is intended to protect the group from the destabilizing impact of *internal* dissent (e.g., the decision of individual members not to follow traditional practices or customs), whereas the second is intended to protect the group from the impact of *external* pressures (e.g., the economic or political decisions of the larger society). To distinguish these two kinds of collective rights, I will call the first "internal restrictions" and the second "external protections."

These two kinds of rights raise very different issues. Internal restrictions involve *intra*group relations. The idea that a national, ethnic, or religious group has rights against its own members raises the danger of individual oppression. Individual freedom may be restricted in the name of group solidarity. Critics of collective rights in this sense often invoke the image of theocratic and patriarchal cultures where women are oppressed and religious orthodoxy enforced as an example of what can happen when the alleged rights of the community are given precedence over the rights of the individual.

External protections involve *inter*group relations—that is, the right of a particular group against the larger society. This raises the issue of fairness between groups. One group may be marginalized or segregated in the name of preserving another group's distinctiveness. Critics of collective rights in this sense often cite the apartheid system in South Africa as an example of what can happen when rights are differentially distributed on the basis of group membership.

It is important to determine whether the three kinds of differentiated citizenship involve internal restrictions or external protections. To some extent, they involve both. However, they are primarily a matter of external protections. The Québécois, Aboriginal peoples, and ethnic minorities are concerned primarily with ensuring that the larger society does not deprive them of the conditions necessary for their survival. Generally speaking, they are not concerned with controlling the extent to which their own members engage in untraditional or unorthodox practices.

The three forms of differentiated citizenship all serve to protect ethnic and national minorities from economic or political pressures from the larger society, although each responds to different pressures. Special representation within the political institutions of the larger society, the devolution of self-government powers from the federal government to the minority, and the protection of cultural practices through polyethnic rights all reduce the vulnerability of minority communities to the economic and political decisions of the larger society.

These various forms of external protections are, I believe, compatible with liberal values. While external protections raise the danger that some groups will dominate others, as in apartheid, this does not seem to be a real danger for the particular external protections currently being claimed in Canada. The special veto powers demanded by French-Canadians, or the land rights demanded by Aboriginals, or the heritage language funding demanded by ethnic minorities will hardly put them in a position to dominate English Canadians. On the contrary, they can be seen as putting the various groups on a more equal footing, in terms of their relative power vis-à-vis one another.

Moreover, none of these external protections need conflict with individual rights, since they do not, by themselves, tell us anything about the power of the ethnic or national group over its own members. The existence of such external protections tells us about the relationship between the majority and minority groups; it does not yet tell us about the relationship between the ethnic or national group and its own members.

There are also some internal restrictions in Canada, although their scope is less clear. Both self-government rights and polyethnic rights can, under some circumstances, be used to oppress the members of the minority group. For example, some Québécois and Aboriginal leaders have sought qualification of, or exemption from, the Canadian Charter of Rights and Freedoms in the name of self-government. These limits on the Charter create the possibility that individuals or groups within Quebec or Aboriginal communities could be oppressed in the name of group solidarity or cultural purity.

Whether there is a real danger of intragroup oppression in Canada is a matter of considerable debate. The most commonly discussed example concerns the potential for sexual discrimination in minority cultures. Some women's groups (mostly from outside Quebec) worried that the Quebec government might use the "distinct society" clause to impose oppressive family policies on women (e.g., restricting access to birth control or abortion to maintain a high birth rate). Whether this was a realistic worry is very dubious. Women's groups within Quebec were quick to reject the idea that collective rights for Quebec were a threat to their equality.

The concern has also been expressed that Aboriginal women might be discriminated against under certain systems of Aboriginal self-government, if these are exempt from the Charter. This concern has been expressed by women's organizations both inside and outside Aboriginal communities. Indeed, the Native Women's Association of Canada has demanded that the decisions of Aboriginal governments be subject to the Canadian Charter (or a future Aboriginal Charter, if it also effectively protects sexual equality).[24]

On the other hand, many Aboriginal leaders insist that this fear of sexual oppression reflects misinformed or prejudiced stereotypes about Aboriginal cultures. They argue that Aboriginal self-government needs to be exempt from the Charter of Rights, not in order to restrict the liberty of women within Aboriginal communities but in order to defend the *external* protections of Aboriginals vis-à-vis the larger society. Their special rights to land, or to guaranteed representation, which help reduce their vulnerability to the economic and political pressure of the larger society, could be struck down as discriminatory under the Charter.[25] Also, Aboriginal leaders fear that white judges may interpret certain rights (e.g., democratic rights) in ways that are culturally biased.[26] Hence many Aboriginal leaders seek exemption from the Charter, but affirm their commitment to the basic human rights and freedoms that underlie it.

Similar debates have occurred over polyethnic rights. There are fears that some immigrant groups and religious minorities may use "multiculturalism" as a pretext for imposing traditional patriarchal practices on women and children. There are fears that some groups will demand the right to stop their children (particularly girls) from receiving a proper education, so as to reduce the chances that the child will leave the community; or the right to continue traditional customs such as clitoridectomy or arranged marriages.

Such internal restrictions clearly do have the potential to deny individual freedom. But these oppressive practices are not part of Canada's current "multiculturalism" policy. While the potential for internal restrictions exists in Canada, there is little public support for the exercise of such rights, even in minority communities. Instead, most collective rights for ethnic and national groups are defended in terms of, and take the form of, external protections against the larger community. Insofar as potential internal restrictions are present in Canada, they are often defended as unavoidable by-products of external protections, rather than as desirable in and of themselves.[27] There is no enthusiasm for the idea that ethnic or national groups should be able to protect their historical customs by limiting the basic civil liberties of their members. For example, there is no public support for restricting freedom of religion in the name of protecting the religious customs of a community.[28]

Social Unity and Differentiated Citizenship

Liberals are also concerned that differentiated citizenship will be a source of disunity, and inhibit the development of a sense of shared Canadian identity. It could lead to the dissolution of the country, or, less drastically, to a reduced willingness to make the mutual sacrifices and accommodations necessary for a functioning democracy.[29]

If groups are encouraged by the very terms of citizenship to turn inward and focus on their "difference" (whether racial, ethnic, religious, sexual, etc.), then citizenship cannot perform its vital integrative function—it ceases to be "a device to cultivate a sense of community and a common sense of purpose."[30] Nothing will bind the various groups in society together, and prevent the spread of mutual mistrust or conflict.

This is a serious concern. In evaluating it, however, we need to keep in mind the distinction between the three forms of differentiated citizenship. Generally speaking, it seems to me that the demand for both representation rights and polyethnic rights is a demand for *inclusion*. Groups that feel excluded want to be included in the larger society, and the recognition and accommodation of their "difference" is intended to facilitate this.

As I noted, the right to special representation can be seen as an extension of the familiar idea of guaranteeing special representation for underrepresented regions (e.g., an equal number of Senate seats for all states or provinces, whatever their population). This practice is widely (and rightly) seen as promoting both participation and fairness, and hence integration. Proponents of special representation simply extend this logic to nonterritorial minorities, who may equally be in need of representation (e.g., ethnic and racial minorities, women, the disabled). There are enormous practical obstacles to such a proposal. For example, how do we decide which groups are entitled to such representation, and how do we ensure that their "representatives" are in fact accountable to the group?[31] Nevertheless, the basic impulse underlying representation rights is integration, not separation.

Similarly, most demands for polyethnic rights are evidence that members of minority groups want to participate within the mainstream of society. Consider the case of Sikhs who wanted to join the Royal Canadian Mounted Police, but, because of their religious requirement to wear a turban, could not do so unless they were exempted from the usual requirements regarding ceremonial headgear. Such an exemption was opposed by many Canadians, who viewed it as a sign of disrespect for one of Canada's "national symbols." But the fact that these men wanted to be a part of the Royal Canadian Mounted Police, and participate in one of Canada's national symbols, is ample evidence of their desire to participate in and contribute to the larger community. The special right they were requesting could only be seen as promoting their integration, not discouraging it.[32]

Self-government rights, however, do raise problems for the integrative function of citizenship. While both representation and polyethnic rights take the larger political community for granted, and seek greater inclusion in it, demands for self-government reflect a desire to weaken the bonds with the larger community, and indeed question its very nature, authority, and permanence. If democracy is the rule of the people, group self-government raises the question of who "the people" really are. National minorities claim that they are distinct peoples, with inherent rights of self-determination that were not relinquished by their (often involuntary) federation into a larger country. Indeed, the retention of certain powers is often explicitly spelled out in the treaties or constitutional agreements that specified the terms of federation. Self-government rights, therefore, are the most complete case of differentiated citizenship, since they divide the people into separate "peoples," each with its own historic rights, territories, and powers of self-government, and each, therefore, with its own political community.

It seems unlikely that differentiated citizenship can serve an integrative function in this context. If citizenship is membership in a political community, then self-government rights necessarily give rise to a sort of dual citizenship, and to conflicts about which community citizens identify with most deeply. Moreover, there seems to be no natural stopping-point to the demands for increasing self-government. If limited autonomy is granted, this may simply fuel the ambitions of nationalist leaders who will be satisfied with nothing short of their own nation-state. Democratic multination states are, it would seem, inherently unstable for this reason.

It might seem tempting, therefore, to ignore the demands of national minorities, avoid any reference to such groups in the constitution, and insist that citizenship is a common identity shared by all individuals, without regard to group membership. This is often described as the American strategy for dealing with cultural pluralism. But with a few exceptions—such as the (mostly outlying) Indian, Eskimo, Puerto Rican, and native Hawaiian populations—the United States is not a multination state. It has faced the problem of assimilating voluntary immigrants and involuntary slaves, who arrived in America as individuals or families, rather than incorporating historically self-governing communities whose homeland has become part of the larger community. And where the "ethnicity-blind" strategy was applied to national minorities—such as Indians—it has often been a spectacular failure.[33] Hence many of these groups are now accorded self-government rights within the United States. Indeed, there are very few democratic multination states that follow the strict "common citizenship" strategy. This is not surprising, because refusing demands for self-government rights may simply aggravate alienation among these groups, and increase the desire for secession.[34]

What, then, is the source of unity in a multination country? Rawls claims that the source of unity is a shared conception of justice: "Although a well-ordered society is divided and pluralistic . . . public agreement on questions of political and social justice supports ties of civic friendship and secures the bonds of association."[35] A similar view underlies the constant reference to "shared values" in many of the federal government's committee reports and constitutional proposals leading up to the Charlottetown Accord. The hope is that focusing on the shared values of freedom and equality will provide the grounds for social unity in Canada.

This seems implausible. The fact that two national groups share the same principles of justice does not necessarily give them any strong reason to join (or remain) together, rather than remaining (or splitting into) two separate countries. The fact that people in Norway and Sweden share the same principles of justice is no reason for them to regret the secession of Norway in 1905. They have common principles, but are quite content pursuing them in separate countries. Similarly, the fact that anglophones and francophones in Canada share the same principles of justice is not a strong reason to remain together, since the Québécois rightly assume that they could continue to pursue these principles in their own independent state. Secession would not require abandoning their principles of justice.

Of course, if anglophones and francophones had a strong desire to live together in a single country, then sharing similar principles of justice would help them do so. But if they no longer desire to live together, it is not clear why the existence of common principles of justice would (or should) rekindle that desire, any more than the commonality of principles among Swedes and Norwegians is a reason for them to reunite in a single country. A shared conception of justice throughout a political community does not necessarily generate a shared *identity*, or sense of solidarity and loyalty, that will supersede rival identities based on nationality.[36]

Constructing a common identity is a fragile and ongoing project in a country like Canada, which contains two or more groups that view themselves as self-governing nations.[37] Of the three kinds of differentiated citizenship, therefore, self-government rights pose the greatest threat to social unity. However, the denial of self-government rights is also likely to threaten social unity, by encouraging resentment and even secession. So concerns about social unity, while valid, leave us more or less back at square one in terms of evaluating self-government claims.

Conclusion

Canada has a long history of accommodating group difference, particularly national and ethnic difference. It is difficult to say whether this history is a successful one. On the one hand, the continued existence of the country has often been in question, and remains so today. On the other hand, Canada has enjoyed 125 years of peaceful co-existence between three national groups, and innumerable ethnic groups, with an almost total absence of political violence. While many groups continue to feel excluded, the political system has proven flexible enough to accommodate many demands for self-government, multicultural recognition, and special representation. It is difficult to find a scale that allows us to add up these successes and disappointments to arrive at some overall judgments of the Canadian experiment in accommodating group difference.

Indeed, perhaps the major lesson to be drawn from the Canadian experience is the sheer heterogeneity of group difference, and of the mechanisms for accommodating them. The sorts of demands made by national, ethnic, and social groups differ greatly in their content and in their relation to traditional liberal democratic principles of equality, freedom, and democracy.

Notes

1. *Andrews v. Law Society of British Columbia* (1989) 10 C.H.R.R. D/5719 (S.C.C.).

2. Allen Buchanan, "Assessing the Communitarian Critique of Liberalism," *Ethics* 99, no. 4 (1989): 852–72; Michael Walzer, "The Communitarian Critique of Liberalism," *Political Theory* 18, no. 1 (1990): 6–23.

3. Iris Marion Young, "Polity and Group Difference: A Critique of the Ideal of Universal Citizenship," *Ethics* 99, no. 2 (1989): 258.

4. It is misleading to describe Aboriginal peoples as a single nation, since the term "aboriginal" covers three categories of Aboriginals (Indian, Inuit, and Métis), and the term "Indian" itself is a legal fiction, behind which there are numerous distinct aboriginal nations with their own histories and separate community identities. See Alan Cairns, "The Fragmentation of Canadian Citizenship," in William Kaplan, ed., *Belonging: The Meaning and Future of Canadian Citizenship* (Montreal: McGill-Queen's University Press, 1993), 188.

5. Throughout this essay, I use "Québécois" to refer to the French-speaking majority in the province of Quebec. There are francophones outside Quebec, and the French nation in Canada was not always identified so closely with the province of Quebec. For the change in self-identity from *la nation canadienne-française* to *québécois*, see Kenneth McRoberts, *Quebec: Social Change and Political Crisis*, 3d ed. (Toronto: McClelland and Stewart, 1988).

6. For example, the provincial legislature in Quebec is called the "National Assembly"; the major organization of Status Indians is known as the "Assembly of First Nations." Similarly, American Indians are recognized in law as "domestic dependent nations." On the adoption of the language of nationhood by Aboriginal groups, see David Long, "Culture, Ideology and Militancy: Movement of Native Indians in Canada." in W. E. Carroll, ed., *Organising Dissent: Contemporary Social Movements in Theory and Practice* (Toronto: Garamond, 1992), 118–34; Jane Jenson, "Naming Nations: Making Nationalist Claims in Canadian Public Discourse," *Canadian Review of Sociology and Anthropology* 30, no. 3 (1993): 337–58.

7. Government of Canada, *Shaping Canada's Future Together: Proposals* (Ottawa: Supply and Services, 1991), 10.

8. This assimilationist policy was adopted in both Canada and the United States, a fact that is obscured by the misleading contrast between the American "melting-pot" and the Canadian "ethnic mosaic." While "ethnic mosaic" implies protecting the integrity of ethnic cultures, in practice it simply meant that immigrants to Canada had a choice of two dominant cultures to assimilate to. Canada is binational, but the "uneasy tolerance which French and English were to show towards each other was not extended to foreigners who resisted assimilation or were believed to be unassimilable" (John Porter, *The Measure of Canadian Society* [Ottawa: Carleton University Press, 1979], 154).

9. As is the United States, although the American self-conception is often that of a polyethnic/immigrant country containing no national minorities. This ignores the existence of the American Indians, Puerto Ricans, native Hawaiians, and others. Conversely, some countries that recognize that they are multinational (e.g., Belgium, Switzerland) have trouble acknowledging that they are polyethnic (and so treat immigrants as second-class citizens).

10. This ambiguity has led to unwarranted criticism of Canada's "multiculturalism policy," the term the federal government uses for its post-1970 policy of promoting polyethnicity rather than assimilation for immigrants. Some Québécois have opposed the "multiculturalism" policy because they think it reduces their claims of nationhood to the level of mere ethnicity. Other people had the opposite fear that the policy was intended to treat immigrant groups as nations, and hence support the development of institutionally complete cultures alongside the French and English. In fact, neither fear was justified, since "multiculturalism" is a policy of supporting polyethnicity within the national institutions of the English and French cultures.

11. Immigration and the incorporation of national minorities are the two most common sources of cultural diversity in modern states. However, not all ethnocultural groups fall into one or the other of these headings. In particular, the situation of African-Americans is distinct. They do not fit the voluntary immigrant pattern, not only because they were brought to America involuntarily as slaves but also because they were prevented (rather than encouraged) from integrating into the institutions of the majority culture (e.g., racial segregation; laws against miscegenation and the teaching of literacy). Nor do they fit the national minority pattern, since they do not have a homeland in America or a common historical language. They came from a variety of African cultures, with different languages, and no attempt was made to keep together those with a common ethnic background. On the contrary, people from the same culture (even from the same family) were typically split up once in America. Moreover, before emancipation, they were legally prohibited from trying to re-create their own cultural structure (e.g., all forms of black association, except churches, were illegal). The situation of African-Americans, therefore, is virtually unique. Given this distinct situation, we should not expect solutions that are appropriate for African-Americans to be appropriate for either voluntary immigrants or national minorities (or vice versa).

12. According to various United Nations Declarations, "all peoples have the right to self-determination." The U.N. does not define "peoples," and it has generally applied

the principle of self-determination only to overseas colonies, not internal national minorities, even when the latter were subject to the same sort of conquest and colonization as the former. However, this is widely seen as arbitrary.

13. A certain degree of de facto asymmetry in powers has been a long-standing aspect of Canadian federalism. However, many Canadians are unwilling to formally recognize this asymmetry in the Constitution. See Charles Taylor, "Shared and Divergent Values," in R. Watts, ed., *Options for a New Canada* (Toronto: University of Toronto Press, 1991), 53–76; A. G. Gagnon and J. Garcea, "Quebec and the Pursuit of Special Status," in R. D. Olling and M. Westmacott, eds., *Perspectives on Canadian Federalism* (Scarborough: Prentice-Hall, 1988), 304–25.

14. On the relation of Aboriginal self-government to federalism, see Frank Cassidy and Robert Bish, *Indian Government: Its Meaning in Practice* (Halifax: Institute for Research on Public Policy, 1989); J. A. Long, "Federalism and Ethnic Self-Determination: Native Indians in Canada," *Journal of Commonwealth and Comparative Politics* 29, no. 2 (1991): 192–211.

15. For detailed discussion of these rights in the British context, see Bhikhu Parekh, "British Citizenship and Cultural Difference," in Geoff Andrews, ed., *Citizenship* (London: Lawrence and Wishart, 1991), 197–204.

16. Of course, some groups' demands take the form of withdrawal from the larger society. However, this is primarily true of religious sects rather than of immigrant communities per se. For example, the Hutterites and Mennonites in Canada (like the Amish in the United States) are allowed to pull their children out of school before the legal age of sixteen, and put severe restrictions on the ability of group members to leave their community. It would be misleading to view this as the result of Canada's multiculturalism policy, since the legal exemptions accorded these Christian sects long predate the multiculturalism policy. In the rest of this essay, therefore, I will concentrate on the demands associated with recent immigrant groups. I discuss the case of religious sects in "Two Models of Pluralism and Tolerance," *Analyze & Kritik* 14, no. 1 (1992): 33–56, reprinted in David Heyd, ed., *Toleration* (Princeton: Princeton University Press, forthcoming).

17. I discuss these proposals in "Group Representation in Canadian Politics," in Leslie Seidle, ed., *Equity and Community: The Charter, Interest Advocacy, and Representation* (Montreal: Institute for Research on Public Policy, 1993), 61–89.

18. Young, "Polity and Group Difference," 259. Cf. Young's *Justice and the Politics of Difference* (Princeton: Princeton University Press, 1990), 183–91; Christine Boyle, "Home-Rule for Women: Power-Sharing between Men and Women," *Dalhousie Law Journal* 7 (1983): 790–807.

19. Quebec is in fact guaranteed three seats (out of nine) on the Supreme Court, and some Aboriginal leaders have demanded guaranteed Aboriginal representation on the Court, at least on those issues that directly affect their rights.

20. This is in fact one of the major obstacles to asymmetrical federalism. There is no accepted model for determining the status of Quebec's Members of Parliament under a system of asymmetrical powers (how many MPs should Quebec have? what issues should they vote on?). An analogous situation concerns the representation of Puerto Rico in the American federal government. Since Puerto Rico is generally self-governing, it has drastically reduced representation in Congress compared to other American citi-

zens. For a more detailed discussion of this issue and of the problems of multination federations more generally, see my forthcoming "Federalism, Nationalism, and Multiculturalism," *Revista Internacional de Filosofia Politica* 6 (1996).

21. They are of course not unique to Canada. Indeed, all three types are included (but not distinguished) in Iris Young's list of group-differentiated policies in the American context. She lumps together land rights for American Indians, language rights for Hispanics, and representation for gays and women, and defends them all as remedies for oppression. I think this is misleading. Of the three forms of differentiated citizenship, only (some of) the demands for special representation are best understood as remedies for group oppression. Claims of oppression are neither necessary nor sufficient for claims of self-government or polyethnic rights.

22. I give a more comprehensive defense of them in *Multicultural Citizenship* (Oxford: Oxford University Press, 1995). It is worth noting that group-differentiated rights were widely accepted within the liberal tradition before the Second World War. I discuss this, and the reasons for the postwar change in liberal views, in "Liberalism and the Politicization of Ethnicity," *Canadian Journal of Law and Jurisprudence* 4, no. 2 (1991): 239–56, reprinted in Julia Stapleton, ed., *Group Rights* (Bristol: Thoemmes Press, 1995).

23. P. E. Trudeau, "The Values of a Just Society," in Thomas Axworthy, ed., *Towards a Just Society* (Toronto: Viking, 1990), 363–64.

24. Similar debates have occurred over the legal protection of sexual equality on American Indian reservations. See Carla Christofferson, "Tribal Courts' Failure to Protect Native American Women: A Reappraisal of the Indian Civil Rights Act," *Yale Law Journal* 101, no. 1 (1991): 169–85; Judith Resnik, "Dependent Sovereigns: Indian Tribes, States, and the Federal Courts," *University of Chicago Law Review* 56 (1989): 671–759.

25. For example, guaranteed representation for Aboriginals could be seen as violating the equality rights of the Charter, as could restrictions on the mobility of non-Aboriginals on Indian lands.

26. For example, traditional Aboriginal methods of consensual political decision-making could be seen as denying the democratic rights guaranteed in sections 3–5 of the Charter. These traditional decision-making procedures do not violate the underlying democratic principle of the Charter—namely, that legitimate authority requires the consent of the governed, subject to periodic review. However, traditional Aboriginal practices do not use the particular method for securing the consent of the governed envisioned by the Charter—namely, periodic election of representatives. Rather, they rely on certain time-honored procedures for ensuring consensual decision-making. Aboriginal leaders worry that white judges will impose their own culturally specific form of democracy, without considering whether traditional Aboriginal practices are an equally valid interpretation of democratic principles.

27. Another example of the way internal restrictions and external protections are combined is the language laws in Quebec. This example is complex, since the laws distinguish between various kinds of language use (government services, education, workplace, and commercial signs) and various groups (resident anglophones, anglophones who move to Quebec from other provinces, francophones, and immigrants). The main justification for these laws is to ensure equal opportunity for francophones against the economic and political pressure of the anglophone majority in North Amer-

ica. As such, they have been quite successful, particularly in enabling francophones to use French in the workplace. However, some aspects of these laws involve unjustified internal restrictions. For example, the former law (recently amended) not only guaranteed that commercial signs include French but also prohibited the use of English on certain signs. This was partly an internal restriction, insofar as it was designed to protect the stability of Québécois society from the choices of its own members. It was also partly an overrestrictive external protection, since it unnecessarily restricted the freedom of anglophones to use their own language. See Robert Yalden, "Liberalism and Language in Quebec: Bill 101, the Courts and Bill 178," *University of Toronto Faculty of Law Review* 47 (1989): 973–94; Gordon Campbell, "Language, Equality and the Charter," *National Journal of Constitutional Law* 4, no. 1 (1994): 29–73.

28. This does occur on some American Indian reservations. See William Weston, "Freedom of Religion and the American Indian," in R. Nichols, ed., *The American Indian: Past and Present*, 2d ed. (New York: John Wiley and Sons, 1981); Frances Svensson, "Liberal Democracy and Group Rights: The Legacy of Individualism and Its Impact on American Indian Tribes," *Political Studies* 27, no. 3 (1979): 421–39. Notice that the threat to individual freedom posed by internal restrictions does not arise just with *minorities*. It is often a majority nation, or an ethnically homogenous nation-state, which seeks to oppress its own members. I discuss the distinction between internal restrictions and external protections, and their relation to liberalism, in *Multicultural Citizenship*, chaps. 3 and 8.

29. Some liberals regard the idea of group-differentiated citizenship not only as divisive but as a contradiction in terms. For them, citizenship is, by definition, a matter of treating people as individuals with equal rights under the law. Hence "the organization of society on the basis of rights or claims that derive from group membership is sharply opposed to the concept of society based on citizenship" (Porter, *The Measure of Canadian Society*, 128).

30. Derek Heater, *Citizenship: The Civic Ideal in World History, Politics and Education* (London: Longman, 1990), 295.

31. I discuss these issues in *Multicultural Citizenship*, chap. 7. See also Anne Phillips's essay in this volume, and her *Politics of Presence* (Oxford: Oxford University Press, 1995).

32. This is in contrast to many Aboriginal communities in Canada, who, as part of their self-government, have been trying to remove the Royal Canadian Mounted Police from their reserves and replace it with an Aboriginal police force.

33. As even its proponents admit. See, e.g., Michael Walzer, "Pluralism in Political Perspective," in M. Walzer, ed., *The Politics of Ethnicity* (Cambridge, Mass.: Harvard University Press, 1982), 27; cf. my "Liberalism and the Politicization of Ethnicity," 248–55.

34. In any event, the state cannot avoid giving public recognition to particular group identities. It must decide which language(s) will serve as the official language(s) of the schools, courts, and legislatures. This shows that the "strict separation of state and ethnicity" view proclaimed by many American liberals is incoherent. I discuss this in *Multicultural Citizenship*, chap. 6.

35. Rawls, "Kantian Constructivism in Moral Theory," *Journal of Philosophy* 77, no. 9 (1980): 540.

36. W. Norman, "The Ideology of Shared Values," in Joseph Carens, ed., *Is Quebec Nationalism Just?* (Montreal: McGill-Queen's University Press, 1995), 137–59. I discuss the relationship between identity and values in *Multicultural Citizenship*, chap. 9; and "Social Unity in a Liberal State," *Social Philosophy and Policy* 13, no. 1 (Winter 1996): 105–36.

37. For interesting speculations on this issue, see Charles Taylor's discussion in "Shared and Divergent Values." The great variation in historical, cultural, and political situations in multination states suggests that there is no generalized answer regarding the role of either a common citizenship identity or a differentiated citizenship identity in promoting or hindering social unity.

Nine

Diversity and Democracy: Representing Differences

CAROL C. GOULD

Introduction

It has become a commonplace in political theory to criticize liberalism for its abstract universality and abstract individualism, in which differences other than those of political opinion are ignored or overridden and assigned to the private sphere. But the alternative theoretical framework in which differences would be adequately recognized and effectively taken into account in the public domain remains undeveloped and problematic. Some basic questions arise here: what differences ought to be recognized, and why these rather than others? Which differences should be ignored, and which would it be pernicious to recognize? What would it mean to recognize differences in political or, more generally, in public or institutional contexts, and what is the normative rationale for this recognition? Does the emphasis on the recognition and representation of differences violate equal rights as a norm of justice?

I would like to explore what light can be shed on these questions from the perspective of a democratic theory that stresses participation in decision-making in contexts broader than the political and which is informed by feminist theory. Because the focus of this essay is on recognizing and representing differences in the public sphere, I will begin with a consideration and critique of Jürgen Habermas's interpretation of this public domain. I will then consider the views of a number of other theorists working within a similar framework or influenced by it. In the second part of this essay, I will present the outlines of an alternative theoretical approach to the question of differences in the public sphere and in this context offer some philosophical groundwork on the conceptions of difference, its domains, and its normative status in political and social activity. I will also consider some of the concrete problems involved in the effective representation of specific differences in public life, in particular, of gender, race, and ethnicity, for example, as to whether one should mandate the representation of women in politics in proportion to their numbers, and whether only women can represent women.

Habermas, the Public Sphere, and
the Problem of Difference

Habermas's early reconstruction of the public sphere locates it as a historically new domain of discourse, with a wide participation across differences of class or political estate and to some degree even of gender. This public domain takes its place outside the institutions of the state and serves as the forum for discussion about public norms. Although Habermas offers this as a descriptive historical account, he subsequently relates it to a normative account of discourse that aims at agreement concerning moral norms and at the formation of a generalizable interest. The features of such a discourse, anticipated in communicative action more generally, are well known. They include reciprocal recognition by the speakers of each other as free and equal in participating in the discourse, and interchangeable in their dialogue roles; they aim at consensus that is rational, in the sense that they are all committed to the sway of the better argument. Such a rational discourse implies criteria of universalizability and impartiality. And more recently Habermas has stressed that it also involves a concern for the welfare of the other and therefore the feature of solidarity.[1] Although not originally intended as a model of democracy, this account of practical discourse has suggested to others that it may be used as an account of deliberative or communicative democratic decision-making. Some problems with such an interpretation will be taken up later.

The features stressed in Habermas's account of discourse—the freedom and equality of participants, the reciprocity of perspectives, and so on—are clearly attractive to any right-minded (or perhaps we should say left-minded) person. His account clearly takes us beyond both traditional liberal and Marxist frameworks. Still, there are difficulties with it, some of them already noted by others (and also by myself[2]), and several of these bear specifically on the recognition and representation of difference.

First, we may question whether the emphasis on the determination of generalizable interests through discourse gives sufficient weight to both individual and group differences and their role within the public domain. It is not that such differences as those of gender, race, culture, or again, the differentiated needs of individuals are simply suppressed or ignored, for all voices are free to enter into the discourse, and no expression of interest is excluded. But the telos of the discourse, what characterizes its aim and method, is agreement. Difference is something to be gotten past. And the reciprocal recognition is for the sake of common agreement rather than also for the sake of enhancing and articulating diversity. Diversity may be the original condition of a polyvocal discourse but univocity is its normative principle. I would argue by contrast that, in addition to common agreement, interaction among people in public, whether discursively or in other modes of activity, is normatively oriented to the articulation, acknowledgment, and sometimes encouragement of differences. Indeed, I would propose that an adequate conception of justice itself would involve not simply universalizability but also the recognition of differences.

It will be argued that the Habermasian framework makes room for the expression or the development of differences either as goods that individuals pursue in private or as expressive concerns in the context of communicative action. Such expression of differences finds its proper development, according to Habermas, in the aesthetic domain. But this separation of domains and therefore the downplaying of the enhancing role of difference at the core of the public sphere is problematic. It removes from the public sphere not only difference but also the creativity that issues forth in imaginative critique and rejection of existing agreement and in the generation of new and unexpected frameworks for agreement. Thus it tends to denigrate the sources of critique and the Socratic subversion of established norms.

A second problem concerns the issue of domain. For one thing, the arena of this public discourse as one of communicative action is systematically separated by Habermas from goal-oriented or purposive-rational activity, which is regarded as strategic or else instrumental. This originally analytical distinction seems to become reified in the demarcation of different spheres of activity. As a sphere of discourse or public opinion that serves only as a democratic dam constraining politics,[3] the public domain leaves out those contexts of practical activity oriented to common goals that I have called common activities, and that in my view ought to be included in the domain of public life. Social, economic, and political institutions are for the most part organized as common activities of this sort. I have further argued that each of these institutional contexts of common activity ought to be democratized—that is, social and economic institutions as well as political ones—to permit joint decision-making concerning common goals and the means of realizing them.[4] Habermas tends to relegate decision-making in such contexts to a strategic type of action either in state administration or economic system. But this does not do justice either to joint goal-setting as practical social activity or to the possibilities of democratic participation and control in the domains of state and economy.

The alternative view of the public that I am proposing would allow for more differentiated and localized centers of activity, representing common interests that are not necessarily global or society-wide. In such diverse common activities and the institutions organized around them, the opportunities for the expression and recognition of differences and for their representation are greater. It is also evident that a condition for the full manifestation of difference in these contexts is their democratization, permitting opportunities for participation by their members. By institutionalized common activities, I mean not only organizations with political programs, or that attempt to influence politics, or the institutions of political democracy themselves, but equally centrally the range of specific and local institutions of work, that is, firms or companies, or again, social and cultural institutions, such as universities and museums, as well as voluntary associations like social clubs and so forth.

Of course, none of this diminishes the significance of the public domain of discourse as Habermas has described it, but as an account of publicness it is incomplete. This is so partly because it sees the state and the economy as falling outside it and hence as themselves not amenable to democratization. Thus it tends to reduce the sphere of the political—as state—to administration and of the economy to the private domain of pure means-ends relations. Further, it is incomplete in construing the public too exclusively in terms of discourse or communication and not also in terms of common practical activities oriented to shared goals.

A third set of difficulties emerges with respect to Habermas's characterization of discourse as having a built-in criterion of consensus as its ultimate and ongoing aim. Not only does the discussion aim at agreement, it aims at the total agreement of all those who could possibly be affected by the adoption of the norm that is the object of the agreement. Now it may be the case that for any kind of agreement to have validity and to be effective, those who have entered into the agreement must consensually have agreed in the procedural sense to abide by the outcome. However, with respect to moral norms, that is, the sort that communicative action aims at grounding or validating, the consensual agreement concerns not merely the legitimation of the procedure but of the normative content or substance of the norms agreed on. The force of the requirement for consensus in these substantive normative contexts might well tend to discourage differences that result in dissension or imperil the achievement of consensus. Even if consensus is taken as a counterfactual norm rather than as something to be empirically achieved within a time constraint, the pressure for agreement at the limit could be expected to exert pressure on arguments in the present and may then unwittingly suppress difference or devalue it. A good example of this in the empirical case is the pressure exerted on dissenting jurors in criminal trials where unanimous or consensual verdicts are required and where the social and psychological cost of a hung jury looms over the expression of difference. True, this is not an analogous case, for here the consensual norm is not counterfactual but actual, yet its moral force may have a similar effect.

It may be objected that this criticism might hold if Habermas's were a theory of democratic decision-making, because in that case a counterfactual norm would have to be replaced by an actual method of reaching decisions within time constraints. Indeed, Habermas had earlier characterized the question of democratic forms as the practical question of "[which] mechanisms are in each case better suited to bring about procedurally legitimate decisions and institutions."[5] One would ordinarily think here of the argument for fair procedures such as majority rule and the requirement for protection of minorities, and so on. But in fact, Habermas goes on to characterize "procedurally legitimate decisions and institutions" as those that "would meet with the unforced agreement of all those involved if they could participate, as free and equal, in discursive will formation."[6] But obviously, no majority or any other procedure short of an actual consensus of "all those involved" could guarantee procedural legitimacy in this case. Even democratic decision procedures are then put under the normative regulation of consensus. In effect, we would have to know what the consensus would be in order to judge that a democratic decision was procedurally legitimate, a requirement impossible to meet.

Another problem with this idea of consensus is one that I can only allude to here. It concerns the grounding for rights that I would argue are needed to protect individual differences and enable their free expression. If, for Habermas, rights are grounded in norms of justice that are validated by consensus, then their grounding is purely procedural. And because consensus has no essential or metaphysical status, a different consensus would ground different rights. But I would argue that rights, especially the basic human rights, have to be grounded more securely than any procedure, even an ideal one, could accomplish. I have argued that rights are grounded in the character of human action itself, an argument that I have developed at length elsewhere.[7] Habermas presupposes the same basic rights, especially the freedom and equality of the participants in the discourse. It is these rights that undergird the validity of the norms that are arrived at because they are acceptable to the participants in the discourse, and acceptable on the condition of their freedom and equality. Without such free consent, the norms would have no moral force. But the very freedom and equality of the participants cannot themselves be grounded in any consensual norm. If they were, this would entail an infinite regress (of procedures that ground rights that ground procedures that ground rights ad infinitum); or else a circle, in which the rights grounded by norms are themselves presupposed in the procedure of grounding these norms. Instead, they are presupposed by Habermas, who sees them as necessary conditions for participation in the communicative action itself. But because this communicative action is itself a procedure for reaching understanding or agreement, the rights are seen as no more than conditions for participation in this procedure. This, it seems to me, is a very weak basis for rights.

We might add that this is especially so for the rights of difference. For one's differences are not themselves required by the process of coming to agreement or for understanding but rather stand apart from what is in the generalizable interest, and therefore the rights to difference cannot be grounded in the requirements of coming to agreement.

A final concern is that although Habermas asserts that everyone is free to enter into the discourse of the public sphere and to be heard, there are voices that are mute in this discussion. There are, for example, those who do not or cannot speak in public, who from inarticulateness, fear, habit, or oppression are removed from participation in public life. There is also the relatively narrow conception of the exclusively discursive rationality that is operative in this sphere and the delimitation of communication to rational verbal discourse. In short, this universal sphere, even within the confines of a nation or a political unit, is less than universal in its constitution.

Discursive Models of Democracy

The natural temptation to interpret Habermas's communicative model as a model of democracy has led some other theorists to a number of interesting variations on Habermasian themes, a few of which I shall take note of here.

When a discursive or communicative model is transformed into a model of democracy, whether as so-called discursive, deliberative, or communicative democracy, it takes on some peculiar features. From the obvious fact that democracy as the form of self-governance always involves discussion, deliberation, or communication among the participants in this self-governance, Habermasian models of democracy seem to appropriate only the discursive element and either deliberately eschew or else ignore the crucial element of joint decision-making and of the self-governance that it enables. Free and equal participation in a public discourse, in an ideal model, may well help to shape public opinion (though in practice public opinion is often shaped by other means), but public opinion by itself does not govern. Governance in a democracy is self-government by means of participation and representation in contexts of decision-making. Again here, presumably because of Habermas's separation of communicative discourse from decision-making, these discursive interpretations of democracy focus exclusively on participation as talk or discussion or deliberation. In effect, it becomes all talk and no action, in the sense of effective decision-making. We may say that while decision without deliberation is blind, deliberation without decision is empty.[8]

The character of this domain of discursive democracy remains that of a general forum where the relations are those of speaking and being heard. Still, almost surreptitiously, the criterion for participation turns out to be "all those affected" by the adoption of a norm or, in effect, by a decision. It cannot simply be all those who are affected by the discourse, for it would be entirely unclear what this means. But the criterion for the demarcation of the domain of membership in any given discourse—that all those must participate in actual dialogue who might possibly be affected by the norm or the decision in question—is also excessively indeterminate, for we cannot know all who may be affected (both because of the global effects of actions and of their effects on future generations, not to speak of the unintended or unforeseeable consequences of actions).

Recent theorists have tried to differentiate the public sphere into a diversity of associations or movements or possibly institutions, that is, more or less informal or loosely configured groupings, where membership is voluntary and not ascriptive and where difference can be represented, at least in discourse. While this is clearly an improvement over an undifferentiated public sphere, I would argue that it leaves out many significant public institutional contexts for democratic decision-making and for the representation of difference. Moreover, the question of the domain of membership in the informal associations or groupings into which the public sphere is divided remains unclear. Once the discursive model is interpreted as a putative model of democratic decision-making, the question then becomes, "Who has a right to participate not only in deliberation but in the decision-making itself?" The answer "everyone affected by the decision" will not work for any practical or real-world context.

One interpretation of the discursive model as an ideal model of democracy is Joshua Cohen's account of deliberative democracy.[9] The virtue of this model for the adequate recognition and representation of differences is that it carries over into democratic deliberation the Habermasian element that every voice be heard as a free and equal participant in the deliberation. Difference is then recognized simply by the presence of the different and no more than this. There is no special representation, for the different but equal status is assured by the elimination of the hindrances and inequalities that may have led in the past to unequal status and inferior representation.

Cohen also proposes a view akin to Habermas's, that the deliberation aim at a consensus, in this case about the common good, or common goods.[10] The requirement of consensus in the context of democratic decisions about the common good is no longer a counterfactual norm but a requirement for actual agreement in real time. This might sometimes occur, especially where the deliberative body is relatively small and homogeneous in its moral outlook, and marked by reciprocal good will. Cohen grants therefore that this is an ideal model and that actual democratic institutions should be judged by how closely they approximate to this ideal. But because agreements on the common good are choices bound by time constraints, Cohen recognizes that when consensus cannot be achieved, the body has to move to majoritarian decision processes. But as Thomas Christiano points out, the reliance on such majoritarian procedures is not normatively justified by Cohen.[11] Further, there would seem to be no consideration of how difference and the interests of the different would be protected against being overridden in such cases of majority rule.

Here, one of the key protections is a set of rights that are constitutionally guaranteed and that may not be violated even by a decision of the majority, and, as suggested in the preceding, this poses difficulties for the discursive model. This difficulty is particularly evident in Iris Young's discussion of what she calls communicative democracy. On her view, the decisions of such a communicative body politic determine what is just if they meet the conditions of free discussion among members of the polity and are acceptable to all, a strong condition of consensus. She writes: "Because there is no theological or socially transcendent ground for claims about justice, just norms and policies are simply those that would be arrived at by members of a polity who freely communicate with one another with the aim of reaching an understanding."[12] There is then no appeal beyond the authority of the decision of such a democratic body. Therefore, there can be no criticism of an unjust decision, which remains undefined in this model. This is what Rawls has designated as pure procedural justice. Rights as having any status independent of a democratic procedure simply do not exist here. Rights are what are consensually taken to be rights, and if the consensus changes then what was once a right may no longer be. Indeed, by what seems to be circular reasoning, the rights to freely participate as equals in the body politic are themselves presupposed rather than the outcome of a procedure that in turn would have to presuppose them in order to authorize or legitimate them. There may be legal rights that may appropriately be subject to such shifting consensual decisions. For example, the right to burn leaves in autumn, which was once legally condoned, has been abrogated because of concerns with pollution. But where the human rights as rights against majorities are concerned, such transiency will not do.

In a related way, Seyla Benhabib claims that basic rights are themselves essentially contestable and therefore presumably open to discursive vindication (citing Baynes) and at the same time holds that though they are contestable they cannot be abrogated or violated without suspending or ending democracy itself, because these are "the constitutive and regulative institutional norms of debate in democratic societies."[13] Benhabib wants to have it both ways, then; for if the rights are really contestable, then one possibility has to be that they can be abrogated. Otherwise, contestation reduces to differences of interpretation and that's not what essential contestability means. But if they are not contestable, this means that they have their authority in something other than the discursive procedure of the genesis and validation of norms. Either the rights are contestable, or they are not.

An alternative interpretation to get us off this hook might be that this is a hypothetical normative argument to the effect that if we want democracy then we have to have rights, no matter how much we pretend to be free to contest them. But in this case, basic rights would simply be instrumental with respect to the higher value of democracy and would have no independent ground apart from this. This would mean that rights are protected against majoritarian violations only as long as the majority decides to protect democracy. But this sounds like a verbal trick, namely, that if these rights are violated, it isn't democracy, and therefore within a democracy basic rights by definition cannot be violated.

Benhabib goes on to propose the renegotiation of the boundary between the public and private spheres, private here referring to the domain of personal relations and the family. She criticizes Habermas for drawing this distinction too rigidly in order to protect individual autonomy from intrusion by the state or the public sphere and for neglecting the feminist critique of domination and oppression within this private sphere.[14] Nancy Fraser has advanced a similar critique.[15]

On Benhabib's view, then, what can be preserved as privacy is as renegotiable and open to discursive contestation as the basic rights, which as we have just seen are also "on the agenda" (though paradoxically). But the private sphere of personal life has never been immune to the intrusion of law or of the legal protection of rights and persons. The extent of such protection has certainly varied, and women's rights within the private sphere—from the right to hold property to the right to be free from marital rape—have certainly grown overall. But changes in the extent of the jurisdiction of legally protected rights does not mean that the principle of there being *some* boundary is contestable. Some domain of privacy both as the condition for free individuality and the development of personal relations must be essentially preserved as a domain free from government intrusion, and this is necessary from a feminist perspective as well.[16]

Benhabib also seems to want to preserve something like this (citing Jean Cohen on the limits that the requirements of moral autonomy put on legality).[17] But on Benhabib's view, the only protection of this autonomy which is the final boundary for privacy is that it is a precondition for democratic legitimacy. However, as we have just seen, even this is essentially contestable and open to discursive validation, according to Benhabib, which means that the boundary is in principle open to being erased altogether. Though this is not a likely outcome, given our liberal preferences for privacy and the continuation of democracy, it is not clear that it could be ruled out on this model and therefore remains a weak basis for the protection of privacy rights as among the basic liberty rights. We may add that some of the discussions in liberal and feminist theory have pointed out that the rights required as necessary conditions for democracy are too narrow to include what we would want included under privacy. While freedom of speech and association, as well as political equality, can clearly be justified simply as necessary for democracy, it is not clear that a full set of liberty rights or the right of privacy, as including for example rights over one's body, can be adequately justified in this way.

A final point here is that there may be a confusion between the domain of legality and rights and the domain of the discourse of the public sphere. Of course, anything can be discussed freely in conversations of the public sphere without putting in question any boundaries between the public and the private, except perhaps the publicly accepted norms concerning personal relations, and the public awareness of domination and oppression. The public sense of justice may be profoundly affected by such discussion, and social movements and organizations for women's equality or for civil rights may affect legislation. Therefore, the public perception of the boundary between what is public and what is private may certainly be renegotiated. But this does not yet determine rights and the extent of their legal protection within the private sphere.

Recognizing and Representing Differences

What then is involved in taking differences seriously in the social and political domain? In part, as I have already suggested, it means taking rights seriously. But I would argue that this involves a conception of rights and of justice different from the classical liberal one. Whereas the latter is difference blind in its principles of equal rights mandating a sameness of treatment, the principle of justice that I propose (and that I develop at some length in my book *Rethinking Democracy*)[18] builds a recognition of difference and responsiveness to individuated needs, as well as the protection of the rights of difference into its basic conception.

If we take justice as equal freedom to entail not only the negative liberties and equal political rights but also equal rights to the conditions of differentiated self-development, that is, as what I call equal positive freedom, then justice requires not the *same* conditions for each one but rather *equivalent* conditions determined by differentiated needs. Justice then entails a recognition and consideration of relevant differences. It sees equal treatment as inherently responsive to and defined by difference. Thus instead of merely adding a conception of nonstandard interests, for example, of the vulnerable, to the standard interests that the liberal theory of justice acknowledges, this principle builds differentiation into the basic requirement of just treatment. It also requires responsiveness to and even empathy with the differentiated needs of others, drawing on the feminist discussion of care.

This principle of justice as equal positive freedom presents a number of difficulties in its application: first is the need for a criterion of relevant vs. irrelevant differences. Not every differentiated need has an equal claim in the context of self-development. Second, at the policy level, it is difficult to make or implement policy that is radically individuated. Practically speaking, people often have to be treated in terms of their group characteristics. Still, as a regulative principle, it leads us to accommodate differences as far as possible both in distributive contexts and at the level of rights. Nonetheless, as presupposing equality in regard to a range of basic human rights, including the negative liberties, equal political rights, and subsistence rights, this alternative conception requires that the differential treatment be compatible with equal human rights. Many hard questions remain open here then, for example, as to whether recognition of a particular group right, for example, of ethnic self-determination, is compatible with political equality. But I would suggest that the principle provides a useful normative guideline even for hard questions such as this.

Taking differences seriously in public life requires more than simply a reformulated principle of justice, however. It requires a radical increase in opportunities for participation in contexts of common activity, including not only in the discourse and associations of the public sphere, in the sense discussed earlier, but also in the institutions of economic, social, and political life. Indeed, such opportunities for democratic participation are required by the principle of justice in my account. For if individuals have an equal right to determine their own actions and further, if engaging in common activity is one of the necessary conditions for their self-development, then it follows that there is an equal right to participate in determining the course of such common activity. This includes participation in decision-making in the institutions of work, that is, in the firm, in social and cultural institutions, as well as in contexts of politics and government. This would also include the voluntary associations, social movements, and informal groupings of the public sphere. Thus the conception here of what I would call the public domain represents a broader arena for activity than that included on the discursive model.

Such participation provides opportunities for the effective expression of difference and for its appropriate recognition in several ways. For one thing, in these normally smaller-scale contexts of participation, difference can be directly expressed by the individual or group and concretely recognized in the social interactions among people engaged in the common activity. Here, difference is directly presented rather than simply talked about. Participation in decision-making also means that effective action can be taken on behalf of the different needs and interests that difference presents. Further, such contexts contribute to individuals' and groups' recognition and articulation of their own differentiated concerns.

I would also suggest that the very diversity of common activities in which participation is possible makes an important contribution to the differentiation of individuals, where this differentiation is a mark of self-development. Such a multiplicity of contexts for one's activity and association with others permits the expression and elaboration of a range of different capacities. The value of such a diversity of contexts and its contribution to the development of individuals was recognized by some earlier pluralist theorists of democracy and of culture—notably, John Dewey.

It remains to consider some alternative approaches to the role and valuation of difference in political and social life and to analyze the status of such group differences as gender, race, and ethnicity. Finally, in view of this analysis, I will consider the question of the representation of group differences in the context of democratic decision-making.

Two alternative approaches to difference present themselves immediately. The first, associated with classical liberalism, takes all differences other than political opinion as indifferent or as to be eliminated from consideration from politics in the name of the universal equality of the citizen. Differences other than political ones are nobody's business but one's own and therefore belong in the private sphere, together with one's religion, one's moral beliefs, and one's family practices. The second view celebrates difference, especially as a cultural value, and encourages diversity and the representation of diversity as a positive social good. That is not to say that it promotes dissension in politics as a version of this good. Rather, it argues for some harmonious variety among reciprocally respectful members of a common polity, who while they respect one another's equal rights also respect and encourage one another's differences. This is, to say the least, a high-minded view.

There are, however, other approaches to difference that fall between these types or go beyond them. One is the pluralist view represented in democratic theory by Schumpeter and the early Dahl, which sees democracy as essentially a mediation among conflicting interest groups for the sake of equilibrium. Another is the compensatory view of differences. Here, the injuries of difference—of race, gender, and ethnicity, which have been the basis for discrimination and unequal treatment in the past—are to be openly recognized as grounds for affirmative action to rectify them. Differences are recognized in order to eliminate their negative effects. Beyond all these views is what I might call an essentialist multiculturalism, which not only affirms group differences but argues for their permanent structural representation in contexts of political democracy or in government. Such a view proposes special representation by gender or race or culture much as states are represented in the U.S. Senate.

The mention of essentialism raises the question of how to characterize group differences. Perhaps the oldest and most backward conception of those social group differences that have played a role in politics is the view that these differences are essential, that is, that they are fixed essences given once and for all, with traits that are homogeneously distributed among all the group members. Essentialism with respect to groups is closely akin to abstract universality:[19] all the individuals of the different group are the same. Something not quite as strong as this is preserved in the notion of ascriptive group identity, where this is seen as given, something that you are "born" into and that constitutes you as being who you are and is ascribed to you by others in a way that makes it involuntary from your point of view. By contrast, groups with which one identifies voluntarily (e.g., voluntary associations) and which one can therefore enter or leave at will do not constitute one as being who one is essentially, though such affiliation may well partly identify one's social or cultural or even personal character.[20]

It seems to me that the distinction between the voluntary and the involuntary or ascriptive nature of a group difference is misleading and not refined enough. For example, take native language, certainly a case of "thrownness"[21] or of a "given" in one's group identity. Yet there is nothing that necessitates that one's native language continue to be spoken past early childhood, and there are numerous instances, for example, in my own family, in which the native language was completely forgotten and the actual language was acquired completely contingently. In this case, what is given is not at all fixed and may be radically transformed either by one's own choice or by someone else's. However, it may be argued that a trait like gender or race that is biologically based, unlike language, is strongly ascriptive and given once and for all. The flaw in this argument, though, is that what constitutes a relevant difference in social and political terms with regard to race and gender is not one's genetic sex determination or one's skin pigment but what has been made of these by social and historical construal, largely by discrimination and oppression. It is not being black or female that constitutes the group difference but being subject to oppression as a black or as a female. This works the other way as well: the positive features of gender, race, or ethnic identity are also historical accomplishments.

To sum up: one needs to distinguish between the givenness of a characteristic and how this is taken or what is done with it, and this blurs the distinction between the ascriptive and the voluntary, which is originally so sharply drawn. This is not to say that individuals can always throw off a characteristic or change its significance by themselves. To do so may well require joint action over a period of time. One need look no further than the changes in the significance of being a woman brought about by the feminist movement, for an obvious case.

I might note in passing that Iris Young's discussion of this ascriptive vs. voluntary distinction in her recent book is not altogether clear on this point. She says, on the one hand, that you are constituted by your group as to who you are but that you may change your group identification if you choose.[22] However, because ascriptive group identity is not a matter of one's own intentions on her view, it is not clear how this can be compatible with changing it by choice. She seems to want to have it both ways, without showing how these can be compatible. Further, with respect to why such group differences should be relevant to politics, Young helpfully points to the experience of oppression, marginality, and so on. But there may also be positive contributions that make such group differences relevant.

This account of the significance of group differences comes closest to the second approach to the valuation of differences in the context of democratic politics, namely, the view that assessed diversity as a positive social good. We may now conceive of this as a nonessentialistic and voluntary social pluralism or multiculturalism. The proviso here would have to be that the representation and satisfaction of group differences be compatible with the priority of equal rights. The compensatory approach to group difference is also compatible with such a perspective. But I would argue that one needs to add to the group differences already discussed the range of group differences that emerge from participation in common activities. These may be characterized as groups identified by shared common interests. But they are not like the interest groups envisioned in the older pluralist democratic theory, in which the interests were aggregative rather than shared.

Finally, what does such a social pluralist account of group differences imply for the question of the representation of such differences in the democratic process? Obviously, being nonessentialist, such an approach cannot endorse any move to permanent special group representation. In addition, it would be critical of the idea that groups can be represented only by those who are members of them, as though all members shared some essential identity. Similarly, one cannot argue that *any* member of a group can equally well represent *all* members of a group. It would be odd indeed to think that Clarence Thomas could represent all African-Americans or that Margaret Thatcher could represent all women. Similarly, some men may sometimes do a better job of representing the interests of women than some women could, especially because there are some women (fortunately few) whose only feminist interest is themselves. Nonetheless, the shared experience of both oppression and achievement that characterizes the members of a group argues that, as a rule, they would be better representatives of the group than would nonmembers.

However, there is a further and complex issue that remains, and that is whether, in the context of democratic decision-making, there ought to be representation of differences in rough proportion to the numbers of the group in the population. Such a representation of disempowered groups could be endorsed even by liberal theory on the grounds that where this is lacking there is presumptive evidence of discrimination, for all things being equal, there should normally be a rough statistical correlation between numbers and representation. Beyond this, more positively, if women, for example, are the best representatives of their group because of shared experiences and understandings, then the political equality of women in the population would argue for their roughly proportional representation in the institutions of democratic self-governance. Moreover, the distinctiveness of the contribution of these representatives to the democratic process would be a benefit to the whole.

If we grant the desirability of such proportionality in the representation of group differences, how could it possibly be implemented? What mechanisms could plausibly effect such a change? The least problematic way from the point of view of structural changes in our current U.S. political forms would be to empower such disadvantaged groups socially and economically so that they would have equal access to the means of participation and election. As unlikely as this is at present, any other structural or procedural means may be even less likely and may be normatively unjustifiable (at least in the U.S. context). For example, one could mandate a quota of congressional representatives to be women, or African-Americans, or Chicanos, etc. But this would intrude on the electoral process, because voting could not be prescribed. However, more reasonably, it could be the aim of the political parties to nominate representatives of such groups judiciously in districts where they are likely to win elections.[23] This would mean that the nomination process itself would have to reflect the recognition of and participation by members of such groups. The Democratic Party institutionalized a representational requirement of this sort for delegates to their national convention some years ago. Other methods used to enhance the representation of differences are in common practice already. They include redistricting so as to empower groups by geographic location (especially where in the past such groups had been previously disempowered by discriminatory redistricting); and caucusing by elected representatives of such groups to focus their effectiveness on certain issues. But I would suggest that we should in principle be wary of any structures that violate fundamental principles of liberty and equality. Apart from such political means, the best hope for the representation of difference—both individual and group difference—within a democratic polity, is the expansion of opportunities for participation in a diversity of common activities, whether in the discourses of the public sphere or in the social, economic, and smaller-scale political institutions that constitute the rest of the public domain. In these contexts, difference can be directly expressed, recognized, and made effective.

Notes

1. Jürgen Habermas, "Justice and Solidarity," in *Hermeneutics and Critical Theory in Ethics and Politics*, ed. Michael Kelly (Cambridge, Mass.: MIT Press, 1990), 47.
2. Carol C. Gould, *Rethinking Democracy* (Cambridge: Cambridge University Press, 1988), 124–27; and "On the Conception of the Common Interest: Between Procedure and Substance," in Kelly, *Hermeneutics and Critical Theory in Ethics and Politics*, 264–267.
3. Habermas, "Further Reflections on the Public Sphere," in *Habermas and the Public Sphere*, ed. Craig C. Calhoun (Cambridge, Mass.: MIT Press, 1992), 444.
4. Gould, *Rethinking Democracy*, esp. chaps. 1, 4, and 9.
5. Habermas, *Communication and the Evolution of Society* (Boston: Beacon Press, 1979), 186.
6. Ibid.
7. Gould, *Rethinking Democracy*, chaps. 1 and 3; and "Hard Questions in Democratic Theory: When Justice and Democracy Conflict," *Working Papers*, no. 5, University Center for Human Values, Princeton University, March 1994.
8. Indeed, even if the domain of communicative participation is the validation of norms rather than particular decisions, legislative or otherwise, this too remains in the

limbo of an infinitely delayed counterfactual consensus, that is, of a process with a telos but no closure.

9. Joshua Cohen, "Deliberation and Democratic Legitimacy," in *The Good Polity*, ed. Alan Hamlin and Philip Pettit (New York: Blackwell, 1989), 18–27.

10. Ibid.

11. Thomas Christiano, "Freedom, Consensus, and Equality in Collective Decision Making," *Ethics* 101 (October 1990): 167.

12. Iris Marion Young, "Justice and Communicative Democracy," in *Radical Philosophy: Tradition, Counter-Tradition, Politics*, ed. Roger S. Gottlieb (Philadelphia: Temple University Press, 1993), 130.

13. Seyla Benhabib, *Situating the Self* (New York: Routledge, 1992), 106.

14. Ibid., 111–13.

15. Nancy Fraser, "Rethinking the Public Sphere," in Calhoun, *Habermas and the Public Sphere*, 128–32.

16. Cf. Anita L. Allen, "Women and Their Privacy: What Is at Stake?" in Carol Gould, ed., *Beyond Domination: New Perspectives on Women and Philosophy* (Totowa, N.J.: Rowman and Allanheld, 1984), 233–49.

17. Benhabib, *Situating the Self*, 111–12.

18. Gould, *Rethinking Democracy*, esp. chaps. 1, 4, and 5.

19. Cf. Carol Gould, "The Woman Question: Philosophy of Liberation and the Liberation of Philosophy," in *Women and Philosophy*, ed. Carol Gould and Marx Wartofsky (New York: G. P. Putnam's, 1976), 5–33.

20. Iris Marion Young, *Justice and the Politics of Difference* (Princeton: Princeton University Press, 1990), 44–45.

21. Ibid., 46.

22. Ibid., 42–48.

23. Cf. Anne Phillips, *Engendering Democracy* (University Park: Pennsylvania State University Press, 1991), chap. 3.

Ten

Democracy, Difference, and the Right of Privacy

JEAN L. COHEN

> A well-protected private autonomy helps secure
> the generation of public autonomy just as much
> as, conversely, the appropriate exercise of public
> autonomy helps secure the genesis of private
> autonomy.
>
> *Jürgen Habermas, "Paradigms of Law"*

> [The point is] . . . to affirm the moral judgment
> that women are entitled to be treated as an
> individuals rather than restricted because of their
> sex, but also the moral judgment that the group to
> which they belong may no longer be relegated
> to an inferior position.
>
> *Nadine Taub and Wendy Williams, "Will Equality
> Require More than Assimilation, Accommodation or
> Separation from the Existing Social Structure?"*

THE RELATIONSHIP between democracy and difference has become a central
concern to contemporary political theorists, and for good reason. The emergence of "identity politics" in the 1970s and early 1980s, analyzed under the
formula "new social movements," has begun to show its dark side. Although
always ambiguous, initially the focus on group identity and pride on the part
of women, gays, blacks, and various ethnic and linguistic groups could be
understood as a reaction to the limits of the politics of inclusion, which
seemed to offer formal legal equality (equal treatment) and full political membership only at the price of assimilation and the renunciation of particularity.
The development and assertion of new interpretations of group identity appeared to involve a sophisticated degree of self-reflection on the part of at least
some of the new collective actors regarding the social processes and power
relations involved in identity formation and in the articulation of social norms.
The aim seemed to be to secure an equal chance for all to participate in these
processes on equal terms. As such, "identity politics" retained a universalistic
thrust—it posed an egalitarian and democratic challenge to the pseudo-

neutrality of existing cultural models, institutionalized social norms, and acknowledged group identities.[1]

Today, however, many protagonists of identity politics seem to have thrown down the gauntlet to the politics of inclusion *tout court*, in both its liberal and democratic versions. Aided and abetted by theories that construe the very categories of universality, normativity, equality, publicity, impartiality, and basic rights as mere strategies of power, partisans of identity politics simply assert difference per se, as if that were sufficient to merit recognition and entitlements. Nowadays particularisms do not even bother to pretend to be egalitarian, impartial, tolerant, or solidary with others, or even fair. In its worst guise, this politics has turned into the very opposite of egalitarian and democratic politics—as the emergence of virulent forms of nationalism, ethnocentrism, and intolerant group particularism all over the world witness. One begins to wonder whether the critical theories that challenged the happy consciousness of Enlightenment universalism and unmasked the leveling and homogenizing thrust of concepts informing the liberal and democratic traditions, have played into the hands of the antidemocrats by depriving us of the language and conceptual resources indispensable for confronting the authoritarian assertions of difference so prevalent today.

In such a context, the revival of interest in normative democratic theory is a welcome development in my view, especially because many of the recent works on the topic have placed the concept of the public sphere and the idea of deliberative democracy at the center of their concerns.[2] Indeed, I remain convinced that the democratization of society is still first and foremost a question of the institutionalization and reinstitutionalization of public space. To this extent we remain in the shadow of Habermas's 1962 *Strukturwandel der Öffentlichkeit*. Nevertheless neither the liberal formula whose passing he documented nor his suggested replacements carry much conviction today. At issue is not only the impossibility of bringing to a single level of analysis a counterfactual normative theory (the discourse ethics) and the sociology of institutions, a problem Habermas repeatedly faced. A central additional concern is the normative and conceptual relation between a discursive model of public space conceptualized in terms of universalistic principles (openness, equality of access, participatory parity, etc.), on the one side, and the articulation, acknowledgment, and protection of particularity, or difference, on the other.

From this perspective, recent attempts by feminist theorists to rethink the normative conception of public space with an eye to representing and empowering "difference" are extremely important. Several have attempted to correct for what they take to be those dimensions of the Habermasian model of public space that allegedly exclude or disempower difference.[3] Nevertheless I believe that these attempts suffer from two interrelated difficulties: in some cases, despite intentions and disclaimers, the tendency is to offer a monistic conception of public space, and they all treat the corollary concept of publicity—namely, privacy—as a residual category. They are consequently unable to deliver a conception that is sufficiently protective of difference and plurality, *and* fully adequate to the complexity of contemporary civil societies.

Here I will focus on remedying the second of these deficiencies—that is, I shall try to provide a "redescription" of the concept of privacy, and of the right to privacy, that focuses on its role in the constitution, protection (and even indirectly, the representation) of difference. But let me begin by making a few brief remarks regarding the first problem. I hope it will be clear from what follows that I see *both* voice and privacy as crucial to any project for democratization that seeks to avoid exclusion, leveling, and homogenization.

Of course, the critical interest of feminists in the public sphere is not new. Rather, critiques of the public/private dichotomy are coeval with feminist theory. From its inception, feminist politics targeted the legal disabilities and discriminatory laws that excluded women from the public spheres of work and politics (and that disadvantaged them once they got there), while feminist theory challenged the cultural stereotypes about gender that justified these exclusions. Indeed, by now we should all be familiar with the charges: despite its obvious inadequacy to the institutional complexity of modern civil societies, the dichotomous conception of the social structure divided into public and private spheres (identified with male and female genders respectively) has played a key role in ideologies justifying both the exclusion of women from full membership in the political community and the denial of equality of opportunity to them in economic life. It has also helped to reinforce cultural stereotypes about gender, to perpetuate the ascription of status on this basis, to screen out so-called private issues from public discussion and debate, and to shield the asymmetrical power relations governing the gendered division of labor and other aspects of "intimate relationships" in the home from the demands of justice. As innumerable feminists have insisted, the public/private dichotomy has thereby served to reinforce and perpetuate social hierarchies and inequity between the sexes in all spheres of life.[4]

And yet it is precisely within the milieu of new identity-oriented movements, spearheaded by feminism, that the most radical rejection of the whole liberal and democratic strategy oriented to the *public* sphere, at least, has been criticized. It is not my task in this essay to try to refute directly the versions of feminism that reject the very distinction between the public and the private. Many feminists have already done a good job here.[5] More important, many have insisted upon the indispensability of the concept of public space for a democratic feminism. Indeed, as already indicated, several of the theorists I have in mind are engaged in the project of rethinking the category of the public to make it "woman- and difference-friendly." Thus while Seyla Benhabib opts for the Habermasian model over liberal and republican alternatives, she challenges what she takes to be Habermas's essentialistic distinction between issues that are public and issues that are private, and tries to reformulate the normative conception of discourse in ways that will not screen out need interpretations, or issues central to women.[6] Similarly, Nancy Fraser embraces the principles of publicity analyzed by Habermas yet rejects his alleged reliance on the liberal ideal of a unitary and weak civil public, advocating instead multiple and strong political publics that actually make decisions regarding policy and thus really empower participants.[7] Finally Iris Young seeks to correct the overly rationalistic bias and the homogenizing effects of the ideal of impartiality to which Habermas's discourse model of public space is allegedly wed, by bringing in and valorizing discursive styles supposedly characteristic of subaltern groups and classifications (greeting, rhetoric, and storytelling).[8]

One problem with all these approaches, however, is the lack of differentiation between the analytic levels of normative justification, the empirical practices of deliberation, and a politics capable of generating binding decisions.[9] For example, Iris Young's stimulating conception seeks to construct a vastly expanded model of the public, but the correctives she proffers to empirical practices of deliberation obviously neither amount to an adequate model of normative justification, nor can they supply the rules for a possible politics capable of generating binding decisions.[10] The result is a monistic conception that could not possibly operate anywhere. My point here is that no single type of public space could conceivably involve a) the continual open-ended discursive process of critical reflection on norms, procedures, and metaprinciples, while simultaneously b) making legally and politically binding decisions; c) serving as the arena for the agonistic formation and enactment of individual and social identities; and d) equalizing de facto substantive inequalities among members of the communication community. It is not enough to insist on the plurality of publics (Benhabib), without noticing the possible *and* desirable plurality of its types. We should not be asked to choose among liberal, agonistic, and discursive models of the public sphere (Benhabib) or between weak and strong publics (Fraser), but rather we should try to identify the appropriate place for each in a highly differentiated society. It is thus crucial to broach the question of the different types of publicity that are possible and desirable in different spheres of society. In other words, one must inquire into the different constraints constitutive of specific discursive rules in specific institutional domains. Finally, we should follow Habermas's lead and continue to counterpose a nonspecialized public sphere to the expert and specialized publics that operate (each in a different way according to different discursive rules) in the various institutions of society.[11] It is crucial to show that alongside the myriad publics of a differentiated society there is, as it were, a general civil public—and here I have in mind the disincorporated society-wide forms of public communication—which, though incapable of decisional power, is able to influence publics specialized in decision-making. The history of social

movements has shown that the influence of the open-ended processes of communication possible in a civil public of this amorphous type (itself in turn
influenced by the discourses of specific publics) can be far-reaching both for
collective learning and *indirectly* for the generation of policy.

However, I would also like to suggest that the difficulties encountered by
recent feminist theories of public space in accommodating difference and plurality flow from the ambition to force a full reconciliation between "democracy
and difference" on this level alone. I shall argue in what follows that the ability
to reconcile identity and difference, universality and particularity, will depend
not only on the proper safeguards for the multiplicity of different voices in
public space ("voice") but also very much on "bringing the private back in,"
even if on this level, too, both universal norms and the defense of particular
identities will inevitably reappear. At the very least, some of the fundamental
preconditions for building and defending different, unique identities will depend on maintaining the necessary political and legal protections of privacy.

To be sure, feminist theory has hardly ignored the private: rather, it has
been engaged in critical and genealogical investigations of the power strategies
subtending privacy discourse for some time. Feminist theorists have long
argued that the "personal is political," meaning that the apparently natural
private domain of intimacy (the family and sexuality) is legally constructed,
culturally defined, and the site of power relations.[12] For the most part, the
emphasis has been on the critical deconstruction of privacy rhetoric as part of
a discourse of domination that legitimizes women's oppression.

But what I am suggesting is that feminist theory take the next step, move
beyond the hermeneutics of suspicion, and attempt to redescribe the good
that privacy rights protect. Since public and private are correlative terms, it
seems obvious that reconstructions of the public from a feminist point of view
call for a reconceptualization of privacy. In this essay I thus attempt to formulate a preliminary (and purposely general) concept of the private that can serve
as the correlative of a differentiated notion of the public, and in the form of a
right to privacy, provide the protections for levels of difference that no combination of democratic publics can directly accommodate.

I will attempt to do this by looking through the prism of the debate in
American legal and political theory over the privacy justification for abortion
rights in the U.S. This controversy provides a useful context for rethinking the
relation between privacy and difference, because it reveals the importance of
privacy rights to women as well as the paradoxes that such rights entail. As is
well known, a woman's right to decide upon an abortion in the U.S. was
constitutionally protected as part of her fundamental right to privacy in the
1973 Supreme Court decision in *Roe v. Wade*.[13] Both abortion rights and the
idea of a constitutional right to privacy have been challenged ever since.

Elsewhere, I consider two recent types of criticisms of the privacy justification for reproductive rights, both of which target what are taken to be its

flawed conceptual and normative presuppositions, albeit from opposite points of view.[14] The first of these criticisms, articulated by feminist legal theorists, charges that privacy analysis reinforces an ideological, liberal model of the public/private dichotomy that has long been used to justify gender inequality and private male power within the patriarchal family, along with exclusionary and discriminatory treatment of women outside the domestic sphere. On this interpretation, privacy rights exclude, silence, and suppress difference.[15]

The second, articulated by communitarian critics of liberalism, argues that constitutionalized individual privacy rights undermine community values and solidarity. This is due to the atomistic and adversarial conception of the individual (the self) that allegedly underlies these rights.[16]

We seem to be facing what I shall call the "paradox of privacy rights." With respect to the first argument, the attempt to correct the flaws of domestic privacy with more privacy seems quixotic: how can private (male) power be undermined by according privacy rights to women? On the other hand, from the communitarian perspective, to accord decisional autonomy to women in family matters through the vehicle of privacy rights is to purchase individual choice at the price of community solidarity.[17] And there is yet a third dimension to the "paradox of privacy" pointed out by critics in both camps: while privacy rights purport to be the means for protecting individuals from state power, they also reinforce the disintegrative, leveling, individualizing tendencies in modern society and expose people to increased regulation by state agencies, thereby destroying both the solidarity of the family community and the autonomy of the individual.

It is my claim that these "paradoxes of privacy" are not unavoidable—they stem from the trap of ideology into which both critiques fall. In short, both approaches assume that what they take to be the liberal interpretation of privacy rights is definitive of such rights, and thus both tend to reject privacy discourse.[18] Their critiques are consequently rather one-sided: the first, because it considers only the subordination of juridical practice to the preservation of a system of domination; the second, because it confuses the symbolic with the ideological meaning of individuality attached to privacy rights. The first approach misses the normative and empowering dimensions of privacy rights because it is preoccupied with unmasking the functional role they can play in preserving inequality and in suppressing plurality. The second is distracted by the old atomistic and possessive individualist assumptions subtending many "liberal" justifications of privacy. Thus both fail to grasp the symbolic and real importance of (privacy) rights in securing decisional autonomy, inviolability of personality (including one's psychic space and "imaginary"), bodily integrity, and a degree of control over one's identity needs as socialized, solidary individuals.

The task before us is to break with functionalist and tired ideological conceptions of privacy without jettisoning the principles protected by privacy rights. In other words, it is time to distinguish between the concept of a right to privacy and the various conceptions of privacy that have gone and might go with it.[19] Precisely because the issues, relations, and arrangements once construed to be private, natural, and thus beyond justice have become matters of public debate and political struggle, precisely when boundaries are being redrawn, and when meanings have become destabilized, it is time to enter the fray and rethink privacy rights in ways that enhance rather than restrict plurality, difference, freedom, and equality. The old certainties are gone, as the heated debate over the very meaning of privacy has revealed. But once we reject one particular conception of privacy, we must face the question of how to articulate recognition for a different conception of personal privacy and why this is important. I see the debate over the meaning of such a right as part of an ongoing contestation over the vocabularies, idioms, and cultural codes available for interpreting needs, for pressing claims, for constituting identity, for asserting difference and for gaining recognition.[20]

I shall limit myself here to countering the objections raised by the communitarian critics of privacy analysis.[21] I shall do so by challenging their interpretation of what privacy justifications presuppose and by redescribing the good that privacy rights are meant to protect. Indeed, I shall argue that one of the most important examples of normative learning in the twentieth century is the recognition that personal privacy ought to be differentiated from private property, freedom of contract, "entity" privacy (attached to the patriarchal family as a unit), and protected in its own right.[22] Many of us intuitively acknowledge the importance of this development, despite the confusion and controversy over the meaning of privacy—a confusion that derives from the old association of privacy with property and the patriarchal family. For reasons that I cannot go into here, the notion of private property used to but can no longer serve as the symbolic center of the personal rights complex.[23] In part this has to do with the rise of the interventionist welfare state and the subsequent demotion of property from a sacred principle to an economic concept. It is thus no accident that over the course of the past thirty years, there have been efforts to reorganize this complex around the principle of personal privacy with the notion of decisional autonomy and inviolate personality at its core. As we shall see, it is this new thrust in privacy doctrine articulated fairly recently by the Court, that the communitarians challenge.

Among the dimensions of personal privacy clearly recognized by the Supreme Court today, the "right to be let alone" (freedom from official intrusion or surveillance) and "decisional privacy" (freedom from undue official regulation or control) in the "domain of intimacy" are central. Of the two, the first, especially as concerns the intimate details of one's personal life, is far less contested than the second. The right to be let alone involves informational privacy—control over access or attention by others and over the possession and spread of information about oneself. This principle, if not its applications, is widely accepted today. The debates are over the extent rather than the very idea of our right to informational privacy.

The controversy I wish to discuss revolves around the second prong of privacy doctrine, namely, privacy construed as involving decisional autonomy vis-à-vis the "zone of intimacy"—marriage, divorce, sexual relations, procreation, child rearing, abortion, and so on. This is the area where the battle rages and where the very principle, rather than the reach, of an individual right to privacy is being contested.

The "Pernicious Development of Privacy Doctrine"

Two influential communitarian critiques of the right to privacy, as it is applied to the zone of intimacy, are provided by Michael Sandel and Mary Ann Glendon.[24] Both argue against the new developments in privacy doctrine in this domain, because they allegedly rest on an unconvincing claim to neutrality vis-à-vis the question of the value of fetal life, and because they privilege individualistic over community values. Both reject the landmark case of *Roe v. Wade* on these grounds. Because of constraints of space, here I can only address the second consideration.[25]

Sandel and Glendon each note, with dismay, the development of privacy doctrine from a "traditional" concern to keep certain personal, intimate facts from public view, or informational privacy, to a contemporary right to engage in certain conduct without governmental restraint, in the name of individual choice.[26] But for both thinkers, the important change is not the application of the notion of privacy to the "zone of intimacy" but rather the shift *within* the intimate zone, from informational privacy to decisional autonomy, and from substantive justifications appealing to communal values and prized traditions or practices, to individualist justifications.

Typical of communitarians, Sandel and Glendon are enamored with "the family" and "family values"; thus they do not object to the reasoning in the landmark case of *Griswold v. Connecticut* where the Court for the first time explicitly recognized a constitutional right to privacy and found it to apply to the right of married couples to use contraceptives.[27] For as Glendon points out, the scope and precise content of the new constitutional right was unclear. Since it applied to married couples, the right to privacy could have been construed as some kind of family right.[28] Sandel argues that the Court justified the privacy right it proclaimed in *Griswold* on teleological rather than voluntarist grounds. The right to privacy was defended not for the sake of letting people lead their sexual lives as they choose but rather for the sake of affirming and protecting the social institution of marriage, and the human goods realized in it. *Griswold* in short protected the prized institution of marriage and the human goods realized in marriage (intimacy, harmony in living, bilateral loyalty, a sacred association) and affirmed a social practice and tradition valued by the community.[29] Moreover, it remained tied to the traditional notion of privacy as the interest in keeping intimate affairs from public view. The violation of privacy consisted in the intrusion required to enforce the law, not in the restriction on the freedom to use contraceptives. As such, privacy protected an entity—the family as a unit—against intrusion, and as such it fit the liberal paradigm distinguishing certain spheres of life as off-limits to state intervention.[30]

The shift within the intimate sphere to voluntarist and individualist arguments began, according to Glendon and Sandel, with the case *Eisenstadt v. Baird* (1972), which involved a law restricting the distribution of contraceptives to unmarried persons.[31] Here the Court struck down the law through the explicit innovation that "redescribed the bearers of privacy rights from persons qua participants in the social institution of marriage to persons qua individuals, *independent of their roles or attachments*."[32] Moreover, privacy was conceived no longer as freedom from surveillance or disclosure of intimate affairs but rather as protecting the freedom to engage in certain activities without governmental restriction. Sandel cites the now famous statement in *Eisenstadt* as proof of these invidious innovations: "If the right of privacy means anything, it is the right of the *individual*, married or single, to be free from unwarranted governmental intrusion into matters so fundamentally affecting a person as the decision whether to bear or beget a child."[33]

As is well known, one year later this reasoning was applied in *Roe* where the privacy right was extended to "encompass a woman's decision whether or not to terminate her pregnancy."[34] Moreover, the language of decisional autonomy was made quite explicit in the 1977 majority opinion in *Carey v. Population Services International*, where Justice Brennan argued that the constitutional protection of individual autonomy in matters of childbearing is not dependent on the element in *Griswold* that forbade the use of contraceptives because it would bring police into marital bedrooms. Rather, Justice Brennan maintained that the autonomy rights of individuals were really at the core of what even Griswold protected.[35] Indeed, Brennan maintained that the teaching of *Griswold*, *Eisenstadt*, and *Roe* is that the Constitution protects individual decisions in matters of childbearing from unjustified intrusion by the state. Later decisions upholding abortion rights also used the language of decisional autonomy to describe the privacy interest at stake. And in his important dissent in *Bowers*, Justice Blackmun summarized what is at issue in the Court's previous privacy decisions: "We protect those rights not because they contribute . . . to the general public welfare, but because they form so central a part of an individual's life. The concept of privacy embodies the moral fact that a person belongs to himself and not others nor to society as a whole. . . . We protect the decision whether to have a child because parenthood alters so dramatically an individual's self-definition."[36] The Court thus clearly construed the new privacy as securing decisional autonomy to individuals over certain intensely personal concerns.

Now it is time to discover just what is so objectionable about this development. Here I can take up only one set of criticisms, to wit, the objection to the conception of the self allegedly underlying the very idea that privacy rights secure decisional autonomy to the individual with respect to personal matters.

Privacy as Autonomy: The Isolated, Disembedded Self?

The communitarian argument leveled against the principle of an individual right to personal privacy protecting decisional autonomy, is that such a right presupposes an atomistic (Glendon) or voluntarist (Sandel) concept of the individual and a philosophical anthropology of the self that is both incoherent and incompatible with moral responsibility. Glendon and Sandel each make this charge, albeit with differing degrees of sophistication. Glendon argues that the Court's rulings protecting decisional autonomy embody a view of society as a collection of separate autonomous self-sufficient individuals.[37] This "flaw" in privacy doctrine is, according to Glendon, distinctively and deplorably American.[38] In short, she construes the right to privacy in American Constitutional Law simply as the *right to be let alone*, which in turn presupposes a conception of the individual as autarchic, isolated, sovereign. It is the atomism of the concept of the individual presupposed by the new privacy doctrine that she dislikes.

Sandel's critique of the principle of privacy as autonomy challenges the voluntarist conception of individual agency that it allegedly presupposes. Recall his famous argument against Rawls, contending that the liberal conception of justice which privileges the idea of equal rights over substantive conceptions of the good rests upon an anthropological concept of the self which is not only isolated, atomistic, and autonomous but also radically unsituated.[39] The essentially unencumbered self is "a subject of possession individuated in advance and given prior to its ends."[40] This self adopts a distanced attitude toward all possible life goals and voluntaristically chooses its own conception of the good as if this were one among many dispensable preferences. Accordingly, the autonomous unencumbered self is construed as external to its own identity. It has no constitutive attachments, but merely a set of preferences from which it can pick and choose.

It is this self that is allegedly presupposed by the new privacy doctrine. Thus in its privacy cases, it is the Court's individualism that Sandel abhors, for the Court seems to conceive intimate relationships as entirely the product of personal choice, instead of as constitutive of the persons who participate in them. In short, the new privacy rights undermine both community (in this case, family) and concrete identity because they rest on a voluntarist, disem-

bedded conception of the self that is in turn subsumed under abstract universalist principles (rights) that deny and even undermine the particular identities of situated individuals.

Against this conception of the self, Sandel insists that everyone is radically
situated—their identities, self-understandings, and values are shaped through
community-mediated communicative processes of socialization. Thus on
theoretical grounds, the liberal conception of the self as a solipsistic presocie-
tal being presupposed by the new privacy rights is impossible. Moreover, our
moral experience belies voluntarism, for in order to have moral intuitions we
must view ourselves as particular persons situated within this family, this
community, this nation or people, as bearers of this history and this particular
identity. We are not separate from, but tied to and defined by our aims and
attachments, and these flow from our embeddedness in a specific context and
community that is constitutive of who we are and to which we owe duties of
loyalty. We also owe particular duties of responsibility to the concrete specific
people with whom we have special relationships. If we assume that subjects
are socialized through communication we must see them as members of
communities, sharing community values and traditions and having concrete
identities and relationships. Individuals do not create their moral vocabulary
ex nihilo, it is inherited from the traditional understandings into which they
are socialized and which in turn nourishes their capacity to be moral agents
as well as their self-understandings, providing the content of their particular
identities. Sandel thus sees us as particular albeit self-interpreting beings, able
to reflect on our history and to revise to some extent our identities but situated nonetheless.

Now if he and Glendon were correct about the conception of the self that
they impute to the new privacy doctrine, they would have a strong case. But
they are not correct. There is no obvious connection between either the
atomist or the voluntarist conception of the self articulated above and the
general notion of the rights-bearing individual. Nor does the new privacy doctrine entail the particular version of liberalism targeted by this critique. In
short, there is no *conceptual* connection between privacy rights that secure
personal decisional autonomy in certain domains and the ideological version
of the self just described.[41] If it has been so interpreted in the past, then it is
time to change the interpretation, not to jettison the principle of individual
privacy rights.[42]

The argument of both Glendon and Sandel is based on a category error:
abstract concepts such as legal personality, fundamental individual rights,
privacy, and decisional autonomy are not equivalent to an ontological description of the self or a particular concept of agency.[43] The principle that individual privacy rights protect decisional autonomy (choice) regarding certain
personal or intimate concerns can go quite well with a recognition of the
intersubjective character of processes of personal identity formation, and an

awareness of the historical, contextual sources of our values. Indeed, decisional autonomy could be said to presuppose the communicatively mediated
processes of moral and ethical development that make practical reflection
and reasoning possible. None of these insights, however, obviate the need
for privacy as decisional autonomy when it comes to certain choices for the
socialized, embedded, interdependent, communicative individual who views
her identity needs as constitutive of who she is. Only if decisional autonomy
is respected in every person, however situated, only if their capacity for moral
deliberation and justification, on the one side, and for ethical-existential self-
reflection and self-interpretation (involving the possibility of partial revision
of their identities and conceptions of the good on the basis of new insights) on
the other, are protected against coercion by the state or the majority of the
"community," can the individual function as a moral agent at all. These values
may come from the "community," but our attitude toward them is not thereby predetermined.

   To be sure, there have been rather controversial attempts to justify the personal rights complex recently secured by the new privacy doctrine that appeal
to a comprehensive conception of the autonomous individual. But one could
accept the critique of the Kantian or Millian concept of autonomy without
assuming that privacy rights entail this sort of justification or, for that matter,
any comprehensive conception of the person or any overarching substantive
moral worldview.[44] One could, in other words, argue that the principle of
privacy rights rests on the *abandonment* of "the cult of wholeness" presupposed
by general philosophies of man. Indeed, it rests on and secures (along with
other sets of rights) the differentiation between our status as *legal persons* and
our functioning as concrete unique individuals involved in specific relationships and particular communities where we may indeed be quite engaged with
others and deeply involved in the pursuit of substantial ideals of the good.[45]
Sandel's critique, in short, mistakenly conflates the legal with the natural person.[46] Legal personhood of course attaches to individuals, but it presupposes
no particular conception of the natural individual or of the self.

   In sum, personal privacy rights are meant to ensure domains of decisional
autonomy for every individual, not an atomist or voluntarist conception of
the individual. They protect one's decisional autonomy vis-à-vis certain crucially personal concerns,[47] they do not dictate the kinds of reasons one gives
for moral or ethical decisions or the reflective processes informing the decision. Thus on the privacy justification for reproductive choice, a woman may
decide for or against abortion on the basis of her community's values or her
religious worldview, or after discussion with "significant others"—her relation
to tradition, community, or loved ones is not in question here. Her right to
decide does not dictate the basis of her decision. Decisional privacy rights
designate the individual as the locus of decision-making when certain kinds
of moral or ethical dilemmas or existential concerns are involved—they do

not dictate to whom one must justify one's ethical choices or the kinds of reasons one must give. As Hannah Arendt argued long ago, such rights ascribe a *legal persona* to individuals that serves as a protective shield for their concrete, unique identities, particular motives, and personal choices, but do not prescribe these. Rather, they provide the formal enabling conditions for her to pursue her conception of the good without unjust interference by the state or by others.

Thus when the language of autonomy or choice appears in Court decisions, there is no reason to impute to the Court a voluntarist ideal of the person.[48] Ascribing decisional autonomy to individuals over certain issues does not commit the concept of privacy rights to a conception of the disembedded individual—it simply militates against state paternalism whether in the guise of "community norms" or "majority will."

Privacy and Identity: The Right to Inviolate Personality

Even though this interpretation of the decisional autonomy can be defended against the preceding criticisms, it is not sufficient to account for the issue of identity raised by the communitarian intervention. According to Sandel, we must proceed in our moral and legal reasoning on the assumption that we are dealing with concrete selves, not abstract persons, with individuals defined in and through their ends, for whom attachments and beliefs are constitutive of who they are, and whose goals are essential to their good and indispensable to their identity. The self-realization of the individual so understood is indeed tied to a social precondition—shared values and membership in solidary communities in which norms and traditions are transmitted, and mutual recognition of concrete identities, granted.

Thus when Sandel and Glendon speak of the community's conception of the good, and of the "right" of the community to institutionalize its values (community self-realization), they have apparently shifted terrain from issues of autonomy/justice to concern with identity/the good.[49] But they are wrong to restrict the issue of the good to the integrity of community values or common identity, as if there were, in highly differentiated and pluralist, and multicultural, civil societies, a single overarching conception of the good, or a single substantive collective identity upon which we all agree.[50] This sort of philosophical realism vis-à-vis common identity is misleading, to say the least.

It also seems as if these theorists assume that the individual and the common good, individual and group identities, completely overlap. Since they patently do not, then the need to protect the integrity of those dimensions of individual identities and conceptions of the good that are *different* from majoritarian interpretations of collective identity, or of the common good on any level, is a crucial one.

If certain versions of liberal theory have operated with a controversial notion of autonomy, the communitarians suffer from the opposite difficulty. They have not only tended to abandon the principle of autonomy altogether, they have also suppressed the problem posed by the *difference* and potential conflict between individual and group identity. Group identity is of course part of the identity of the members of the group. But in modern pluralist, differentiated, civil societies, individuals belong to many different groups, play a variety of social roles, and have "communal" identifications that are operative on different levels of the social structure. The sources and inputs into individual identity are multiple and heterogeneous. Indeed, the fact that one is situated within a plurality of communities—that one must act out a number of often conflicting roles—ought to lead back to the acknowledgment of the centrality of individual agency and choice in the shaping of a life.[51] The personal dynamics of shifting involvements among separate spheres, roles, commitments required by life in a highly differentiated modern society is what creates the need and the possibility for each individual to develop a strong sense of self along with the ability to form, self-reflectively affirm, and express *her unique identity* in an open multiplicity of contexts.

Although people do not invent the traditions, patterns, and norms into which they are at first socialized, as they become individualized, they do invent and reinvent (or more fashionably, perform) the unity of their lives and their unique identities (of course in interactive, communicative processes). They also contribute to reinterpreting and reinventing meanings, norms, traditions, and narratives. Both constituted and constituting, the identity of the concrete individual is not just a set of preferences among which we can pick and choose like clothes. But nor is it simply the product of communal values, social embeddedness, shared traditions, or a set of social roles. Indeed, all these are open to conflicting interpretations on the part of individuals and subgroups within a particular society. Precisely because it is the individual's task to develop and express their self-conceptions out of (and within) the multiplicity of memberships and affiliations, roles and structures they are involved in, precisely because they require recognition for their concrete personalities, their opportunity for self-development, and experimental self-presentation require protection. Such protection affords to the individual *a sense of control* over her self-definitions, over the self-creative synthesis that only she can fashion out of her various locations and background, in part, through communicative interaction with others.[52] It is my thesis that in highly differentiated societies, the new privacy rights—precisely because they include both informational and decisional-autonomy aspects—play an important role in protecting the capacities of individuals to form, maintain, and present to others a coherent and distinct self-conception. It is also my claim that *by narrowing down privacy rights to the right to be let alone, by assuming that deci-*

sional autonomy has to entail an arbitrary relation between the individual and her ends, by saddling the new privacy with an abstract conception of the individual that allegedly ignores the real individuality of members of concrete communities, the communitarian critics are deprived of an important source of protection for the integrity of individual as well as group identities which may differ from that which the state at any time seeks to promote.

In short, I contend that we can take up the concern for the situated dimensions of identity and argue that the new privacy rights protect both agency *and* identity, both self-determination *and* self-realization, without prescribing a particular concept of the self on either level. What, if not a right to personal privacy (securing control over access and decision-making to the individual), protects the variety of identities of individuals and groups living in modern civil societies from leveling in the name of some vague idea of community values or the majority's conception of the common good? To be sure, provisions for the participation of every group on equal terms in the public spaces of civil and political society, such that no perspective is excluded, is an important way to empower people (through "voice") to assert, protect, and further develop their different individual and collective identities in public. Voice and participation in democratic public spaces certainly can help protect difference. But individual personal privacy rights are nonetheless indispensable. Personal privacy rights protect the constitutive minimal preconditions for having an identity of one's own. Moreover, they ensure respect and protection for *individual difference*—for individual identities that seem to deviate from the "norm" embraced by society at large (in law) or by one's particular subgroup.[53]

Thus more is involved here than the right to be let alone. I am referring to the protection of concrete, fragile identities and self-formative processes that are, indeed, constitutive of who we are *and* who we wish to be. I want to argue that when properly understood, privacy rights guaranteeing decisional autonomy in certain personal matters protect these as well as the chance for each individual to develop, revise, and pursue her own conception of the good, that is, her identity needs. Let me formulate the standard that underlies this aspect of privacy as *the right not to have an identity imposed upon one by the state or third parties that one cannot freely affirm and embrace*. Indeed, even if one's personal identity needs conflict with the majority's interpretation of community values, personal privacy rights protect them unless, and only unless, they violate universal moral principles. This is why personal privacy rights (together, of course, with communicative rights) secure the right to be different.

Personal privacy rights do not prescribe what identities should be like; rather, they secure to every individual the preconditions for developing intact identities that they can embrace as their own.[54] On the one hand, by securing everyone's juridical personhood and decisional autonomy *equally*, privacy rights protect the claim of every concrete individual, no matter how different or odd, to be treated as a peer by members of the community.[55] On the other hand, privacy rights shield the personal dimensions of one's life from undue scrutiny or interference. As such they protect the processes of self development and self-realization that go into identity formation. The principle that articulates this idea in American privacy doctrine, is the principle of *inviolate personality*.[56]

Of course, the crucial question of which personal concerns should be covered by privacy rights remains to be answered. Here we cannot avoid the issue of where to draw the boundary line between public and private. As we have seen, feminists have criticized traditional modes of drawing the boundary. Our success in bringing a wide range of previously excluded "personal" issues into the public view and debate, including abortion itself, is certainly to be seen as a democratization of public space. Indeed, the discursive conception of public space embraced by democratic feminists presupposes that the agenda is open, and that there is no way to predefine the nature of issues that can be publicly discussed as being in essence, either public or private. It is *within* a generalized public discourse that the determination of what should fall under the protective cover of privacy rights and what should not is ultimately to be made. Moreover the boundary line is permanently open to contestation, and of course it shifts over time. Nevertheless, the boundary line must be drawn somewhere. Indeed, I have argued elsewhere that while processes of discursive will-formation determine the boundary between the private and the public, they cannot entirely abolish the private.[57] At the time I was concerned with articulating what a normatively defensible model of discursive public space presupposed. Now I am concerned with a normative conception of privacy. Let me turn to this directly and then return to the issue of what should fall under the protective shield of privacy rights in the next section of this paper.

Here I want to indicate what it means to enjoy a privacy right to decisional autonomy regarding certain personal concerns before identifying these concerns. In short, it means that one cannot be obliged either to reveal one's personal motives for one's choices or to accept as one's own the group's reasons or evaluations. Neither the source nor the particular content of the individual's motives for action can be regulated by the state in this domain. In other words, a right to personal privacy involves precisely the liberation from the obligation to justify one's actions in a discursive process by giving reasons that everyone together could accept as their own. To put it another way, privacy as decisional autonomy frees one from the pressure to adopt as one's own reasons the reasons that everyone accepts. Such a telos toward consensus holds for moral discourse, strictly speaking, and might be an ideal for some political decisions backed up by state sanctions, but it is not required for existential or ethical decisions covered by personal privacy rights. To put this another way, a privacy right entitles one to choose with whom one will attempt to justify one's existential decisions, with whom one will communicatively rethink conceptions of the good, and indeed, whether one will discuss certain matters with anyone at all. For with respect to personal decisions shielded by the protective cover of decisional and informational privacy, it does not matter whether the reasons decisive for me could also be accepted by everyone else.[58] This means that the state may not require me to reveal my reasons for acting in the domain in which I have the right to act on my own reasons. Thus the decisional autonomy of the legal subject in the domain protected by personal privacy rights involves informational privacy as well. This means that one has the liberty to withdraw certain concerns, motives, and aspects of the self from the public scrutiny and control.[59] But it also means that one has the liberty to embrace and present (perform) self-identifications of one's choosing in different contexts and to different people as one wishes.

Thus as Glendon has noted, privacy rights do indeed mark off a protected sphere surrounding the individual, constituting an invisible shield around the person.[60] But this is not an institutional sphere—individuals carry their protective shield, their legal persona, with them wherever they are—within and in withdrawal from interaction. They are not thereby burdened with an asocial conception of individuality as she seems to believe. Instead, privacy rights shielding personality provide a boundary that protects the integrity and inviolability of *socialized* interacting individuals. It is ultimately in a political process of deliberation and decision that the question of what content comes under the rubric of privacy is answered. But once the boundary line is drawn, privacy rights place discretionary control over the boundary (access to the self) in the hands of the individual.

It is by now a commonplace that although the practices and rituals of privacy vary across cultures, *every* society acknowledges the normative importance of privacy.[61] Every society establishes what Robert Post has recently called rules of civility, which safeguard respect for individual personal privacy and are in a sense constitutive of both individuals and community.[62] Echoing Erving Goffman, Post argues that the integrity of individual personality is dependent in part upon the observance of social rules of deference and demeanor that bind the actor and recipient together. In following these "rules of civility," individuals establish and affirm ritual and sacred aspects of their own and the other's identities while confirming the social order.[63] The violation of these rules indicates a lack of recognition for personal dignity and can damage a person by discrediting her identity and injuring her personality, thereby disconfirming her sense of self. Thus the reciprocal recognition of privacy is the condition of the possibility of successful social interaction based on mutual recognition of the integrity of the participants.

Indeed, the normative nature of privacy lies precisely in the protection of what Erving Goffman has called the "territories of the self"—a preserve to which an individual can claim "entitlement to possess, control, use, dispose of."[64] Defined by normative and social factors, territories are a vehicle for the exchange of meaning: they serve as a kind of language through which persons communicate with one another.[65] But they are also central to the subjective sense that the individual has concerning her selfhood. What counts is not whether a preserve is exclusively maintained or shared, or given up entirely,

> but rather the role that the individual is allowed in determining what happens to his claim. An apparently self-determined, active deciding as to how one's preserves will be used allows these preserves to provide the bases of a ritual idiom. Thus, on the issue of will and self-determination turns the whole possibility of using territories of the self in a dual way, with comings-into-touch avoided as a means of *maintaining respect* and engaged in as a *means of establishing regard*. . . . It is no wonder that felt self-determination is crucial to one's sense of what it means to be a full-fledged person.[66]

On this normative conception of privacy it is clearly the *sense of control* over one's identity, over access to oneself, over which aspects of oneself one will present at which time and to whom, along with the ability to press or to waive territorial claims, that is crucial and *empowering*—indeed, it is the sine qua non for understanding oneself to be an independent person, an individual worthy of respect and capable of establishing regard. In our society, the new privacy doctrine thus secures more than the abstract principle of respect for persons as choosers, more than secrecy and solitude: privacy rights conferring decisional autonomy over certain personal matters secure to the individual a sense of control over her self-definitions and over the decision regarding which aspects of herself she will bring into play at which times and with whom. Privacy rights thus protect and even help constitute a structure of mutual recognition and the social ritual by means of which one's identity is acknowledged and one's selfhood guaranteed.

"Privacy is an essential part of the complex social practice by means of which the social group recognizes and communicates to the individual—that his existence is his own . . . this is a precondition of personhood. . . . And this in turn presupposes that he believes that the concrete reality which he is . . . belongs to him in a moral sense."[67]

The language of possession here should not mislead us—what is meant is that by virtue of privacy, one is able to maintain a sense of selfhood, of agency and personal identity, not that these are a form of alienable property.[68] While a right to privacy that protects *inviolate personality* thus is universalistic, in that it establishes every individual as a legal person meriting equal concern and respect, what it protects is our particularity—our concrete and fragile identities.[69] The right to inviolate personality protected by privacy rights articulates intersubjectively recognized personal boundaries that are the sine qua non for the establishment and maintenance of autonomous identities.[70] It also protects the communicative infrastructure (the rules and rituals of civility) crucial to interaction.

Privacy Redescribed: Bringing the Body Back In

Let me return to the problem of what "personal concerns" should be covered by the new privacy. Here I can only offer my own intervention in what I see as a highly politicized debate on this matter. For of course, as indicated earlier, the answer would ultimately depend upon the cultural self-understanding and ethical views of societies and on the outcome of political contestation over cultural norms, codes, and social relations that constitute the practices, domains, and understandings of privacy at any given time.

Here I shall briefly address this issue by drawing out the implications of the normative meaning of privacy rights securing decisional autonomy to women in the area of procreation—an interpretation that does not proceed on the possessive individualist or voluntarist model of the person but rather builds upon the notion of situated, embodied, interactive individuality. Indeed, in order to understand *why* abortion rights among other procreative concerns are central to the concrete as well as the abstract dimension of ourselves, we must replace the possessive-individualist conception of the relation of self and body that has dominated our thinking for so long, with something better.

Because I have no space to make the argument in the philosophical depth it requires, I will simply summarize the results of recent work on the topic with the phrase "We are all embodied selves."[71] We do not happen to have bodies or choose to take them with us where we go, as with our purses; we are our bodies. By this I mean that our bodies, our symbolic interpretation of our bodies, our imaginary identification of our bodies and selves, and our sense of control over our bodies are central to our most basic sense of self, to our identity and our personal dignity. My body is not extrinsic to who I am. Of course, this is not a simple physical fact, for we can lose some body parts without losing our identity and the symbolic meaning we give to our bodies is communicatively mediated, varying across cultures and over time. Nevertheless, our selves, our identities, are intricately implicated in our bodies and in what we make of them—for our bodies are our mode of being in the world.

Indeed, Goffman views the body as one of the core territories of the self. He argues that a sense of control over one's own body is crucial to maintaining an intact sense of self and to the ability to interact with others.[72] Self-confidence is predicated upon the sense that one can dispose freely over one's own body: that one can coordinate its functions autonomously and regulate access to it.[73]

Without recognition by others of one's autonomous control over one's body, of one's bodily integrity, without at least this most basic acknowledgment of one's dignity, the individual's self-image is crippled (loss of self-confidence), as is the security she needs in order to interact successfully with others and to express her own needs and feelings. Thus the slogan "Our bodies, our selves," employed by women to defend their abortion rights, rings quite true—for what is at stake in the abortion controversy, is precisely a woman's selfhood and identity. This is why the liberty interest in this case is deemed to be so personal, so intimate, so fundamental, and meriting protection.

Now it is or should be obvious that to force a woman to endure an unwanted pregnancy is to force an identity upon her—the identity of pregnant woman and mother.[74] And clearly her bodily integrity in the physical and emotional sense are at stake in laws that criminalize abortion. But so is her inviolate personality. Indeed, these are intimately interrelated. This is not because women are identical to or own their wombs, or because a woman is or owns her fetus, but because the experience of pregnancy constitutes a fundamental change in her embodiment on the physical, emotional, symbolic, and imaginary levels, and thus in her identity and sense of self. Not only does an unwanted pregnancy impose a very powerful form of embodiment on the woman in which she very much fears losing control over her bodily functions and her sense of self, it also imposes a new and undesired identity and a new intimate relationship onto the woman,[75] requiring heavy investments of herself with implications that go well beyond the physical discomfort or mere life-style issues that antichoice thinkers believe sums up the problem of an unwanted pregnancy for women. To assert the importance of bodily integrity to privacy analysis is not to revive the paradigm of property or to claim an absolute right to do with one's body as one pleases.[76] Rather, it is to argue that bodily integrity is central to an individual's identity and should be protected by privacy rights as fundamental, to be overruled only if a truly compelling state interest is at stake. In this respect I agree with Kendall Thomas's argument that the emphasis of privacy analysis on protected places, intimate associations, and autonomous choice is insufficient, for it fails to recognize "that 'privacy' is always *body-mediated*."[77] Thus when women claim the "right to control our own bodies" they are claiming the right to define themselves.[78]

Nevertheless, the idea of bodily integrity, I would argue, gets at one crucial dimension of our situated identity, but not all dimensions of it. We are also situated individuals in the sense highlighted by communitarians: we develop self-definitions on the basis of culturally available resources in our life-world, we draw on our location in a specific set of institutions, relationships, and contexts, we make use (often creatively) of discourses that prestructure in part what can be said and thought, and out of all this, we add imaginary significations unique to ourselves and fashion our own creative contribution to our

self-formative processes—our identity. Our relation to our body, our embodiment, is the crucial substratum of our identity, but not the whole of it. Once
we recognize that identity formation takes place throughout our lives, we can
see that the symbolic meaning we give to our bodies and our selves has many
sources and presuppositions. Respect for an individual's bodily integrity involves, as do the other components of privacy, recognition *within* interaction
of the individual's own judgment, in regulating access and information, and in
decisions involving her basic identity needs. Although privacy in the sense of
concealment is also a component of bodily integrity, it is not the whole of it.
Like the other dimensions of privacy, we need bodily integrity within as well
as apart from interaction with others.

   Thus procreative issues are fundamental, and not only because, as Ronald
Dworkin has argued, the "moral" issues on which such decisions hinge are
quasi-religious, touching on the ultimate point and value of human life.[79]
Reproductive freedom is fundamental also because what is at stake is a
woman's ability to have control over her identity: her embodiment, her self-
formative processes, her life projects, and her self-understanding are all at
stake, or would be if she were denied reproductive freedom. All individuals
need to have some sense of control over their bodies, over their self-definitions, over the self-creative synthesis that only the individual can make out of
her various locations, and background and future projects. Inviolability of
personality, and the sense of control over the territories of the self including
the body, remain indispensable for any conception of freedom. In the abortion
issue in particular and in reproductive issues in general, the abstract and situated dimensions of a woman's inviolability are involved. Moral autonomy,
psychic integrity, and the integrity of individual processes of identity-forma-
tion, to which our bodies are central—thus bodily integrity—are the core of
what a right to personal privacy does or should protect.

   One's inviolate personality, bodily integrity, psychic processes of identification, and decisional autonomy over the "territories of the self" deserve protection no matter where one is. The concept of a general, fundamental, constitutionally protected right to privacy covers all these. Understood in this way,
privacy could and should replace property as the symbolic principle around
which the key complex of personal civil rights is articulated.[80] To cast the right
to abortion as a privacy right is to acknowledge women's "difference" while
leaving it up to each individual woman how to define this difference.[81] Although women as women acquire "special protection" for their unique capacities (abortion rights are women's rights), their "difference" is not thereby reified; rather, it is simultaneously acknowledged and left to them to construct.
Once we realize that privacy rights protect the abstract, situated, and embodied dimensions of inviolate personality, then it is certainly worth the effort to
fight for these rights *and* for the inclusion of a woman's decision whether or
not to procreate under the cover of such a right.

Notes

1. See Jean L. Cohen and Andrew Arato, *Civil Society and Political Theory* (Cambridge, Mass.: MIT Press, 1992), 492–563.

2. See the essays in Craig Calhoun, ed., *Habermas and the Public Sphere* (Cambridge, Mass.: MIT Press, 1992), along with John Dryzek, *Discursive Democracy* (Cambridge: Cambridge University Press, 1990), James Fishkin, *Deliberative Democracy* (New Haven: Yale University Press, 1991), Thomas Spragens, *Reason and Democracy* (Durham, N.C.: Duke University Press, 1991), and Anne Phillips, *Engendering Democracy* (University Park: Pennsylvania State University Press, 1991).

3. I have in mind recent work of Seyla Benhabib, *Situating the Self* (New York: Routledge, 1992), chaps. 3, 5, and 6; Nancy Fraser, "Rethinking the Public Sphere: A Contribution to the Critique of Actually Existing Democracy," in Calhoun, *Habermas and the Public Sphere*, and Iris Marion Young, *Justice and the Politics of Difference* (Princeton: Princeton University Press, 1990), especially chaps. 4 and 6.

4. For a classic statement of these problems see Carole Pateman, "Feminist Critiques of the Public/Private Dichotomy," in S. I. Benn and G. F. Gaus, *Public and Private in Social Life* (Kent: Croom Helm, 1983), 281–303.

5. For a recent summary see Anne Phillips, *Engendering Democracy*, 92–119.

6. Benhabib, *Situating the Self*, 111.

7. Fraser, "Rethinking the Public Sphere," 113, 115. Fraser, however errs in ascribing to Habermas a unitary conception of the public. Any cursory reading of *The Structural Transformation of the Public Sphere* would show that he was perfectly aware of the existence of multiple publics and of different types of publics, not to mention the gendered character of various types of public space. See 27–56, 141–80.

8. Young, *Justice and the Politics of Difference*, 117–19. See also Young's essay in this volume.

9. Benhabib and Young reason from discourse ethics as if one can move from this level of analysis directly to the institutional level. Fraser reasons from Habermas's institutional analysis and, to her credit, sees the distinction between weak and strong publics. However, she makes no effort to explain why some publics must be strong, or why others must be weak. She seems to think that the normative model of deliberative public space (suitably corrected) distilled by Habermas from his analysis of the generalized, society-wide emergent civil public could be applied to bodies engaged in actual policy-making for society as a whole. But this would collapse the distinction between the locus of legitimacy and the locus of "sovereignty" that is central to the understanding of modern public space.

10. Her discussion of greeting, rhetoric, and narrative in effect proffers these as useful techniques for ensuring discursive virtues—e.g., for ensuring that we listen to one another, and that we avoid silencing those who speak differently—but these techniques are not arguments. Nor does the correct claim that the goal of our discussion need not be the discovery of a general interest obviate the need for agreement, even if what we agree to is that we disagree and will accept the play of our differences with regard to certain concerns. Impartiality in *this* need not mean a homogenizing standpoint that is really the point of view of a privileged group parading around as if it were neutral. Rather, it means that only what all of us can agree to, having expressed our

concrete situated views or interests or needs, can stand as a legitimate norm including the agreement to disagree and tolerate, even solidarize with difference.

11. Above all one must avoid identifying the generalized public sphere of civil society *either* with the temporally, socially, and substantively constrained publics of parliaments and courts *or* with the particular discrete, nongeneralized associational publics and discursive counterpublics that proliferate on the terrain of civil society. I do not wish to be misunderstood here. I am not advancing the equivalent of the restraints on public discourse that Rawls's concept of "public reason" proposes (see John Rawls, "The Idea of Public Reason," in *Political Liberalism* [New York: Columbia University Press, 1993], 212–55). But there are constraints nonetheless that are operative in institutionalized political publics and in less institutionalized yet organized and structured associational publics and that delimit the kinds of reasons one can give for decisions. Such constraints are inoperative in the generalized public sphere of civil society first and foremost because it does not determine public policy or even make organizational decisions. For a recent informative discussion of the difference between Habermas and Rawls on this matter see Thomas McCarthy, "Kantian Constructivism and Reconstructivism: Rawls and Habermas in Dialogue," *Ethics* 105 (October 1994): 44–63.

12. The boundaries between public and private, personal and communal, have been shown to be conventional rather than natural, as are the cultural codes that assign specific roles and places to different genders. They are thus open to social and political contestation. Indeed feminists have quite convincingly argued that the rigid "traditional" construction of a whole chain of polarities usually associated with the private/public distinction is deeply gendered—I have in mind the oppositions of nature/culture, body/mind, emotion/reason, passion/interest, particular/universal, concrete/abstract, and home/the world of work or politics, and their association with the difference of female/male.

13. *Roe v. Wade*, 410 U.S. 113 (1973).

14. Jean L. Cohen, "Redescribing Privacy: Identity, Difference and the Abortion Controversy," *Columbia Journal of Gender and Law* 3, no. 1 (1992): 43–117.

15. Ibid., 48–65.

16. Ibid., 65–117.

17. There is a feminist version to this communitarian argument: namely, that such a move from "status" to "contract" apparently frees women to shape their own lives at the price of buying into a possessive individualist model of the self that denies the reality women know: the centrality of interdependence and interconnectedness, and of relationships and care in constituting the self.

18. They assume that the "liberal" conception of a right to privacy is tied to a philosophical theory of possessive individualism, to an atomistic or methodological individualism, and to naturalistic conceptions of what falls under the heading of "private" and what falls under "public." This conception is deployed to justify considering the family and gender relations in general as "beyond" justice. Thus whatever relations of power, inequality, and injustice exist in the "domestic sphere" are thereby shielded from public scrutiny or considered natural and hence not unjust.

19. In this essay I am arguing that the concept of a right to privacy need not be tied to conceptions of privacy that are modeled on the paradigm of property ownership, justified by a philosophical theory of possessive individualism, and that presuppose an

atomistic, disembedded, or expressivist conception of the self. I am offering a different conception of privacy, one that places inviolate personality, bodily integrity, and the right not to have an identity imposed upon one that one cannot affirm and embrace at its center. As will become clear, I do not link this conception of privacy to the property paradigm of rights or to the theory of possessive individualism. Nor do I derive this conception of privacy from a theory of natural or moral rights. The philosophical justification for a legal (constitutional) right to privacy is a complex issue that I shall address in a longer book on the subject. Let me simply say here that I do not believe it is convincing to proceed by positing substantive natural or moral rights of the individual and then deducing legal rights from these. For the distinction between concept and conception see John Rawls, *A Theory of Justice* (Cambridge, Mass.: Harvard University Press, 1971), 3–11.

20. Indeed, the meaning of all basic rights, whether it is freedom of speech, equality, liberty, or privacy that is at stake, shifts over time and is in principle indeterminate and open to dispute. By indeterminate, however, I do not mean that the content of rights is wholly arbitrary or simply "politically" determined by the judges or legislators. For a discussion see Jean L. Cohen, "Is There a Duty of Privacy? Law, Sexual Orientation and the Construction of Identity," unpublished typescript, 1995.

21. There is another important set of criticisms raised by communitarians, and by Michael Sandel in particular—namely, that the decision to construe the abortion issue as a matter of individual privacy is not a neutral decision on the part of the Court, but rather rests on a substantive moral position that the Court simply papered over with its privacy and neutrality rhetoric. In short, Sandel contests the claim to legal neutrality over the "value of life," raising important constitutional and doctrinal legal issues. For an in-depth discussion and rebuttal of his argument, I refer the reader to my "Redescribing Privacy," 69–92. For an extensive analysis of the objections put forth by feminist "equality" theorists to privacy analysis, see the same article, 48–65.

22. For a discussion of the distinction between entity and personal privacy, see Martha Fineman, "Intimacy Outside of the Natural Family: The Limits of Privacy," *Connecticut Law Review* 23 (1992): 955.

23. Hannah Arendt was one of the first to notice the connection between the decline of property from its sacrosanct status, the rise and deepening of intimacy, and the concern with rights of personal privacy and autonomy. On her view these developments are part of an attempt to protect against the dedifferentiation between public and private entailed in the rise of the social. Private property served as the age-old remedy against the tendency of public power to expand and trespass on private concerns. The Bill of Rights and the articulation of rights of liberty and privacy as civil rights are in her view a key attempt to erect a legal bulwark for personal autonomy against public power. On the other hand, the only remedy against another danger, that of corruption of public concerns by private power and private interests is, in her view, the vitality of the public realm itself. Moreover, without a vital public realm, civil rights would not be strong enough to protect against state penetration. Thus despite her ambivalence toward "liberal" foundations for rights, Arendt nonetheless saw quite clearly the importance of personal privacy rights, although it is true that she always privileged public over private happiness. See Hannah Arendt, *The Human Condition* (Chicago: University of Chicago Press, 1958), 58–72; and *On Revolution* (New York: Viking, 1963), 252–53. See also Jean L. Cohen, "Redescribing Privacy," 105–12, and Jennifer Nedelsky, "American Con-

stitutionalism and the Paradox of Private Property," in Jon Elster and Rune Slagstad, eds., *Constitutionalism and Democracy* (Cambridge: Cambridge University Press, 1988), 241–73.

24. Michael J. Sandel, "Moral Argument and Liberal Toleration: Abortion and Homosexuality," *California Law Review* 77, no. 3 (May 1989): 521–38. See also Michael J. Sandel, "Religious Liberty—Freedom of Conscience or Freedom of Choice?" *Utah Law Review*, no. 3 (1989): 597–615; and Michael J. Sandel, "The Procedural Republic and the Unencumbered Self," *Political Theory* 12, no.1 (February 1984): 81–96, Mary Ann Glendon, *Abortion and Divorce in Western Law* (Cambridge, Mass.: Harvard University Press, 1987), and *Rights Talk* (New York: Free Press/Macmillan, 1991).

25. For a discussion of the first objection see Jean L. Cohen, "Redescribing Privacy," 69–92.

26. Sandel, "Moral Argument and Liberal Toleration," 324, and Glendon, *Abortion and Divorce in Western Law*, 36–37.

27. *Griswold v. Connecticut*, 381 U.S. 479 (1965). Of course, serious constitutional critics of privacy doctrine object very strongly to the right to privacy discovered in *Griswold*. Their position is that since a right to privacy appears nowhere in the text of the Constitution, we have no such right. On these grounds, *Griswold* is as flawed as *Eisenstadt*. See Robert Bork, *The Tempting of America* (New York: Free Press, 1990), 112, 115–16; and John Hart Ely, "The Wages of Crying Wolf: A Comment on *Roe v. Wade*," *Yale Law Journal* 82 (1973), 920.

28. Glendon, *Abortion and Divorce in Western Law*, 36. See also Glendon, *Rights Talk*, 47–75.

29. Sandel, "Moral Argument," 527. According to Glendon, what *Griswold* protected could thus be construed as some sort of family right. Glendon, *Abortion and Divorce in Western Law*, 36. As such, privacy protected an entity—the family as a unit—against intrusion and seemed continuous with the traditional common law concept of family or "entity" privacy. See Fineman, "Intimacy Outside of the Natural Family," 966–72.

30. In this sense *Griswold* was continuous with the traditional common law concept of family privacy or "entity privacy" that had been used to preclude the principles of justice from being applied within the family unit. This did serve to keep issues off the public agenda and to reinforce patriarchal power and to deny women and children needed rights and protections in the "domestic" sphere. See Fineman, "Intimacy Outside the Natural Family," 966–72.

31. Cited in Glendon, *Abortion and Divorce in Western Law*, 36; and Sandel, "Moral Argument and Liberal Toleration," 527.

32. Sandel, "Moral Argument and Liberal Toleration," 527.

33. *Eisenstadt v. Baird*, 405 U.S. 438, 453 (1972). Cited in Sandel, "Moral Argument and Liberal Toleration," 528.

34. *Roe v. Wade*, 410 U.S. 113 (1973).

35. *Carey v. Population Services International*, 431 U.S. 678 (1977), cited in Gerald Gunther, *Constitutional Law*, 11th ed. (New York: Foundation Press, 1988), 515–16.

36. *Bowers v. Hardwick*, 478 U.S. 186 (1986). This case involved a challenge to the constitutionality of a Georgia statue criminalizing consensual sodomy. But the Court's majority decision rejected the claim that the right to personal privacy applied to homosexual activity. Justice Blackmun wrote a vigorous dissent to this decision.

37. Glendon, *Abortion and Divorce in Western Law*, 35; *Rights Talk*, 47–75.

38. Ibid., 50–51.

39. See Michael J. Sandel, *Liberalism and the Limits of Justice* (Cambridge: Cambridge University Press, 1982), 179–83.

40. Michael J. Sandel, ed., *Liberalism and Its Critics* (New York: New York University Press, 1984), 162.

41. Of course it is possible that one might be able to show that certain opinions by certain Justices do presuppose this conception of the self. But that does not mean that there is a conceptual relation between the new privacy doctrine and the voluntarist ideal of the self, or that the new privacy doctrine could not rest on very different assumptions. It is, in short, indeterminate in this regard.

42. See Claude Lefort, *The Political Forms of Modern Society*, ed. John B. Thompson (Cambridge, Mass.: MIT Press, 1986) for a critique of the "bourgeois" or "liberal" understanding of what rights entail and for providing a solution to the second paradox of privacy rights mentioned in the introduction of this essay:

"The paradox is this: the rights of man appear as those of individuals, individuals appear as so many little independent sovereigns, each reigning over his private world, like so many micro-entities separated off from the social whole. But this representation destroys another: that of a totality which transcends its parts. It discloses a transversal dimension of social relations, relations of which individuals are the terms but which confer on those individuals their identity, just as much as they are produced by them" (257).

Lefort's point is that what appears to be separation reinforced or created by individual rights, especially privacy rights, is actually a modality of one's relation to others, but one that escapes all corporate models of the social whole. As such, basic rights construct the conditions for interaction and communication (i.e., certain structures of mutual recognition)—they do not presuppose atomism.

43. See Jeremy Waldron, ed., *Nonsense upon Stilts* (New York: Methuen, 1987), 166–90, for a cogent reply to the claims that personal rights entail an abstract or atomist conception of the individual.

44. See Charles Larmore, *Patterns of Moral Complexity* (New York: Cambridge University Press, 1987), 40–91; and Larmore, "Political Liberalism," *Political Theory* 18, no.3 (August 1990): 339–60. There are other ways to justify this complex. Bruce Ackerman offers a hermeneutic justification of the development in privacy doctrine that avoids natural rights arguments entirely. See Bruce Ackerman, *We the People* (Cambridge, Mass.: Harvard University Press, 1991). Jürgen Habermas in *Between Facts and Norms*, trans. William Rehg (Cambridge, Mass.: MIT Press, 1996), on the other hand, attempts to provide a philosophical justification for the complex of rights protecting personal autonomy that relies entirely on communication-theoretical arguments of the theory of discourse ethics.

45. Although I agree with Larmore on this point I do not follow him in labeling all that is nonstate the "private realm." For a model of civil society that breaks with the public/private dichotomy as a paradigm for the social structure, see Jean L. Cohen and Andrew Arato, *Civil Society and Political Theory*.

46. Sandel seems to conflate three different levels of meaning of the word "autonomy": the moral, the legal, and the empirical (psychological or social). But privacy rights securing decisional autonomy or choice to individual legal subjects over "per-

sonal matters," however construed, do not describe the ideal properties of moral actors or of moral judgments. Nor do they refer to the empirical ability of concrete subjects to determine their lives without constraint (a matter of psychical maturity and social context). The legal meaning of constitutionally protected rights to privacy with respect to personal matters is that such rights *confer* decisional autonomy onto the individual thereby acknowledging their agency in the relevant domains. They do not *presuppose* autonomous individuals or any particular ideal of the self. Constituted as the rights holder, it is up to the individual to choose whether and how to exercise her legally recognized agency.

Just who is deemed capable of legal personhood in this sense is another matter. In the past, many groups, including workers, African-Americans, certain immigrants, women, and children have been denied legal personhood on the grounds that they are, by definition, incapable of autonomy. But the content of the conception of autonomy operative here was not dictated by the abstract conception of legal personhood. Rather, it was drawn from a cultural and ideological conception modeled on the bourgeois market actor, construed as the male breadwinner. The theory of possessive individualism associated with this model construed the "autonomous individual" as self-sufficient and independent of the will or (economic) support of others. This, of course, meant that women were denied recognition as full-fledged persons. But we can extend legal personhood, privacy, and decisional autonomy to natural persons, without, however buying into this ideology. We must realize that by conferring legal personhood in general, and privacy rights in particular, the law constitutes and protects a structure of recognition whereby one is acknowledged as a person whose integrity must be respected.

47. Needless to say, what counts as a crucial personal concern changes over time and can be the stakes of intense debate and conflict. Surely this is the case for abortion.

48. Sandel, "Moral Argument and Liberal Toleration," 524. To be sure, there is little agreement today over how to define a *philosophical* concept of autonomy. It is one thing to say that the individual has the right to make decisions, when intensely personal matters involving quasi-religious worldviews, bodily integrity, and constitutive identity needs are at stake. It is quite another thing to explicate what conditions render that choice autonomous, what capacities are entailed, and what autonomy actually means. Critiques from Marxist, communitarian, feminist, and postmodern points of view of the liberal concept autonomy, targeting the individualistic, metaphysical, and rationalist presuppositions with which it has been burdened, are myriad. More interesting now are the attempts to rethink the concept of autonomy in light of such criticisms. For recent efforts to develop a nonmetaphysical, intersubjective, and woman-friendly concept of autonomy, see Jennifer Nedelsky, "Reconceiving Autonomy: Sources, Thoughts and Possibilities," *Yale Journal of Law and Feminism* 1 (1989): 7–33; Maeve Cooke, "Habermas, Autonomy and the Identity of the Self," forthcoming in *Philosophy and Social Criticism*; and Kenneth Baynes, "Autonomy, Reason and Intersubjectivity," an unpublished typescript. For a critique of this enterprise see Christine Di Stefano, "Rethinking Autonomy," a paper prepared for delivery at the 1990 annual meeting of the American Political Science Association, August 30–September 2, 1990.

49. Needless to say, the abortion issue straddles this fault line.

50. For an amusing critique of what he calls the phantom community, see Stephen Holmes, "The Permanent Structure of Anti-Liberal Thought," in Nancy Rosenblum, ed., *Liberalism and the Moral Life* (Cambridge, Mass.: Harvard University Press, 1989).

51. To point out that individual identities are developed through communicative interaction and require recognition by others to survive intact in no way undermines this claim.

52. I do hope that I shall not be accused of realism and essentialism vis-à-vis individual identity, or of reinscribing a naive modernist conception of the unitary self and the fully autonomous rational subject because of these statements. I acknowledge the multiple and often conflicting sources of identity as well as the frequent contestation over the cultural codes and social practices that go into identity formation. But I also believe that the ability to develop and maintain a coherent sense of self is the sine qua non of successful individuation—a fragile process that needs protection. The sign that one is relatively successful in this project is one's ability to present one's sense of self through narratives that construct and reconstruct one's identity for affirmation and acknowledgment by others.

53. This is hardly a new idea for liberals. However, my point is that such protection need not entail atomistic, voluntarist, or possessive individualist conceptions of the self. Personal privacy rights can be severed from the property paradigm as well as from patriarchal assumptions regarding "entity" privacy.

54. The right to personal privacy protects the capacity of interdependent, socialized, individuals to evaluate, reflect upon, and rethink received ideas and identity needs, to affirm or redefine them, to think and act on reasons, and to debate or attempt to justify these to others, but it does not *impose* critical reflection, a detached stance, onto them.

55. See Hannah Arendt, *The Origins of Totalitarianism* (New York: Harcourt Brace Jovanovich, 1951), 267–302, for an excellent discussion of the protective role of the legal persona, and the principle of equality that is attached to it.

56. For the classic statement of this principle as the core of what privacy rights should protect, see Samuel D. Warren and Louis D. Brandeis, "The Right to Privacy," reprinted in F. Shoeman, ed., *Philosophical Dimensions of Privacy* (Cambridge: Cambridge University Press, 1984), 85. Most commentators have focused only on the famous "right to be let alone," also articulated by Brandeis and Warren in this article. But this has led to a one-sided interpretation of our current privacy doctrine as evidenced by Glendon's approach. The original version of the article appeared as Samuel D. Warren and Louis D. Brandeis, "The Right to Privacy," *Harvard Law Review* 4 (1890): 193ff. See also Cohen, "Redescribing Privacy," 98–112.

57. Jean Cohen, "Discourse Ethics and Civil Society," and David Rasmussen, ed., *Universalism vs. Communitarianism* (Cambridge, Mass.: MIT Press, 1990), 83–109.

58. I owe this formulation to Klaus Guenter's paper, "Communicative and Negative Liberty," delivered at the conference on Habermas's book *Faktizität und Geltung* at Cardozo Law School, New York City, in fall of 1992.

Thus regarding the abortion decision, this means that if my right to an early, safe abortion is covered by a general right to privacy, then the reasons for my decision remain my own and I do not have to submit these to boards of doctors, judges, or any other external authority for approval.

59. It would, however, be false to interpret this as implying that the individual's need interpretations are fixed and pregiven, that she does not engage in existential discourses in which her personal judgments and needs are articulated and possibly revised, or that she solipsistically opts out of any and every dialogic community when she makes personal decisions. My point is that it is up to her to choose with whom,

when, and what to discuss regarding personal concerns. While her own reasons can be clarified or altered in such a discussion, what counts is not that she take on the reasons of the community at large but that she arrive at personal reasons acceptable to herself for her projects, which one hopes can be acknowledged by particular significant others as appropriate for her. For, of course, no one can stand alone or affirm an identity by herself.

60. Glendon, *Rights Talk*, 40, 52.

61. See Barrington Moore, *Privacy*; and Robert R. Murphy, "Social Distance and the Veil," in Ferdinand Shoeman, ed., *Philosophical Dimensions of Privacy*, 34–55.

62. Robert Post, "The Social Foundations of Privacy: Community and Self in Common Law Tort," in *California Law Review* 77, no. 3 (May 1989): 963.

63. Ibid.

64. Erving Goffman, "Territories of the Self," in *Relations in Public* (New York: Harper, 1971), 28. On this see also Georg Simmel, *The Sociology of Georg Simmel*, 321, n. 66, where he speaks of an ideal sphere around every human being that cannot be penetrated unless the personality value of the individual is thereby destroyed. Quoted in Post, "The Social Foundations of Privacy," 971.

65. Goffman, "The Territories of the Self," 29–41.

66. Ibid., 60.

67. See J. Reiman, "Privacy, Intimacy and Personhood," in Shoeman, *Philosophical Dimensions of Privacy*, 310, for a discussion of the normative coherence of the concept of privacy and of a right to privacy that rejects the possessive individualist model of the self and challenges objectivistic interpretations.

68. For a discussion of the distinction between property rights and privacy rights and a rebuttal of Glendon on this issue see Cohen, "Redescribing Privacy," 105–12.

69. This includes protection for our psychic space and the imaginary identifications each individual makes within that space that make her unique. The right of privacy must not be misread along rationalistic lines as protecting only the freedom of individual (moral) conscience or of the individual as rational chooser. Rather, inviolability refers also to the inner psychic space of individuals and to their bodily integrity.

70. For an enlightening discussion of the importance of this dimension of rights to the maintenance of an intact sense of self and self-respect to African-Americans in particular, see Patricia Williams, *The Alchemy of Race and Rights* (Cambridge, Mass.: Harvard University Press, 1991). Against the critique of rights fashionable in certain legal circles, Williams argues that rights help establish boundaries that eliminate the overly personalized and contemptuous character of relationships between dominant (white) and subordinate (black) groups. Thus personal privacy rights serve to prohibit others from acting upon the presumed transparency and utter availability of the bodies and identities of others. "But where one's experience is rooted not just in a sense of illegitimacy but in *being* illegitimate, in being raped, and in the fear of being murdered, then the black adherence to a scheme of both positive and negative rights—to the self, to the sanctity of one's own personal boundaries—makes sense" (154).

71. There is a burgeoning literature on the body. See John O'Neill, *Five Bodies: The Human Shape of Modern Society* (Ithaca: Cornell University Press, 1985); and *The Communicative Body* (Evanston: Northwestern University Press, 1989); Brian Turner, *The Body and Society* (Oxford: Blackwell, 1984); Maurice Merleau-Ponty, *The Phenomenology of Perception* (London: Routledge and Kegan Paul, 1962); Kendall Thomas, "Beyond

the Privacy Principle," *Columbia Law Review* 92, no. 6 (October 1992): 1431–1516; and Zillah Eisenstein, *The Female Body and the Law* (Berkeley and Los Angeles: University of California Press, 1988); Thomas Laqueur, *Making Sex: Body and Gender from the Greeks to Freud* (Cambridge, Mass.: Harvard University Press, 1990); Elaine Scarry, *The Body in Pain: The Making and Unmaking of the World* (New York: Oxford University Press, 1985).

72. Erving Goffman, "Territories of the Self," 38. See also Reiman, "Privacy, Intimacy and Personhood," 310–14.

73. Goffman was one of the first to study the destructive impact on the sense of self experienced by individuals in total institutions, subjected to the total loss of privacy and bodily integrity. More recently, Elaine Scarry has focused on the destructive impact on the self when one's bodily integrity is purposefully attacked, as in the experience of torture. See Scarry, *The Body in Pain*, 49. Building upon this analysis, Axel Honneth has analyzed the sense of humiliation and the loss of the sense of self and of a coherent sense of reality when one's bodily integrity (one's control) is not recognized by others. See Axel Honneth, "Integrity and Disrespect: Principles of a Conception of Morality Based on a Theory of Recognition," *Political Theory* 20, no. 2 (May 1992), 190–93.

74. This does *not* mean that the choice to have a child or to abort is a choice of an identity. "Women should be able to abort their pregnancies so that they may avoid being forced into an identity, not because they are defining their identities through the decision itself. Resisting an enforced identity is not the same as defining oneself." Jed Rubenfeld, "The Right to Privacy," *Harvard Law Review* 102 (1989): 737–82.

75. See Karst, "The Freedom of Intimate Association," *Yale Law Journal* 89 (1980): 624.

76. No right is absolute in this sense. The state may, for example, insist upon inoculation of children attending public school against certain diseases, and it may take measures to protect public health that involve inoculation of adults as well. In the longer version of this essay I address the questions of limits to the right to abortion in terms of the stages of pregnancy. See Cohen, "Redescribing Privacy," 87–92.

77. Here I agree with Kendall Thomas when he argues that we must acknowledge that privacy is always body-mediated, and that this is a key dimension of arguments regarding the limits of state power over the sexualities of its citizens. "Beyond the Privacy Principle," 15–16. But this is an argument that points to redescribing, not abandoning, privacy analysis. Thus I reject Thomas's suggestion that we drop privacy analysis altogether.

78. The harm in denying women this right is that it denies to her the sense that her body and her self are *hers* to imagine and construct. If the woman is cast as the container for the fetus, her sexuality and her identity are reduced to the maternal function. Small wonder that the debate over abortion is very much a debate over discourses and how the issue should be framed. Whether women are to be construed as creators or as containers, whether fetuses are cast as persons with a right to life or as potential life, potential persons, whether we see abortion as continuous with contraception and as preventing a fertilized egg from becoming a baby or as killing—all this depends very much on how the issue is framed and on the definition of women and their place in society. See Kristin Luker, *Abortion and the Politics of Motherhood* (Berkeley and Los Angeles: University of California Press, 1984) for what is now a classic analysis of the genesis and stakes in competing discourses of the abortion debate in the U.S. See also

Barbara Katz Rothman, *Recreating Motherhood: Ideology and Technology in a Patriarchy* (New York: Norton, 1989).

In my view, this is also a debate over who gets to define women's "difference," i.e., their ability to become pregnant and create a child—the individual woman herself, or others.

79. Ronald Dworkin, *Life's Dominion* (New York: Knopf, 1993), 1–101.

80. For an excellent discussion of this issue, see Bruce Ackerman, *We the People*, 159ff. See my discussion of Bruce Ackerman in "Redescribing Privacy," 105–12.

81. In the longer version of this essay I also make the equality argument for abortion rights, arguing for a synthetic use of equal protection analysis, privacy analysis, and bodily integrity arguments. See Cohen, "Redescribing Privacy," 48–65.

Eleven

Gender Equity and the Welfare State: A Postindustrial Thought Experiment

NANCY FRASER

THE CURRENT crisis of the welfare state has many roots—global economic trends, massive movements of refugees and immigrants, popular hostility to taxes, the weakening of trade unions and labor parties, the rise of national and "racial"-ethnic antagonisms, the decline of solidaristic ideologies, and the collapse of state socialism. One absolutely crucial factor, however, is the crumbling of the old gender order. Existing welfare states are premised on assumptions about gender that are increasingly out of phase with many people's lives and self-understandings. They therefore do not provide adequate social protections, especially for women and children.

The gender order that is now disappearing descends from the industrial era of capitalism and reflects the social world of its origin. It was centered on the ideal of *the family wage*. In this world people were supposed to be organized into heterosexual, male-headed nuclear families, which lived principally from the man's labor market earnings. The male head of the household would be paid a family wage, sufficient to support children and a wife/mother, who performed domestic labor without pay. Of course countless lives never fit this pattern. Still, it provided the normative picture of a proper family.

The family-wage ideal was inscribed in the structure of most industrial-era welfare states.[1] That structure had three tiers, with social-insurance programs occupying the first rank. Designed to protect people from the vagaries of the labor market (and to protect the economy from shortages of demand), these programs replaced the breadwinner's wage in case of sickness, disability, un-

An earlier version of this article appeared under the title "After the Family Wage: Gender Equity and Social Welfare," in *Political Theory* 22, no. 4 (November 1994): 591–618. Because of production problems, that version did not contain a final round of important revisions, which are incorporated here. The present version, then, is the version of record. Portions of the *Political Theory* article are reprinted here with permission. Research for the article was supported by the Center for Urban Affairs and Policy Research, Northwestern University. For helpful comments, I am indebted to Rebecca Blank, Joshua Cohen, Fay Cook, Barbara Hobson, Axel Honneth, Jenny Mansbridge, Linda Nicholson, Ann Shola Orloff, John Roemer, Ian Shapiro, Tracy Strong, Peter Taylor-Gooby, Judy Wittner, Eli Zaretsky, and the members of the Feminist Public Policy Work Group of the Center for Urban Affairs and Policy Research, Northwestern University.

employment, or old age. Many countries also featured a second tier of programs, providing direct support for full-time female homemaking and mothering. A third tier served the "residuum." Largely a holdover from traditional poor relief, public assistance programs provided paltry, stigmatized, means-tested aid to needy people who had no claim to honorable support because they did not fit the family-wage scenario.[2]

Today, however, the family-wage assumption is no longer tenable—either empirically or normatively. We are currently experiencing the death throes of the old, industrial gender order with the transition to new, *postindustrial* phase of capitalism. The crisis of the welfare state is bound up with these epochal changes. It is rooted in part in the collapse of the world of the family wage, and of its central assumptions about labor markets and families.

In the labor markets of postindustrial capitalism, few jobs pay wages sufficient to support a family single-handedly; many, in fact, are temporary or part-time and do not carry standard benefits.[3] Women's employment is increasingly common, moreover—although far less well paid than men's.[4] Postindustrial families, meanwhile, are less conventional and more diverse.[5] Heterosexuals are marrying less often and later, and divorcing more often and sooner. And gays and lesbians are pioneering new kinds of domestic arrangements.[6] Gender norms and family forms are highly contested, finally. Thanks in part to the feminist and gay- and lesbian-liberation movements, many people no longer prefer the male breadwinner/female homemaker model. One result of these trends is a steep increase in solo-mother families: growing numbers of women, both divorced and never married, are struggling to support themselves and their families without access to a male breadwinner's wage. Their families have high rates of poverty.

In short, a new world of economic production and social reproduction is emerging—a world of less stable employment and more diverse families. Though no one can be certain about its ultimate shape, this much seems clear: the emerging world, no less than the world of the family wage, will require a welfare state that effectively insures people against uncertainties. It is clear, too, that the old forms of welfare state, built on assumptions of male-headed families and relatively stable jobs, are no longer suited to providing this protection. We need something new, a postindustrial welfare state suited to radically new conditions of employment and reproduction.

What, then, should a postindustrial welfare state look like? Conservatives have lately had a lot to say about "restructuring the welfare state," but their vision is counterhistorical and contradictory; they seek to reinstate the male breadwinner/female homemaker family for the middle class, while demanding that poor single mothers "work." Neoliberal proposals have recently emerged in the United States but they, too, are inadequate in the current context. Punitive, androcentric, and obsessed with employment despite the absence of good jobs, they are unable to provide security in a postindustrial world.[7]

Both these approaches ignore one crucial thing: a postindustrial welfare state, like its industrial predecessor, must support a gender order. But the only kind of gender order that can be acceptable today is one premised on *gender equity*.

Feminists, therefore, are in a good position to generate an emancipatory vision for the coming period. They, more than anyone, appreciate the importance of gender relations to the current crisis of the industrial welfare state and the centrality of gender equity to any satisfactory resolution. Feminists also appreciate the importance of care-work for human well-being and the effects of its social organization on women's standing. They are attuned, finally, to potential conflicts of interest within families and to the inadequacy of androcentric definitions of work.

To date, however, feminists have tended to shy away from systematic reconstructive thinking about the welfare state. Nor have we yet developed a satisfactory account of gender equity that can inform an emancipatory vision. We need now to undertake such thinking. We should ask, What new, postindustrial gender order should replace the family wage? And what sort of welfare state can best support such a new gender order? What account of gender equity best captures our highest aspirations? And what vision of social welfare comes closest to embodying it?

Two different sorts of answers are currently conceivable, I think, both of which qualify as feminist. The first I call the universal breadwinner model. It is the vision implicit in the current political practice of most U.S. feminists and liberals. It aims to foster gender equity by promoting women's employment; the centerpiece of this model is state provision of employment-enabling services such as day care. The second possible answer I call the caregiver parity model. It is the vision implicit in the current political practice of most Western European feminists and social democrats. It aims to promote gender equity chiefly by supporting informal care-work; the centerpiece of this model is state provision of caregiver allowances.

Which of these two approaches should command our loyalties in the coming period? Which expresses the most attractive vision of a postindustrial gender order? Which best embodies the ideal of gender equity?

In this essay, I outline a framework for thinking systematically about these questions. I analyze highly idealized versions of universal breadwinner and caregiver parity in the manner of a thought experiment. I postulate, contrary to fact, a world in which both these models are feasible in that their economic and political preconditions are in place. Assuming very favorable conditions, then, I assess the respective strengths and weaknesses of each.

The result is not a standard policy analysis. For neither universal breadwinner nor caregiver parity will in fact be realized in the near future; and my discussion is not directed primarily at policy-making elites. My intent, rather, is theoretical and political in a broader sense. I aim, first, to clarify some dilemmas surrounding "equality" and "difference" by reconsidering what is meant by gender equity. In so doing, I also aim to spur increased reflection on feminist strategies and goals by spelling out some assumptions that are implicit in current practice and subjecting them to critical scrutiny.

My discussion proceeds in four parts. In the first section, I propose an analysis of gender equity that generates a set of evaluative standards. Then, in the second and third sections, I apply those standards to universal breadwinner and caregiver parity, respectively. I conclude, in the fourth section, that neither of those approaches, even in an idealized form, can deliver full gender equity. To have a shot at *that*, I contend, we must develop a new vision of a postindustrial welfare state, which effectively dismantles the gender division of labor.

Gender Equity: A Complex Conception

In order to evaluate alternative visions of a postindustrial welfare state, we need some normative criteria. Gender equity, I have said, is one indispensable standard. But in what precisely does it consist?

Feminists have so far associated gender equity with either equality or difference, where "equality" means treating women exactly like men and "difference" means treating women differently insofar as they differ from men. Theorists have debated the relative merits of these two approaches as if they represented two antithetical poles of an absolute dichotomy.[8] These arguments have generally ended in stalemate. Proponents of "difference" have successfully shown that equality strategies typically presuppose "the male as norm," thereby disadvantaging women and imposing a distorted standard on everyone. Egalitarians have argued just as cogently, however, that difference approaches typically rely on essentialist notions of femininity, thereby reinforcing existing stereotypes and confining women within existing gender divisions. Neither equality nor difference, then, is a workable conception of gender equity.[9]

What, then, *would* be a workable conception?

I propose we reconceptualize gender equity as a complex idea, not a simple one. This means breaking with the assumption that gender equity can be identified with any single value or norm, whether it be equality, difference, or something else. Instead we should treat it as a complex notion comprising a plurality of distinct normative principles. The plurality will include some notions associated with the equality side of the debate, as well as some associated with the difference side. It will also encompass still other normative ideas that neither side has accorded due weight. Wherever they come from, however, the important point is this: each of several distinct norms must be respected simultaneously in order that gender equity be achieved. Failure to satisfy any one of them means failure to realize the full meaning of gender equity.

In what follows, I assume that gender equity is complex in this way. And I propose an account of it that is designed for the specific purpose of evaluating alternative pictures of a postindustrial welfare state. For issues other than welfare, a somewhat different package of norms might be called for. Nevertheless, I believe that the general idea of treating gender equity as a complex conception is widely applicable. The analysis here may serve as a paradigm case demonstrating the usefulness of this approach.

For this particular thought experiment, in any case, I unpack the idea of gender equity as a compound of seven distinct normative principles. Let me enumerate them one by one.

The antipoverty principle. The first and most obvious objective of social-welfare provision is to prevent poverty. Preventing poverty is crucial to achieving gender equity now, after the family wage, given the high rates of poverty in solo-mother families and the vastly increased likelihood that U.S. women and children will live in such families.[10] If it accomplishes nothing else, a welfare state should at least relieve suffering by meeting otherwise unmet basic needs. Arrangements, such as those in the United States, that leave women, children, and men in poverty are unacceptable according to this criterion. Any postindustrial welfare state that prevented such poverty would constitute a major advance. So far, however, this does not say enough. The antipoverty principle might be satisfied in a variety of different ways, not all of which are acceptable. Some ways, such as the provision of targeted, isolating and stigmatized poor relief for solo-mother families, fail to respect several of the following normative principles, which are also essential to gender equity in social welfare.

The antiexploitation principle. Antipoverty measures are important not only in themselves but also as a means to another basic objective: preventing exploitation of vulnerable people.[11] This principle, too, is central to achieving gender equity after the family wage. Needy women with no other way to feed themselves and their children, for example, are liable to exploitation—by abusive husbands, by sweatshop foremen, and by pimps. In guaranteeing relief of poverty, then, welfare provision should also aim to mitigate exploitable dependency.[12] The availability of an alternative source of income enhances the bargaining position of subordinates in unequal relationships. The nonemployed wife who knows she can support herself and her children outside of her marriage has more leverage within it; her "voice" is enhanced as her possibilities of "exit" increase.[13] The same holds for the low-paid nursing-home attendant in relation to her boss.[14] For welfare measures to have this effect, however, support must be provided as a matter of right. When receipt of aid is highly stigmatized or discretionary, the antiexploitation principle is not satisfied.[15] At best the claimant would trade exploitable dependence on a husband or a boss for exploitable dependence on a caseworker's whim.[16] The goal should be to prevent at least three kinds of exploitable dependencies: exploitable dependence on an individual family member, such as a husband or an adult child; exploitable dependence on employers and supervisors; and exploitable dependence on the personal whims of state officials. Rather than shuttle people back and forth among these exploitable dependencies, an adequate approach must prevent all three simultaneously.[17] This principle rules out arrangements that channel a homemaker's benefits through her husband. It is likewise incompatible with arrangements that provide essential goods, such as health insurance, only in forms linked conditionally to scarce employment. Any postindustrial welfare state that satisfied the antiexploitation principle would represent a major improvement over current U.S. arrangements. But even it might not be satisfactory. Some ways of satisfying this principle would fail to respect several of the following normative principles, which are also essential to gender equity in social welfare.

The equality principles. A postindustrial welfare state could prevent women's poverty and exploitation and yet still tolerate severe gender inequality. Such a welfare state is not satisfactory. A further dimension of gender equity in social provision is redistribution, reducing inequality between women and men. Equality, as we saw, has been criticized by some feminists. They have argued that it entails treating women exactly like men according to male-defined standards, and that this necessarily disadvantages women. That argument expresses a legitimate worry, which I shall address under another rubric in what follows. But it does not undermine the ideal of equality per se. The worry pertains only to certain inadequate ways of conceiving equality, which I do not presuppose here. At least three distinct conceptions of equality escape the objection. These are essential to gender equity in social welfare.

Income equality. One form of equality that is crucial to gender equity concerns the distribution of real per capita income. This sort of equality is highly pressing now, after the family wage, when U.S. women's earnings are approximately 70 percent of men's, when much of women's labor is not compensated at all, and when many women suffer from "hidden poverty" due to unequal distribution within families.[18] As I interpret it, the principle of income equality does not require absolute leveling. But it does rule out arrangements that reduce women's incomes after divorce by nearly half, while men's incomes nearly double.[19] It likewise rules out unequal pay for equal work and the wholesale undervaluation of women's labor and skills. The income-equality principle requires a substantial reduction in the vast discrepancy between men's and women's incomes. In so doing, it tends, as well, to help equalize the life-chances of children, for a majority of U.S. children are currently likely to live at some point in solo-mother families.[20]

Leisure-time equality. Another kind of equality that is crucial to gender equity concerns the distribution of leisure time. This sort of equality is highly pressing now, after the family wage, when many women, but only a few men, do both paid work and unpaid primary care-work and when women suffer disproportionately from "time poverty."[21] One recent British study found that 52 percent of women surveyed, compared to 21 percent of men, said they "felt tired most of the time."[22] The leisure-time–equality principle rules out welfare arrangements that would equalize incomes while requiring a double shift of work from women, but only a single shift from men. It likewise rules out arrangements that would require women, but not men, to do either the "work of claiming" or the time-consuming "patchwork" of piecing together income from several sources and of coordinating services from different agencies and associations.[23]

Equality of respect. Equality of respect is also crucial to gender equity. This kind of equality is especially pressing now, after the family wage, when postindustrial culture routinely represents women as sexual objects for the pleasure of male subjects. The principle of equal respect rules out social arrangements that objectify and denigrate women—even if those arrangements prevent poverty and exploitation, and even if in addition they equalize income and leisure time. It is incompatible with welfare programs that trivialize women's activities and ignore women's contributions—hence with "welfare reforms" in the United States that assume Aid to Families with Dependent Children (AFDC) claimants do not "work." Equality of respect requires recognition of women's personhood and recognition of women's work.

A postindustrial welfare state should promote equality in all three of these dimensions. Such a state would constitute an enormous advance over present arrangements, but even it might not go far enough. Some ways of satisfying the equality principles would fail to respect the following principle, which is also essential to gender equity in social welfare.

The antimarginalization principle. A welfare state could satisfy all the preceding principles and still function to marginalize women. By limiting support to generous mothers' pensions, for example, it could render women independent, well provided for, well rested, and respected, but enclaved in a separate domestic sphere, removed from the life of the larger society. Such a welfare state would be unacceptable. Social policy should promote women's full participation on a par with men in all areas of social life—in employment, in politics, in the associational life of civil society. The antimarginalization principle requires provision of the necessary conditions for women's participation, including day care, elder care, and provision for breastfeeding in public. It also requires the dismantling of masculinist work cultures and woman-hostile political environments. Any postindustrial welfare state that provided these things would represent a great improvement over current arrangements. Yet even it might leave something to be desired. Some ways of satisfying the antimarginalization principle would fail to respect the last principle, which is also essential to gender equity in social welfare.

The antiandrocentrism principle. A welfare state that satisfied many of the foregoing principles could still entrench some obnoxious gender norms. It could assume the androcentric view that men's current life patterns represent the human norm and that women ought to assimilate to them. (This is the real issue behind the previously noted worry about equality.) Such a welfare state is unacceptable. Social policy should not require women to become like men, or to fit into institutions designed for men, in order to enjoy comparable levels of well-being. Policy should aim instead to restructure androcentric institutions so as to welcome human beings who can give birth and who often care for relatives and friends, treating them not as exceptions, but as ideal-typical participants. The antiandrocentrism principle requires decentering masculinist norms—in part by revaluing practices and traits that are currently undervalued because they are associated with women. It entails changing men as well as changing women.

Here, then, is an account of gender equity in social welfare. On this account, gender equity is a complex idea comprising seven distinct normative principles, each of which is necessary and essential. No postindustrial welfare state can realize gender equity unless it satisfies them all.

How, then, do the principles interrelate? Here everything depends on context. Some institutional arrangements permit simultaneous satisfaction of several principles with a minimum of mutual interference; other arrangements, in contrast, set up zero-sum situations, in which attempts to satisfy one principle interfere with attempts to satisfy another. Promoting gender equity after the family wage, therefore, means attending to multiple aims that are potentially in conflict. The goal should be to find approaches that avoid trade-offs and maximize prospects for satisfying all—or at least most—of the seven principles.

In the next sections, I use this approach to assess two alternative models of a postindustrial welfare state. First, however, I want to flag three sets of relevant issues. One concerns the social organization of care-work. Precisely how this work is organized is crucial to human well-being in general and to the social standing of women in particular. In the era of the family wage, care-work was treated as the private responsibility of individual women. Today, however, it can no longer be treated in that way. Some other way of organizing it is required, but a number of different scenarios are conceivable. In evaluating postindustrial welfare state models, then, we must ask, How is responsibility for care-work allocated between such institutions as the family, the market, civil society, and the state? And how is responsibility for this work assigned within such institutions: by gender? by class? by "race"-ethnicity? by age?

A second set of issues concerns differences among women. Gender is the principal focus of this essay, to be sure, but it cannot be treated *en bloc*. The lives of women and men are cross-cut by several other salient social divisions, including class, "race"-ethnicity, sexuality, and age. Models of postindustrial welfare states, then, will not affect all women—or all men—in the same way; they will generate different outcomes for differently situated people. For example, some policies will affect women who have children differently from those who do not; some, likewise, will affect women who have access to a second income differently from those who do not; and some, finally, will affect women employed full-time differently from those employed part-time, and differently yet again from those who are not employed. For each model, then, we must ask, Which groups of women would be advantaged, and which groups disadvantaged?

A third set of issues concerns desiderata for postindustrial welfare states other than gender equity. Gender equity, after all, is not the only goal of social welfare. Also important are nonequity goals, such as efficiency, community, and individual liberty. In addition there remain other equity goals, such as "racial"-ethnic equity, generational equity, class equity, and equity among nations. All these issues are necessarily backgrounded here. Some of them, however, such as "racial"-ethnic equity, could be handled via parallel thought experiments: one might define "racial"-ethnic equity as a complex idea, analogous to the way gender equity is treated here, and then use it, too, to assess competing visions of a postindustrial welfare state.[24]

With these considerations in mind, let us now examine two strikingly different feminist visions of a postindustrial welfare state. And let us ask ourselves which comes closest to achieving gender equity in the sense I have elaborated here.

The Universal Breadwinner Model

In one vision of postindustrial society, the age of the family wage would give way to the age of the universal breadwinner. This is the vision implicit in the current political practice of most U.S. feminists and liberals. (It was also assumed in the former communist countries!) It aims to achieve gender equity principally by promoting women's employment. The point is to enable women to support themselves and their families through their own wage-earning. The breadwinner role is to be universalized, in sum, so that women, too, can be citizen-workers.

Universal breadwinner is a very ambitious postindustrial scenario, requiring major new programs and policies. One crucial element is a set of employment-enabling services, such as day care and elder care, aimed at freeing women from unpaid responsibilities so they could take full-time employment on terms comparable to men.[25] Another essential element is a set of workplace reforms aimed at removing equal-opportunity obstacles, such as sex discrimination and sexual harassment. Reforming the workplace requires reforming the culture, however—eliminating sexist stereotypes and breaking the cultural association of breadwinning with masculinity. Also required are policies to help change socialization, so as, first, to reorient women's aspirations toward employment and away from domesticity, and second, to reorient men's expectations toward acceptance of women's new role. None of this would work, however, without one additional ingredient: macroeconomic policies to create full-time, high-paying, permanent jobs for women.[26] These would have to be true breadwinner jobs in the primary labor force, carrying full, first-class social-insurance entitlements. Social insurance, finally, is central to universal breadwinner. The aim here is to bring women up to parity with men in an institution that has traditionally disadvantaged them.

How would this model organize care-work? The bulk of such work would be shifted from the family to the market and the state, where it would be performed by employees for pay.[27] Who, then, are these employees likely to be? In many countries today, including the United States, paid institutional care-work is poorly remunerated, feminized, and largely racialized and/or performed by immigrants.[28] But such arrangements are precluded in this model. If the model is to succeed in enabling *all* women to be breadwinners, it must upgrade the status and pay attached to care-work employment, making it, too, into primary-labor-force work. Universal breadwinner, then, is necessarily committed to a policy of "comparable worth"; it must redress the widespread undervaluation of skills and jobs currently coded as feminine or "nonwhite," and it must remunerate such jobs with breadwinner-level pay.

Universal breadwinner would link many benefits to employment and distribute them through social insurance, with levels varying according to earnings. In this respect, the model resembles the industrial-era welfare state.[29] The difference is that many more women would be covered on the basis of their own employment records. And many more women's employment records would look considerably more like men's.

Not all adults can be employed, however. Some will be unable to work for medical reasons, including some not previously employed. Others will be unable to get jobs. Some, finally, will have care-work responsibilities that they are unable or unwilling to shift elsewhere. Most of these last will be women. To provide for these people, universal breadwinner must include a residual tier of social welfare that provides need-based, means-tested wage replacements.[30]

Universal breadwinner is far removed from present realities. It requires massive creation of primary-labor-force jobs—jobs sufficient to support a family single-handedly. That, of course, is wildly askew of current postindustrial trends, which generate jobs not for breadwinners but for "disposable work-

228 EQUALITY, DIFFERENCE, PUBLIC REPRESENTATION

ers."[31] Let us assume for the sake of the thought experiment, however, that its conditions of possibility could be met. And let us consider whether the resulting postindustrial welfare state could claim title to gender equity.

Antipoverty. We can acknowledge straight off that universal breadwinner would do a good job of preventing poverty. A policy that created secure breadwinner-quality jobs for all employable women and men—while providing the services that would enable women to take such jobs—would keep most families out of poverty. And generous levels of residual support would keep the rest out of poverty through transfers.[32]

Antiexploitation. The model should also succeed in preventing exploitable dependency for most women. Women with secure breadwinner jobs are able to exit unsatisfactory relations with men. And those who do not have such jobs but know they can get them will also be less vulnerable to exploitation. Failing that, the residual system of income support provides back-up protection against exploitable dependency—assuming that it is generous, nondiscretionary, and honorable.[33]

Income equality. Universal breadwinner is only fair, however, at achieving income equality. Granted, secure breadwinner jobs for women—plus the services that would enable women to take them—would narrow the gender wage gap.[34] Reduced inequality in earnings, moreover, translates into reduced inequality in social-insurance benefits. And the availability of exit options from marriage should encourage a more equitable distribution of resources within it. But the model is not otherwise egalitarian. It contains a basic social fault line dividing breadwinners from others, to the considerable disadvantage of the others—most of whom would be women. Apart from comparable worth, moreover, it does not reduce pay inequality among breadwinner jobs. To be sure, the model reduces the weight of gender in assigning individuals to unequally compensated breadwinner jobs; but it thereby increases the weight of other variables, presumably class, education, "race"-ethnicity, and age. Women—and men—who are disadvantaged in relation to those variables will earn less than those who are not.

Leisure-time equality. The model is quite poor, moreover, with respect to equality of leisure time, as we can see from the communist experience. It assumes that all of women's current domestic and care-work responsibilities can be shifted to the market or the state. But that assumption is patently unrealistic. Some things, such as childbearing, attending to family emergencies, and much parenting work cannot be shifted—short of universal surrogacy and other presumably undesirable arrangements. Other things, such as cooking and (some) housekeeping, could—provided we were prepared to accept collective living arrangements or high levels of commodification. Even those tasks that are shifted, finally, do not disappear without a trace, but give rise to burdensome new tasks of coordination. Women's chances for equal leisure, then, depend on whether men can be induced to do their fair share of this work. On this, the model does not inspire confidence. Not only does it offer no disincentives to free-riding, but in valorizing paid work, it implicitly denigrates unpaid work, thereby fueling the motivation to shirk.[35] Women without partners would in any case be on their own. And those in lower-income households would be less able to purchase replacement services. Employed women would have a second shift on this model, then, albeit a less burdensome one than some have now; and there would be many more women employed full-time. Universal breadwinner, in sum, is not likely to deliver equal leisure. Anyone who does not free-ride in this possible postindustrial world is likely to be harried and tired.

Equality of respect. The model is only fair, moreover, at delivering equality of respect. Because it holds men and women to the single standard of the citizen-worker, its only chance of eliminating the gender respect gap is to admit women to that status on the same terms as men. This, however, is unlikely to occur. A more likely outcome is that women would retain more connection to reproduction and domesticity than men, thus appearing as breadwinners manqué. In addition, the model is likely to generate another kind of respect gap. By putting a high premium on breadwinner status, it invites disrespect for others. Participants in the means-tested residual system will be liable to stigmatization; and most of these will be women. Any employment-centered model, even a feminist one, has a hard time constructing an honorable status for those it defines as "nonworkers."

Antimarginalization. This model is also only fair at combating women's marginalization. Granted, it promotes women's participation in employment, but its definition of participation is narrow. Expecting full-time employment of all who are able, the model may actually impede participation in politics and civil society. Certainly, it does nothing to promote women's participation in those arenas. It fights women's marginalization, then, in a one-sided, "workerist" way.

Antiandrocentrism. Last, the model performs poorly in overcoming androcentrism. It valorizes men's traditional sphere—employment—and simply tries to help women fit in. Traditionally female care-work, in contrast, is treated instrumentally; it is what must be sloughed off in order to become a breadwinner. It is not itself accorded social value. The ideal-typical citizen here is the breadwinner, now nominally gender-neutral. But the content of the status is implicitly masculine; it is the male half of the old breadwinner/homemaker couple, now universalized and required of everyone. The female half of the couple has simply disappeared. None of her distinctive virtues and capacities has been preserved for women, let alone universalized to men. The model is androcentric.

We can summarize the merits of universal breadwinner in table 1.

TABLE 1
The Universal Breadwinner Model

	Universal Breadwinner
Antipoverty	good
Antiexploitation	good
Income equality	fair
Leisure-time equality	poor
Equality of respect	fair
Antimarginalization	fair
Antiandrocentrism	poor

Not surprisingly, universal breadwinner delivers the best outcomes to women whose lives most closely resemble the male half of the old family-wage ideal couple. It is especially good to childless women and to women without other major domestic responsibilities that cannot easily be shifted to social services. But for those women, as well as for others, it falls short of full gender equity.

The Caregiver Parity Model

In a second vision of postindustrial society, the era of the family wage would give way to the era of caregiver parity. This is the picture implicit in the political practice of most Western European feminists and social democrats. It aims to promote gender equity principally by supporting informal care-work. The point is to enable women with significant domestic responsibilities to support themselves and their families either through care-work alone or through care-work plus part-time employment. (Women without significant domestic responsibilities would presumably support themselves through employment.) The aim is not to make women's lives the same as men's but rather to "make difference costless."[36] Thus childbearing, child-rearing, and informal domestic labor are to be elevated to parity with formal paid labor. The caregiver role is to be put on a par with the breadwinner role—so that women and men can enjoy equivalent levels of dignity and well-being.

Caregiver parity is also extremely ambitious. On this model, many (though not all) women will follow the current U.S. female practice of alternating spells of full-time employment, spells of full-time care-work, and spells that combine part-time care-work with part-time employment. The aim is to make such a life pattern costless. To this end, several major new programs are necessary. One is a program of caregiver allowances to compensate childbearing, child-raising, housework, and other forms of socially necessary domestic labor; the allowances must be sufficiently generous at the full-time rate to support a family—hence equivalent to a breadwinner wage.[37] Also required is a program of workplace reforms. These must facilitate the possibility of combining supported care-work with part-time employment and of making the transition between different life-states. The key here is flexibility. One obvious necessity is a generous program of mandated pregnancy and family leave so that caregivers can exit and enter employment without losing security or seniority. Another is a program of retraining and job search for those not returning to old jobs. Also essential is mandated flextime so that caregivers can shift their hours to accommodate their care-work responsibilities, including shifts between full- and part-time employment. Finally, in the wake of all this flexibility, there must be programs to ensure continuity of all the basic social-welfare benefits, including health, unemployment, disability, and retirement insurance.

This model organizes care-work very differently from universal breadwinner. Whereas that approach shifted care-work to the market and the state, this one keeps the bulk of such work in the household and supports it with public funds.[38] Caregiver parity's social-insurance system also differs sharply. To assure continuous coverage for people alternating between care-work and employment, benefits attached to both must be integrated in a single system. In this system, part-time jobs and supported care-work must be covered on the same basis as full-time jobs. Thus a woman finishing a spell of supported care-work would be eligible for unemployment insurance benefits on the same basis as a recently laid-off employee in the event she could not find a suitable job. And a supported care-worker who became disabled would receive disability payments on the same basis as a disabled employee. Years of supported care-work would count on a par with years of employment toward eligibility for retirement pensions. Benefit levels would be fixed in ways that treat care-work and employment equivalently.

Caregiver parity also requires another, residual tier of social-welfare. Some adults will be unable to do either care-work or waged work, including some without prior work records of either type. Most of these people will probably be men. To provide for them, the model must offer means-tested wage-and-allowance replacements.[39] Caregiver parity's residual tier should be smaller than universal breadwinner's, however; nearly all adults should be covered in the integrated breadwinner-caregiver system of social insurance.

Caregiver parity, too, is far removed from current U.S. arrangements. It requires large outlays of public funds to pay caregiver allowances, hence major structural tax reform and a sea-change in political culture. Let us assume for the sake of the thought experiment, however, that its conditions of possibility could be met. And let us consider whether the resulting postindustrial welfare state could claim title to gender equity.

Antipoverty. Caregiver parity would do a good job of preventing poverty— including for those women and children who are currently most vulnerable. Sufficiently generous allowances would keep solo-mother families out of poverty during spells of full-time care-work. And a combination of allowances and wages would do the same during spells of part-time supported care-work and part-time employment.[40] Since each of these options would carry the basic social-insurance package, moreover, women with "feminine" work patterns would have considerable security.[41]

Antiexploitation. Caregiver parity should also succeed in preventing exploitation for most women, including for those who are most vulnerable today. By providing income directly to nonemployed wives, it reduces their economic dependence on husbands. It also provides economic security to single women with children, reducing their liability to exploitation by employers. Insofar as caregiver allowances are honorable and nondiscretionary, finally, recipients are not subject to caseworkers' whims.[42]

Income equality. Caregiver parity performs quite poorly, however, with respect to income equality, as we can see from the Nordic experience. Although the system of allowances-plus-wages provides the equivalent of a basic minimum breadwinner wage, it also institutes a "mommy track" in employment— a market in flexible, noncontinuous full- or part-time jobs. Most of these jobs will pay considerably less even at the full-time rate than comparable breadwinner-track jobs. Two-partner families will have an economic incentive to keep one partner on the breadwinner track rather than to share spells of care-work between them; and given current labor markets, making the breadwinner the man will be most advantageous for heterosexual couples. Given current culture and socialization, moreover, men are generally unlikely to choose the mommy track in the same proportions as women. So the two employment tracks will carry traditional gender associations. Those associations are likely in turn to produce discrimination against women in the breadwinner track. Caregiver parity may make difference cost less, then, but it will not make difference costless.

Leisure-time equality. Caregiver parity does somewhat better, however, with respect to equality of leisure time. It makes it possible for all women to avoid the double shift if they choose, by opting for full- or part-time supported care-work at various stages in their lives. (Currently, this choice is available only to a small percentage of privileged U.S. women.) We just saw, however, that this choice is not truly costless. Some women with families will not want to forego the benefits of breadwinner-track employment and will try to combine it with care-work. Those not partnered with someone on the caregiver track will be significantly disadvantaged with respect to leisure time, and probably in their employment as well. Men, in contrast, will largely be insulated from this dilemma. On leisure time, then, the model is only fair.

Equality of respect. Caregiver parity is also only fair at promoting equality of respect. Unlike universal breadwinner, it offers two different routes to that end. Theoretically, citizen-workers and citizen-caregivers are statuses of equivalent dignity. But are they really on a par with each other? Caregiving is certainly treated more respectfully in this model than in current U.S. society, but it remains associated with femininity. Breadwinning likewise remains associated with masculinity. Given those traditional gender associations, plus the economic differential between the two life-styles, caregiving is unlikely to attain true parity with breadwinning. In general, it is hard to imagine how "separate but equal" gender roles could provide genuine equality of respect today.

Antimarginalization. Caregiver parity performs poorly, moreover, in preventing women's marginalization. By supporting women's informal carework, it reinforces the view of such work as women's work and consolidates the gender division of domestic labor. By consolidating dual labor markets for breadwinners and caregivers, moreover, the model marginalizes women within the employment sector. By reinforcing the association of caregiving with femininity, finally, it may also impede women's participation in other spheres of life, such as politics and civil society.

Antiandrocentrism. Yet caregiver parity is better than universal breadwinner at combating androcentrism. It treats caregiving as intrinsically valuable, not as a mere obstacle to employment, thus challenging the view that only men's traditional activities are fully human. It also accommodates "feminine" life patterns, thereby rejecting the demand that women assimilate to "masculine" patterns. But the model still leaves something to be desired. Caregiver parity stops short of affirming the universal value of activities and life patterns associated with women. It does not value caregiving enough to demand that men do it, too; it does not ask men to change. Thus, caregiver parity represents only one-half of a full-scale challenge to androcentrism. Here, too, its performance is only fair.

Caregiver parity's strengths and weaknesses are summarized in table 2.

TABLE 2
The Caregiver Parity Model

	Caregiver Parity
Antipoverty	good
Antiexploitation	good
Income equality	poor
Leisure-time equality	fair
Equality of respect	fair
Antimarginalization	poor
Antiandrocentrism	fair

In general, caregiver parity improves the lot of women with significant carework responsibilities. But for those women, as well as for others, it fails to deliver full gender equity.

Conclusion: Toward Universal Caregiver

Both universal breadwinner and caregiver parity are highly utopian visions of a postindustrial welfare state. Either one of them would represent a major improvement over current U.S. arrangements. Yet neither is likely to be realized soon. Both models assume background preconditions that are strikingly absent today. Both presuppose major political-economic restructuring, including significant public control over corporations, the capacity to direct investment to create high-quality permanent jobs, and the ability to tax profits *and wealth* at rates sufficient to fund expanded high-quality social programs. Both models also assume broad popular support for a postindustrial welfare state that is committed to gender equity.

If both models are utopian in this sense, neither is utopian enough. Neither universal breadwinner nor caregiver parity can actually make good on its promise of gender equity—even under very favorable conditions. Although both are good at preventing women's poverty and exploitation, both are only fair at redressing inequality of respect.[43] And after that their strengths and weaknesses diverge. Universal breadwinner fails especially to promote equality of leisure time and to combat androcentrism, while caregiver parity fails especially to promote income equality and to prevent women's marginalization.[44] (The relative merits of universal breadwinner and caregiver parity are summarized in table 3.) Neither model, in sum, provides everything feminists want. Even in a highly idealized form neither delivers full gender equity.

TABLE 3
Relative merits of the Universal Breadwinner and Caregiver Parity Models

	Universal Breadwinner	Caregiver Parity
Antipoverty	good	good
Antiexploitation	good	good
Income equality	fair	poor
Leisure-time equality	poor	fair
Equality of respect	fair	fair
Antimarginalization	fair	poor
Antiandrocentrism	poor	fair

If these were the only possibilities, we would face a very difficult set of trade-offs. Suppose, however, we reject this Hobson's choice and try to develop a third alternative. The trick is to envision a postindustrial welfare state that combines the best of universal breadwinner with the best of caregiver parity, while jettisoning the worst features of each. What third alternative is possible?

So far we have examined—and found wanting—two initially plausible approaches: one aiming to make women more like men are now; the other leaving men and women pretty much unchanged, while aiming to make women's difference costless. A third possibility is to *induce men to become more like most women are now*—namely, people who do primary care-work.

Consider the effects of this one change on the models we have just examined. If men were to do their fair share of care-work, universal breadwinner would come much closer to equalizing leisure time and eliminating androcentrism, while caregiver parity would do a much better job of equalizing income and reducing women's marginalization. Both models, in addition, would tend to promote equality of respect. If men were to become more like women are now, in sum, both models would begin to approach gender equity.

The key to achieving gender equity in a postindustrial welfare state, then, is to make women's current life patterns the norm for everyone. Women today often combine breadwinning and caregiving, albeit with great difficulty and strain. A postindustrial welfare state must ensure that men do the same, while redesigning institutions so as to eliminate the difficulty and strain.[45]

We might call this vision *universal caregiver*.

What, then, might such a welfare state look like? Unlike caregiver parity, its employment sector would not be divided into two different tracks; all jobs would assume workers who are caregivers, too; all would have a shorter work week than full-time jobs have now; and all would have employment-enabling services. Unlike universal breadwinner, however, employees would not be assumed to shift all care-work to social services. Some informal care-work would be publicly supported and integrated on a par with paid work in a single social-insurance system. Some would be performed in households by relatives and friends, but such households would not necessarily be heterosexual nuclear families. Other supported care-work would be located outside households altogether—in civil society. In state-funded but locally organized institutions, childless adults, older people and others without kin-based responsibilities would join parents and others in democratic, self-managed care-work activities.[46]

Much more work needs to be done to develop this third—universal caregiver—vision of a postindustrial welfare state. A key is to develop policies that discourage free-riding. *Contra* conservatives, the real free-riders in the current system are not poor solo mothers who shirk employment. Rather they are men of all classes who shirk care-work and domestic labor, as well as corporations who free-ride on the labor of working people, both underpaid and unpaid.

A good statement of the universal caregiver vision comes from the Swedish Ministry of Labor: "To make it possible for both men and women to combine parenthood and gainful employment, a new view of the male role and a radical change in the organization of working life are required."[47] The trick is to imagine a social world in which citizens' lives integrate wage-earning, caregiving,

community activism, political participation, and involvement in the associational life of civil society—while also leaving time for some fun. This world is
not likely to come into being in the immediate future. But it is the only imag-
inable postindustrial world that promises true gender equity. And unless we
are guided by this vision now, we will never get any closer to achieving it.

Notes

1. Mimi Abramowitz, *Regulating the Lives of Women: Social Welfare Policy from Colo-
nial Times to the Present* (Boston: South End Press, 1988); Nancy Fraser, "Women,
Welfare, and the Politics of Need Interpretation," *Hypatia* 2, no. 1 (Winter 1987): 103–
21, reprinted in Fraser, *Unruly Practices: Power, Discourse, and Gender in Contemporary
Social Theory* (Minneapolis: University of Minnesota Press, 1989); Linda Gordon, "What
Does Welfare Regulate?" *Social Research* 55, no. 4 (Winter 1988): 609–30; and Hilary
Land, "Who Cares for the Family?" *Journal of Social Policy* 7, no. 3 (July 1978): 257–84.
An exception is France, which from early on accepted high levels of female waged work.
Jane Jenson, "Representations of Gender: Policies to 'Protect' Women Workers and
Infants in France and the United States before 1914," in *Women, the State, and Welfare*,
ed. Linda Gordon (Madison: University of Wisconsin Press, 1990).

2. This account of the tripartite structure of the welfare state represents a modifica-
tion of my earlier view in "Women, Welfare, and the Politics of Need Interpretation."
Heretofore, I followed Barbara Nelson in positing a two-tier structure of ideal-typically
"masculine" social insurance programs and ideal-typically "feminine" family support
programs. See Nelson, "Women's Poverty and Women's Citizenship: Some Political
Consequences of Economic Marginality," *Signs: Journal of Women in Culture and Society*
10, no. 2 (Winter 1984): 209–31; and "The Origins of the Two-Channel Welfare State:
Workmen's Compensation and Mother's Aid," in *Women, the State, and Welfare*, ed.
Linda Gordon (Madison: University of Wisconsin Press, 1990). Although that view was
a relatively accurate picture of the U.S. social-welfare system, I now consider it analytically misleading. The United States is unusual in that the second and third tiers are
conflated. The main program of means-tested poor relief—Aid to Families with Dependent Children (AFDC)—is also the main program that supports women's child-raising.
Analytically, these are best understood as two distinct tiers of social welfare. When
social insurance is added, we get a three-tier welfare state.

3. David Harvey, *The Condition of Postmodernity: An Inquiry into the Origins of Cultural
Change* (Oxford: Blackwell, 1979); Scott Lash and John Urry, *The End of Organized
Capitalism* (Cambridge: Polity Press, 1987); and Robert Reich, *The Work of Nations:
Preparing Ourselves for Twenty-First-Century Capitalism* (New York: Knopf, 1991).

4. Joan Smith, "The Paradox of Women's Poverty: Wage-Earning Women and Economic Transformation," *Signs: Journal of Women in Culture and Society* 9, no. 2 (Winter
1984): 291–310.

5. Judith Stacey, "Sexism by a Subtler Name? Postindustrial Conditions and
Postfeminist Consciousness in the Silicon Valley," *Socialist Review* no. 96 (1987): 7–28.

6. Kath Weston, *Families We Choose: Lesbians, Gays, Kinship* (New York: Columbia
University Press, 1991).

7. Nancy Fraser, "Clintonism, Welfare, and the Antisocial Wage: The Emergence of a Neoliberal Political Imaginary," *Rethinking Marxism* 6, no. 1 (Spring 1993): 9–23.

8. See the essays in *Feminist Legal Theory: Readings in Law and Gender*, ed. Katharine T. Bartlett and Rosanne Kennedy (Boulder, Colo.: Westview Press, 1991).

9. Feminists have responded to this stalemate in several different ways. Some have tried to resolve the dilemma by reconceiving one or another of its horns; they have reinterpreted difference or equality in what they consider a more defensible form. Others have concluded "a plague on both your houses" and sought some third, wholly other, normative principle. Still others have tried to embrace the dilemma as an enabling paradox, a resource to be treasured, not an impasse to be gotten around. Many feminists, finally, have retreated altogether from normative theorizing—into cultural positivism, piecemeal reformism, or postmodern antinomianism. None of these responses is satisfactory. Normative theorizing remains an indispensable intellectual enterprise for feminism, indeed for all emancipatory social movements. We need a vision or picture of where we are trying to go, and a set of standards for evaluating various proposals as to how we might get there. The equality/difference theoretical impasse is real, moreover; it cannot be simply sidestepped or embraced. Nor is there any "wholly other" third term that can magically catapult us beyond it.

10. David T. Ellwood, *Poor Support: Poverty in the American Family* (New York: Basic Books, 1988).

11. Robert Goodin, *Reasons for Welfare: The Political Theory of the Welfare State* (Princeton: Princeton University Press, 1988).

12. Not all dependencies are exploitable. Goodin (ibid., 175–76) specifies the following four conditions that must be met if a dependency is to be exploitable: 1) the relationship must be asymmetrical; 2) the subordinate party must need the resource that the superordinate supplies; 3) the subordinate must depend on some particular superordinate for the supply of needed resources; 4) the superordinate must enjoy discretionary control over the resources that the subordinate needs from him or her.

13. Albert O. Hirschman, *Exit, Voice, and Loyalty: Responses to Decline in Firms, Organizations, and States* (Cambridge, Mass.: Harvard University Press, 1970); Susan Moller Okin, *Justice, Gender, and the Family* (New York: Basic Books, 1989); and Barbara Hobson, "No Exit, No Voice: Women's Economic Dependency and the Welfare State," *Acta Sociologica* 33, no. 3 (Fall 1990): 235–50.

14. Frances Fox Piven and Richard A. Cloward, *Regulating the Poor* (New York: Random House, 1971); Gosta Esping-Andersen, *The Three Worlds of Welfare Capitalism* (Princeton: Princeton University Press, 1990).

15. Goodin, *Reasons for Welfare*.

16. Edward V. Sparer, "The Right to Welfare," in Norman Dorsen, ed., *The Rights of Americans: What They Are—What They Should Be* (New York: Pantheon, 1970).

17. Ann Shola Orloff, "Gender and the Social Rights of Citizenship: The Comparative Analysis of Gender Relations and Welfare States," *American Sociological Review* 58, no. 3 (June 1993): 303–28. The antiexploitation objective should not be confused with current U.S. attacks on "welfare dependency," which are highly ideological. These attacks define "dependency" exclusively as receipt of public assistance. They ignore the ways in which such receipt can promote claimants' independence by preventing exploitable dependence on husbands and employers. Nancy Fraser and Linda Gordon, "A

Genealogy of 'Dependency': Tracing a Keyword of the U.S. Welfare State," *Signs: Journal of Women in Culture and Society* 19, no. 2 (1994): 309–36.

18. Ruth Lister, "Women, Economic Dependency, and Citizenship," *Journal of Social Policy* 19, no. 4 (1990): 445–67; and Amartya Sen, "More than 100 Million Women Are Missing," *New York Review of Books* 37, no. 20 (December 20, 1990): 61–66.

19. Lenore Weitzman, *The Divorce Revolution: The Unexpected Social Consequences for Women and Children in America* (New York: Free Press, 1985).

20. Ellwood, *Poor Support*, 45.

21. Lois Bryson, "Citizenship, Caring and Commodification," an unpublished paper presented at the conference on "Crossing Borders: International Dialogues on Gender, Social Politics and Citizenship," Stockholm, May 27–29, 1994; Arlie Hochschild, *The Second Shift: Working Parents and the Revolution at Home* (New York: Viking, 1989); Juliet Schor, *The Overworked American: The Unexpected Decline of Leisure* (New York: Basic Books, 1991).

22. See Lister, "Women, Economic Dependency, and Citizenship."

23. Laura Balbo, "Crazy Quilts," in *Women and the State*, ed. Ann Showstack Sassoon (London: Hutchinson, 1987).

24. A fourth set of issues is also extremely important, but I do not have space to consider it here. It concerns the bases of entitlement to provision. Every welfare state assigns its benefits according to a specific mix of distributive principles, which defines its basic moral quality. That mix, in each case, needs to be scrutinized. Usually it contains varying proportions of three basic principles of entitlement: need, desert, and citizenship. Need-based provision is the most redistributive, but it risks isolating and stigmatizing the needy; it has been the basis of traditional poor relief and of modern public assistance, the least honorable forms of provision. The most honorable, in contrast, is entitlement based on desert, but it tends to be antiegalitarian and exclusionary. Here one receives benefits according to one's "contributions," usually tax payments, work, and service—where "tax payments" means wage deductions paid into a special fund, "work" means primary labor-force employment, and "service" means the military, all interpretations of those terms that disadvantage women. Desert has usually been seen as the primary basis of earnings-linked social insurance in the industrial welfare state. (But for a critique of this view as androcentric and ideological, see Nancy Fraser and Linda Gordon, "Contract versus Charity: Why Is There No Social Citizenship in the United States?" *Socialist Review* 22, no. 3 [July–September 1992]: 45–68.) The third principle, citizenship, allocates provision on the basis of membership in society. It is honorable, egalitarian, and universalist, but also expensive, hence hard to sustain at high levels of quality and generosity; some theorists worry, too, that it encourages free-riding. (The free-rider worry, too, is typically defined androcentrically, as a worry about shirking paid employment. Little attention is paid, in contrast, to a far more widespread problem, namely, men's free-riding on women's unpaid domestic labor. A welcome exception is Peter Taylor-Gooby, "Scrounging, Moral Hazard, and Unwaged Work: Citizenship and Human Need," an unpublished typescript [1993].) Citizenship-based entitlements are most often found in social-democratic countries, where they may include single-payer universal health insurance systems, universal family or child allowances, and universal flat-rate old age pensions; they are virtually unknown in the United States—except for public education. In examining models of postindustrial welfare states, then, one must look closely at the construction of entitlement. It makes

considerable difference to women's and children's well-being, for example, whether day care places are distributed as citizenship entitlements or as desert-based entitlements, i.e. whether or not they are conditional on prior employment. It likewise matters, to take another example, whether care-work is supported on the basis of need, in the form of a means-tested benefit for the poor, or whether it is supported on the basis of desert, as return for "work" or "service," now interpreted nonandrocentrically, or whether, finally, it is supported on the basis of citizenship under a universal basic income scheme.

25. Employment-enabling services could be distributed according to need, desert, or citizenship, but citizenship accords best with the spirit of the model. Means-tested day care targeted for the poor cannot help but signify a failure to achieve genuine breadwinner status; and desert-based day care sets up a catch-22: one must already be employed in order to get what is needed for employment. Citizenship-based entitlement is best, then, but it must make services available to all. This rules out Swedish-type arrangements, which fail to guarantee sufficient day care places and are plagued by long queues. Barbara Hobson, "Economic Dependency and Women's Social Citizenship: Some Thoughts on Esping-Andersen's Welfare State Regimes," an unpublished typescript.

26. That, incidentally, would be to break decisively with U.S. policy, which typically assumes that job creation is for men; Bill Clinton's much-touted "industrial" and "infrastructural investment" policies are no exception in this regard. Fraser, "Clintonism, Welfare, and the Antisocial Wage."

27. Government could itself provide care-work services in the form of public goods, or it could fund marketized provision through a system of vouchers. Alternatively, employers could be mandated to provide employment-enabling services for their employees, either through vouchers or in-house arrangements. The state option means higher taxes, of course, but it may be preferable nevertheless. Mandating employer responsibility creates a disincentive to hire workers with dependents, to the likely disadvantage of women.

28. Evelyn Nakano Glenn, "From Servitude to Service Work: Historical Continuities in the Racial Division of Paid Reproductive Labor," *Signs: Journal of Women in Culture and Society* 18, no. 1 (Autumn 1992): 1–43.

29. It, too, conditions entitlement on desert and defines "contribution" in traditional androcentric terms as employment and wage deductions.

30. Exactly what else must be provided inside the residual system will depend on the balance of entitlements outside it. If health insurance is provided universally as a citizen benefit, for example, then there need be no means-tested health system for the nonemployed. If, however, mainstream health insurance is linked to employment, then a residual health care system will be necessary. The same holds for unemployment, retirement, and disability insurance. In general, the more that is provided on the basis of citizenship, instead of on the basis of desert, the less has to be provided on the basis of need. One could even say that desert-based entitlements create the necessity of need-based provision; thus employment-linked social insurance creates the need for means-tested public assistance.

31. Peter Kilborn, "New Jobs Lack the Old Security in Time of 'Disposable Workers,'" *New York Times*, March 15, 1993, A1, A6.

32. Failing that, however, several groups are especially vulnerable to poverty in this

model: those who cannot work, those who cannot get secure, permanent, full-time, good-paying jobs—disproportionately women and/or people of color; and those with heavy, hard-to-shift, unpaid care-work responsibilities—disproportionately women.

33. Failing that, however, the groups mentioned in the previous note remain especially vulnerable to exploitation—by abusive men, by unfair or predatory employers, by capricious state officials.

34. Exactly how much remains depends on the government's success in eliminating discrimination and in implementing comparable worth.

35. Universal breadwinner apparently relies on persuasion to induce men to do their fair share of unpaid work. The chances of that working would be improved if the model succeeded in promoting cultural change and in enhancing women's voice within marriage. But it is doubtful that this alone would suffice, as the communist experience suggests.

36. Christine A. Littleton, "Reconstructing Sexual Equality," in Bartlett and Kennedy, *Feminist Legal Theory*.

37. Caregiver allowances could be distributed on the basis of need, as a means-tested benefit for the poor—as they have always been in the United States. But that would contravene the spirit of caregiver parity. One cannot consistently claim that the caregiver life is equivalent in dignity to the breadwinner life, while supporting it only as a last-resort stopgap against poverty. (This contradiction has always bedeviled mothers' pensions—and later Aid to Dependent Children—in the United States. Although these programs were intended by some advocates to exalt motherhood, they sent a contradictory message by virtue of being means-tested and morals-tested.) Means-tested allowances, moreover, would impede easy transitions between employment and care-work. Since the aim is to make caregiving as deserving as breadwinning, caregiver allowances must be based on desert. Treated as compensation for socially necessary "service" or "work," they alter the standard androcentric meanings of those terms.

38. Susan Okin (in *Justice, Gender, and the Family*) has proposed an alternative way to fund care-work. In her scheme the funds would come from what are now considered to be the earnings of the caregiver's partner. A man with a nonemployed wife, for example, would receive a paycheck for one-half of "his" salary; his employer would cut a second check in the same amount payable directly to the wife. Intriguing as this idea is, one may wonder whether it is really the best way to promote a wife's independence from her husband, as it ties her income so directly to his. In addition, Okin's proposal does not provide any care-work support for women without employed partners. Caregiver parity, in contrast, provides public support for all who perform informal care-work. Who, then, are its beneficiaries likely to be? With the exception of pregnancy leave, all the model's benefits are open to everyone; so men as well as women can opt for a "feminine" life. Women, however, are considerably more likely to do so. Although the model aims to make such a life costless, it includes no positive incentives for men to change. Some men, of course, may simply prefer such a life and will choose it when offered the chance; most will not, however, given current socialization and culture. We shall see, moreover, that caregiver parity contains some hidden disincentives to male caregiving.

39. In this respect, it resembles the universal breadwinner model: whatever additional essential goods are normally offered on the basis of desert must be offered here too on the basis of need.

40. Wages from full-time employment must also be sufficient to support a family with dignity.

41. Adults with neither care-work nor employment records would be most vulnerable to poverty in this model; most of these would be men. Children, in contrast, would be well protected.

42. Once again, it is adults with neither care-work nor employment records who are most vulnerable to exploitation in this model; and the majority of them would be men.

43. Universal breadwinner holds women to the same standard as men, while constructing arrangements that prevent them from meeting it fully; caregiver parity, in contrast, sets up a double standard to accommodate gender difference, while institutionalizing policies that fail to assure equivalent respect for "feminine" activities and life patterns.

44. Neither model, moreover, promotes women's full participation on a par with men in politics and civil society. And neither values female-associated practices enough to ask men to do them, too; neither asks men to change.

45. Such a welfare state would effectively promote gender equity by dismantling the gendered opposition between breadwinning and caregiving. It would integrate activities that are currently separated from one another, eliminate their gender-coding, and encourage men to perform them too. This, however, is tantamount to a wholesale restructuring of the institution of gender. The construction of breadwinning and caregiving as separate roles, coded masculine and feminine respectively, is a principal undergirding of the current gender order. To dismantle those roles and their cultural coding is in effect to overturn that order. It means subverting the existing gender division of labor and reducing the salience of gender as a structural principle of social organization (Okin, *Justice, Gender, and the Family*). At the limit, it suggests deconstructing gender (Joan Williams, "Deconstructing Gender," in Bartlett and Kennedy, *Feminist Legal Theory*). Only by embracing this aim, it seems, can we mitigate potential conflicts among our seven component principles of gender equity, thereby minimizing the necessity of trade-offs. Rejecting that aim, in contrast, makes such conflicts, and hence trade-offs, more likely. *Achieving gender equity in a postindustrial welfare state, then, requires deconstructing gender.*

46. Not only would this approach deconstruct the opposition between breadwinning and caregiving; it would also deconstruct the associated opposition between bureaucratized public institutional settings and intimate private domestic settings. Treating civil society as a site for care-work offers a wide range of new possibilities for promoting equal participation in social life, now no longer restricted to formal employment.

47. Quoted in Lister, "Women, Economic Dependency, and Citizenship," 463.

Part Three

CULTURE, IDENTITY, AND DEMOCRACY

Twelve

Democracy, Power, and the "Political"

CHANTAL MOUFFE

IN RECENT DECADES categories like "human nature," "universal reason," and "rational autonomous subject" have increasingly been put into question. From different standpoints, a variety of thinkers have criticized the ideas of a universal human nature, of a universal canon of rationality through which that human nature could be known, as well as the possibility of an unconditional universal truth. Such a critique of Enlightenment's universalism and rationalism—which is sometimes referred to as "postmodern"—has been presented by some authors, like Jürgen Habermas, as constituting a threat to the modern democratic project. They consider that the link existing between the democratic ideal of the Enlightenment and its rationalistic and universalistic perspective is such that rejecting the latter necessarily jeopardizes the former.

In this essay I want to take issue with such a view and defend the opposite thesis. Indeed, I am going to argue that it is only in the context of a political theory that takes account of the critique of essentialism—which I see as the crucial contribution of the so-called postmodern approach—that it is possible to formulate the aims of a radical democratic politics in a way that makes room for the contemporary proliferation of political spaces and the multiplicity of democratic demands.[1]

Pluralism and Modern Democracy

Before developing my argument, I would like to make a few remarks to specify the way I envisage modern liberal democracy. First, I consider that it is important to distinguish liberal democracy from democratic capitalism, and to understand it in terms of classical political philosophy as a *regime*, a political form of society that is defined exclusively at the level of the political, leaving aside its possible articulation with an economic system. Liberal democracy in its various appellations—constitutional democracy, representative democracy, parliamentary democracy, modern democracy—is not the application of the democratic model to a wider context, as some would have it; understood as a *regime*, it concerns the symbolic ordering of social relations and is much more than a mere "form of government." It is a specific form of organizing human coexistence politically that results from the articulation between two different traditions: on one side, political liberalism (rule of law, separation of powers and individual rights), and, on the other side, the democratic tradition of popular sovereignty.

In other words, the difference between ancient and modern democracy is not one of *size* but of *nature*. The crucial difference resides in the acceptance of *pluralism*, which is constitutive of modern liberal democracy. By pluralism I mean the end of a substantive idea of the good life, what Claude Lefort calls "the dissolution of the markers of certainty." Such a recognition of pluralism implies a profound transformation in the symbolic ordering of social relations. This is something that is totally missed when one refers, like John Rawls, to the *fact* of pluralism. There is, of course, a fact, which is the diversity of the conceptions of the good that we find in a liberal society. But the important difference is not an empirical one; it concerns the *symbolic* level. What is at stake is the legitimation of conflict and division, the emergence of individual liberty, and the assertion of equal liberty for all.

Once pluralism is recognized as the defining feature of modern democracy, we can inquire into the best way to approach the scope and nature of a pluralist democratic politics. My contention is that it is only in the context of a perspective according to which *différance* is construed as the condition of possibility of being that a radical democratic project informed by pluralism can be adequately formulated. Indeed, I submit that all forms of pluralism that depend on a logic of the social that implies the idea of "being as presence" and sees "objectivity" as belonging to the "things themselves," necessarily lead to the reduction of plurality and to its ultimate negation. This is indeed the case with the main forms of liberal pluralism, which generally start by stressing what they call "the fact of pluralism" and then proceed to find procedures to deal with differences whose objective is actually to make those differences irrelevant and to relegate pluralism to the sphere of the private.

Envisaged from an antiessentialist theoretical perspective, on the contrary, pluralism is not merely a *fact*, something that we must bear grudgingly or try to reduce, but an axiological principle. It is taken to be constitutive *at the conceptual level* of the very nature of modern democracy and considered as something that we should celebrate and enhance. This is why the type of pluralism that I am advocating gives a positive status to differences and that it refuses the objective of unanimity and homogeneity which is always revealed as fictitious and based on acts of exclusion.

However, such a view does not allow a total pluralism, and it is important to recognize the limits to pluralism which are required by a democratic politics that aims at challenging a wide range of relations of subordination. It is therefore necessary to distinguish the position I am defending here from the type of extreme pluralism that emphasizes heterogeneity and incommensurability and according to which pluralism—understood as valorization of all differences—should have no limits. I consider that, despite its claim to be more democratic, such a perspective is an impediment to recognizing how certain differences are constructed as relations of subordination and should therefore be challenged by a radical democratic politics. There is only a multiplicity of identities without any common denominator, and it is impossible to distinguish between differences that exist but should not exist and differences that do not exist but should exist.

What such a pluralism misses is the dimension of the *political*. Relations of power and antagonisms are erased, and we are left with the typical liberal illusion of a pluralism without antagonism. Indeed, although it tends to be very critical of liberalism, that type of extreme pluralism, because of its refusal of any attempt to construct a "we," a collective identity that would articulate the demands found in the different struggles against subordination, partakes of the liberal evasion of the political. To deny the need for a construction of collective identities and to conceive democratic politics exclusively in terms of a struggle of a multiplicity of interest groups or of minorities for the assertion of their rights is to remain blind to the relations of power. It is to ignore the limits imposed on the extension of the sphere of rights by the fact that some existing rights have been constructed on the very exclusion or subordination of others.

Pluralism, Power, and Antagonism

In coming to terms with pluralism, what is really at stake is power and antagonism and their ineradicable character. This can only be grasped from a perspective that puts into question the objectivism and essentialism that is dominant in democratic theory. In *Hegemony and Socialist Strategy*,[2] we delineated an approach that asserts that any social objectivity is constituted through acts of power. This means that any social objectivity is ultimately political and has to show the traces of the acts of exclusion that govern its constitution—what, following Derrida, can be referred to as its "constitutive outside."

This point is decisive. It is because every object has inscribed in its very being something other than itself and that as a result, everything is constructed as *différence*, that its being cannot be conceived as pure "presence" or "objectivity." Since the constitutive outside is present within the inside as its always real possibility, every identity becomes purely contingent. This implies that we should conceptualize power not as an *external* relation taking place between two preconstituted identities but rather as constituting the identities themselves. This point of confluence between objectivity and power is what we have called "hegemony."

When we envisage democratic politics from such an antiessentialist perspective, we can begin to understand that for democracy to exist, no social agent should be able to claim any mastery of the *foundation* of society. This signifies that the relation between social agents becomes more democratic only insofar as they accept the particularity and the limitation of their claims; that is only insofar as they recognize their mutual relations as one from which power is ineradicable. The democratic society cannot be conceived any more as a society that would have realized the dream of a perfect harmony in social relations. Its democratic character can be given only by the fact that no limited social actor can attribute to herself the representation of the totality. The main question of democratic politics, then, becomes not how to eliminate power but how to constitute forms of power that are compatible with democratic values.

To acknowledge the existence of relations of power and the need to transform them, while renouncing the illusion that we could free ourselves completely from power: this is what is specific to the project that we have called "radical and plural democracy." Such a project recognizes that the specificity of modern pluralist democracy—even a well-ordered one—resides not in the absence of domination and of violence but in the establishment of a set of institutions through which they can be limited and contested. To negate the ineradicable character of antagonism and aim at a universal rational consensus—this is the real threat to democracy. Indeed, this can lead to violence being unrecognized and hidden behind appeals to "rationality," as is often the case in liberal thinking, which disguises the necessary frontiers and forms of exclusion behind pretenses of "neutrality."

Political Liberalism

To illustrate the dangerous consequences of the rationalist approach and show the superiority of the one I am delineating here, I have chosen to take the example of "political liberalism" elaborated by John Rawls. In his recent work, Rawls intends to give a new solution to the traditional liberal problem of how to establish peaceful coexistence among individuals with different conceptions of the good. For a long time liberals have seen the solution to that problem in the creation of a modus vivendi or, following Schumpeter, a "modus procedendi" that regulates the conflict among different views. Hence the generally accepted view of democracy as a procedural form, neutral with respect to any particular set of values, a mere method for making public decisions.

Recently, liberals like Rawls—and, in a slightly different way, Charles Larmore—have taken issue with such an interpretation of the liberal principle of neutrality. They affirm that a liberal democratic society needs a form of consensus that is deeper than a simple modus vivendi on mere procedures. Its aim should be the creation of a moral and not merely prudential type of consensus around its basic institutions. Their objective is to provide a moral, albeit min-

imal, consensus on political fundamentals. Their "political liberalism" aims at
defining a core morality that specifies the terms under which people with
different conceptions of the good can live together in political association. It
is an understanding of liberalism that is compatible with the fact of pluralism
and the existence of moral and religious disagreement and that must be distinguished from comprehensive views like those of Kant and Mill. Given that it
is neutral with respect to controversial views of the good life, they believe that
such a liberalism can provide the political principles that should be accepted
by all despite their differences.[3]

According to Rawls, the problem of political liberalism can be formulated
in the following way: "How is it possible that there may exist over time a stable
and just society of free and equal citizens profoundly divided by reasonable
religious, philosophical and moral doctrines?"[4] The problem is, in his view,
one of political *justice*, and it requires the establishment of fair terms of social
cooperation between citizens envisaged as free and equal but also as divided
by profound doctrinal conflict. His solution, as reformulated in his recent
book *Political Liberalism*, puts a new emphasis on the notion of "reasonable
pluralism." He invites us to distinguish between what would be a mere empirical recognition of opposed conceptions of the good, the fact of "simple" pluralism, and what is the real problem facing liberals: how to deal with a plurality of incompatible yet *reasonable* doctrines. He sees such a plurality as the
normal result of the exercise of human reason within the framework of a constitutional democratic regime. This is why a conception of justice must be able
to gain the support of all "reasonable" citizens despite their deep doctrinal
disagreements on other matters.

Let us examine this distinction between "simple" and "reasonable" pluralism. Avowedly it is supposed to secure the moral character of the consensus
on justice, which precludes that a compromise should be made with "unreasonable" views—that is, those that would oppose the basic principles of political morality. But in fact, it allows Rawls to present as a moral exigency what
is really a political decision. For Rawls, reasonable persons are persons "who
have realized their two moral powers to a degree sufficient to be free and equal
citizens in a constitutional regime, and who have an enduring desire to honor
fair terms of cooperation and to be fully cooperating members of society."[5]

What is this if not an indirect form of asserting that reasonable persons are
those who accept the fundamentals of liberalism? In other words, the distinction between "reasonable" and "unreasonable" helps to draw a frontier between those who accept the liberal principles and those who oppose them. It
means that its function is *political* and that it aims at discriminating between
a permissible pluralism of religious, moral, or philosophical conceptions—as
long as those views can be relegated to the sphere of the private and satisfy the
liberal principles—and what would be an unacceptable pluralism because it
would jeopardize the dominance of liberal principles in the public sphere.

What Rawls is really indicating with such a distinction is that there cannot be pluralism as far as the principles of the political association are concerned and that conceptions which refuse the principles of liberalism are to be excluded. I have no quarrel with him on this issue. But this is the expression of an eminently *political* decision, not of a moral requirement. To call the anti-liberals "unreasonable" is a way of stating that such views cannot be admitted as legitimate within the framework of a liberal democratic regime. This is indeed the case, but the reason for such an exclusion is not a moral one. It is because antagonistic principles of legitimacy cannot coexist within the same political association without putting in question the political reality of the state. However, to be properly formulated, such a thesis calls for a theoretical framework that asserts that the political is always constitutive—which is precisely what liberalism denies.

Rawls tries to avoid the problem by presenting his priority of the right over the good as a moral distinction. But that does not solve the problem. First, a question arises concerning the status of his assertion of the priority of the right over the good. To be consistent, Rawls cannot derive it from any comprehensive doctrine. Is it, then, only an "intuitive idea" that we all share? The communitarians would certainly object to such a view. So, what can it be? The answer is, of course, that it is one of the main features of liberal democracy understood as a distinctive political form of society; it is part of the "grammar" of such a "regime." But an answer along those lines is not available to Rawls because there is no place for such a constitutive role of the political in his theory. This is why he cannot provide a convincing argument for justifying the frontiers of his pluralism, and why he gets caught in a circular form of argumentation: political liberalism can provide a consensus among reasonable persons who *by definition* are persons who accept the principles of political liberalism.

Overlapping Consensus or Constitutional Consensus

Another consequence of Rawls's incapacity to apprehend the constitutive role of the political is revealed when we scrutinize another aspect of his solution to the liberal problem: the creation of an "overlapping consensus" of reasonable comprehensive doctrines in which each of them endorses the political conception from its own point of view. He declares that when the society is well-ordered, it is around the principles of his theory of justice as fairness that the overlapping consensus is established. Because they are chosen thanks to the device of the original position with its "veil of ignorance," those principles of fair terms of cooperation satisfy the liberal principle of legitimacy that requires that they are endorsed by all citizens as free and equal—as well as reasonable and rational—and addressed to their public reason. According to the standpoint of political liberalism, those principles are expressly designed to gain the reasoned support of citizens who affirm reasonable though conflicting comprehensive doctrines. Indeed, the very purpose of the veil of ignorance is to preclude the knowledge of citizens' comprehensive conceptions of the good and to force them to proceed from shared conceptions of society and personality required in applying the ideals and principles of practical reason.[6]

In line with his project of establishing the moral character of his "political liberalism," Rawls is at pains to indicate that such an overlapping consensus must not be confused with a simple modus vivendi. He insists that it is not merely a consensus on a set of institutional arrangements based on self-interest but the affirmation on moral grounds of principles of justice that have themselves a moral character. Moreover, the overlapping consensus also differs from a constitutional form of consensus which, in his view, is not deep or wide enough to secure justice and stability. In a constitutional consensus, he states, "while there is agreement on certain basic political rights and liberties—on the right to vote and freedom of political speech and association, and whatever else is required for the electoral and legislative procedures of democracy—there is disagreement among those holding liberal principles as to the more exact content and boundaries of these rights and liberties, as well as on what further rights and liberties are to be counted as basic and so merit legal if not constitutional protection."[7]

Rawls grants that a constitutional consensus is better than a modus vivendi because there is a real allegiance to the principles of a liberal constitution that guarantees certain basic rights and liberties and establishes democratic procedures for moderating political rivalry. Nevertheless, given that those principles are not grounded in certain ideas of society and personality of a political conception, disagreements persist concerning the status and content of those rights and liberties, and they create insecurity and hostility in public life. Hence, he says, the importance of fixing *once and for all* their content. This is provided by an overlapping consensus on a conception of justice as fairness, which establishes a much deeper consensus than one that would be restricted to constitutional essentials.

While admitting that those constitutional essentials (i.e., fundamental principles that specify the general structure of government and the political process as well as basic rights and liberties of citizenship)[8] are more urgent to settle, Rawls considers that they must be distinguished from the principles governing social and economic inequalities. The aim of justice of fairness is to establish a consensus on a public reason whose content is given by a political conception of justice. "This content has two parts: substantive principles of justice for the basic structure (the political values of justice); and guidelines of enquiry and conceptions of virtue that make public reason possible (the political values of public reason)."[9]

Rawls seems to believe that, whereas rational agreement among comprehensive moral religious and philosophical doctrine is impossible, in the political domain such an agreement can be reached. Once the controversial doctrines have been relegated to the sphere of the private, it is possible, in his view, to establish in the public sphere a type of consensus grounded on Reason (with its two sides: the rational and the reasonable). This is a consensus that it would be illegitimate to put into question once it has been reached, and the only possibility of its destabilization would be an attack from the outside by the "unreasonable" forces. This implies that, when a well-ordered society has been achieved, those who take part in the overlapping consensus should have no right to question the existing arrangements since they embody the principles of justice. If somebody does not comply, it must be because of "irrationality" or "unreasonableness."

At this point, the picture of the Rawlsian well-ordered society begins to emerge more clearly, and it looks very much like a dangerous utopia of reconciliation. To be sure, Rawls recognizes that a fully overlapping consensus might never be achieved, but at best approximated. It is more likely, he says, that the focus of an overlapping consensus will be a class of liberal conceptions acting as political rivals.[10] Nevertheless, he urges us to strive for a well-ordered society where, given that there is no more conflict between political and economic interests, this rivalry has been overcome. Such a society would see the realization of justice as fairness, which is the correct and definite interpretation of how the democratic principles of equality and liberty should be implemented in the basic institutions. It is independent of any interest, and does not represent any form of compromise, but is truly the expression of free public democratic reason.

The way he envisages the nature of the overlapping consensus clearly indicates that, for Rawls, a well-ordered society is a society from which politics has been eliminated. A conception of justice is mutually recognized by reasonable and rational citizens who act according to its injunctions. They probably have very different and even conflicting conceptions of the good, but those are strictly private matters and do not interfere with their public life. Conflicts of interests about economic and social issues—if they still arise—are resolved smoothly through discussions within the framework of public reason, by invoking the principles of justice that everybody endorses. If an unreasonable or irrational person happens to disagree with that state of affairs and intends to disrupt that nice consensus, she must be forced, through coercion, to submit to the principles of justice. Such a coercion, however, has nothing to do with oppression, for it is justified by the exercise of reason.

If it was ever to be realized, Rawls's "liberal utopia" would, then, be a society in which legitimate dissent would have been eliminated from the public sphere. This is, indeed, worrying. How has he been led to defend such a position? Why is there not any space left in his well-ordered society for contested interpretations of the shared liberal democratic principles? The answer lies, I believe, in his flawed conception of politics, which is reduced to a mere activity of allocating among competing interests susceptible to a rational solution. This is why he thinks that political conflicts can be eliminated thanks to a conception of justice that appeals to individuals' idea of rational advantage within the constraints established by the reasonable.

According to his theory, citizens need as free and equal persons the same goods because their conceptions of the good—however distinct their content—"require for their advancement roughly the same primary goods, that is, the same basic rights, liberties, and opportunities, and the same all-purpose means such as income and wealth, with all of these supported by the same social bases of self-respect."[11] Therefore, once the just answer to the problem of distribution of those primary goods has been found, the rivalry that previously existed in the political domain disappears.

Rawls's scenario presupposes that political actors are driven only by what they see as their rational self-advantage. Passions are erased from the realm of politics, which is reduced to a neutral field of competing interests. Completely missing from such an approach is "the political" in its dimension of power, antagonism, and relationships of forces. What "political liberalism" is at pains to eliminate is the element of "undecidability" that is present in human relations. It offers us a picture of the well-ordered society as one from which—through rational agreement on justice—antagonism, violence, power, and repression have disappeared. But it is only because they have been made invisible through a clever strategem: the distinction between "simple" and "reasonable pluralism." In that way, exclusions can be denied by declaring that they are the product of the "free exercise of practical reason" that establishes the limits of possible consensus. When a point of view is excluded it is because this is required by the exercise of reason; therefore the frontiers between what is legitimate and what is not legitimate appear as independent of power relations. Thanks to this legerdemain, rationality and morality provide the key to solving the "paradox of liberalism": how to eliminate its adversaries while remaining neutral.

Alas, it is not enough to eliminate the political in its dimension of antagonism and exclusion from one's theory to make it vanish from the real world. It does come back, and with a vengeance. Once the liberal approach has created a framework in which its dynamics cannot be grasped, the political becomes its unthought and repressed side, the "dark forces of irrationality" that condemns this type of liberalism to perpetual irrelevance.

Democracy and Undecidability

By bringing to light the potential consequences of Rawls's project, my aim was to reveal the danger of postulating that there could be a rational definite solution to the question of justice in a democratic society. Such an idea leads to the closing of the gap between justice and law that is a constitutive space of modern democracy. To avoid such a closure, we should relinquish the very idea that there could be such a thing as a "rational" political consensus—that is, one that would not be based on any form of exclusion. To present the institutions of liberal democracy as the outcome of a pure deliberative rationality is to reify them and make them impossible to transform. It is to deny the fact that, like any other regime, modern pluralist democracy constitutes a system of relations of power and to render the democratic challenging of those forms of power illegitimate.

In the end, the rationalist defense of liberal democracy, in searching for an argument that is beyond argumentation and in wanting to define the meaning of the universal, makes the same mistake for which it criticizes totalitarianism: the rejection of democratic indeterminacy and the identification of the universal with a given particular. Modern democratic politics, linked as it is to the declaration of human rights, does indeed imply a reference to universality. But this universality is conceived as a horizon that can never be reached. Every pretension to occupy the place of the universal, to fix its final meaning through rationality must be rejected since the recognition of undecidability is the condition of existence of democratic politics.

To believe that a final resolution of conflicts is eventually possible—even if it is seen as an asymptotic approach to the regulative idea of a rational consensus—far from providing the necessary horizon of the democratic project, is something that puts it at risk. Indeed, such an illusion carries implicity the desire for a reconciled society where pluralism would have been superseded. When it is conceived in such a way, pluralist democracy becomes a "self-refuting ideal" because the very moment of its realization would coincide with its disintegration.

With its insistence on the irreducible alterity that represents both a condition of possibility and a condition of impossibility of every identity, a perspective informed by poststructuralism provides a much better theoretical framework to grasp the specificity of modern democracy than rationalist approaches. The notion of the "constitutive outside" forces us come to terms with the idea that pluralism implies the permanence of conflict and antagonism. Indeed it helps us to understand that conflict and division are to be seen neither as disturbances that unfortunately cannot be completely eliminated nor as empirical impediments that render impossible the full realization of a good constituted by an unreachable harmony, because we will never be completely able to coincide with our rational universal self.

Thanks to the insights of poststructuralism the project of radical and plural democracy is able to acknowledge that difference is the condition of possibility of constituting unity and totality as the same time that it provides their essential limits. In such a view, plurality cannot be eliminated; it becomes irreducible. We have therefore to abandon the very idea of a complete reabsorption of alterity into oneness and harmony. It is an alterity that cannot be domesticated; rather, as Rodolphe Gasché indicates, it "forever undermines, but also makes possible, the dream of autonomy achieved through a reflexive coiling upon self, since it names the precondition of such a desired state, a precondition that represents the limit of such a possibility."[12]

Contrary to other projects of radical or participatory democracy informed by a rationalistic framework, radical and *plural* democracy rejects the very possibility of a nonexclusive public sphere of rational argument where a non-coercive consensus could be attained. By showing that such a consensus is a *conceptual* impossibility, it does not put in jeopardy the democratic ideal as some would argue. On the contrary, it protects pluralist democracy against any attempts of closure. Indeed, such a rejection constitutes an important guarantee that the dynamics of the democratic process will be kept alive.

Instead of trying to erase the traces of power and exclusion, democratic politics requires bringing them to the fore, making them visible so that they can enter the terrain of contestation. The fact that this must be envisaged as an unending process should not be cause for despair, because the desire to reach a final destination can only lead to the elimination of the political and to the destruction of democracy. In a democratic polity, conflicts and confrontations, far from being a sign of imperfection, indicate that democracy is alive and inhabited by pluralism.

To the Kantian-inspired model of democracy, which envisages its realization under the form of an ideal community of communication, as a task conceived of as infinite, to be sure, but which nevertheless has a clearly defined shape, we should oppose a conception of democracy that, far from aiming at consensus and transparency, is suspicious of any attempt to impose a univocal model of democratic discussion. Aware of the dangers of rationalism, this is a view that does not dream of mastering or eliminating undecidability, for it recognizes that it is the very condition of possibility of decision and therefore of freedom and pluralism.

Notes

1. I have on several occasions pointed out the disingenuous move that consists in conflating poststructuralism with postmodernism, and I will not repeat this argument here. Let us just recall that the antiessentialism that I am endorsing, far from being restricted to poststructuralism, constitutes the point of convergence of many different currents of thought and that it can be found in authors as different as Derrida, Rorty, Wittgenstein, Heidegger, Gadamer, Dewey, Lacan, and Foucault.

2. Ernesto Laclau and Chantal Mouffe, *Hegemony and Socialist Strategy: Towards a Radical Democratic Politics* (London: Verso, 1985).

3. For a critique of this attempt by Larmore and Rawls to reformulate the liberal notion of neutrality, see Chantal Mouffe, *The Return of the Political* (London: Verso, 1993), chap. 9.

4. John Rawls, *Political Liberalism* (New York: Columbia University Press, 1993), xviii.

5. Ibid., 55.

6. Ibid., 141.

7. Ibid., 159.

8. Ibid., 227.

9. Ibid., 253.

10. Ibid., 164.

11. Ibid., 180.

12. Rodolphe Gasché, *The Tain of the Mirror* (Cambridge, Mass.: Harvard University Press, 1986), 105.

Thirteen

Difference, Dilemmas, and the Politics of Home

BONNIE HONIG

> Given the limitation on human action, it is naive to
> suppose that there is a solution to every moral
> problem with which the world can face us. We
> have always known that the world is a bad place.
> It appears that it may be an evil place as well.
> *Thomas Nagel*

> I feel like telling him why I feel a connection to the
> Inuits. That it's because of their ability to know,
> without a shadow of a doubt that life is
> meaningful. Because of the way, in their
> consciousness, they can live with the tension
> between irreconcilable contradictions, without
> sinking into despair and without looking for a
> simplified solution. Because of their short, short
> path to ecstasy.
> Smilla's Sense of Snow, *Peter Hoeg*

WHAT SORT of problem does "difference" pose for democratic theory and practice? Most of the essays in this volume treat difference as nothing more than identities that are *different from* "ours." In the title phrase "democracy and difference," for example, difference is just another word for what used to be called pluralism. Recent work in political and feminist theory, however, suggests that difference is not simply a different identity, nor is it merely (*pace* Hegel) the constitutive matter out of which identity is formed; it is also that

For their comments and criticisms, thanks to Jane Bennett, Josh Cohen, Jill Frank, Marcie Frank, Sally Gibbons, Morris Kaplan, David Mapel, Patchen Markell, Kirstie McClure, Pratap Mehta, Michael Sandel, Dennis Thompson, Michael Whinston, and Linda Zerilli. Early drafts of this essay were presented at the University of Texas at Austin, Amherst College, the Conference for the Study of Political Thought at Yale University, and the University of California at Berkeley. This essay is a moderately revised version of a paper that appeared in *Social Research*'s special issue on liberalism (Fall 1994). The essay was completed while the author was a fellow at the Center for Advanced Study in the Behavioral Sciences. I am grateful for financial support provided by the National Science Foundation, Grant #SES-9022192.

which resists or exceeds the closure of identity. It signals not a difference *from* others but a difference that troubles identity from with*in* its would-be economy of the same. Difference is what identity perpetually seeks (and fails) to expunge, fix, or hold in place. In short, difference is a problem for identity, not one of its adjectives.

Pluralists and, more recently, multiculturalists tend to domesticate or conceal this sort of difference by taking group identities and affiliations as their starting point. Treating difference as simply a different identity enables them to affirm a diversity that is potentially unruly but that is also reassuring insofar as it does not threaten to be ungovernable.

And yet ungovernability is precisely what difference threatens us with. To take difference—and not just identity—seriously in democratic theory is to affirm the inescapability of conflict and the ineradicability of resistance to the political and moral projects of ordering subjects, institutions, and values. Moreover, it requires that we recast the task of democratic theory, and move it beyond that of simply orchestrating multiple and conflicting group needs and toward a new responsiveness to that first task's propensity to involve democratic cultures and institutions in violent and resentful dynamics of identity/difference.[1] It is to give up on the dream of a place called home, a place free of power, conflict, and struggle, a place—an identity, a form of life, a group vision—unmarked or unriven by difference and untouched by the power brought to bear upon it by the identities that strive to ground themselves in its place.

In this essay, I turn to moral and political theoretical treatments of dilemmas to explore some of the issues posed by difference and these two ways of reading it. Dilemmas—situations in which two values, obligations, or commitments conflict and there seems to be no right thing to do—pose the question of difference and the ineradicability of conflict in a specific and ordinarily familiar setting. I focus on Bernard Williams's analysis of dilemmas and value pluralism, first, because he *affirms* that ineradicable conflict and second, because he nonetheless goes on to treat dilemmas in a way that parallels the approach taken by pluralists and multiculturalists to difference.

For Williams, dilemmas are not expressive or symptomatic of rifts in subjectivity or identity. Instead, dilemmas are the spectral bearers of fragmentation from which unitary subjects must be protected. Thus even while Williams claims to affirm dilemmas as a valuable part of the terrain of moral life, his dilemma narratives (in the form of his examples) betray his tendency simultaneously to fence off serious conflicts, guarding safe spaces of predictability and order for his moral subjects. Williams's premised primacy of the unitary subject of integrity ultimately enables him to resecure the kind of moral closure he claims to eschew, not by obviating dilemmas philosophically (as his Kantian and utilitarian adversaries might) but by holding them at bay rhetorically, psychologically, and politically.

In contrast to Williams, I argue that the circumstances of their subject constitution position all moral subjects in what I call *dilemmatic spaces*. Indeed, we might think of the subject as positioned on multiple, conflictual axes of identity/difference such that her agency itself is constituted, even enabled—and not simply paralyzed—by daily dilemmatic choices and negotiations. The perspectives of this subject suggest that we ought not to think only in terms of dilemmas as discrete events onto which unitary agents with diverse commitments stumble occasionally (as Williams does) but perhaps also in terms of a dilemmatic space or spaces that both constitute us and form the terrain of our existence. These dilemmatic spaces vary in intensity and gravity but none is untouched by conflict and incommensurability.

The notion of a dilemmatic space treats dilemmas as expressive of more than a mere value pluralism. It relocates difference from the outside of moral agency (where it is called pluralism and engenders episodic conflicts) to its inside (where difference looms as incoherence and engenders unending and never-quite-mastered struggles of resistance, adjustment, and negotiation). In short, it treats dilemmas not only as a symptom of value pluralism but also as a sign of the ineradicability of difference from identity.

This identification of dilemmas with the (admittedly) more amorphous notion of a dilemmatic space does not deny the felt eventfulness of particular dilemmas. But it insists on a particular (Nietzschean) meaning for the term—event. Rather than springing up *ab initio*, dilemmas are actually the eventful eruptions of a turbulence that is always already there. They are the periodic crystallizations of incoherences and conflicts in social orders and their subjects.

This notion of a dilemmatic space calls attention to the institutional and discursive *constructions* of value conflicts or struggles as *dilemmas*, that is, as hard and fast and episodic choices between binary, discrete, and mutually exclusive alternatives. Williams himself contributes to this construction, but he also attenuates it. Hence my focus on him. He resists the mutually exclusive dimension of dilemmas by combating the corresponding will to invoke closure on moral choices once made. In the aftermath of dilemmatic choice, he refuses to erase the unchosen alternatives or remainders, affirming the fidelity to them expressed by the moral emotions of regret and remorse, and rejecting the charge made by other moral theorists that these emotions are irrational or pathological.

However, Williams's attenuations do not finally counteract the effects of his dilemma narratives, which tend to return dilemmas to the margins of ethics and politics in order to protect the boundaries of agentic integrity from the disruption, danger, and harm with which he associates dilemmas. These narratives buttress and animate Williams's repeated counsels to subjects to withdraw from dilemmas—often the scene of political involvement—for the sake of their integrity whenever possible.

From a more political perspective than that taken by Williams, however, dilemmas appear not only as specters of agentic fragmentation but also always as markers of a potential space of (gender) politics, empowerment, and political engagement. The resistance of dilemmas to ordinary rule-governance—precisely their apparent ungovernability and undecidability—enables them to serve as a site from which to interrogate and perhaps even transcend the very decidable ordinary rules and cultural constructs that support and stabilize conventional gender differences, value pluralism, agentic integrity, and the construction of "homes" as spaces of safety and withdrawal from the tumult of politics.

This political possibility demands (*inter alia*) that the seductions of home be rigorously engaged and challenged, but they rarely are. Perhaps unwittingly, Williams himself reinscribes those seductions as he distances himself and his moral subjects from the dilemmas that so captivate and repel him. But for the feminist theorists upon whom I draw in contrast to Williams, for Teresa de Lauretis and Bernice Johnson Reagon in particular, there are promising possibilities of democratic empowerment available to those who interrogate the processes that construct home as a site of safety (for some), and who give up the privileges of that ideological place called home (though not the much needed respite of periodic withdrawals from political action) to affirm the risks and the ineradicability of difference, dilemmas, and conflict for the sake of the promise of social democratic struggle.

Moving Dilemmas: From the Margins to the Center and Back Again

Bernard Williams puts dilemmas at the center of his moral theory because, following Isaiah Berlin, he begins from the premise that human values are plural and incommensurable, and therefore bound to conflict in any social order. Both Berlin and Williams affirm this condition; they do not regret it. It occasions a richness, creativity, and courage that Berlin celebrates as the mark of a specifically "liberal consciousness," a consciousness that responds to conflicts one at a time, "not trying to eliminate them on more than a piecemeal basis."[2]

Williams criticizes Kantianism and utilitarianism for rejecting this piecemeal approach in favor of a more systematic moral theory.[3] Both deny the reality and salience of moral dilemmas by developing formulas designed to adduce right answers in cases where two moral "oughts" appear to conflict.[4] With the Kantian or utilitarian right answer in hand, one of the competing oughts is eliminated from the scene, exposed as false, secondary or irrational, and the dilemma is dissolved. Kantians and utilitarians think this elimination is necessary if the foundational "ought implies can" is to be kept safe. When two oughts conflict, only one of them can be performed; if both are authentic oughts then only one implies "can," and morality is left open to the charge that it imposes undue burdens upon its agents, obligating them to perform the impossible.

Williams's insight is that morality is open to that charge either way.[5] Its elimination of one of the oughts in a dilemma situation may protect it from the undue burden charge by preserving the connection between ought and can, but morality reopens itself to that very same charge with its insistence that the agent disconnect herself from the unperformed (and allegedly unobligating) ought. Conflicts of oughts are not structurally like conflicts of belief, Williams explains. Whereas the discovery of a conflict between two beliefs does tend "*eo ipso* to weaken one" of them, the discovery of a conflict between two oughts tends, on the contrary, to generate a struggle.[6] In this respect, oughts are more like desires. The discovery of a conflict between two of them, *in itself*, weakens neither one.

Against Kantian and utilitarian moral theory, Williams argues that when two oughts conflict, "I do not think in terms of banishing error." The problem is not to discover which of the two oughts is the impostor and which the authentic obligation. Nor is the problem in the agent's "thought about the moral situation. . . . [W]hat is wrong lies in his situation."[7] Both oughts are compelling, and the situation that stages their conflict is inescapable. In such cases, "I think, if constructively at all, in terms of acting for the best and this is a frame of mind that acknowledges the presence [and the validity] of both the two oughts."[8] Indeed, the ought not acted upon often persists in the form of regret, a moral emotion not inconsistent with the feeling that one has acted for the best, but also awkwardly obstructive of the desire for moral closure that drives the Kantian and utilitarian projects.[9]

On morality's rule-governed (but still fortune-ridden) terrain, Williams's moral agents regularly encounter moments of conflict and struggle, moments in which two oughts compel them but only one can be acted upon. Since "moral conflicts are neither systematically avoidable, nor all soluble without remainder,"[10] Williams's moral theory focuses not on rule-following but on the places where rules break off, not only on how to decide what to do but also on how to deal with undecidability, less on the need to do the right thing than on how to act for the best. His account of the moral life stresses its unruliness, putting contingency, moral luck, and struggle at the center of moral theory, and finally focusing considerable attention on the phenomenon of tragic situations—those radically undecidable situations in which there is no right thing to do, in which whatever one does will be horribly, awfully wrong.

But, as Williams turns his attention from ordinary cases of conflict to extraordinary cases of tragedy, his strategy changes. The (increasingly intensified) experience of moral struggle is moved from the center back to the pe-

riphery of his moral world. This is because tragic situations are different from
mere dilemmas. "Conflicts of obligation," Williams says, "are peculiar in presenting a conflict between determinately specified actions, [but] the tragic
ones among them are further peculiar in lying beyond the ordinary routes of
moral thought."[11] In tragic situations like Agamemnon's, for example, even the
relatively unambitious goal of "'acting for the best' may very well lose its content."[12] Here any regret that follows an act is not for the ought that was left
undone but for the very thing that *was* done. Here struggle, regret, acting for
the best, the entire constellation of values and practices that Williams develops to empower agents to negotiate their ways through conflicts of oughts
loses whatever salvational and regulative powers it had.

Perhaps because of the sheer horror of tragic situations, Williams quickly
reassures us that they are rare, exceptional, extraordinary. With that reassur-
ance, however, he marginalizes the radical undecidability that, on his own
account, touches all moral experience.[13] The distinction between ordinary dilemmas and extraordinary or tragic dilemmas becomes a distinction of
kind, and ordinary life is once again scripted as a site of relative safety that is
only very occasionally interrupted by the exceptional, tragic incursion of undecidability.

Integrity at Risk: Dilemmas at Home and Abroad

Why is it important to Williams to distinguish ordinary from extraordinary
dilemmas? How does he ground and maintain that distinction, to what conceptual and rhetorical lengths will he go to sustain it, and what effect does
it have on the way we think about dilemmas in relation to ethical and political life?

In "A Critique of Utilitarianism," Williams concedes that utilitarian calculation may be the most appropriate form of moral reasoning in "extreme
situations." But he worries about (what he sees as) utilitarianism's cold willingness to calculate in every situation, its failure to appreciate the ethicality of
the refusal to calculate.[14] Hence his need for a qualitative distinction between
ordinary and extreme situations: If that distinction is allowed to slide into
a mere difference "between the greater and the less," then, "the consequen-
tial thoughts one was prepared to deploy in the greater it may seem quite
irrational not to deploy in the less."[15] In short, without a *qualitative* distinction between ordinary and extreme situations, utilitarian calculation
might become hegemonic, the privileged mode of moral reasoning, appropriate in all cases.

Here, Williams's opposition to utilitarianism focuses less on its relentless
will to resolve dilemmas without remainder (a feature it shares with Kantianism) and more on its treatment of moral agents as the agents of utility rather

than as the bearers of integrity (a feature that sharply distinguishes utilitarianism from its Kantian alternative). Because utilitarianism treats agents as points
in the line of a satisfaction system, it obligates them to perform even very
unpalatable actions if those actions are necessary to produce utilitarianly preferred outcomes.[16] It requires that agents alienate themselves even from their
deepest commitments and projects. From the perspective of utility, the agent's
refusal to do that looks like "moral self-indulgence" and not like the admirable
act of integrity Williams judges it to be.

Displayed by the sort of agent who "acts from those dispositions and motives that are *most deeply his* and [who] has the virtues that enable him to do
that,"[17] integrity's catch-phrase is "not through me"—as in, "That outcome
might indeed be a good one, but I cannot allow it to be brought about through
me." The reflexivity of the catch-phrase may appear to "express a motivation
of the suspect 'self-indulgent' kind," but "in itself, it does not represent any
motivation at all."[18] The motivation is in the moral emotion, or feeling, or
principle to which the agent declares her fidelity, in the "ought" that she cannot give up. Integrity consists in her being the sort of person who refuses to or
is unable to dissociate herself from her emotions, feelings, principles, or projects even for the sake of a larger or more general good.

Williams outlines the stakes of the opposition between utility and integrity
by way of two examples. I center the rest of my argument around these two
examples because they (like most examples in philosophical writing) bear
the burden of assumptions for which their author does not take explicit responsibility. Williams is not completely unaware of the problem. He notes
that "examples in moral philosophy tend to beg important questions" and he
knows that his own may be "defective" in that way. Those who cannot just
accept his examples as they are, he says, are invited to "rework them in richer
and less question begging form."[19] I take him up on his offer, enhancing and
extending his examples in order to make apparent the subtle ways in which
they collude to make the world safe for integrity by resolving or displacing
impossible choices. I forward these enhancements and extensions in the spirit
in which Teresa de Lauretis calls for the remaking, not the replacement, of
conventional narratives, in order to enable "an interruption of the triple track
by which narrative, meaning and pleasure are constructed from [the hero's]
point of view."[20]

In the first example, the hero is George, an unemployed chemist who is
offered a job pursuing research at a biochemical warfare lab. George is opposed to that sort of research but he also finds himself in difficult circumstances. As a result of his own unemployment and poor health, his wife is
working to support the family and this "causes a great deal of strain, since
they have small children and there are severe problems about looking after
them," problems that would, Williams implies, be alleviated were George's
wife restored to the home. The situation is complicated further by the fact

that the older chemist who secures the job offer for George shares George's reservations about biochemical warfare and even confides in him that if George does not take the job it will be offered to another chemist, whose "excess of zeal" is what initially moved George's supporter to "use his influence to get George the job."

The second example is set not in England but in an unnamed South American country. The hero, Jim, a hapless English botanist, has lost his way and stumbles onto the central square of a small town. Lined up there are twenty Indians, guarded by several armed, uniformed men. The captain in charge ("a heavy man in a sweat-stained khaki shirt") questions Jim. Satisfied that he got there by accident, the captain explains that the Indians were randomly chosen from a town that had been protesting against the government and the execution is meant to induce the rest of the town to curtail its resistances to the regime. "However, since Jim is an honoured visitor from another land, the captain is happy to offer him a guest's privilege of killing one of the Indians himself. If Jim accepts, then as a special mark of the occasion the other Indians will be let off." If Jim refuses, the mass execution will proceed as planned and Pedro, the captain's underling, will carry it out. All the villagers, including the twenty lined up for execution, "understand the situation and are obviously begging Jim to accept."[21]

From a utilitarian perspective, Williams argues, both George and Jim ought to accept the offers made to them. George ought to take the job, and Jim ought to shoot one Indian. Both will thereby bring greater pleasure and less pain into the world. But Williams disagrees. For the sake of his integrity, George should turn down the job and stay home, even though it means continued domestic unhappiness and even though it means that the biochemical warfare research he opposes will be in the hands of a zealot. The alternative involves George in a daily compromise of himself and his pacifist principles.

Jim's case is "different, and harder." The utilitarian solution "is probably right in this case"—he probably ought to shoot one of the men held hostage—but not necessarily so.[22] His case is more radically undecidable in part because Jim, unlike George, cannot just go home. Jim's case is also harder, less decidable, partly because Jim is facing the people who might die as a result of his (in)action—"the people at risk are *actual and there*"—while George is in a position to affect the lives only of people who are "hypothetical, future or *elsewhere*."[23]

These last considerations do make a difference to the phenomenology of dilemmas. But why does Williams stop there? Why not interrogate that difference? Why not draw attention to the institutional and discursive practices—never mentioned by Williams—that distinguish home from elsewhere, thereby enabling and inviting George to secure his integrity *by* staying home, in this case, literally? Is that not a privilege provided by the institutions—like the very research lab in question here—that frame and constitute George's horizons and secure for him a stable distinction between home and elsewhere, in part by producing the sorts of weapons that never let their users see their targets?[24] If so, then George's integrity is both supportive of and supported by the institutions from which George would like to stay away. Indeed, if he is able to announce his integrity with the celebrated catchphrase "not through me," that is because he is positioned to do so by a variety of forces—discourses, powers, privileges—that are very much at work through him, and through those around him.[25] And these forces are very much at work within Williams's own rendering of the two dramas, as well.

Positioned on a North-South axis, Williams's examples take advantage of a temporal/geographic scheme of development (which suggests that South America is "the past that the [North] has already lived out"[26]) to construct for us a home that provides a safe and nurturing space for integrity. The ordinariness of George's dilemma is secured by contrast with the extraordinariness of Jim's, and the contrast effectively reassures us that extreme situations, terrible bad luck, sweat-stained khaki shirts, and unmediated violence happen elsewhere, not here. Together, Williams's two examples combine to locate agentic integrity firmly at home, in England, where it is challenged by a merely ordinary dilemma posed by Others who are only hypothetical or elsewhere; meanwhile, a more radical undecidability and (its only match) the calculating morality of consequentialism are exiled abroad, where a violence that is graphic and unmediated attaches itself to a subject whose integrity is already a casualty of an extreme, truly tragic situation in which the Others he encounters are actual and there. All this in order to establish between George and Jim a clear, demarcating distance and difference that mirror, enable, and animate George's own project of establishing a similar distance and difference between himself and the laboratory whose research agenda threatens to compromise him.

The multiple oppositions layered and mapped by Williams's examples effect a displacement and projection of violences and conflicts that are inside the U.K. and its subjects onto an external Other that is safely distant from the home terrain. Why is this displacement important? Because it disempowers subjects of the U.K., leaving them unprepared to engage the violences and conflicts they *do* face at home, and because the displacement subtly affects the way those subjects view—and treat—the Others that serve as the screen for their projections. Specifically, Williams's second example tacitly suggests that South Americans are less damaged than are the British by exposure to utilitarianism, and that they, the South Americans, are more used to it: The scene interrupted by Jim is, after all, an instance of utilitarian punishment, performed for its expected didactic effects, inflicted not on those who are specifically guilty, but on a random sample of the population being "educated." This example subtly makes the point that Williams makes explicitly throughout: utilitarians may rule there—in South America? in nineteenth-century India?—

but not here. And where utilitarians rule, the integrity of the developed world and its citizens is always already—structurally—at risk.

These oppositions and their political effects are interrogated and resisted from the postcolonial, feminist perspective developed by Teresa de Lauretis. In contrast to Williams, de Lauretis emphasizes not the separability but "the *interrelatedness* of discourses and social practices," not the unitariness of integrity but "the *multiplicity* of positionalities concurrently available in the social field." That social field is "a tangle of distinct and variable relations of power and points of resistance" in which one is always already entangled in the forces one opposes.[27] For de Lauretis's subjects, therefore, the question is not *whether* to become involved in the discourses, practices, and institutions of which they are critical, but *how*. How best to position themselves given their complicity with and resistance to the discourses, practices, and institutions they seek to overcome or transform? From this perspective, withdrawal, staying home—in the purest and least complicated sense of that place—is simply not an option.[28]

Unsurprisingly, de Lauretis's project entails "leaving or giving up a place that is safe, that is 'home'—physically, emotionally, linguistically, epistemologically—for another place that is unknown and risky." It entails the rejection of all that to which George clings: "a family, a self, a 'home' . . . held together by the exclusions and repression that enable any ideology of the same," for the sake of the "position of resistance and agency" that such a rejection might enact.[29]

From such a position of resistance and agency, from a position that resists the seductions of home, we are empowered to ask after, and to theorize, the possible *connections* between home and elsewhere, between George's situation and Jim's. Once the question is posed, we might find that the lab that offers George a research position is owned by the same company that ships arms to the unnamed South American country in which Jim finds himself. Further investigation might reveal that a subsidiary of that company employs the local Indians to work on its agribusiness farms. Indeed, things might turn out to be even more complicated than that. Perhaps another branch of the same company funds botanical and genetic research. It may have provided the financial support for Jim's botanical expedition. It may even be financing his chair at his "home" university in England. With each new answer to these questions, with each new question, the easy line between home and elsewhere is increasingly attenuated.

That line—the line (re)produced by Williams's two examples in combination and also held fast by a tangle of social-political-cultural-economic-juridical-academic institutions and discourses—is the line that keeps the dilemmatic at bay, the line held fast by a series of displacements and projections that reassures "us" that we are safe from a radical undecidability that assaults Others elsewhere but only haunts us, from a distance, here.

"There's No Place like Home"

Williams's efforts both to affirm dilemmas and to keep them at bay mirror the efforts of those who, in the process of theorizing democracy and difference, affirm difference but relocate it in the safety of a different identity that is elsewhere, not here. Thus the differences and conflicts that are always already inside the subject are occluded, the possibility of safe spaces called home is resecured, and politics is returned to the familiar and relatively reassuring terrains of pluralism and multiculturalism.

These home-making strategies are challenged by Bernice Johnson Reagon, in her essay "Coalition Politics." Reagon chastizes those who turn to feminist politics seeking a homelike refuge. Women do not share a common experience or identity as women, she argues, feminism is always riven by differences, and so feminist politics must be coalitional, not homelike, in structure.

Coalition politics is not easy. It involves "trying to team up with someone who could possibly kill you because that's the only way you can figure you can stay alive." When you feel like you might "keel over at any minute and die," when "you feel threatened to the core," then "you're really doing coalition work."[30] Thus for Reagon, the transformation of women-only music festivals from sites of refuge to increasingly diverse, fractious, and unsafe gatherings—places of coalition—is to be celebrated, not mourned, because the festivals became "places of crisis and you can do wonderful things in a crisis."[31]

The yearning for home, the quest for safety, a home, a "barred room" a "womb," leaves people unprepared for "surviving in a world with other peoples," unprepared for conflict. "Some people will come to a coalition and they rate the success of the coalition on whether or not they feel good when they get there. They're not looking for a coalition; they're looking for a home! They're looking for a bottle with some milk in it and a nipple, which does not happen in a coalition. You don't get a lot of food in a coalition. You don't get fed a lot in coalition. In a coalition you have to give and it is *different* from your home."[32]

Like Williams, Reagon relies on that difference, deploying an opposition of home vs. elsewhere-coalition, but she departs from Williams in two important respects: first, she relies on the contrast between home and elsewhere to create a space for political involvement rather than to vouchsafe the privilege of withdrawal. Second, she repeatedly disrupts and confuses the terms of the opposition even as she continues to redeploy it. "It is very important not to confuse them—home and coalition," she says, but she then goes on to do just that.[33]

She begins by using the opposition conventionally. Home is a site of safety and identity; coalition politics is a site of danger and difference. Coalition politics requires a willingness to take risks, and that depends upon the reassuring prospect of periodic withdrawal from political involvement to safe spaces of refuge. "You can't stay there all the time. You go to coalition for a few hours and then you go back and take your bottle wherever it is, and then you go back and coalesce some more." Coalition, Reagon adds, "is a monster. It never gets enough. It always wants more. So you better be sure you got your home someplace for you to go to so that you will not become a martyr to the coalition."[34]

These conventional juxtapositions of home and coalition hearken back to Hobbes's account of the state of nature, which, no less than Reagon's coalition politics, is a monster that never gets enough, a place where people are martyred, and where survival mandates teaming up with "someone who could possibly kill you." Hobbes, too, juxtaposed that place with home, the private, safe, and stable place secured by Leviathan. And yet, as anyone with siblings must know, and as spouses in all domestic situations can surely attest, the practice of teaming up with someone who could possibly kill you is not the opposite of home, it perfectly captures one of the defining features of family life itself. What children or spouses do not establish temporary alliances with and against one another? Hobbes cast these terrors out of the home and projected them elsewhere, onto the screen of the state of nature.[35] Reagon repeats the Hobbesian projection, substituting her coalition politics for Hobbes's state of nature, ("coalition *can* kill people"[36]), mapping her home onto his (on both accounts, home is where life is preserved and people are fed).

But Reagon does not leave these Hobbesian structures intact. The irony with which she characterizes home as a womb or an infant's bottle unsettles her characterization of home as essentially a site of nurturance, free of difference, violence, conflict, and death: who but a recently fed infant could believe that? And, conversely, the exhilaration with which Reagon speaks of coalition politics unsettles her conventional identification of political involvement with danger and death. Indeed, as it turns out, coalition is "not by nature fatal";[37] it can also be a site of vitality and vigor, as Reagon makes clear in her concluding message: take the experience of coalition politics home with you, she tells her audience, "go around, apply it. And then do it everyday you get up and find yourself alive."[38] The monster that was all-consuming now appears as a generative power. And the homes so valued as vital sites of refuge from coalition are now seen to be themselves reinvigorated by the vitality and energy of political engagement. The classic Hobbesian opposition is unsteadied as the womb (home as life-preserving, nurturing refuge) is seen to be in danger of becoming its former opposite, a tomb, if deprived of the inspiration—the life-giving breath—of politics.

Coalition's life-giving powers do depend upon the support of spaces of withdrawal, recovery, and preparation, spaces like bell hooks's "homeplaces" where marginal peoples, objectified by a dominant racist and sexist culture, treat each other as subjects and further develop their capacities for agency, care, and respect.[39] Analogously, in totalitarian regimes, homeplaces serve as invaluable sites that enable not only care but also resistance, including the writing and preservation of secret counterhistories, and hidden transcripts. But the need for spaces of preparation, withdrawal, and resistance does not settle the question of how we ought to conceive of them. Reagon suggests that it is best to value them in context and to treat them as temporary (as with nationalism, a variety of homeplace that is both "crucial to a people if you are ever going to impact as a group in your own *interest*" and also potentially a "reactionary" force, zealously intolerant of others and of otherness[40]). I would add that home itself must also be resignified—a move Reagon stops short of. If home is to be a positive force in politics, it must itself be recast in coalitional terms as the site of necessary, nurturing, but also strategic, conflicted, and temporary alliances.

Moreover, as Reagon's rhetoric suggests, the resignification of home (and nation) entails another resignification—that of the womb, which has historically and psychoanalytically anchored the dream of home. The conventional figuration of the womb as a site free of difference, conflict, and struggle is as phantasmatic as the perfect, homeful bliss with which the mother-child dyad is conventionally viewed. This resignification might be enabled by the recent findings of the evolutionary biologist David Haig, who argues that the relationship between fetus and mother during pregnancy is not after all "a delicate process of cooperation between a woman and her fetus" but instead a series of genetic conflicts, a set of struggles over the resources needed for survival. Notably, Haig attributes the conflict to (what is effectively) the ineliminability of difference from identity. Instead of being a relation of perfect identity, it turns out that even the mother-fetus relation is riven by difference. The fetus (in the *New York Times*' gloss) "shares only half of its genes with the mother; the other half comes from the father. As a result, the evolutionary interests of a mother and her offspring can be different." They can even conflict.[41]

Parties to the scientific debate on this topic (as represented by the *New York Times*) fall into two camps: the relationship between mother and fetus is either cooperative or conflictual. In his quest for a more moderate position, Haig does not escape the binary but spatializes it, characterizing the situation as "a conflict of interest within a basically peaceful society." But in fact there is no basic peace on Haig's account, only a convergence of interests between mother and child. The fetus needs the mother-host to stay alive at least until it is born (and it has a further evolutionary interest in having future siblings who share half its genes). The mother has an interest in the birth of this child and future others because her "offspring is her [genetic] legacy to posterity."[42]

The construct of "interests"—as both Haig and Reagon rely on it—may occlude more than it discloses in this setting. The difficult, simultaneously rewarding, but altogether complicated set of relationships between mother and fetus (in the context of a wanted pregnancy), or between a nation and its

members, might be better characterized as a coalitional partnership in which
not interests per se but life itself is at stake, an arrangement in which parties
team up with an Other with the power to kill them because each one's life—
whether emotional, psychological, or as gene pool (in some larger sense)—is
deeply dependent upon the Other. Indeed, the fact that Reagon speaks of the
power, but not the propensity, of the Other to "kill" its coalitional partner
suggests that the metaphor's purpose is precisely to mark the coalitional relation's vulnerability, not to overdetermine its outcome.

These recastings of home and womb as coalitional in structure move from
the interest-anchored conceptions of Reagon and Haig to a more psychoanalytic perspective on the self's relation to difference and otherness as a set of
relations marked simultaneously by rage, struggle, mutuality, and debt. In so
doing, the recastings resist those remnants of (pre-) colonial home-yearning
that linger in Reagon's account, such as her identification of nationalism with
the achievement or location of a self-identical or authentic group interest un-
troubled by difference, and they deepen her critique of the will to home *in
politics* by stressing the uncontainability of home-yearning to particular (apolitical) sites for particular (political) purposes. The phantasmatic imaginary of
home (as safe haven in a heartless world) leaks into the politics of its bearers,
animating a longing for a more homelike, (would-be) womblike universe, unriven by difference, conflicts, or dilemmas, a well-ordered and welcoming
place. The phantasmatic imaginary of the womb is no less leaky; hence the
need to engage and resignify it, too.

The dream of home is dangerous, particularly in postcolonial settings, because it animates and exacerbates the inability of constituted subjects—or
nations—to accept their own internal differences and divisions, and it engenders zealotry, the will to bring the dream of unitariness or home into being. It
leads the subject to project its internal differences onto external Others and
then to rage against them for standing in the way of its dream—both at home
and elsewhere. (This maneuver parallels Williams's relocation of the dilemmatic from the inside of subjectivity to its outside where it takes shape as
discrete and episodic dilemmas that can and ought to be avoided whenever
possible.) This zealotry takes shape as a propensity either to withdraw from
conflicts or to conquer them: withdrawal (to a supposedly safe home that is
elsewhere, away from all this tumult) and conquest (of that tumultuous disorder in order to build a supposedly safe home here) are two sides of the same,
zealot's, coin. Both signal an unwillingness—on the part of constituted subjects or formed nations—to settle for anything less than a phantasmatic imaginary of home.[43]

To resignify home as a coalitional arrangement and to accept the impossibility of the conventional home's promised safety from conflict, dilemmas,
and difference is not to reject home but to recover it for the sake of an alternative, future practice of politics. The recovery does, however, admit and em-

brace a vulnerability that may *look like* homelessness from the perspectives of both Williams and his Kantian and utilitarian adversaries. That vulnerability is what Williams both theorizes (as tragedy) and seeks to fend off. For her part, Reagon struggles to resist both Williams's impulses by insisting that "you can do wonderful things *in* a crisis." But her success depends not only upon the capacity to see opportunity in crisis. It also depends upon the ability to resist the forces that imbue us with an often overwhelming desire to go home, or to found a home where we are, or to make a home out of the "I" that each of us is(n't).

Beyond the Womb Stage: The Democratic Energies of Decentered Subjects

What difference does "difference" make to democratic theory and practice? It disrupts liberal-democratic dreams of home, but it posits alternative, and perhaps broader, sites of potential empowerment. It disables certain conceptions of agency, but it enables others at the same time. It renders problematic (but not impossible) certain identity- and interest-based conceptions of pluralism, but it also animates more coalitional varieties of social democratic organization and affiliation.

All this is resisted by concepts like Bernard Williams's "integrity," which express a phantasmatic yearning for a clear, central principle, commitment, or disposition upon which a singular (individual or group) subjectivity can be grounded and secured. In opposition to this fantasy of safety and impermeability, however, another conception of subjectivity emerges, a coalitional (and psychoanalytic) conception in which the fragments, differences, and identities that constitute subjectivity do not simply coexist within a single if plural self but actually cross-cut and inhabit each other, cooperating with and waging war against each other in a perpetual motion of mutuality, engagement, struggle, and debt.

This alternative conception complicates Williams's first example, raising the possibility that George's dilemma between chemistry and pacifism is not external to him, but internal. That internal rift is occluded by Williams's identification of George's pacifism with his "most deeply" held ethical principles and by his positing for George the possibility and, indeed, obligation of withdrawal from the conflict occasioned by the lab's offer of employment. Williams never considers the possibility that George's devotion to chemistry is a sign that he is also deeply resistant to his own pacifism, or that George's identity as a pacifist depends upon—and is shaped by its partnership with—that moment of difference within him. Instead, he assumes that George's devotion to chemistry is an entirely separate project or commitment that is secondary, incidental, and certainly dispensable, while his pacifism, by contrast, is deep.

These assumptions enable Williams to lock into place the externality of the dilemma facing George, occluding and displacing the dilemmatic dimensions of intrasubjective conflict that are most deeply disturbing to the agentic integrity he values. Like Jim in South America, George simply happens upon his dilemma. George differs from Jim only in having the good luck to face his conflict not in the anarchy of South America but in the contrastingly stable, law-governed terrain called England. This enables (and even obligates) him to withdraw from the scene of conflict, his integrity intact—shaken, perhaps, but not stirred.

All this suggests that although Williams does not seek (in Berlin's terms) to eliminate conflict from the moral universe in a wholesale way, he does theorize an agency that is not really at risk from the *ordinary* conflicts it encounters, an agency that can and does withdraw from the dilemmatic even if only in the mild and unheroically piecemeal way that bespeaks a liberal—rather than a rationalist or absolutist—consciousness. This is an agency whose respect or tolerance for the sometime, quotidian unrulinesses of the moral and political world is grounded in Reagon's womb stage, in the certain knowledge that it can go home—to the conceptual-spiritual space of integrity or to the territorial terrain of hearth and family. This is an agency whose integrity depends upon a problematic political quiescence or withdrawalism, an agency that could stand to learn a great deal from the uneasy examples of figures like Robert Oppenheimer, Primo Levi, or the group Physicists for Nuclear Responsibility, all of which serve as salient counterheroes to Williams's George.[44]

"At home, they want more home," George Kateb argues in a brief note on homelessness, exile, and alienation.[45] There is truth in that. But away from home, we want more home, too. Home-yearning never goes away. The solution lies neither in the consolidation of new and improved homes that claim really to deliver on the dream nor in the exile of self-alienation sought by Kateb, which is, after all, never a fait accompli either. Instead, as Bruce Robbins suggests, if "there is no 'home' [in the sense of a place] free of all material encumbrance and social entanglement," then instead of "trying to return there again and again," we should try, rather, to "take the true measure of the real but relative freedoms we have." We cannot do this, however, unless and until we "stop positing spaces of freedom, which . . . inevitably mask someone else's servitude,"[46] spaces of privacy and integrity that depend upon the displacement of abjection onto Others, spaces of identity that seem to require for their survival the displacement, conquest, or conversion of the difference and Otherness that relentlessly intrude upon us.

Some of the real but relative energies and freedoms available to democratic agencies come from decentered subjects (excentric subjects, in de Lauretis's pun on "eccentricity") who are plural, differentiated, and conflicted because they are constituted as subjects-citizens in and by a world that is not—no more than they themselves are—rationally and singly authored. The social dimensions of the self's formation as a subject-citizen require and generate an openness to its continual renegotiation of its boundaries and affiliations in relation to a variety of (often incommensurable) groups, networks, discourses, and ideologies, both within its "home" state and abroad.[47] Social democracies—insofar as they are committed to the perpetuity of political contest and to the generation of new (domestic as well as international or extrastatist) social movements *in addition* to the more rather than less egalitarian distribution of scarce resources—have the greatest potential to permit and even energize the sorts of mobilities and settlements that these renegotiations require.[48] And when decentered subjects, aware of the role that difference plays in relation to identity, engage in these renegotiations they, in turn, have the power to energize their social democracies, while pressing upon them claims of justice, fairness, fidelity, and ethicality on behalf of those differences to which social democratic regimes tend to become deaf in their eagerness to administer to represented identities that are established, stable, and familiar.

With their activisms, these decentered subjects endorse Jean-François Lyotard's observation that "politics is only business and culture is only tradition unless both of them are worked over by a sense of the differend."[49] In so doing, these decentered subjects also display a greater sensitivity and fidelity to Bernard Williams's remainders than do his own agents of integrity. And, with their political practices of activism and amendment, they come closer to realizing Williams's own worthy vision of a practice of ethics that is responsive to the ineliminability of conflict and difference from the human condition.

Notes

1. On the need for a shift from an administrative to a politicizing democratic theory, see my *Political Theory and the Displacement of Politics* (Ithaca: Cornell University Press, 1993). For an exploration of identity/difference dynamics in their political and ethical settings, see William E. Connolly, *Identity\Difference: Democratic Negotiations of Political Paradox* (Ithaca: Cornell University Press, 1991). Connolly theorizes the identity/difference relation as an inescapable relation of debt and struggle with ethical ramifications, while also insisting that the self is not exhausted by this relation but, instead, always exceeds it. That excess, also marked by the Derridean term *différance* (and, according to Connolly, by the Nietzschean concept of "life"), is another of the elements that goes missing with the pluralist and multicultural conversions of "difference" into mere, different identities.

2. *Concepts and Categories: Philosophical Essays* (New York: Viking, 1979), xvi. A liberal consciousness, in Williams's gloss, "is prepared to try to build a life around the recognition that those different values do each have a real and intelligible human significance, and are not just errors, misdirections, or poor expressions of human nature" (*Concepts and Categories*, xviii).

3. The claim goes further: both mistake the nature of the need to overcome conflicts. The need is not logical or rational; it is social or personal ("Conflicts of Values," in Bernard Williams, *Moral Luck: Philosophical Papers, 1973–1980* [Cambridge: Cambridge University Press, 1981], 73, 81).

4. For Williams, "oughts" are possible courses of action that have a moral or ethical pull on the agent, but they are not necessarily obligations in the strict moral sense. In *Ethics and the Limits of Philosophy* (Cambridge, Mass.: Harvard University Press, 1985), 182, Williams argues that one problem with the "morality system" is its insistence on converting all oughts into obligations. This distinction (between some oughts and moral obligations) is what Williams seems to have in mind when he says that in discussing conflicts of oughts he is "considering what has traditionally though *misleadingly* been called 'conflicts of obligation'" ("Ethical Consistency," in Bernard Williams, *Problems of the Self: Philosophical Papers, 1956–1972* [Cambridge: Cambridge University Press, 1973], 170–71). Ruminations like this one are what have led some to identify Williams as one of an increasing number of Anglo-American theorists who see morality as a problem rather than a solution. See Bernd Magnus, Stanley Stewart, and Jean-Pierre Mileur, *Nietzsche's Case: Philosophy as/and Literature* (New York: Routledge, 1993).

5. Morality's openness to the charge either way is partly due to its own misguided treatment of every ought as an obligation, narrowly understood. See n. 4.

6. "Ethical Consistency," 172.

7. "Conflicts of Values," 75.

8. "Ethical Consistency," 172. Cf. 183–84: "It is surely falsifying of moral thought to represent its logic as demanding that in a conflict situation one of the conflicting oughts must be totally rejected." True, one of the oughts is rejected in the sense of not being acted upon, "but this does not mean that they do not both apply to the situation; or that I was mistaken in thinking that these were both things that I ought to do."

9. "Ethical Consistency," 179.

10. Ibid.

11. "Conflicts of Values," 75.

12. "Ethical Consistency," 173.

13. "What would have to be true of the world and of an agent that it should be impossible for him to be in such a situation where whatever he did was wrong? I doubt in fact that there is anything that could produce such a guarantee short of the existence of a rather interventionist [sic: providential] God or else the total reduction of moral life to rules of efficient behaviour—two extremes which precisely leave out the actual location of moral experience" (*Moral Luck*, 75).

14. Utilitarianism "will have something to say even on the difference between massacring seven million and massacring seven million and one." It leaves no room for "the unthinkable" as a "moral category." It deems irrational or cowardly the "refusal to follow out one's moral thoughts ("A Critique of Utilitarianism," in *Utilitarianism For and Against* [Cambridge: Cambridge University Press, 1973], 92–93).

15. Ibid., 91–92; emphasis added.

16. Utility makes the agent into a "channel between the input of everyone else's projects, including his own, and an output of optimific decision" ("A Critique of Utilitarianism," 116–17). Of course, one could argue, as Mill effectively does with regard to other traditional moral virtues, that it is a utilitarianly good thing that agents have integrity, and therefore respect for it ought to be built in to every calculation. I note this possibility, however, only to leave it aside; my interest here is not in the debate between utility and integrity but in the range of moral and political issues that that debate forecloses.

17. "Utilitarianism and Moral Self-Indulgence," in *Moral Luck*, 49; emphasis added. Cf. "A Critique of Utilitarianism," 116–17.

18. "Utilitarianism and Moral Self-Indulgence," 50–51.

19. "A Critique of Utilitarianism," 97.

20. "Desire in Narrative," in *Alice Doesn't: Feminism, Semiotics, Cinema* (Blooming-ton: Indiana University Press, 1984), 157. Within the moral theoretical literature, the question that suggests itself in response to dilemmas is precisely that forwarded by the hero's point of view: "What should I do?" My aim in this essay, and in the larger project from which this essay is drawn, is to make room for a more *political* set of questions also to emerge in response to dilemmas. Specifically: how do dilemmas work to fragment and consolidate certain forms of subjectivity, to shape our attitudes toward identity, difference, conflict, and pluralism, to generate felt needs for certain kinds of institu-tional arrangements? I explore these questions in more detail in *"There's No Place Like Home": Democratic Politics in Cosmopolitan Times* (Princeton: Princeton University Press, forthcoming).

21. "A Critique of Utilitarianism," 97–99.

22. Ibid., 117.

23. Ibid.; emphasis added. Williams further uses these examples to assess the differ-ent conceptions of responsibility and moral emotions operative in utilitarian thinking. He argues that from a utilitarian perspective the agent's reservations about participating in murder look like mere squeamishness. Moreover, the agent who refuses to act will be liable to the charge of negative responsibility: "You could have prevented it," the rela-tives of the murdered will say to Jim, and they will be right (108). But does that—should that—make *him* responsible for the outcome? I leave these interesting questions aside, while also leaving unassessed the merits of Williams's argument as a critique of utilitarianism. My interest at this point lies in Williams's own construction and treat-ment of these extreme and ordinary ethical conflicts and the subjectivities (un)settled by them.

24. These sorts of questions were recently raised by the Gulf War, which powerfully illustrated anew the astounding ability of advanced technological societies to conduct wars and kill people with the appearance of ease and cleanliness. That appearance has since slipped. For a deft discussion of its phantasmatic character, see Judith Butler, "Contingent Foundations," in *Feminists Theorize the Political*, ed. Judith Butler and Joan W. Scott (New York: Routledge, 1992), 10–11.

25. The phrase "not through me" articulates the fantasy of subjectivity—that the subject is a fixed point of origin and not (also) a contingent location and effect of discursive and social-institutional sedimentations (what Williams refers to only as "dis-positions and motives") that constitute its agency. That is, the capacity to say "not through me" with all the intensity that Williams imagines is enabled precisely by the falsity of the utterance and all that it presupposes.

26. I adapt the phrase from Shiv Visvanthan, who uses it with reference to the East-West divide. "From the Annals of the Laboratory State," in *Alternatives: A Journal of World Policy* 12 (1987): 41.

27. "Eccentric Subjects: Feminist Theory and Historical Consciousness," in *Feminist Studies* 16, no. 1 (Spring 1990): 131; emphases added.

28. Toward the end of *The Crying Game*, as the tentacles of the tragedy are wending their way around the film's major players, Fergus/Jimmy looks at a picture of Jody and says (to Dil, to himself), "He should never have left home." But where or what was Jody's home? The film suggests: Africa, the jungle, Jamaica, Tottenham, London, the U.K., the Metro (a pub named for a *transportation* system), or his heterosexual "nature"

and the home life to which it should have destined him. In this postcolonial landscape, home is not a stable site. Nor is it *really* a desirable site. Fergus's/Jimmy's wish is uttered in a preoccupied manner, as if his mind is elsewhere. He speaks these words with pain, but not in raw pain or anguish. He has been transformed by knowing Jody, and he does not seem—this late in the crying game—unequivocally disposed to wish those transformations away.

29. It involves "recognizing our location" and pursuing a consciousness of its "relation to or possible complicity with" the "socio-cultural formations (discourses, forms of representation, ideologies)" that it seeks to overcome or transform. ("Eccentric Subjects," 138–39; de Lauretis is quoting from Adrienne Rich's "Notes Towards a Politics of Location," in *Blood, Bread, and Poetry: Selected Prose, 1979–1985* [New York: Norton, 1986]).

30. "Coalition Politics: Turning the Century," in *Home Girls: A Black Feminist Anthology* (New York: Kitchen Table–Women of Color Press, 1983), 356–57.

31. Ibid., 360 and 368. The ancient Chinese character *chi* signified both crisis and opportunity. In modern Chinese, a supplement is added to make the distinction—*chi wei* signifies crisis or danger, and *chi hui* signifies opportunity or coming together in a positive way—while *chi* itself, true to its original signification as a *critical juncture*, now means a joint in a machine. Thanks to Arthur Kleinman and Yi ling Mao on this point.

32. Ibid., 358–9; emphasis added.

33. Ibid., 360.

34. Ibid., 359, 361.

35. This projection is somewhat attenuated, however, on Richard Flathman's recent account of Hobbes, in which the relationship between home and state of nature is not finally one of separation but one of "commingling." See *Thomas Hobbes: Skepticism, Individuality and Chastened Politics* (Newbury Park, Calif.: Sage, 1993).

36. "Coalition Politics," 361; emphasis in the original.

37. Ibid.

38. Ibid., 368.

39. *Yearning: Race, Gender, and Cultural Politics* (Boston: South End Press, 1990), 41–49. Reagon puts the point a bit differently: in your "barred room," she says, "you act out community" ("Coalition Politics," 358). But Reagon's barred rooms are not free of difference and conflict. Hence the need for community to be *acted out*.

40. "Coalition Politics," 361.

41. Haig concludes that "a lot of difficulties in pregnancy probably come about because there are genetic conflicts between what is best for the mother's genes and what is best for the fetal genes."

42. That convergence of interests expires at birth. Others may take its place subsequently. "Medical Science," *New York Times*, July 20, 1993, C3; citing David Haig, evolutionary biology, Harvard and Margie Profet, Division of Biochemistry and Molecular Biology, University of California, Berkeley.

43. These two sides of the zealot's coin are personified in Williams's first example by George and by his alternate, the chemist who pursues his research with an "excess of zeal." Indeed, these two characters make what is effectively—structurally—the same choice: both choose the relative safety of home over the risk of life in a dilemmatic (and potentially political) space. George withdraws to his home (which, though, not an unproblematic place, given his wife's absence and his children's attendant difficulties,

is a place of withdrawal and political uninvolvement), taking his regrets with him, while his alternate—let us call him Geoff—turns his work into a home, a place free of conflict and dilemmas. Why is Geoff so zealous in his labors? Again expanding upon Williams's examples, we might conjecture that Geoff was, perhaps, once a pacifist himself. Having long since abandoned that youthful commitment, however, he now proclaims, loudly and often, the incompatibility of political involvement with the objective, scientific pursuit of knowledge. His zealousness in research suggests that the remnants of past choices still haunt him, that he is still troubled by remorse or regret, unsteadied by those moments in his self that resist his proclamations, moments that he is determined to silence. *Both* George's and Geoff's are the responses of zealots. George's zeal is a little more attenuated, the home to which he withdraws may be a little more complicated, his sensitivity to the remainders of past choices may be a bit more nuanced, but his home-making strategies and the political-professional withdrawalism they enable are no less worthy of remark.

44. I discuss these counterexamples in detail in an expanded version of this essay, chap. 2 of *"There's No Place like Home."*

45. *Social Research* 58, no. 1 (Spring 1991), 137 (special issue on "Home: A Place in the World").

46. *Secular Vocations: Intellectuals, Professionalism, Culture* (London: Verso, 1993), 10.

47. In a recent essay, Michael Walzer forwards some initially similar sounding claims about social democratic agency and action, but Walzer's civil society is a pluralist rather than a dilemmatic space, in which no single or "singular answer" suffices in response to the civil society question, and in which citizens find in their "associational networks" many "partial fulfilments" but no "one clinching fulfilment." Walzer leaves the conflicts among the plural, partial answers to the civil society question undertheorized, even absent from the scene, never raising or exploring their cross-cutting intra- and intersubjective dimensions. In the absence of a more contestatory vision of social democracy and its agencies, it remains to some extent unclear what it is that *generates* the social democratic energies and actions Walzer means to celebrate. The outcome is little different from that produced by Williams's value pluralism: an effective if unwitting reinscription of home—in Walzer's case, mapped onto a relatively conflict-free civil society—and a recentering of a subject, unriven by difference, who is the beneficiary, as consumer and citizen, of a fairly benign social democratic pluralism. See Michael Walzer, "The Civil Society Argument," in *Dimensions of Radical Democracy: Pluralism, Citizenship, Community,* ed. Chantal Mouffe (London: Verso, 1992), 90, 99.

48. These sorts of renegotiations are one element of what I have called elsewhere a "magnanimous, democratic politics of augmentation and amendment." See *Political Theory and the Displacement of Politics,* chap. 7.

49. *Political Writings,* trans. Bill Readings and Kevin Paul Geiman. Minneapolis: University of Minnesota Press, 1993, 10.

Fourteen

Democracy and Multiculturalism

FRED DALLMAYR

IN RECOUNTING the Spanish conquest of America and the ensuing subjugation or annihilation of the native Indians, Tzvetan Todorov advances an important thesis: that "there exist two major forms of communication, one between man and man, the other between man and the world." In large measure, Todorov's account of the conquest revolves around the relation or conflict between these two modes of communication, with the Indians cultivating resonances with the world and the Spaniards interhuman discourse. The "exemplary history" of the Spanish conquest, he writes, teaches us "that Western civilization has conquered, among other reasons, because of its superiority in human communication; but also that this superiority has been asserted at the cost of communication with the world." Being heir to the Spanish colonizing effort, modern Western thought tends to conceive communication as "only inter-human"—a conception predicated on the notion that "world" cannot be a grammatical subject or a partner in dialogue. While granting the possibility of an evolutionary ascendancy, Todorov considers the latter conception as "perhaps a narrow view of the matter," one that unduly flatters "our feeling of superiority in this regard."

Properly construed, communication in Todorov's view should be extended to include, alongside intersubjective relations, also the interaction that occurs "between the person and his/her social group, the person and the natural world, the person and the religious universe." It was this second type of communication that played a crucial part in Aztec culture, which interpreted "the divine, the natural, and the social through indices and omens, and with the help of that professional, the prophet-priest." By privileging world-communication, the Indians were unable to cope with, and ultimately fell prey to, the rationalizing, disenchanting discourse of the Spaniards; in fact, it seems as if "everything happened because the Mayas and the Aztecs lost control of communication." Summarizing his findings on this score, Todorov's study offers an assessment that is judicious as well as haunting and full of portents for our time:

> The Spaniards win the war. They are incontestably superior to the Indians in the realm of interhuman communication. But their victory is problematic, for there is not just one form of communication, one dimension of symbolic activity. . . . The

encounter of Montezuma with Cortés, of the Indians with the Spaniards, is first of all a human encounter and we cannot be surprised that the specialists in human communication should triumph in it. But this victory, from which we all derive, Europeans and Americans both, delivers as well a terrible blow to our capacity to feel in harmony with the world, to belong to a preestablished order; its effect is to repress man's communication with the world, to produce the illusion that all communication is interhuman communication; the silence of the gods weighs upon the camp of the Europeans as much as on that of the Indians. By winning on one side, the Europeans lost on the other; by imposing their superiority upon the entire country, they destroyed their own capacity to integrate themselves into the world. . . . The victory was already big with its defeat.[1]

Beyond their focal concern, Todorov's comments (I believe) carry a broader significance. Uncannily, the Spanish-Indian encounter appears in many ways as a precursor of recent and contemporary developments, now projected onto a global scale. While, as Todorov says, the Spaniards managed to impose their superiority "upon the entire country" (meaning America), Western culture today is in the process of imprinting its mark upon the entire world. And since this process of globalization is primarily an interhuman encounter, we should once again not be surprised that the "specialists in human communication" (now including radar and telecommunication) should triumph or prevail. To be sure, the mission or spirit of Western culture today differs from that animating the conquistadors. Whereas—apart from the quest for lucre—Spanish colonizers aimed at (or justified their conduct in terms of) religious conversion and evangelization, modern Western culture is dedicated to the yardsticks of science and democracy, both secular in character. Yet the difference is deceptive, disguising a deeper linkage or connecting bond.

On this point again, Todorov provides telling clues. Devoted to the model of world-communication, he notes, Aztec culture gave a large space to religious belief—which seems to be paralleled by Spanish missionary zeal. But here a crucial contrast surfaces, one that separates that zeal sharply from all kinds of "pagan" religion. "What matters here," he writes, "is that Christianity is, fundamentally, universalist and egalitarian. 'God' is not a proper noun: this word can be translated into any language, for it designates not *a* god . . . but *the* god." In seeking to be universal and egalitarian, Christian religion—like modern science—transcends and cuts down all local or regional kinds of faith—and thereby is intolerant (despite its egalitarianism). While Aztecs managed to worship many divinities and even were willing to integrate Christ into their own pantheon, this option was not available to Christians—and in fact was harshly refused by Cortés, for a basic reason: the Christian god "is not one incarnation which can be added to the rest; it is *one* in an exclusive and intolerant fashion." This fact, Todorov notes wryly, contributed "not a little to the Spaniards' victory: intransigence has always defeated tolerance."[2]

Looked at from our contemporary vantage, the story of the Spanish conquest is instructive or "exemplary" in ways that are not fully developed in Todorov's study. Apart from pointing to continuing dangers of imperialism (cloaked today behind "one world" formulas), the story brings into view a tension or tensional opposition that is not merely accidental but has a basic or paradigmatic status: the opposition between the egalitarian universalism of modern Western culture and the array of particular ethnic cultures and religious traditions, that is, between a rationalized worldview and indigenous life-worlds. To the extent that it forms part and parcel of the Western syndrome, modern democracy—meaning here liberal-egalitarian democracy—necessarily stands opposed to alternative cultures and life forms, both at home and abroad—notwithstanding pragmatic attempts at accommodation. Being wedded to universalist principles (of equal liberty), modern democracy cannot readily accommodate radical cultural diversity—just as little as modern science can integrate alchemy (or Christianity accept the pagan pantheon).

In the following I would like to explore this tensional nexus of democracy (or democratic citizenship) and "multiculturalism," paying attention both to issues in democratic theory and to some concrete political experiences in our time. Taking a leaf from Todorov, one might say that the tension involves two modes of communication: the first being intersubjective (linking speaking subjects or agents), the second being "worldly" or holistic; using slightly different terms, the first might be described as linear and horizontal, the second as circular and (in a sense) vertical. A preliminary word of caution: in taking world-communication seriously, the point is not to endorse ethnocentrism or to ignore or downplay dangers of communal repression and aggression. While troubling and far from imaginary, these dangers (in fairness) must be complemented by perils lurking from the opposite side. Despite a complacent sense of moral "superiority" in the West, universalist ambitions are far from blameless or innocent, having often entailed violent or destructive consequences—a fact amply documented by the Spanish conquest.

I

In recent American discussions, the issue of "multiculturalism" (under this label) is often styled as a debate over curricular structure and reform, with defenders of mainstream education arrayed against advocates of "postmodern" pluralism or heterogeneity. Approached from this angle, the issue is largely (or only) of academic interest; reduced to curricular wrangles, the sharper edges of multiculturalism are likely to be dulled or ignored.[3] In a more direct and tangible fashion, the issue penetrates into contemporary ethical-political and constitutional theory in America—but again in a manner that rarely touches on the deeper level of cultural paradigms and existential life forms. In the scholarly literature in this field, (multi)cultural concerns surface primarily in the form of a controversy over the nature and status of the ethical bond in the public arena, that is, over the relative weight to be assigned to formal rules of justice vis-à-vis more substantive conceptions of the "common good." Customarily, the controversy boils down to the opposition between two major camps labeled respectively "liberalism" (or liberal universalism) and "communitarianism," with the first camp sponsoring universal principles derived from individual or interhuman consent, and the second a more historically nurtured vision of holistic goodness. In the vocabulary of moral theory, the first perspective may be said to subscribe to a "deontological" ethics revolving around individual "rights" and freedoms, while the second center-stages the cultivation of "virtue(s)" in the context of a moral-political community.[4]

It cannot be my purpose here to review in detail the liberal-communitarian controversy—something that has been done frequently and expertly by many others. At this point, I merely want to single out a few salient features of this debate—before proceeding to arguments that appear to me more telling and revealing with respect to multiculturalism. One feature that can hardly be overlooked is the somewhat abstract or ahistorical character of the debate, the tendency on both sides to treat "liberalism" or "communitarianism" as invariant essences or ideal types that can be instantiated at any time or place. While useful for polemical purposes, this essentializing tendency blends out significant aspects of locality and history (quite apart from downplaying multiple modes of syncretism or overlap).[5] Most important, theoretical essentialism sidesteps the historical situatedness of the debate, the fact that it arose in a distinct historical setting and for distinct reasons. Without oversimplifying unduly, one might say that the debate arose in the context of—and in response to perceived quandaries besetting—American liberal democracy, with one side seeking to shore up and vindicate the core tenets of that democracy and the other side pointing to weaknesses with the intent of providing remedies or antidotes for such defects. Seen in this light, it is clear that the debate was carried out on the terrain and under the auspices of liberal universalism, with communitarianism playing at best a subsidiary or remedial role. Moreover, placed on this terrain communitarians often were tempted to adopt the vocabulary of the host paradigm with its built-in polarity—which accounts for their proclivity to replace individual with communal goals or ego identity with collective identity. (In this manner, one might add as an aside, communitarians misconstrued the fabric of traditional life forms whose porous, unsystematic character eluded the individual-collective bifurcation.)[6]

I do not intend to linger further on this debate, which today is somewhat dated. In the meantime, the battle lines have shifted, and new arguments have been introduced that are more directly pertinent to multicultural concerns. Instructive in this respect is the work of Iris Young, especially her study *Justice and the Politics of Difference*. As Young makes it clear at the very beginning of her study, her approach steers a course between and beyond the alternatives of atomistic individualism and collectivist communitarianism—namely, by taking more seriously the existence of ethnic and cultural groups and their diversity. While liberal universalism tends to abstract from distinct cultural traditions and beliefs (in the interest of normative neutrality), prevalent modes of communitarianism integrate such traditions into a unified or collective worldview (often linked with the modern nation-state). Without relinquishing concern with equity and the rule of law, Young's study advances a view of justice more sensitive to historical and social contexts, especially to the rich texture of cultural life forms. In terms of this view, liberal universalism and egalitarianism need to be tempered and corrected through closer attention to cultural heterogeneity and the "politics of difference." As Young writes:

> The principle of equal treatment originally arose as a formal guarantee of fair inclusive treatment; this mechanical interpretation of fairness, however, also suppresses difference. The politics of difference sometimes implies overriding a principle of equal treatment with the principle that group differences should be acknowledged in public policy . . . in order to reduce actual or potential oppression. Using examples from contemporary legal debate, including debates about equality and difference in women's liberation, bilingual education, and American Indian rights, I argue that sometimes recognizing particular rights for groups is the only way to promote their full participation.[7]

In shifting the focus to cultural groups, Young's book departs sharply from liberal accounts of social pluralism, accounts in which groups figure merely as aggregates of individuals or as combinations for the pursuit of shared interests. Instead, Young places the accent on historically grown life forms, with each life form being differentiated from other groups by virtue of "cultural forms, practices, or way of life." Under the impact of modern individualism and utilitarianism, she notes, Western social and political theory has tended to construe groups "either on the model of aggregates or on the model of associations," both of which are "methodologically individualist concepts." In this usage, "aggregate" refers to a classification of people according to some substantive-empirical attributes, like skin color, gender, or age. Apart from other defects, this model neglects the deeper existential wellsprings of cultural life forms, the fact that cultural groups are defined not by extrinsic attributes but by "a sense of identity," that is, by shared practices and by shared historical experiences and agonies.

As distinguished from aggregates, "associations" are voluntary combinations formed for the promotion of particular interests. Although more practice-related, associations share a crucial premise with aggregates: like the latter, the association model "implicitly conceives the individual as ontologically prior to the collective, as making up or constituting groups." This premise, however, has been debunked by the main strands of "poststructuralist philosophy," which have exposed as illusory the metaphysics of a "unified self-making subjectivity." Following this line of deconstructive theorizing, Young's study not surprisingly invokes some Heideggerian insights regarding human "being-in-the-world." While membership in associations, she notes, derives from arbitrary choice, group affiliation by contrast "has the character of what Martin Heidegger calls 'thrownness': one *finds oneself* as a member of a group, which one experiences as always already having been." Yet existential affiliation does not signify an inescapable fate, nor does it support the reification of group life.[8]

As presented by Young, a politics of difference involves a commitment to justice and the rule of law coupled with a firm recognition and promotion of cultural life forms and group diversity. As she points out, liberal Enlightenment principles—enshrined in the American constitution—aim at equal legal treatment and at human and political emancipation construed as an exodus from parochial group loyalties. Under liberal auspices, justice means a focus on rights applicable "equally to all," while group differences are reduced to "a purely accidental and private matter." Liberalism thus construed, she concedes, has been "enormously important" in the history of modern politics by providing weapons in the "struggle against exclusion and status differentiation" and by making possible "the assertion of equal worth of all persons." Yet recent decades have brought to the fore the downside of this liberal program by showing the oppressive aspects of a homogenizing universalism. In Young's account, by construing liberation as the "transcendence" or "elimination of group difference," liberalism subscribes to a conception of justice that implicitly embraces an "ideal of assimilation," that is, a melting-pot vision of social integration. From the vantage of a politics of difference, by contrast, recognition of equal worth "sometimes requires different treatment for oppressed or disadvantaged groups."

Young's study at this juncture points to the upsurge of such a differential politics in the American context—as exemplified by the Black Power movement (with its celebration of Afro-American culture), the American Indian movement (with its stress on Red Power), the emergence of gay cultural expression, and more radical, gynocentric strands in the feminist movement (with their opposition to a liberal-humanist feminism). What emerges from these diverse movements and initiatives is not a denial of emancipation but rather a reformulation of the sense and direction of liberation—where the latter means no longer liberation from, but rather in and through culture and cultural diversity. As opposed to an assimilationist ideal, the politics of difference to this extent sponsors an outlook of "democratic cultural pluralism." In this vision, Young writes, the good society "does not eliminate or transcend group difference"; rather, it entails "equality among socially and culturally differentiated groups who mutually respect and affirm one another in their differences."[9]

As one should note—and as Young repeatedly emphasizes—recognition of group differences in the public realm must not be confused with a return to social hierarchies or to invidious sorts of cultural prejudice and exclusivism. From the vantage of radical democracy, pluralist politics completely rejects the lure of "essentializing" cultural groups or of endowing them with invariant (empirical or cultural) traits. While traditional politics, in devaluing some people, assumed an "essentialist meaning of difference" and defined groups as having "different natures," Young notes, a democratic politics of difference construes difference "more fluidly and relationally as the product of social processes," that is, as the outgrowth of cultural practices in interaction with other practices. Seen in this light, democratic multiculturalism assigns to cultural difference a transitive, transformative, and emancipatory meaning rather than confining it to an "exclusionary" mode. In the latter mode, assertion of group distinctness implies the denial of other groups and thus obeys the antinomial frame of self and other, thesis and negation.

As Young observes, the nondemocratic and "oppressive" meaning of difference defines it as "absolute otherness, mutual exclusion, categorical opposition," thereby submitting difference to the "logic of identity" where the dominant group embodies the norm from which others deviate. Construed as categorical opposition, difference represses not only interactions between groups but also differences *within* groups; thus in a curious reversal, difference as exclusion "actually denies difference." In contrast to this outcome, radical democratic pluralism adopts a flexible, open-ended stance; its understanding of group difference sees the latter as "indeed ambiguous, relational, shifting, without clear borders that keep people straight," as "entailing neither amorphous unity nor pure individuality." Most important, differential politics does not conceive difference in terms of timeless categories or attributes; instead, it focuses on the porous character of cultural traditions and on the "relations between groups" and between groups and public institutions. As Young comments, ably summarizing this part of her study, "Difference now comes to mean not otherness, exclusive opposition, but specificity, variation, heterogeneity. Difference names relations of similarity and dissimilarity that can be reduced to neither coextensive identity nor nonoverlapping otherness."[10]

II

In her study, Young discusses the implications of democratic difference chiefly with reference to salient domestic issues in the United States—specifically, women's liberation, bilingual education, and American Indian rights. In an epilogue she suggests that arguments of her book might be extended to other societies and even to the international or global context—leaving the matter, however, to broad hints. As it happens, multicultural pressures are felt today in several industrial countries and—perhaps most acutely—in non-Western societies rent by the conflict between modernizing life-styles and indigenous cultural traditions. Among industrial countries, a prominent example is Canada, marked by the rift between Anglophone and Francophone communities (not to mention the upsurge of native Indian claims to autonomy).

There are several aspects that render the Canadian case noteworthy and instructive. One aspect is the high political saliency of cultural pluralism and diversity. More than elsewhere (in the West), multiculturalism has been the topic of intense public and constitutional debates—which may have to do with the fact that Canada has never fully subscribed to the assimilationist or "melting pot" ideal of her neighbor. In 1967, a Royal Commission on Bilingualism and Biculturalism issued a report that focused attention both on rights of citizenship and on problems of cultural diversity. Largely in response to this report, the national government four years later announced an explicitly "multicultural" policy that, while stressing equal rights of all Canadians, also sought to protect the distinct life forms or cultures of minorities. A similar outlook was embodied a decade later in the Canadian "Charter of Rights and Freedoms," which, while clearly center-staging the liberal principle of equal individual freedom, also made reference to the "preservation and enhancement of the multicultural heritage of Canadians."[11] Apart from such official pronouncements, another important feature of multiculturalism in Canada is the sustained attention it has received from top-rate intellectuals and social theorists. For present purposes, I want to lift up for comment the views of one of Canada's leading philosophers, Charles Taylor, especially as articulated in the book *Multiculturalism and "The Politics of Recognition."*

Although often labeled a "communitarian" and hence accused of collectivist tendencies, Taylor's approach in that study is highly nuanced and circumspect; like Iris Young, his argument completely sidesteps established school doctrines, especially the conundrums of individualism-collectivism. In his contribution to the book—an essay titled "The Politics of Recognition"—Taylor pays ample tribute to the liberal legacy of individual freedom enshrined in the idea of a general human "dignity." As he points out, the collapse of feudal regimes wedded to social hierarchy (governed by the principle of honor) gave way in modernity to the notion of dignity, now used in "a universalist and egalitarian sense" where it refers to an "inherent dignity of human beings" or a "citizen dignity" uniformly shared by everyone. This notion was further deepened, but also complicated, by the postrevolutionary stress on a differentiated "identity," and particularly by the Romantic idea of an inwardly constituted "authenticity" lending distinctiveness both to individuals and to historically grown cultures. As formulated by Herder and his heirs, the maxim of authentic identity centerstaged "originality" of life-styles on two levels: that of the individual person among other persons and that of a "culture-bearing people among other people."[12]

The sketched key notions of the modern era, according to Taylor, have spawned a complex and tensional legacy. In his presentation, modernity has given rise to two competing conceptions of public life: the conceptions of liberal universalism (anchored in rights) and of cultural distinctiveness. With the move from feudal hierarchy to dignity, he writes, has come "a politics of universalism emphasizing the equal dignity of all citizens" and dedicated to the progressive "equalization of rights and entitlements." In modern (Western) democracies, the principle of "equal citizenship" and of growing equalization has become a central if not the chief governing maxim. On the other hand, the notion of authenticity or authentic identity has buttressed the emergence of a different conception: namely, a "politics of difference" focused on individual and cultural distinctiveness. Thus whereas the politics of universalism seeks to safeguard a general human sameness (termed "equal dignity"), the politics of difference insists on the need to recognize the "unique identity of this individual or group," that is, their differentiation from everyone else.

By seeking to secure unique distinctness to everyone alike, the latter politics obviously harbors an inner paradox—which is the paradox of democratic pluralism. Rigorously construed, Taylor notes, the politics of difference requires us to give general assent to what is not universal but particular; differently phrased, it insists on paying homage to what is universally present— that everyone has an identity—"through recognizing what is peculiar to each." Hence, a universal demand here "powers an acknowledgment of specificity." The contrast between the two types of modern politics is obvious and quite naturally fuels tensions and mutual accusations. While the politics of dignity seeks to promote nondiscrimination among all citizens in a "difference-blind" manner, the politics of difference often redefines nondiscrimination as requiring differential treatment based on individual and cultural distinctness. Whereas traditional liberals man the bastion of equal citizenship, advocates of difference are liable to attack the largely fictional character of liberal universalism, by asserting its complicity with prevailing power differentials (specifically with a "hegemonic culture" to which minority or suppressed cultures are required to adapt).[13] To exemplify these issues more concretely, Taylor at this point turns to the situation in Canada, as it has emerged in the wake of the Canadian Charter of Rights and Freedoms and of the so-called Meech Lake accord (which aimed to recognize Quebec as a "distinct society").

In Taylor's interpretation, the Canadian Charter basically center-stages individual rights and entitlements in a manner similar to the Bill of Rights of the American constitution. To this extent, Canada, like the rest of the Western world—and "perhaps the world as a whole"—is following the "American precedent" of a liberal, rights-based universalism. Relying on this aspect of the Charter, opponents of the Meech Lake accord (with its promise of cultural distinctness) in essence sponsored the priority of rights over "goodness," that is, the principle that individual rights together with nondiscrimination provisions must always "take precedence over collective goals." Inspired by "profound philosophical assumptions" traceable to Kant, this conception of politics understands dignity to consist chiefly in human "autonomy," that is, in "the ability of each person to determine for himself or herself a view of the good life." Promoted "with great force and intelligence" by prominent thinkers in the United States, the postulate of self-determining individual autonomy forms the core of what Michael Sandel has called the "procedural republic" with its privileging of procedural rules (including judicial review) over substantive goals or shared forms of life.[14]

While appreciating its "profound" assumptions and also some of its concrete effects, Taylor does not ultimately subscribe to this procedural model. As he indicates, liberal universalism is not as innocently neutral or nondiscriminatory as it claims to be. In the Canadian case, application of proceduralism does not impartially enhance or cultivate a distinct Francophone culture but rather undercuts or demolishes the latter. Generally speaking, political society cannot remain "neutral" between those seeking to maintain cultural traditions and those wishing to "cut loose" to promote individual self-interest. To this extent, proceduralism can be charged with being "inhospitable to difference" (or at least reducing difference to private preference). For committed Quebecers, what was at issue in constitutional debates was not only an individual right to bilingualism but the "survival and flourishing of French culture" seen as a shared "good" and its preservation for both present *and* future generations.

Pursuit of this goal, in Taylor's account, is not so much illiberal as rather inspired by a different conception of public life: that of a politics of difference. What is involved or presupposed in this conception is a distinction between two levels of rights: a level of basic or "fundamental" rights construed along the lines of liberal universalism (and the Canadian Charter), and a level of cultural rights that permits public regulation; while the former requires uniform treatment and should "never be infringed," the latter allows for cultural diversity. On this view, Taylor notes, a society with shared or common goals can still be "liberal," provided it is also capable of "respecting diversity," especially when dealing with dissenters, and of maintaining "adequate safeguards for fundamental rights." As is evident throughout, Taylor's own sympathies are with such a differential view of politics—purged of repressive-collectivist traces. Properly construed, he adds, a politics of difference is

> willing to weigh the importance of certain forms of uniform treatment against the importance of cultural survival, and opt sometimes in favor of the latter. . . . Although I cannot argue it here, obviously I would endorse this kind of model. Indis-

putably, though, more and more societies today are turning out to be multicultural, in the sense of including more than one cultural community that wants to
survive. The rigidities of procedural liberalism may rapidly become impractical in
tomorrow's world.[15]

As one should note, Taylor's endorsement of differential politics is qualified
in several ways. Apart from insisting on basic liberal safeguards (on the level
of fundamental rights), his essay also takes exception to an uncritical acceptance of all kinds of cultural diversity—something occasionally demanded by
radical multiculturalists (including proponents of "subjectivist neo-Nietz-
schean" theories). In Taylor's view, uncritical acceptance of this sort is ultimately a form of condescension, because it does not derive from a "genuine act
of respect." From his perspective, the claim to attention and respect on the
part of other cultures operates only in the form of a presumption—to the
effect that, having animated societies over long stretches of time, such cultures
have presumably something to teach the rest of the world. Although the
presumption is not invulnerable, it cannot be dislodged without close engagement and a serious effort at understanding. Phrased differently, the presumption requires not a "peremptory" acceptance of all cultural beliefs and practices but "a willingness to be open to comparative cultural study of the kind
that must displace our horizons in the resulting fusions."[16]

III

The presumption stated by Taylor implies a readiness for cross-cultural engagement and certainly a rejection of any kind of Eurocentrism or Western
cultural imperialism. Seriously applied, the presumption unhinges prevailing
hegemonic relations, including the taken-for-granted superiority of modern
Western life-styles. At this point it seems appropriate to turn to the broader
global repercussions of contemporary multiculturalism, that is, to the tension
between liberal-Western universalism and cultural loyalties in a worldwide
setting. The tension is clearly evident in many of the (so-called) "developing"
societies where "nation-building" along Western lines has led to the juxtaposition of two highly diverse, nearly incompatible life-styles and political discourses: on the one hand, the discourse of secularism, legal proceduralism,
and individual rights; on the other hand, the complex fabric of vernacular
traditions and indigenous cultural beliefs. The abruptness of the juxtaposition
accounts in good measure for the volatile, near-explosive character of political
conditions in large parts of Africa; the same volatility extends in modified form
into the Near East and portions of Asia.[17]

Under provocation, the unsteady mix of life forms and discourses can readily tilt into one or the other direction—although political contexts constrain

the available range of options. Wherever one turns in the non-Western world today, one finds oscillation between secular-modernizing and religious (some-times fundamentalist) regimes or movements. Given Western global hege-mony in economic, military, and scientific domains, long-range trends augur ill for the maintenance of indigenous practices or vernacular narratives. To grasp the effects of hegemonic cultural imposition, one does not have to ven-ture far afield. A telling case is the fate and present condition of native Indian communities in North America, particularly in the United States. With some adjustments, a similar story can be told about (postindependence) develop-ments in Central and South America—where the rhetoric of liberal procedur-alism (with an accent on individual property rights) has often been used to erode and disaggregate native communities.[18]

The fate of American Indians provides a sobering reminder of the dangers and defects of modern universalism—a reminder that offers no brief or vindi-cation for xenophobia or ethnic self-seclusion. No doubt, the hazards of our age are immense on all sides—and can be met only if responses rise to the level of contemporary challenges. As it seems to me, our time is urgently in need of political imagination and a readiness for experimentation (qualities that often are in short supply). Clearly, to avoid the pitfalls of communalism as well as universalist assimilation, new paths need to be explored on the levels of both institutional arrangements and political reflection. With regard to public insti-tutions, proponents of liberal individualism sometimes assert the superior and indeed incorrigible character of existing Western structures and procedures—an assertion that neglects the variety among Western regimes as well as the long period of experimentation preceding prevailing arrangements. In a democratic setting hostile to both ethnocentrism and universalist leveling, cultivation of diversity cannot solely rely on existing procedural safeguards—although the latter must not lightly be discarded or set aside.

More than ever in politics, democratic multiculturalism provides the op-portunity and the need for institutional inventiveness and flexibility. Among the diverse possibilities of institutionalizing or giving public recognition to cultural diversity, attention might be given—and is sometimes given in the literature—to such institutional devices as the extension of individual rights to group or collective rights (especially rights of ethnic and cultural minorities); the establishment of "ethnic federalism," that is, a regime that grants a degree of autonomy and self-government to ethnic groups within a broader constitu-tional framework; the promotion of "consociational" policies (in Arend Lijphart's sense) involving the consensual or agonal interaction between group leaders in multiethnic societies; and finally the diversification of parliamentary government through novel forms of bicameralism (or multicameralism) allow-ing representation of different constituencies. None of these devices are free of problems or possible abuses; hence, all need to be carefully screened and calibrated to ensure the democratic character of multiculturalism.[19]

On the plane of theoretical reflection, multicultural politics forces a reconsideration of many issues that were presumed to be settled under Enlightenment or post-Enlightenment auspices. In important ways, this reconsideration
inserts itself into the contemporary questioning of the status of "modernity"
(which, in my view, has no truck with a facile antimodernism). One way to
approach these issues is by returning to Tzvetan Todorov, and especially to his
differentiation between two chief modes of communication. Ever since the rise
of contractarian theories in early modernity, interhuman (or subject-subject)
communication has been at the heart of Western conceptions of social and
political life, while "world" has been progressively distanced into a target of
objective-scientific analysis. To be sure, the manner of conceptualization has
been progressively refined during recent centuries—though without changing
the basic direction. Thus contractarian assumptions still surface in a new guise
in contemporary rational choice models, in versions of "speech-act" theory,
and especially in the conception of communicative rationality and "communicative action" (formulated by Habermas). As Alessandro Ferrara has noted, the
conception of communicative rationality and of a consensus among equal
partners "presupposes a *modern* frame of reference. It would make no sense to
speak of rational agreement on the soundness of a validity claim within a
tradition-oriented culture. Furthermore, the distinction of three kinds of validity claims presupposes the differentiation of objective, social and subjective
world—a differentiation which takes place only with modernity."[20]

Although prominent (and valuable in many respects), the primacy accorded to interhuman communication today is no longer unequivocal or un-
disputed; as it happens, several intellectual developments are afoot aiming at
a retrieval of the world-dimension. Particularly noteworthy in this respect is
Husserl's turn to the "life-world" and Heidegger's insistence on the worldliness
of human life and his portrayal of human *Dasein* as a "being-in-the-world,"
that is, as a creature intimately enmeshed in a complex, multifaceted context.
As one should note, "world" for Heidegger does not signify an external container (a *res extensa*) amenable to objectifying analysis, but rather a constitutive feature of *Dasein* itself—the latter no longer seen as a subjective ego but
as a participant embroiled in the ongoing happening or disclosure of "being."
Without neglecting interhuman speech or discourse (on the level of human
co-being or *Mitsein*), world relations in this framework extend to a nonobjecti-
fying and interpretive engagement with nature as well as an attuned sensitivity
to the "call of conscience" (as *vox Dei*)—that is, to a multilayered fabric of
experiences and linguistic modalities. World-communication in this sense is
further developed and fleshed out in Heidegger's later reflections on language—where language is seen no longer as a mere means or instrument of
human communication but as an inexhaustible reservoir or endowment allowing human thought and speech to proceed in the first place. In Heidegger's

account, language has its own mode of speaking and disclosure that establishes a primordial space for world-communication and world-experience, a space making room for the interactive entwinement of human life and nature, and of human finitude and the divine.[21]

These considerations clearly have a bearing on multiculturalism—given that cultures are life forms or forms of world-communion where meaning is structured along horizontal as well as vertical-holistic lines. What additionally needs to be taken into account here is the close linkage between cultures and vernacular or indigenous languages—a linkage that resists streamlining under the auspices of universalist discourses. At this point complaints or concerns are likely to be raised again regarding communalism or ethnocentric myopia—complaints that are not spurious given the widespread upsurge of ethnic antagonisms and violence in our time. As will be remembered, liberal universalism arose precisely as an antidote and corrective to feudal parochialism and to the proliferation of status distinctions in feudal society. To this extent, liberalism heralded an emancipation from parochial bondage and from the fetters of social inequality; in Kant's celebrated phrase, Enlightenment signaled a release from external tutelage and an ascent to the level of a self-governing maturity. Yet there are reasons to believe that our age holds out the challenge of a new and different kind of maturity: one where freedom is willing to recognize and cultivate cultural diversity (without restoring invidious hierarchies).

What has been called "lateral universalism" may precisely be a corollary of this mature stance—a stance where universal principles are no longer found outside or beyond concrete differences, but in the heart of the local or particular itself, that is, in the distinct topography of the world. This view resonates with another aspect of Heidegger's later work: his accent on the "fourfold" topology of being, that is, the capacity of every individual thing to gather in itself all the constitutive dimensions of the world. This conception, in turn, resonates with a view prominent in Asian thought: the view of the "suchness" of all beings as an emblem not of self-centered seclusion but of an ingathering hospitable to all other beings. In the context of Zen Buddhism, Keiji Nishitani elucidates suchness with the help of the (medieval) notion of "circuminsession," stating that, by virtue of this circuminsessional relation, every individual being is the ground of all others, and hence all things "are gathered together and as such render possible an order of being, a 'world.'" A similar outlook is expressed by Lao Tzu in the *Tao Te Ching*, in a passage that is sometimes interpreted in terms of a narrow parochialism:

> There is no need to run outside
> For better seeing,
> Nor to peer from a window. Rather abide
> At the heart of your being.[22]

Notes

1. Tzvetan Todorov, *The Conquest of America: The Question of the Other*, trans. Richard Howard (New York: Harper Perennial, 1992), 61, 69, 97, 251.

2. Ibid., 105–6. As he elaborates (106), "Christianity's egalitarianism is part of its universalism: since God belongs to all, all belong to God; there is not, in this regard, a difference among peoples nor among individuals."

3. For aspects of the academic debate cf. Allan D. Bloom, *The Closing of the American Mind* (New York: Simon & Schuster, 1987) and *Liberal Education and Its Enemies* (Colorado Springs: Air Force Academy, 1991); Dinesh D'Souza, *Illiberal Education: The Politics of Race and Sex on Campus* (New York: Free Press, 1991); Nancy Warehime, *To Be One of Us: Cultural Conflict, Creative Democracy and Education* (Albany: SUNY Press, 1993); Russell Kirk, *America's British Culture* (New Brunswick, N.J.: Transaction, 1993); also Bruce Wilshire, *The Moral Collapse of the University* (Albany: SUNY Press, 1990).

4. Cf., e.g., David Rasmussen, ed., *Universalism vs. Communitarianism: Contemporary Debates in Ethics* (Cambridge, Mass.: MIT Press, 1990); Shlomo Avineri and Avner de-Shalit, eds., *Communitarianism and Individualism* (New York: Oxford University Press, 1992); Stephen Mulhall and Adam Swift, eds., *Liberals and Communitarians* (Oxford: Blackwell, 1992); Will Kymlicka, *Liberalism, Community and Culture* (New York: Oxford University Press, 1989); and Michael Sandel, ed., *Liberalism and Its Critics* (New York: New York University Press, 1984).

5. The historical dimension has been recognized at least by some (presumed) communitarians. As Charles Taylor has noted: "The basic error of [liberal] atomism in all its forms is that it fails to take account of the degree to which the free individual with his own goals and aspirations . . . is only possible within a certain kind of civilization; that it took a long development of certain institutions and practices, of the rule of law, of rules of equal respect, of habits of common deliberation, of common association, of cultural development, and so on, to produce the modern individual." See his *Philosophy and the Human Sciences: Philosophical Papers* (Cambridge: Cambridge University Press, 1985), vol. 2, 309.

6. As Michael Sandel, a leading communitarian, candidly admitted: "Despite its philosophical failure, this liberal vision is the one by which we live. For in late-twentieth-century America, it is our vision, the theory most thoroughly embodied in the practices and institutions most central to our public life." See his "The Procedural Republic," in Avineri and de-Shalit, *Communitarianism and Individualism*, 14. The aspect that traditional life forms are streamlined into collective identities only under the impact of modern ideologies (especially the ideology of nationalism) is widely recognized in the literature; cf., e.g., Partha Chatterjee, *Nationalist Thought and the Colonial World* (Minneapolis: University of Minnesota Press, 1993).

7. Iris Marion Young, *Justice and the Politics of Difference* (Princeton: Princeton University Press, 1990), 4, 11. Young acknowledges a number of intellectual mentors—who are appropriately diverse. Her attitude toward Habermasian critical theory (a "communicative" variant of liberalism) is instructive: while appreciating the accent on dialogue and critical reflection, she takes exception to Habermas's rationalist universalism (his concern with ideal consensus, his separation of reason and affectivity). On the other hand, she invokes selectively "postmodern" writers, including Adorno, Hei-

degger, Derrida, Lyotard, Foucault, Kristeva, and Irigaray (7, 106–7, 117–18). See also Young's essay in this volume.

8. Ibid., 43–47.

9. Ibid., 156–63. Curiously, while invoking the good society and attacking liberal neutrality, Young at other points supports the liberal separation of justice from the "good life" and the primacy of rights over goodness; see 36, 103–4.

10. Ibid., 157, 169–71. In taking this approach, Young clearly rejects the notion of radical cultural "incommensurability." Cf. in this context also Richard J. Bernstein, "Incommensurability and Otherness Revisited," in his *The New Constellation: The Ethical-Political Horizons of Modernity/Postmodernity* (Oxford: Polity Press, 1991), 57–78.

11. On the Charter of Rights and Freedoms see Huguette Labelle, "Multiculturalism and Government," in James S. Frideres, ed., *Multiculturalism and Intergroup Relations* (New York: Greenwood Press, 1989), 1–4.

12. Charles Taylor, "The Politics of Recognition," in *Multiculturalism and "The Politics of Recognition"* (Princeton: Princeton University Press, 1992), 24–35.

13. "The Politics of Recognition," 37–39, 43. See also Will Kymlicka's essay in this volume.

14. "The Politics of Recognition," 43–44, 52–58. See also Michael Sandel, "The Procedural Republic and the Unencumbered Self," *Political Theory* 12 (1984): 81–96. Among prominent American spokesmen of liberal universalism, Taylor mentions especially Rawls, Dworkin, and Ackerman.

15. Taylor, "The Politics of Recognition," 58–61. The essay gives a succinct summary of the debates surrounding the Meech Lake accord (60): "The rest of Canada saw that the distinct society clause legitimated collective goals [in violation of liberal proceduralism]. And Quebec saw that the move to give the Charter precedence imposed a form of liberal society that was alien to it, and to which Quebec could never accommodate itself without surrendering its identity."

16. "The Politics of Recognition," 66–67, 70–73. The requirements of cross-cultural understanding have been discussed by Taylor in greater detail in "Comparison, History, Truth," in Frank E. Reynolds and David Tracy, eds., *Myth and Philosophy* (Albany: SUNY Press, 1990), 37–55, and in "Understanding and Ethnocentricity," in Taylor's *Philosophy and the Human Sciences*, 116–33. For discussions of the Canadian situation from different angles see George Grant, *English-Speaking Justice* (Notre Dame, Ind.: University of Notre Dame Press, 1974), and *Lament for a Nation: The Defeat of Canadian Nationalism* (Toronto: Macmillan of Canada, 1978); also Pierre Vadeboncoeur, *Un génocide en douce* (Montreal: Parti pris, 1976), and Louis Sabourin, *Passion d'être, Désire d'avoir: Le dilemme Québec-Canada dans un univers en mutation* (Montreal: Editions du Boréal, 1992). In Vadeboncoeur's view, modern liberal universalism inevitably dismantles traditional cultures (through a process of "gentle genocide" that cannot be reversed).

17. Cf. in this context Mark Juergensmeyer, *The New Cold War? Religious Nationalism Confronts the Secular State* (Berkeley and Los Angeles: University of California Press, 1993); and Crawford Young, ed., *The Rising Tide of Cultural Pluralism: The Nation-State at Bay?* (Madison: University of Wisconsin Press, 1993).

18. The disruption of Indian communities in favor of individual or corporate property rights is discussed by Jeffrey L. Gould with special reference to developments in Nicaragua; see his "They Don't Care about Our History: Politics and Ethnicity in Nicaragua, 1920–1980" (an unpublished typscript). For a plea to revitalize native voices in the

global arena see Franke Wilmer, *The Indigenous Voice in World Politics* (Newbury Park, Calif.: Sage, 1993).

19. Some of these devices, with particular reference to Yugoslavia, are explored by Vojislav Stanovcic in "Problems and Options in Institutionalizing Ethnic Relations," *International Political Science Review* 13 (1992): 359–79. See also Arend Lijphart, *Democracy in Plural Societies: A Comparative Exploration*, 2d ed. (New Haven: Yale University Press, 1980); Will Kymlicka, *Multicultural Citizenship: A Liberal Theory of Minority Rights* (Oxford: Clarendon, 1995); and Kymlicka, ed., *The Rights of Minority Cultures* (Oxford: Oxford University Press, 1995). Regarding the issue of diverse constituencies, cf. Robert C. Grady, *Restoring Real Representation* (Champaign: University of Illinois Press, 1993).

20. Alessandro Ferrara, "Universalisms: Procedural, Contextualist and Prudential," in Rasmussen, *Universalism v. Communitarianism*, 16. Sharpening his critique, Ferrara (17) describes Habermasian theory as a "generalization of the parochialism of modernity," adding: "The universality of the complexes of rationality brought about by modernity is questionable, the superiority of modern rationality over that of pre-modern and primitive societies is questionable, and the factual irreversibility of modernization cannot lend normative force to the modern conception of validity."

21. See Martin Heidegger, *On the Way to Language*, trans. Peter D. Hertz (New York: Harper & Row, 1971); and Gerald L. Bruns, *Heidegger's Estrangements: Language, Truth, and Poetry in the Later Writings* (New Haven: Yale University Press, 1989). A similar view is reflected in Gadamer's notion of the "speculative" character of language revealing its quality of world-disclosure; see Hans-Georg Gadamer, *Truth and Method*, 2d rev. ed., trans. Joel Weinsheimer and Donald G. Marshall (New York: Crossroad, 1989), 469.

22. See Lao Tzu, *The Way of Life*, trans. Witter Bynner (New York: Perigee Books, 1972), 75; Keiji Nishitani, *Religion and Nothingness*, trans. Jan Van Bragt (Berkeley and Los Angeles: University of California Press, 1982), 159; and Heidegger, "The Thing," in *Poetry, Language, Thought*, trans. Albert Hofstadter (New York: Harper & Row, 1971), 163–86. Cf. also Masao Abe, "Emptiness Is Suchness," in his *Zen and Western Thought*, ed. William R. LaFleur (Honolulu: University of Hawaii Press, 1985), 223–27; and my discussion of Nishitani in *The Other Heidegger* (Ithaca: Cornell University Press, 1993), 200–226. The notion of a "lateral universalism" was put forth by Maurice Merleau-Ponty in *Signs*, trans. Richard C. McCleary (Evanston: Northwestern University Press, 1964), 119–20. What Sabourin calls "endogénéité" seems to point in a similar direction; see *Passion d'être, Désir d'avoir*, 112–34.

Fifteen

The Performance of Citizenship: Democracy, Gender, and Difference in the French Revolution

JOAN B. LANDES

THERE HAS BEEN considerable discussion of late over the gendered character of the bourgeois public sphere, which I have elsewhere characterized as being "essentially, not just contingently, masculinist."[1] My aim is not to rehearse these disagreements here, and I would endorse the efforts of those who seek to realize the promises of freedom, equality, and reason within enlightened discourse. Yet I would note that the long-deferred emancipation of women, like racial minorities and the working classes, cannot be laid solely at the door of the political choices made in France in 1789, or what Keith Baker refers to as the privileging of the "republican discourse of political will, which found its fullest expression in the Terror."[2] I do not share Baker's confidence that competing discursive positions in the eighteenth-century milieu were radically independent of one another. I also question the value of exempting the discourse of rational social progress from the charge of masculinism if, as Baker himself admits, those who held to this rationalist discourse also allowed (what he deems to be) "contingent grounds for denying women (and others) full and immediate participation in the exercise of universal individual rights."[3] Certainly, liberal rational discourse opened up opportunities for women to claim rights and new political identities, but so too did republican ideology; both, in turn, foreclosed the possibility of full gender equality. With respect to the question of female citizenship, at least, what appears most striking are the overlapping vocabularies and political practices of seemingly distinctive orientations to democratic politics in the eighteenth century.

The dramatic exclusion of women from the full rights of citizenship arrested the movement toward gender equality during the French Revolution. Additionally, the paradox of the gendered determination of modern democratic sovereignty and republican freedom is nowhere more dramatically played out during the eighteenth century than in the popular revolution in France. However, the cumulative record of women's rights in the "age of democratic revolution" is far from encouraging. Republican France is an exception only in the extent to which women actually participated in national politics (as opposed to community life) and simultaneously staked out substantive claims to political citizenship. It may be true that revolutionaries in France, compared to England and America, were more deeply invested in a Rousseauist version of republicanism and hence committed to the doctrine of naturally derived sexual difference.[4] Equally pertinent, though, is Harriet Branson Applewhite's and Darline Gay Levy's striking observation that "the age of democratic revolution nowhere produced political democracy that included women as citizens; nowhere did women achieve political and civil rights that middle-class white male proprietors had established for themselves. . . . At the same time, however, self-conscious demands for the improvement of women's condition through education, welfare, extensions of civil rights, and reform of family law became an irradicable part of the political agenda. Simultaneously, men's awareness of women's claims and of their challenge to male dominance and hegemonic power brought to the surface the deep-seated anxieties and ambivalence of the governing elites."[5] Like Applewhite and Levy, I am impressed that "*everywhere* in the Western world, women's available repertoires of words and symbols were derived from a male political language" (my emphasis).[6]

I do acknowledge the existence of competing discourses in enlightened thought on the position of women.[7] However, I would argue that neither liberals, rationalists, nor republicans wholly met the challenge of gender equality, nor was this a consequence of some lapse of attention or traditional prejudice on their part. From the outset, democracy in the modern world produced not only a discourse but a practice of gender difference. Gender, in turn, was caught in the webs of modern politics, and marked by oppositions between individual and community, particularity and universality. With this in mind, I want to reconsider the constitution of democratic social space during the Revolution from the perspective of the staging of the new political body of the democratic sovereign. Surely, just as democratic space was partitioned into gendered territories and legal barriers to women's equality were established, women were fated to political, civil, and personal subordination. Likewise, the representation of power in the democratic public sphere was premised on the fiction of a neutral, but embodied (because natural) subject; one capable of subjecting (his) individual passions and interests to the rule of reason. Only men's bodies seemed to fulfill the ideal requirements of this contained form of subjectivity. In contrast, women were deemed to inhabit bodies that, rather than guaranteeing their political liberties, were marked by their physically distinctive sexualities and irrational, hence apolitical, qualities.

In his report to the Convention on behalf of the Committee of General Security on the occasion of the Convention's decision in fall 1793 to outlaw all women's societies and popular clubs, André Amar summed up well the fear that women's unloosed nature spelled for many men. Citizen Amar stated that women's presence in popular societies "would give an active role in govern-

ment to people more exposed to error and seduction. . . . Women are disposed by their organization to an over-excitation which would be deadly in
public affairs and . . . interests of state would soon be sacrificed to everything
which ardor in passions can generate in the way of error and disorder. Delivered over to the heat of public debate, they would teach their children not
love of country but hatreds and suspicions."[8] Amar's suspicions are certainly
characteristic of radical Jacobin worries about women's public presence; and
Rousseau is the obvious source for such rank sentiments. But Rousseau is
certainly not alone in his culpability. Indeed, Carole Pateman has argued per-
suasively that "it is only in the modern world that 'disorder of women' constitutes a general social and political problem." She states, "more specifically, it
is only with the development of liberal individualism and the arguments of its
democratic and socialist critics that beliefs about women become an acute,
though not always acknowledged problem in social and political theory and
practice."[9] Additionally, Pateman claims that "the body of the 'individual' is
very different from women's bodies. His body is tightly enclosed within
boundaries, but women's bodies are permeable, their contours change shape
and they are subject to cyclical processes. All these differences are summed up
in the natural bodily process of birth. . . . Women lack neither strength nor
ability in a general sense, but, according to the classic contract theorists, they
are naturally deficient in a specifically *political* capacity, the capacity to create
and maintain political right."[10]

Pateman is no doubt right to notice the repeated efforts of male theorists
and political activists to confine women to a "naturally defined" role in the
private sphere of the family. Yet for her this amounts to the circumstances of
patriarchal rule, anchored by a nearly permanent constitution of "our very
identity as embodied women and men."[11] Conversely, by way of a brief exploration of the counterdiscourse on women's rights, along with several instances
of feminine performances during the Revolution, I hope to demonstrate the
extent to which women's seemingly essential(ized) gender identities were subject to disruption and friction.[12] By charting the ambiguities in discourse and
practice during the Revolution, I certainly do not mean to suggest that these
marginal efforts to expand women's freedom were in the main successful.
Rather, my purpose is to review this history with an eye to the present and,
concurrently, to suggest that feminism need no longer be caught in the "iden-
tity-difference" trap or look to history to find "women" as we always knew
them.[13] I would urge that we affirm instead the still unrealized, universalistic
promise of democratic and liberal theory, while appreciating that difference(s)
may provide the grounds for unity rather than division. We need not fear
diversity but rather the univocal, homogenizing, sedimented identities of race,
sex, religion, ethnicity, or nationality that undermine the grounds for commonality among individuals and deny the multiplicity of (always changing)
associations, allegiances, locations and positions through which personal

identity is constituted.[14] As Christina Crosby has advised, "The question . . . is whether feminisms which 'deal with the differences between us' break out of this vicious circle in which women are self-evident and history mirrors the present."[15]

Bodies and Rights: Feminist Counterdiscourses

Articulate demands for the equality of the sexes during the Revolution were relatively few in number, and largely drowned out by the chorus of voices asserting the difference between the sexes and deriving powerful new authority from the claims of medical science.[16] The Marquis de Condorcet and Olympe de Gouges were two of the most notable opponents of the prevailing view that natural, sexual difference ought to dictate the domestication and subordination of women. The liberal aristocrat Condorcet authored "On the Admission of Women to the Rights of Citizenship" in 1790 and other tracts on the political liberty of women and blacks. He has won consistent praise for expanding on the egalitarianism of the seventeenth-century rationalist thinker Poullain de la Barre and for anticipating modern feminism. Condorcet argued that without the inclusion of women, the nation would have no recourse to a "free constitution." He deemed women to be "sentient beings, capable of acquiring moral ideas and of reasoning concerning those ideas," and therefore entitled to equal rights.[17] He even compared the inconveniences of motherhood to such "passing indispositions" as gout and bronchitis, suggesting that neither women's bodies nor their duties ought to disqualify them from participating in the political sphere.[18] Condorcet met his compatriot's strong objections that women reason differently or perhaps do not reason at all by advocating raised educational standards and the equalization of the social circumstances between the sexes. Only then, he allowed, would women escape the pull of vanity and self-interest and respond to the rigorous order of justice and positive law. Accordingly, Condorcet held that superstition and ignorance, not nature, accounted for women's prejudice and their illicit powers. He looked to education and publicity to eliminate the secret sway exercised by women in Old Regime society.

Yet even Condorcet admitted the force of bodily differences between the sexes when he moved to reassure his opponents that representative government need not lead to women's abandonment of their domestic affairs or to their governance of others. While contemptuously dismissing appeals to "utility" as mere pretexts of tyrants for denying "a true right" (among which he includes freedom for slaves, press liberty, and freedom from unjust imprisonment), Condorcet still perseveres in order "to leave no argument unanswered."[19] Indeed, he finds it necessary not merely to answer utilitarian objections to women's rights but equally to assuage men's fears that (in the vocabulary of the day) female citizens might become "femmes-hommes" or, like royal mistresses, come to exercise power over men. So, he states, "it is unnecessary to believe that because women could become members of national assemblies, they would immediately abandon their children, their homes, and their needles. They would be only the better fitted to educate their children and to rear men. It is natural for a woman to suckle her children and watch over their early years. Detained in the home by these cares, and less strong than the man, it is also natural that she should lead a more retiring, more domestic life." Reaffirming his commitment to women's rights, Condorcet did add that although the necessity of performing certain natural duties might be a motive for not voting for a woman in an election, it is not sufficient reason for women's legal exclusion.[20]

These are powerful claims on behalf of women. However, from our perspective, it is especially interesting to discover that even this forceful advocate of sexual equality introduced an asymmetry between the sexes into this otherwise egalitarian and rationalist defense of women's rights. Moreover, Condorcet located that disproportion directly on the reproductive and maternal body of woman. Despite his efforts to lay to rest the argument of natural difference, Condorcet was not entirely persuaded that sexual differences would not continue to have a decided social effect in a more rationally organized society.

Keith Baker objects that Condorcet made no retreat on this issue, avouching that whereas the philosopher assumed that most women would continue their domestic duties, "he sees no basis in women's nature to confine them to these functions, to exclude them from active participation in political life, or to deny them full access to the public instruction upon which rational politics and the progress of society must depend. Condorcet does not need, then, to extract arguments for women's emancipation from the recalcitrant lode of republican discourse. He finds them abundantly available in the competing discourse of rational social progress underlying his entire philosophy."[21] Baker's point is well taken. Indeed, in closing, Condorcet challenges his critics to "show me a natural difference between men and women which may legitimately serve as foundation for the deprivation of a right."[22] What Condorcet could not fully reconcile himself to, however, was the possibility that once having achieved full political rights, women might be led (in men's eyes) to just such an abandonment of their seemingly "natural" domestic duties. Accordingly, in the face of women's heightened political involvement during the popular revolution, those few representatives still favoring political equality for women appear to have retracted their former support. Despite his pronounced early commitment to women's voting rights, Condorcet remained silent on the issue when presenting his introductory report on the draft constitution to the Convention in early 1793—the period following the removal of the distinction between active and passive voters, so that the denial of women's rights was made more explicitly a matter of gender difference than one of property or class position; a time when women's activism in the streets and in the galleries of the Convention was accelerating, and during which an antifeminine campaign in the revolutionary press was already well advanced.

Yet despite Condorcet's apparent equivocation, as noted by his official silence on the issue of women's rights, there was some discussion of the question, especially among Condorcet's own friends and political allies. David Williams—friend of the Girondins, participant in Sophie de Condorcet's salon, author of *Lettres sur la liberté politique*, and participant in the preparatory work for the Constitution—wrote his *Observations sur la dernière constitution de la France avec des vues pour la formulation de la nouvelle constitution*. Williams supported education for women, their right to testify in cases involving members of their own sex, and political rights for single women, spinsters as well as widows.[23] In addition, the constitutional draft commission discussed an appeal for women's voting rights by deputy Pierre Guyomar entitled *le Partisan de l'égalité des droits et de l'inégalité en fait*. Much like Condorcet in his earlier tract, Guyomar compared prejudice in sexual matters to those of race, calling for its outright abolition. However, Guyomar went further, accusing the Declaration of Rights of perpetuating an aristocracy of men and smuggling in Old Regime principles. Despite these few voices of concern, the Commission concluded in April 1793 that women lacked sufficient education to participate in the nation's political life.[24]

The difficulties that Condorcet confronted in his efforts to ground sexuality in an argument for natural rights are even more pronounced in "The Declaration of the Rights of Woman" by the playwright, actress, pamphleteer, and condemned royalist Olympe de Gouges.[25] Whereas Condorcet (the man) spoke as an impartial though sympathetic observer, Gouges wrote from the site of the female body itself. She boldly announced that "it is a woman who dares to show herself so strong and so courageous for her King and her country." Similarly, she asked the "people, unhappy citizens, [to] listen to the voice of a just and feeling woman."[26] Thus Gouges unequivocally declared herself an "interested" party to the cause of women's rights. Refusing to efface her identity behind the language of abstract individuality, she called attention to her femaleness. Her work is riddled with a series of ambiguities having to do with the embodied and particularistic nature of female subjectivity. In an illuminating discussion, Joan Wallach Scott cautions against expunging the contradictory, illogical, or inconsistent aspects of Gouges's discourse. She advises that we attend to Gouges's equivocations not as a deficiency on her part (as others have been tempted to do) but as "an effect of the exclusions and contradictions of the [liberal] political theory within and against which it was articulated."[27] Thus for Scott the ambiguities and paradoxes in Gouges's defense of women's rights "expose the operations of particularity and exclusion in the abstract concept of universal Man."[28] In effect, Gouges refused the easy but ultimately unsatisfactory solution of securing woman's status as an abstract individual in the face of its masculine embodiment. "In order to claim the general status of 'human' for women, she insisted on their particular qualifications; in the process of insisting on equality, she constantly pointed out and acknowledged difference."[29]

Scott situates the dilemmas of the body in Gouges's thought against the hegemonic view among revolutionaries that sexual difference was a founding principle of the natural, hence of the social and political order. In the telling estimation of the physician Jacques-Louis Moreau, women were "thoroughly saturated with their sex."[30] Rather than denying women's bodily particularity, however, Gouges argued from women's different standpoint for universal rights. As a consequence, she risked providing ammunition to those who made women's distinctiveness the basis of their ineligibility for equal treatment and protection under the law. On the other hand, however imperfect, Gouges's disruptive arguments pointed to the need "to think differently about the whole question of rights."[31] In Article XI of "The Declaration," Gouges curiously tied the right of free speech to the distinctive needs of woman to name the father of their child. She linked this in turn to a guarantee of paternal obligation, for example, that fathers will (be made to) recognize their children. Acknowledging women's subjection to men in the family, Gouges connected the right to speech to women's ability to enforce paternal duty. Simultaneously, she made a claim on masculine prerogatives and exposed the abuses of patriarchal power. Yet precisely because it is in the area of pregnancy "that a woman's speech is simultaneously most authoritative and most open to doubt," Scott observes that "the terms by which de Gouges claims the rights of speech for women . . . raise the spectre of the unreliable feminine, the devious and calculating opponent of rational, truth-speaking man, and so they are literally fraught with uncertainty."[32]

Similarly, while extolling the mothers, daughters, and sisters of the nation, Gouges remained ambivalent about actually existing women. She scorned the "nocturnal administration of women" that characterized Old Regime practice and requested that prostitutes be placed in designated quarters. She prophesied that in the new republic the "powerful empire of nature" would lead women to disavow their former illicit and immoral behavior, their former "empire." As I have argued elsewhere, what is remarkable is that these pleas for the rights of wives and mothers of the new republic were proffered by a woman whose very occupation in the theater and way of being in the (public) world were in tension with the republican revolutionary code of female domesticity to which she appealed. Yet she resorted to domestic metaphors, for example, when she spoke of the relationships between the Assembly and the monarchy as "two powers [executive and legislative], [which] like man and woman, should be united but equal in force and virtue to make a good household."[33]

How, then, does nature figure for Gouges? Scott proposes that while Gouges reinterpreted nature's meaningfulness as a ground for rights, she nonetheless adhered to the notion of natural justifications for political arrangements. For example, she rejected the differentiation of bodies into fixed binary categories, insisting on "multiplicity, variety, ranges of difference, spectra of colors and functions, confusion of roles—the ultimate undecidability and indeterminacy of the social significance of physical bodies."[34] Not only did this lead Gouges to challenge the fixity of sexual nature, but she applied this same reasoning to the question of racial division which, as we have seen, was a concern of Condorcet's as well. Gouges argued on the basis of the undecidability of color against the prerogatives of whites and the enslavement of blacks. On the other hand, like many of her contemporaries, she also sought in nature the grounds for the legitimization of universal, human rights. Consequently, because Gouges held rights to be at once embodied and universal, she never resolved the paradox in her thinking whereby physical differences were at the same time irrelevant and essential to the meaning of equality. Like Condorcet, Gouges's formulation makes apparent dilemmas that continue to trouble rights discourse down to the present. But by eschewing a more logical or rigorous approach to the problem, Gouges highlights even more acutely the stakes involved in foundational arguments for human and political rights.

Bodies in Space: Women and Revolutionary Politics

From the early events of 1789, the Revolution opened up dramatically new political spaces within which women as well as men participated.[35] Despite the prevalence of masculine discourse, the paucity of demands by women for the suffrage, and the strong legal barriers facing women—the Constitution of 1791 denied women the right granted to active citizens to vote or to bear arms, and the Constitution of 1793 denied women full rights as democratic citizens—there is still considerable evidence of women's presence in the articulate, mobilized citizenry.[36] What is more, for a few critical years until the Jacobin repression of October 1793 banning women from membership in revolutionary clubs and societies or from making deputations to the Paris Commune, the revolutionary leadership exhibited something of an uncertain response toward women's formulations of revolutionary citizenship and civic virtue. As Darline Gay Levy and Harriet Branson Applewhite explain, the authorities "hesitated, they veered between co-opting, directing, and exploiting women's claim to a political identity and political power; they ridiculed it, symbolically recast it in order to defuse it, and [finally] repressed it. [But] in the spaces opened up by ambivalence and vacillation, women assumed political identities as *citoyennes*."[37]

Moreover, despite the pronounced misogyny that they exhibited in 1793, Jacobin men were not always the first to object to politically active women. During the insurrection of May 31 to June 2, 1793 (the ouster of the Girondin moderates from the National Convention, which the Society of Revolutionary Republican Women had helped to bring about), the Jacobin leaders as well as sans-culotte section officials lauded the members of the society for the "purest civic mindedness." In contrast, Girondins such as the deputy and journalist A.-J. Gorsas spoke of the threat of armed militant women or "drunken bacchanalians" as "furies . . . armed with pistols and daggers; they make public declarations and rush to all the public places of the city, bearing before them the standard of license."[38] Additionally, Levy and Applewhite allow that even the Jacobin repression of women in fall 1793 was not fore-ordained but rather "overdetermined" and advance three factors for consideration: 1) In the context of their own efforts to rein in the popular, grassroots proponents of regulated political economy, the Jacobins came to see the republican revolutionary women as absolutely ungovernable; indeed, not subject to the usual mechanisms of political coercion, co-optation, and control precisely because as women they were not part of the formal political system; they neither voted, held office, nor sat in the assemblies or committees. 2) The Jacobin leadership came to perceive the practice of militant, republican women as threatening to the stability of the family, and to women's role as moderators of the inflexible civic virtue of male citizens. 3) By exceeding tolerated definitions of femininity as weakness, lack, and incapacity, the revolutionary republican women (who claimed military as well as political powers) posed a threat of castration or impotence to Jacobin men.[39]

In a study of provincial Jacobin women's clubs, Suzanne Desan finds similar evidence of women's broad political involvement on issues ranging from women's rights to the regulation of the price of grain and the dismantling of the Constitutional church. She, too, notes the initial approbation with which male revolutionaries greeted women's clubs, especially in the years 1791–92: as a bulwark against the power of nonjuring clergy, as useful adjuncts to revolutionary ceremony and educational programs, and for their benevolent activities. Yet Desan points to three major troubling challenges posed by women's clubs: 1) the disagreement among patriots as to whether women's role as cultural missionaries and patriotic educators required public meetings and sessions of clubs; 2) the growing unease about the impact of women's increased power over men in the private realm; and 3) the fear that revolutionary education would change the interior nature of women from softness, frivolity, sensibilité, mystery, seduction, and deception to rationality and "transparency" as required of the new revolutionary man.[40] Indeed, while affirming that women's primary role was in the home, members of women's clubs embraced their maternal role as a call to women "to *politicize their relationships* with their husbands and lovers, to bring political judgment as well as moral lessons to the bedroom." Desan observes that frequent attacks on feminine caprice—the tie to aristocratic and deceitful bedroom politics of the Old Regime—"was riddled with ambiguity, coupled as it often was with an appeal to women to exercise private influence on their men through seduction to the patrie." Moreover, during the turbulent years of 1792 and 1793 men were continually open to accusations of having been trompés, tricked, fooled, or duped. In contrast, mobilized women spoke with growing confidence of their transformation by revolutionary rationalism; thanks to revolutionary education such women believed themselves to have become more rational, less easily deceived.[41] Not unlike Levy and Applewhite, then, Desan concludes that the factors contributing to men's suppression of women's clubs were multiple, stemming from powerful anxieties about the threat to male control, which politicized women posed in the private as well as the public sphere.

In the context of revolutionary public spaces and republican ideology, then, we find striking efforts by women to fashion new political and personal identities and to contribute to an expanded definition of democratic rights and sovereignty. What emerges from several superb studies is a concept of militant female citizenship, enacted by women who demanded the right to bear arms, in self-defense or against the nation's enemies, and the right to sanction laws, even at times exercising the vote which they formally lacked.[42] For example, during the summer of 1793, when the Constitution was being accepted, large numbers of women from Paris and the provinces wrote to the Convention that "although the law deprives them of the precious right of voting for the acceptance of the Constitution," they adhere to it.[43] More commonly, women joined in collective demonstrations, often with the application of force; they petitioned the authorities, and made their presence known in clubs, section assemblies, popular societies, festivals, street demonstrations, on bread lines, and at the markets. They frequented the galleries of the Convention and appeared at revolutionary tribunals and executions. The most militant among them practiced a politics of intimidation, unrelenting surveillance and control, either through legal or insurrectionary means. Women also became particularly adept at inciting action through the use of words. As Dominique Godineau notes, women "made it their work to jolt masculine apathy. They took on the role of 'firebrands': 'if they began the dance, the men would follow.'"[44] As a consequence of all their actions, revolutionary women helped to legitimate and to expand dramatically the newly achieved popular sovereignty.

Throughout this period, the revolutionary leadership remained decidedly ambivalent toward those women who exceeded what were deemed to be innate, naturally sanctioned female traits of passivity and domesticity. Women demonstrated that even a category like domesticity was open to reinterpretation. The militants who demanded the right to bear arms did so on behalf of an expanded notion of home: as mothers and daughters of the nation, they sought the right to defend the patria on its own turf. In general, the dual dynamic of democratic mobilization and liberal legislative reform opened avenues for women's political engagement; and elicited their involvement as critical members of the newly fashioned revolutionary body politic, as mothers, daughters, sisters, and occasionally as seeming citizens in their own right. As Levy and Applewhite observe, "In calculating the power of [the] general will, the revolutionary leadership continued, reluctantly, episodically, to include women; and women persisted in including themselves."[45] In effect,

> During this period, gender roles became one focus of political power struggles, including struggles for control of the revolutionary vocabulary, with its definitions of virtue, vice, and the parameters of citizenship. As part of that struggle, women repeatedly challenged, eluded, or subverted cultural constructs that dictated rigidly defined gender roles and limits (including those based on a presumption of women's innate or socially determined incapacity for assuming political identities). In discourse and act, they forced real, if short-lived and incomplete, transformations and expansions of the meaning and practice of citizenship and sovereignty.[46]

Female Citizenship

In short, we are left to contemplate the irony of women's performance of citizenship in a contested environment where legal, practical, and discursive barriers were being erected to their becoming full citizens, and, ultimately, to their participating at all in the public domain. Even at the crest of their political involvement, as Dominique Godineau reminds us, women were "*citoyennes* without citizenship"; they were, at best, "de facto" participants, to borrow Levy's and Applewhite's terminology.[47] Women's citizenship was episodic, and their efforts to extend the terms of gendered politics were defeated. Still, those women who acted out various possible roles for female citizens in the public sphere radically disrupted the terms of natural femininity expressed in the official gender ideology. Nor were their actions without effects, even for future generations. Notwithstanding their own ambivalences toward public women, we need to recall that thereafter republican, socialist, and anarchist movements tied the memory of women's involvement in the French Revolution to an open endorsement of the cause of female emancipation.[48] To borrow Claude Lefort's formulation, "democracy is instituted and sustained by the *dissolution of the markers of certainty*. It inaugurates a history in which people experience a fundamental indeterminacy as to the basis of power, law and knowledge and as to the basis of relations between self and other, at every level of social life."[49]

306 CULTURE, IDENTITY, DEMOCRACY

In *The Family Romance of the French Revolution*, Lynn Hunt traces further the implications of the political invasion of virtually every aspect of life, even the most intimate details of existence. She underscores how the claims of liberal individualism during the Revolution led to a rejection of Old Regime patriarchal family organization. As a result of revolutionary family legislation, fathers granted autonomy to their children, daughters and sons had equal rights of inheritance, and wives as well as husbands could sue for divorce. However, these reforms in the civil law introduced further paradoxes concerning the status of women: "Women had been incorporated into the new civil order, they were civil individuals under the law; but they had been excluded from certain political rights, with no evident explanation." Thus, Hunt concludes, "the exclusion of women was not theoretically necessary in liberal politics; because of its notions of the autonomous individual, liberal political theory actually made the exclusion of women much more problematic." Indeed, she sees the emergence of domestic ideology in France as a political and cultural response to the need to justify systematically the continuing exclusion of women from politics, "while they were admitted to many of the legal rights of civil society."[50]

No doubt, Hunt is right to notice the uncomfortable fit between liberal individualism and sexual inequality. The same point could be made even more emphatically with respect to the contradictions between democratic principles of equality and the sexual order of inequality. While I would acknowledge the importance (and continuing ramifications) of such ideological and social contradictions, I would still insist that we must account for the gendered cultural and political frameworks within which modern liberal and democratic thought have developed. Hunt herself seems to acknowledge that gender exclusion is not just a consequence of an after-the-fact justification in that her purpose in this book is to uncover the "collective fantasies" and "political unconscious" of revolutionary France. In any event, an adequate treatment of the (historically concrete) embedding of discourse in cultural and political practices is beyond the scope of this essay; though I would caution that the shared critical project of the moment, to reinvigorate both liberal and democratic ideals, requires more than a mere tidying up of the bodily and sexual metaphors through which freedom and equality have been articulated in the past. In that respect, Olympe de Gouges's troubles with rights discourse and democratic practice are far from resolved. As stated earlier, I endorse Hunt's hope, like Baker's, for the realization of the democratic promise of liberal theory. But such a task would also involve, as Chantal Mouffe argues, "the transformation of all the discourses, practices, and social relations where the category 'woman' is constructed in a way that implies subordination." As Mouffe states, "What a project of radical and plural democracy needs is not a sexually differentiated model of citizenship in which the specific tasks of both men and women would be valued equally, but a truly different conception of what it means to be a citizen and to act as a member of a democratic community."[51]

Mouffe's stirring vision is a call for action in the present. What of the past? An exploration of the performative dimension of women's involvement in the revolutionary public sphere has demonstrated the extent to which female identity was far from being homogeneous, static, one-dimensional, or univocal: even in the face of legal subordination, the enactment of citizenship by women pluralized its possibilities. Women's actions demonstrated the multiplicity of possibilities open to the self. Militants did not straddle or even violate some imaginary line between public and private as their opponents accused. Instead, their activities demonstrated that every action has a public and private consequence. They also challenged the normative outlines of natural femininity, which were being drawn in this period. They exceeded the terms of what it commonly meant to be female. For that reason they were decried as furies, labeled as "femmes-hommes," scorned as "public," immoral women, and perhaps most distressing of all for the long run, re-called to the honorable but circumscribed position of domestic womanhood.

Yet politically active women never experienced themselves or their actions as being inconsistent with their status as females. Olympe de Gouges claimed rights for women, and remained ever cognizant of their role as mothers. Militant women were motivated to claim rights and occupy space on the basis of a continuing exploration of the very meaning of femininity in the new democratic public sphere. The sites in which women established their identity were multiple—and subject to ceaseless revision and expansion. Bonnie Honig's valuable feminist reformulation of the thought of Hannah Arendt defines well the implications of the peformative practice of these revolutionary women. Paraphrasing Arendt, Honig writes: "A politics of performativity . . . instead of reproducing and re-representing 'what' we are, agonistically generates 'who' we are by episodically producing new identities, identities whose 'newness' becomes 'the beginning of a new story, started—though unwittingly—by acting [wo]men [and] to be enacted further, to be augmented and spun out by their posterity."[52]

We have come full circle to an appreciation of the mutual implications of ideology and practice under circumstances where neither the subject nor the discourse exists as a seamless web. The special paradox of popular representation bears consideration: wherein the sovereign is relentlessly faceless and plural, where the ability to speak for or represent the people is always at risk and open to challenge. For these same reasons, the democratic body politic demands a stage, and requires a constant performance. In fact, democracy has many performances and multiple scenes. Certainly, during the Revolution, there were determined efforts by the revolutionary leadership to enact and also reify the gendered divisions of the new body politic: in festivals, women and men, adults and children were assigned places and costumes to conform with their new public and private duties; women were first assigned the role of spectators of the political assemblies and societies, and later banned from political space, to be retired to the domestic sphere;[53] real women's contributions to the revolutionary movement were transposed onto a mythological canvas where goddesses embodied political qualities such as liberty, reason, truth, justice, philosophy, and fraternity, and functioned as a kind of dea ex machina effacing human (especially women's) efforts.[54]

However, the democratic polity also introduces a radical departure from its authoritarian alternatives or antecedents. Whereas in the past, authority was anchored in God, king, and tradition, democracy establishes a new source of authority in the republic—what Arendt regards as the specifically political capacity for change: an openness to change, resistance, and creativity.[55] In the revolutionary public sphere, feminist counterdiscourses and a radical performativity by women did exist, overriding at least temporarily the constraints imposed on women by republican morality or laws. Militant women's discordant, egalitarian actions and words expressed the contingent, fragile, yet expansive possibilities within the political practice of democracy. As Claude Lefort remarks: "Without the actors being aware of it, a process of questioning is implicit in social practice, that no one has the answer to the questions that arise, and that the work of ideology, which is always dedicated to the task of restoring certainty, cannot put an end to this practice."[56]

Notes

1. Joan B. Landes, *Women and the Public Sphere in the Age of the French Revolution* (Ithaca: Cornell University Press, 1988), 7.

2. Keith Michael Baker, "Defining the Public Sphere in Eighteenth-Century France: Variations on a Theme by Habermas," in *Habermas and the Public Sphere*, ed. Craig Calhoun (Cambridge, Mass.: MIT Press, 1992), 207. For further discussions of the public sphere's masculinist character, see Nancy Fraser, "Rethinking the Public Sphere: A Contribution to the Critique of Actually Existing Democracy"; Mary P. Ryan, "Gender and Public Access: Women's Politics in Nineteenth-Century America"; and Geoff Eley, "Nations, Publics, and Political Cultures: Placing Habermas in the Nineteenth Century," all in Calhoun, *Habermas and the Public Sphere*; the Forum on the Public Sphere in the Eighteenth Century, with contributions by Daniel Gordon, "Philosophy, Sociology, and Gender in the Enlightenment Conception of Public Opinion"; David A. Bell, "The 'Public Sphere,' the State, and the World of Law in Eighteenth-Century France"; and Sarah Maza, "Women, the Bourgeoisie, and the Public Sphere: Response to Daniel Gordon and David Bell," in *French Historical Studies* 17, no. 4 (Fall 1992): 882–978; Dena Goodman, "Public Sphere and Private Life: Toward a Synthesis of Current Historiographical Approaches to the Old Regime," *History and Theory* 31, no. 1 (February 1992): 58–77; Anthony J. La Volpa, "Conceiving a Public: Ideas and Society in Eigh-

teenth-Century Europe" *Journal of Modern History* 64, no. 1 (March 1992): 79–116; Dorinda Outram, "Revolution, Domesticity and Feminism: Women in France after 1789," *Historical Journal* 32, no. 4 (1989): 971–79. On a related theme, feminists have sought to expand on the potentialities of Habermas's communicative theory stripped of its transcendental or masculinist assumptions. See Iris Marion Young, "The Ideal of Impartiality and the Civic Public," in *Justice and the Politics of Difference* (Princeton: Princeton University Press, 1990); and Seyla Benhabib, "Models of Public Space: Hannah Arendt, the Liberal Tradition and Jürgen Habermas," in *Habermas and the Public Sphere*, 73–99.

3. According to Baker, republican and rationalist conceptions of the public sphere derived from radically competing discourses in the eighteenth-century context: "Rousseau's reworking of the discourse of classical republicanism, fundamentally concerned with the recovery of sovereignty by a community of autonomous citizens, was couched in quite different terms than the rationalist discourse of the social, grounded on notions of the rights of man, the division of labor and the apolitical rule of reason. This latter conception of the public sphere was contingently masculinist to the extent that it admitted contingent grounds for denying women (and others) full and immediate participation in the exercise of universal individual rights, but it was not essentially masculinist in the sense that women were excluded from the exercise of such rights by definition of their very nature." Keith Michael Baker, "Defining the Public Sphere in Eighteenth-Century France," 202.

4. For an essential account of the genesis, and differing outcomes, of republicanism in France and America, see Patrice Higonnet, *Sister Republics: The Origins of French and American Republicanism* (Cambridge, Mass.: Harvard University Press, 1988). Cf. Thomas L. Pangle, *The Spirit of Modern Republicanism: The Moral Vision of the American Founders and the Philosophy of Locke* (Chicago: University of Chicago Press, 1988), on the moral and political principles guiding the founding fathers; Mark E. Kann, *On the Man Question: Gender and Civic Virtue in America* (Philadelphia: Temple University Press, 1991), for a discussion of the consequences of the republican-liberal synthesis in America; and Kenneth Lockridge, *On the Sources of Patriarchal Rage: The Commonplace Books of William Byrd and Thomas Jefferson and the Gendering of Power in the Eighteenth Century* (New York: New York University Press, 1992), on the gender crisis in eighteenth-century America. Finally, in *The Family Romance of the French Revolution* (Berkeley and Los Angeles: University of California Press, 1992), Lynn Hunt probes the impact of gender relations on the political imaginary of the French nation.

Daniel Gordon distinguishes between an Anglo(Scottish)-American model of enlightened sociability and French epistemological theories of public opinion. Moreover, like Baker, he treats Rousseau and the revolutionaries as radical opponents of Enlightenment ideals of public opinion and private communication. And in the latter, he finds a greater openness to women's claims (in the ideology of sociability) and women's concrete presence (in salon culture). Yet he admits that only individual women were advantaged, and only to the extent that they "contribute to a mythical social consensus." He acknowledges the difficulties of a "functionalist theory," wherein as "in the French theories of the public sphere women are portrayed as an important element of 'civilized' society. But this means that the presence of women in the public sphere is legitimate only to the extent that they appear as a civilizing force, a force helping to create that

310   CULTURE, IDENTITY, DEMOCRACY

mythical entity, public opinion." Gordon, "Philosophy, Sociology and Gender," 886, 902, 904.

5. Harriet Branson Applewhite and Darline Gay Levy, editors' introduction to *Women and Politics in the Age of Democratic Revolution* (Ann Arbor: University of Michigan Press, 1990), 18–19.

6. Ibid., 18.

7. See Elisabeth Roudinesco, *Theroigne de Mericourt: A Melancholic Woman during the French Revolution*, trans. Martin Thom (London: Verso, 1991), chap. 1; and Christine Fauré, *Democracy without Women: Feminism and the Rise of Liberal Individualism in France*, trans. Claudia Gorbman and John Berks (Bloomington: Indiana University Press, 1991).

8. "Réimpression de l'Ancien Monitor," vol. 18, pp. 298–300, translated and cited in *Women in Revolutionary Paris, 1789–1795, Selected Documents*, ed. and trans. Darline Gay Levy, Harriet Branson Applewhite, and Mary Durham Johnson (Urbana: University of Illinois Press, 1979), 216–17.

9. Carole Pateman, *The Disorder of Women* (Stanford: Stanford University Press, 1989), 17–18.

10. Carole Pateman, *The Sexual Contract* (Stanford: Stanford University Press, 1988), 96. Cf. Dorinda Outram, *The Body and the French Revolution: Sex, Class, and Political Culture* (New Haven: Yale University Press, 1989).

11. Pateman, *The Disorder of Women*, p. 15.

12. As I stated previously with respect specifically to the suppression of women's clubs and associations, and, more generally, to the overall shift from a public sphere in which women had symbolic importance to a contractual polity dominated by men: "I reject the claim that this outcome was inevitable; rather, I ask how it is that women revolutionaries (as political women) became unnatural during the course of the Revolution." *Women and the Public Sphere*, 12.

13. For two important perspectives on the question of identity and difference within feminist theory, see Nancy Fraser and Linda J. Nicholson, "Social Criticism without Philosophy: An Encounter between Feminism and Postmodernism"; and Christine Di Stefano, "Dilemmas of Difference: Feminism, Modernity, and Postmodernism," in *Feminism/Postmodernism*, ed. and with an introduction by Linda J. Nicholson (New York: Routledge, 1990), 19–38, 63–82.

14. See Donna Haraway, "A Manifesto for Cyborgs: Science, Technology, and Socialist Feminism in the 1980s," in *Feminism/Postmodernism*, 190–233.

15. Christina Crosby, "Dealing with Differences," in *Feminists Theorize the Political*, ed. Judith Butler and Joan Scott (New York: Routledge, 1992), 133.

16. See Thomas Laqueur, *Making Sex: Body and Gender from the Greeks to Freud* (Cambridge, Mass.: Harvard University Press, 1990); Paul Hoffman, *La Femme dans la pensée des lumières* (Paris, 1977); Ludmilla J. Jordanova, "Guarding the Body Politic: Volney's Catechism of 1793," in *1789: Reading, Writing Revolution*, ed. Francis Barker et al. (University of Essex, Proceedings of the Essex Conference on the Sociology of Literature, July 1981, 1982); Jordanova, "Naturalizing the Family: Literature and the Bio-Medical Sciences in the Late Eighteenth Century," in Jordanova, *Languages of Nature* (London: Free Association Books, 1986); Dorinda Outram, *The Body and the French Revolution*, chap. 4, "The Eighteenth-Century Medical Revolution: Bodies, Souls, and Social Classes."

17. Marie Jean Antoine Nicolas de Caritat, Marquis de Condorcet, "On the Admission of Women to the Rights of Citizenship (1790)," in Condorcet, *Selected Writings*, ed. Keith Michael Baker, 100, 98.

18. Ibid., 99–100.

19. Ibid., 100–101.

20. Ibid., 102.

21. Keith Michael Baker, "Defining the Public Sphere in Eighteenth-Century France," 203.

22. Condorcet, "On the Admission of Women," 102.

23. Roudinesco, *Theroigne de Mericourt*, 129–30.

24. Ibid., 130. Additionally, Roudinesco points out that although his own draft plan for egalitarian public education presupposed peace, Condorcet voted for war in April 1792. Ibid., 102. Cf. Elisabeth and Robert Badinter, *Condorcet (1743–1794): Un intellectuel en politique* (Paris: Fayard, 1988), 400–405; 533–44.

25. Gouges, "The Declaration of the Rights of Woman," in Levy, Applewhite, and Johnson, *Women in Revolutionary Paris, 1789–1795, Selected Documents*. Unlike Condorcet and Wollstonecraft, Gouges has only recently secured a certain place in the feminist pantheon. Benoîte Groult is determined to rectify the imbalance. See his editor's introduction to Olympe de Gouges, *Oeuvres* (Paris: Mercure de France, 1986). For a biographical account, see Olivier Blanc, *Olympe de Gouges* (Paris: Syros, 1981).

26. Gouges, "Remarques patriotiques: par la citoyenne, Auteur de la lettre au Peuple, 1788" and "Le cri du sage, par une femme, 1789," in Groult, *Olympe de Gouges*, 73, 91, cited in Joan Wallach Scott, "'A Woman Who Has Only Paradoxes to Offer': Olympe de Gouges Claims Rights for Women," in *Rebel Daughters: Women and the French Revolution*, ed. Sara E. Melzer and Leslie W. Rabine (New York: Oxford University Press, 1992).

27. Scott, "A Woman Who Has Only Paradoxes to Offer," 116.

28. Ibid., 107.

29. Ibid., 108.

30. Ibid., 104–5.

31. Ibid., 110.

32. Ibid.

33. Gouges, "The Declaration of the Rights of Woman," cited in Landes, *Women and the Public Sphere*, 126–27.

34. Scott, "A Woman Who Has Only Paradoxes to Offer," 112.

35. I am drawing the following portrait of female activism and consciousness during the Revolution from the following: Dominique Godineau, "Masculine and Feminine Political Practice during the French Revolution, 1793–Year III," and Darline Gay Levy and Harriet Branson Applewhite, "Women, Radicalization, and the Fall of the French Monarchy," in *Women and Politics in the Age of the Democratic Revolution*, 61–80, 81–107; Levy and Applewhite, "Women and Militant Citizenship in Revolutionary Paris"; Dominique Godineau, *Citoyennes Tricoteuses* (Paris: Alinea, 1988); and Levy, Applewhite, and Johnson, *Women in Revolutionary Paris, 1789–1795, Selected Documents*. See also Landes, *Women and the Public Sphere*; Christine Fauré, *Democracy without Women*.

36. On masculine language, see Dorinda Outram, "Le langage mâle de la vertu: Women and the Discourse of the French Revolution," in Peter Burke and Roy Porter,

eds., *The Social History of Language* (Cambridge: Cambridge University Press, 1988), 120–35.

37. Darline Gay Levy and Harriet Branson Applewhite, "Women and Militant Citizenship in Revolutionary Paris," in *Rebel Daughters: Women and the French Revolution*, 80.

38. Ibid., 93–94.

39. Ibid., 96–97.

40. Suzanne Desan, "'Constitutional Amazons': Jacobin Women's Clubs in the French Revolution," in *Re-Creating Authority in Revolutionary France*, ed. Bryant T. Ragan, Jr., and Elizabeth A. Williams, with a foreword by Lynn Hunt (New Brunswick, N.J.: Rutgers University Press, 1992), 20.

41. Desan, "Constitutional Amazons," 25, 28, 29.

42. The full extent of women's involvement in the revolutionary movement is manifested in a series of key episodes: the women's march on Versailles in October 1789, women's participation in armed processions of the spring and summer 1792, the organized insurgency of women in the Society of Revolutionary Republican Women in May–October 1793, and women's participation in the opening demonstrations of the insurrections of May 1795.

43. Dominique Godineau, "Masculine and Feminine Political Practice during the French Revolution," 69. Cf. Godineau, *Citoyennes Tricoteuses*.

44. Godineau, "Masculine and Feminine Political Practice during the French Revolution," 75.

45. Levy and Applewhite, "Women and Militant Citizenship in Revolutionary Paris," 85.

46. Ibid., 98.

47. Godineau, "Masculine and Feminine Political Practice during the French Revolution," 68; and Levy and Applewhite, "Women and Militant Citizenship in Revolutionary Paris," 81.

48. I am speaking here of stated goals, not living practice. With respect to women, modern movements of emancipation have fallen short on both dimensions. I address aspects of this issue in my "Marxism and the Woman Question," in *Promissory Notes: Women in the Transition to Socialism*, ed. Sonia Kruks, Rayna Rapp, and Marilyn Young (New York: Monthly Review Press, 1989a).

49. Claude Lefort, *Democracy and Political Theory*, trans. David Macey (Minneapolis: University of Minnesota Press, 1988), 19.

50. Lynn Hunt, *The Family Romance of the French Revolution*, 202–3.

51. Chantal Mouffe, "Feminism and Radical Politics," in *Feminists Theorize the Political*, 377, 382.

52. B. Honig, "Toward an Agonistic Politics: Hannah Arendt and the Politics of Identity," in *Feminists Theorize the Political*, 225.

53. Nineteenth-century working women's visible place in the markets and industries occasioned considerable concern on the part of journalists, police, and writers. See Victoria Thompson, "Contamination and Control: The Public Presence of Working Women in Nineteenth-Century Paris," a paper delivered at the Ninth Berkshire Conference on the History of Women, Vassar College, June 11–13, 1993; Mary P. Ryan, *Women in Public: Between Banners and Ballots, 1825–1880* (Baltimore: Johns Hopkins University Press, 1990); Susan Buck-Morss, "The Flâneur, the Sandwichman, and the

Whore: The Politics of Loitering," *New German Critique* 13, no. 39 (1986); Christine Stansell, *City of Women: Sex and Class in New York, 1789–1860* (New York: Knopf, 1986); Elizabeth Wilson, *The Sphinx in the City: Urban Life, the Control of Disorder, and Women* (Berkeley and Los Angeles: University of California Press, 1992); and Janet Wolff, *Feminine Sentences: Essays on Women and Culture* (Berkeley and Los Angeles: University of California Press, 1990), esp. chaps. 2–4.

54. I discuss these issues in an unpublished typescript, "The Embodiment of Female Virtue in Revolutionary Political Culture," to be included in my forthcoming *Visualizing Freedom: Politics, Culture, and Gender in Eighteenth-Century France*. On the role of Liberty as "dea ex machina," subsuming the "heroines of October" at the Festival of August 10, 1793, choreographed by J. L. David, see Levy and Applewhite, "Women and Militant Citizenship in Revolutionary Paris," 94.

55. See Honig, "Toward an Agonistic Feminism," 217.

56. Lefort, *Democracy and Political Theory*, 19.

Sixteen

Peripheral Peoples and Narrative Identities: Arendtian Reflections on Late Modernity

CARLOS A. FORMENT

SURVEYING the political landscape of late modernity with Arendtian lenses has persuaded me that "peripheral peoples" are emblematic of contemporary public life in the same way that their immediate predecessors, Jewish pariahs and political refugees, were once associated with modernity.[1] The first part of the essay discusses the "who-ness" of peripheral peoples, highlighting their uniqueness as political agents; the second addresses their "what-ness," the way their identities have been shaped by hybrid narratives; and the concluding section reviews some basic differences between peripheral peoples and pariahs and refugees in order to underscore the changes in public life that have taken place since midcentury when Arendt wrote her reflections on the nature of modern totalitarian regimes.[2] The affinity between modernity and totalitarianism, according to Arendt, had been made possible in part by the marginalization of pariahs and Jews and the decline of the "nation-state," the main guarantor of "political rights." Late modern public life continues to be marked by social exclusion and an erosion of national and state boundaries, however, because both these are now occurring in a radically different context, made possible by the defeat of totalitarian and the triumph of democratic regimes, and the sociopolitical constellation resulting from them is also quite distinct. Democracy and marginalization have become intertwined in late modernity, contributing to the formation of a new type of regime: "caste democracy."

Peripheral Peoples as Political Agents

The term "peripheral peoples" is admittedly imprecise, and perhaps inevitably so, alluding at once to a new type of political agent, ex-colonials and second-class citizens, and to their distinct experience, cultural hybridness. In spite of its many shortcomings, this term, like any other term, has the advantage of giving contoured shape and recognizable form to a set of practices that too often go unnoticed and unobserved.

Ex-Colonial Subjects

When employed as a noun, the term "peripheral peoples" refers to "ex-colonials" who, since the postwar period, have been emigrating in unprecedented numbers and settling in postimperial countries (England, Spain, Italy, France, Germany, the U.S.) of the North Atlantic Basin.[3] While their legal status is relatively assured, their experience of citizenship remains ambiguous. The majority of these peoples are by now "dual nationals," "permanent residents," or "naturalized citizens," with civic and political attachments extending to their compatriots in their homeland and to those in their adopted country. Dualistic loyalties are exemplified, among others, by Turks currently residing in Germany; Latin Americans in Spain and the U.S.; Arabs and Israelis in Great Britain, France, and the U.S.; Pakistanis, subcontinent Indians, and islanders from the English- and Spanish-speaking Caribbean in Great Britain and the U.S.; and Africans, especially those from the Maghreb, who live and work in France, Spain, Italy, Great Britain, and U.S.[4] Judith Shklar was surely on mark when she noted that "citizenship must always refer primarily to nationality," but the problem is that nations, since the postwar period, have become profoundly pluralized, and this has redefined the way peoples experience their citizenship.[5] The boundaries of nations and states have seldom coincided, but this disjuncture seems more profound and widespread today than ever before.[6] Late modern conceptions of citizenship have assimilated the experience of dual loyalty without receiving formal endorsement from state officials who, nevertheless, tolerate the practice.[7]

Large numbers of these ex-colonials are "neonomads," and their unique experience of duality merits special attention. These persons shuttle back and forth between host country and country of origin in patterned cycles, timed to the alternating rhythms of the international economy and geopolitical context.[8] Migrants and seasonal and guest workers from countries located along the entire perimeter of the imperial core, stretching all the way from Mexico, Central America and the Caribbean, eastward, across the Atlantic Ocean to the Maghreb region of North Africa, over to the Middle East and northward to Turkey, rely on civic ties to shuttle north and south and back again, across this great arch. Neonomads rely on family bonds, "fictive" kinships and weak ties based on work and collegial networks to travel between countries for periods of varying durations, lasting from several months to several years.[9]

Second-Class Citizens

The term "peripheral peoples" also refers to "second-class citizens" (racial, ethnic, national, religious, and gendered minorities) who have been driven by the discriminatory practices of their compatriots to occupy marginal positions in the "central institutions" of their own homeland.[10] While their legal status has always been relatively stable and secure, second-class citizens associate political rights with social degradation. Second-class citizens have been marked by social dishonor linked to public and private experiences of humiliation, discrimination, and prejudice, making them skeptical of, although not hostile to, political rights. In the absence of full political equality and social inclusion, second-class citizens have become increasingly concerned with "human and civil rights," in their homeland and elsewhere, in order to correct the wrongs they and their counterparts have experienced.[11] Second- and third-generation ex-colonials born and raised in Great Britain, Germany, France, and Italy form part of this group.[12] It also includes the Basque in Spain, as well as the Irish in Great Britain and, perhaps, southern Italians, now that the Lombardi League in the north has launched a vigorous campaign against them, and, in alliance with neofascists, against second-generation immigrants from Tunisia, Nigeria, and other parts of Africa.[13] In the U.S., the list is even longer, including Afro-Americans, Native Americans, Asians, Hispanics, and Arabs, to mention the most familiar cases.[14] Religious groups, including Jews and Muslims, continue to face difficulties in several European countries and also in the U.S., as do gendered peoples, such as women and same-sex couples.[15]

There are, to be sure, significant differences internal to any of these peripheral groups, a result of dissimilar social status, economic class, cultural capital, and access to sources of power and institutional influence.[16] But their commonalities remain durable and enduring, and these merit reviewing.

Hybrid Narratives and Collective Identities

Ex-colonial subjects and second-class citizens were shaped, even if in dissimilar ways, by the central institutions and narrative stories that were already in place across the countries of the Atlantic basin. Peripheral peoples entered each country's public sphere under the aegis of liberal regimes, at a time when its central institutions were sturdy in spite of the increasing demands placed on them; its economies stable even during moments of contraction; its national boundaries porous although relatively fixed; its societies meritocratic yet with traces of ascription; and its narratives broadly accepted and, therefore, capable of infusing peripheral peoples with liberal precepts.[17] Liberal narratives constituted, and became constitutive of, the experiences of most peripheral groups who had entered the basin from the postwar period onward.[18] Peripheral peoples relied on these stories to retool their own narratives, eventually using them to question the liberal stories they had been inculcated with.

Liberalism as Cartography

Michael Walzer has suggested that we consider liberalism as a way of mapping and partitioning the sociopolitical landscape:

> Think of liberalism as a certain way of drawing the map of the social and political world. The . . . preliberal map showed a largely undifferentiated land mass, with rivers and mountains, cities and towns, but no borders. . . . Society was conceived as an organic and integrated whole. . . . Confronting this world, liberal theorists preached and practiced the art of separation. They drew lines, marked off different realms, and created the socio-political map with which we are still familiar. . . . Liberalism is a world of walls, and each one creates a new liberty. [19]

The many distinctions and demarcations made by liberal writers are designed to preserve "liberty" and "equality" in the modern world. One of the ways they do this is by attributing agents with certain cultural features, and by erecting institutional boundaries between civil and political society. This enables them, on the one hand, to protect individuals from the double threat of state despotism and the "tyranny of the majority," and, on the other hand, to preserve the impartiality, autonomy, and neutrality of public institutions.

Liberal stories classify agents into either "learners"—those who, for reasons of age, intellectual or moral endowments, and, less so today than before, gender and race, are not yet fully qualified for citizenship—or "choosers"—those who have met the doctrine's standard by demonstrating a sustained capacity for toleration, justice, fairness, and reasonableness.[20] The threshold between learners and choosers is seldom clear, often driving liberal storytellers to rely on the conventional "self-images" of the age to draw this distinction. Like any other group, liberal narratives rests on the ruling prejudices of their day, but in spite of this and other shortcomings, they remain compelling stories among late moderns.

The sociopolitical terrain described by liberals in their stories usually include two major landmarks: political society and civil society.[21] The former is composed of the state apparatus, including congress and the courts, political parties and social movements, with notions of citizenship and patriotism at its symbolic core. The latter is made up of formal and informal voluntary associations, ranging from families, neighborhoods, religious, communal, and pressure groups, and, in some accounts, the economy, with nationhood and civility as its core. Most liberal stories contain lengthy accounts defining the boundaries between political and civil society, a division meant to protect each from the excessive demands of the other.

From these simple stories late moderns have developed more complex ones. For example, the issue of political participation and deliberation, which until now had not featured prominently in liberal doctrine because of its focus on "negative liberty," gained importance among some English, French, Italian, and U.S. thinkers, who shared a concern for its "positive," republican aspects and were seeking to revive citizenship as a way of remaking public life.[22] The communitarian-liberal exchange that recently swept the basin responded to varied conditions there. In the U.S., it came about as a result of the brittle-ness in civic ties and apparent decline in public life; in Spain it was an attempt to tame political passions and create a convivial public sphere capable of ac-commodating ideological foes; and in Germany it was part of a much broader effort by liberals seeking to redefine nationhood in contractual (*jus solis*) in-stead of Romantic (*jus sanguinis*) terms.[23] Finally, the "communicative con-troversy" of the last decade followed separate tracks. In England the concern was with understanding "speech acts" and how "political texts" are willful interventions in public life, while in Germany the focus was on the way "validity claims" contribute in the production and regulation of "ideal speech situations."[24] These and other stories have enriched liberalism in countless ways.[25]

One of the reasons why the liberal narrative remains so compelling derives from the way its storytellers structure their accounts. From a set of simple binaries, liberals are able to generate a series of complex dualities, which they then use to compose major and minor stories, harmonizing them in a contra-puntal manner, as in a fugue.[26] Liberal stories about universal, abstract reason are counterpointed to stories about traditional customary practices; stories about legal rights are counterpointed with those based on substantive virtues; stories about procedural rules based on fairness are counterpointed with those based on substantive arguments about consensual values; and stories related to individual autonomy are counterpointed with those of collective solidarity. These are what liberal stories are made of, providing its authors the basic elements they need to produce dramatic tension, resolution, and release. But the most gifted go beyond them, using a variety of literary tools and devices, including metaphors and similes, to soften and blur the hard edges of each antinomy until they become paradoxes and oxymorons. The usage of literary tropes enables these writers to relax their most cherished assumption, and to reach beyond the boundaries of their narrative to explore its perimeter.

Liberalism, like any other narrative, is constituted through contestation, through the argumentative retellings that are forever taking place among its practitioners over the changing meaning and significance of its stories. In the words of Alasdair McIntyre, "What constitutes a tradition is a conflict of inter-pretation of that tradition, a conflict which itself is susceptible to rival inter-pretations. . . . For it is not merely that different participants in a tradition disagree; they also disagree about how to characterize their disagreements and as to how to resolve them. . . . A tradition then not only embodies the narrative of an argument, but is only to be rediscovered by an argumentative retelling of that narrative which will itself be in conflict with other argumentative retellings."[27] Liberalism is not a mummified doctrine, a dead language; rather, it is a vital form of life.

Ex-Colonial Subjects and Postimperial Narratives

When ex-colonials entered the countries of the postimperial metropole, they did more than just exchange passports and currency at the custom office; they appropriated liberal stories and then used them to reinterpret a century and a half of imperial-colonial relations. The story of bondage between master and servant, put forward originally by Hegel and made familiar to postwar thinkers through the writings of Kojève, summarizes the core experience of the imperial-colonial encounter.[28] Ex-colonials borrowed liberal stories about equality, autonomy, and fairness in order to reinterpret and transform their past experiences of hierarchical domination, social dependency, and lack of recognition.

Replotment followed. Imperialists no longer were portrayed simply as aggressive champions of domination, nor were colonial peoples depicted as its passive, pitiful victims. The notion that these groups represented an antagonistic and irreconcilable form of life also came under intense scrutiny with the aid of liberal stories. What emerged from this "fusion of horizons" was the creation of an alternate tradition: "postcolonial narrative."[29] In this revised version, relations of domination and servitude became internal and constitutive, not external and incidental, to postimperialist and postcolonial groups across the basin. In this narrative, the future belongs neither to the defiant slave, as Gilles Deleuze claimed, nor to the absolute master, as other neo-Nietzscheans maintained, but rather to those who practiced recognition.[30]

After his first visit to his homeland, Jamaica, in the early 1960s, Stuart Hall, a writer in the postcolonial tradition, retells how he became aware of this narrative, and its usefulness for understanding his unfolding selves. In the course of a conversation with his mother, he realized that he had been raised in the island as the product of "a lower-middle-class family that was trying to be a middle-class Jamaican family trying to be an upper-middle-class Jamaican family trying to be an English Victorian family."[31] Back in England, Hall became identified as an immigrant and a black in a country that was virulently antiforeign and racist. The semifictional quality of all three of Hall's narrative identities—parvenu, immigrant, and black—made him aware that his self, like any other self, including those of the British, was fissured and unstable, and marked by a range of discourses, such as those related to social status, nationalism, race and empire.

Postcolonial narratives do not aspire to provide a definitive account of the encounter between ex-colonials and ex-imperialist masters, rather they pro-

vide normative and literary resources for both groups to undergo a transformation that takes them beyond their previous experiences of each other. Postcolonial narratives, in contrast to Enlightenment stories, do not hold out the
promise of complete mastery and transparent understanding. Instead, what
they offer its practitioners is an acknowledgment of differences and a tolerance
for the mobile, nonfixed, fluid nature of sociopolitical meaning, which is why
those who identify with this tradition will, as a matter of strategy, prefer to
postpone and defer the "conversation" until another day, to articulate a loud
silence, when neither interlocutor has the narrative resources required to adequately translate their experiences into partially comprehensible terms.[32] Liberal stories enabled peripheral peoples to "retool" and "reinvent" their own
traditions in new and surprising ways.

Second-Class Citizens and Prophetic Stories

"Second-class citizens" refers to those groups, including gendered, racial, and
ethnic minorities, who occupy a subordinate and marginal place in their own
homeland, but the experiences shared by these groups differs from those
of ex-colonials in ways that need underscoring. Second-class citizens have
always maneuvered inside liberal regimes, and it has been their public experiences in these regimes that has made them quite familiar and knowledge-
able of its public practices. Mastery over liberal narratives has enabled these
second-class citizens to become some of its most creative storytellers and
loyal critics.

Second-class groups who have experienced some of liberalism's shortcomings have not simply rejected its stories about liberty, justice, equality, reasonableness, fairness, toleration, and rights. Instead, they have woven these
strands with a variety of ethnonational and religious narratives associated with
and internal to their own submerged communities. In striking contrast to
liberal orthodoxy, these other narratives contain an especially rich, complex,
and appreciative set of stories about the importance of communal solidarity,
collective memory, social honor, rendering service to one's community, and
becoming personally engaged in struggles for social justice as a way of renewing and remaking one's self.

The hybrid stories that second-class citizens put together were, eventually,
christened by authors on both sides of the Atlantic with the name of "prophetic narrative."[33] Patterned on classical tales from the Bible, these narratives
are usually in three parts: they begin with an account of "public malaise and
personal suffering," depicting the injustices and indignations of an entire community; they continue with stories of "deliverance from oppression and cap-
tivity," the "hidden transcripts," and overt forms of resistance used by the
oppressed to challenge their political rivals; and they end with "promises of

redemption," a renewal of one's commitment to a just and freer life, and a reawakening of one's yearning to live in this type of society. Martin Luther King's famous "I Have a Dream" speech, delivered before the Lincoln Memorial on August 28, 1963, as the keynote address of the "March on Washington D.C.," is perhaps the single most eloquent example of this type of narrative. Prophetic narratives, in contrast to the "discourse of modernity," contribute to a reenchantment of public life, infusing it with tales of historically grounded forms of everyday forms of justice.

Liberalism's narrative and institutional practices had successfully transformed peripheral groups. The stories they narrated contained new inflections, and these pronounced with a slightly different accent. Hybrid peoples had borrowed liberal stories to reinvent their traditions in light of late modern conditions.

Liberal Purism as Narratives of Normalization

Liberal institutions organized public practices across the basin, with its representatives using stories from their repertoire to educate, discipline, and at times compel peripheral peoples to make sense of their own experiences, past and present. Peripheral groups were encouraged to select those stories from the list of liberal antinomies that shed light on their own experiences. Selecting the first term of each paired antinomy was construed as evidence that the person had graduated from learner to chooser, thus earning the status of citizen. Selecting the second term was an indication that the person had lingering traces of preliberal (not antiliberal) notions and hence was still a learner. But what gave unity to the liberal narrative was not, paradoxically, these discrete and separate choices; rather, it was the binary structure of the list itself. Voting for one or the other option was simply a way of reaffirming the liberalism's narrative of modernity. The liberal tradition was reproduced by the dichotomies themselves, and not by embracing or rejecting any one, single story from the list.

The road to liberalism allowed for errors and setbacks, but any attempt by peripheral groups to develop an alternate list based on hybrid stories was prohibited. They had to select from among the standardized list of pre-fixed options; they were not allowed to reconfigure them in a systematic manner. Peripheral peoples learned to select, in a coherent and consistent manner, those stories in the repertoire that were most relevant to their own experiences, even if these were too rich and excessive to be contained by them. Even preliberal learners who occasionally selected wrongly from the list still had to observe and respect its internal dichotomies and external boundaries. Violating either was conceived by liberal purists as a willful declaration of antiliberal intent.

Purist liberals successfully stripped peripheral groups of their anti-and non-modern outlook; however, they failed to remake them in their own image and likeness. Instead of adhering to the dichotomous alternatives on the list, adopting each time a liberal story and discarding its opposite, peripheral groups came together and improvised their own list. They gathered bits and pieces from each story, those with liberal and nonliberal plots alike; fused them with their newly composed hybrid narrative, an amalgam of postcolonial, ethnonationalist, and religious accounts that, to begin with, were not featured in the original list; and combined all three—liberal, nonliberal, and hybrid—into a lumpy, dense narrative, accommodating each plot in light of the rest. Peripheral groups relied on their own historical experiences and prudential judgments to rework the language of liberalism in ways neither they nor their tutors had foreseen. Like master bricoleurs, peripheral groups tinkered with those elements that liberalism had left behind as refuse, cobbling them together with unexpected results.

Peripheral peoples entered late modernity through the language of liberalism, en route becoming marked by its stories. But at the end of the assembly line, they did not turn into "coherent, continuous, centered selves"; "unencumbered, thin, and privatized selves"; or authors of "Grand Narratives." How could they? They were already acquainted with liberalism's shadowy practices in the colonial fringe and imperial core, and these were to remain etched across their faces and bodies, as they gained an understanding of modernity's sublime and sordid features, its idealistic visions and corrupt baseness, its ethical magnanimity and pettiness, its private delights and anguishes. The paradoxical stories that hybrids used to characterize these bountiful experiences drove them to look beyond liberalism, which seemed unable or unwilling to accommodate and contain them. According to hybrids, liberalism and late modernity were competing, noncomplementary forms of life.

Hybrids who embraced liberalism to deny their past, distort their present, and misrecognize their unfolding selves violated one of its central precepts: "self-interest properly understood." Those who memorized their script and played their assigned roles became, paradoxically, its worst students; those who resisted normalization became its finest, spinning stories that reconciled political liberty with social equality, and both of these with cultural differences. Some liberal storytellers retrenched, portraying recalcitrants as deficient citizens and as irresponsible agents, as a late-modern residue from the immediate totalitarian past.[34] By depicting hybrids as "reactionary irrationalists" and themselves as champions of "enlightened rationalism," purists were once again resorting to well-worn tropes to describe, in a highly stylized manner, the "project of modernity."[35] Hybrid groups rejected these stories and challenged liberalism's imaginary, both its fanciful conceptions of itself and its mythical accounts of modernity.

Purists became increasingly fundamentalist in their stories, resorting to a literary genre that, while not exactly new, had not until now formed such an important part of the liberal repertoire: morality plays, based on a ceaseless struggle between the forces of "purity and pollution," to borrow Mary Douglas's anthropological terms.[36] In these plays, characters are made to exemplify, through word and deed, one or another aspect of this struggle; and as the plot unfolds, each protagonist, regardless of his or her initial condition, becomes cleansed or tarnished, as the case might be, by exercising his or her free will. According to Douglas, these plays are most frequently produced and performed during moments of cognitive confusion and moral exhaustion, brought on by sudden encounters with unfamiliar forms of life. Liberals, like besieged tribal peoples, sometimes gather round their totem, to spin and weave stories that cast aspersions on hybrids. They are too complex and intricate to review here, but their effect can be summarized in a few words: restoration of faith in communal truths, and creation of social distance between "us" and "them."

Hybrid discourses, admittedly, remain as flawed and deficient as any other narrative, but they are not fundamentalist in outlook, intolerant in sensibility, or antiliberal in conviction. But as long as the discussion is framed in these minimalist, stark terms, peripheral groups will lack the vocabulary they need to articulate their views. Hybrid stories, as stated earlier, develop through mutual recognition, and when this is lacking, so too will the narrative resources needed by peripheral groups to convey their views. Hybrid stories can become only as sophisticated as the conversations in which they partake.

Pariahs, Exiles, and Hybrids

Interpreting public life from the perspective of disenfranchised, marginalized groups also helps define some of the differences between modern and late modern forms of political life. Although peripheral peoples bear a family resemblance to Arendt's "pariahs" and "exiles," the differences between them are undeniable, as is the political landscape in which they each have maneuvered.

First: Arendt claimed that midcentury public life was populated by "parvenus" and "assimilationists" along with "pariahs" and "exiles," and that the former did better than the latter in most countries of the basin because, in part, of the support they received from liberals (and others).[37] According to MacIntyre, the landscape of late modernity now includes rich aesthetes, managers, and therapists, and these characters, it can be said, are the heirs of liberal upstarts and conformists across the basin.[38] But we need to enlarge Arendt's and MacIntyre's list of characters to make room for peripherals and newly cleansed hybrids. They are central figures in late modern life and must be made part of the story. Perhaps if the previous and present generation of liberals had been more purist, that is, more sustaining of pariahs, exiles, and hybrids, and less inclined toward parvenus, assimilationists, aesthetes, managers, therapists, and cleansed hybrids, the debate underway over democracy and difference might be slightly more interesting.

Second: hybrid peoples, unlike their immediate precursors, are neither "culturally deracinated" nor de facto "social separatists," as Arendt portrayed them. Rather, they are embedded in hybrid forms of life; engaged in "social politics" aimed at protecting their civil societies; and in constant dialogue with their heritage. Moreover, the citizenship status of peripheral peoples, although ambiguous, is stable and secure. Furthermore, their numbers are growing, not diminishing, and, finally, because they no longer have, strictly speaking, a "homeland" or "traditional community" to return to, nor will they be given access to one by political fiat, they cannot take the "exit" option, only the "voice and loyalty" alternatives.

Third: when totalitarian regimes emerged in midcentury, they posed a major threat to democratic public life, but that is not the case today. Democracy is threatened today by orthodox purists who have marginalized and excluded hybrid groups, turning late modern regimes into a castelike society. These new untouchables are not, clearly, the same as those found in rigidly stratified, socially closed, hierarchical caste societies; however, they play just as integral a role and form a vital part of late modernity as their counterparts did in their societies. Late modern caste regimes are unique in their capacity to blur social boundaries and dissolve cultural and political markers, but at the same time they have an unmatched institutional capacity for generating social distance among groups based on nonascriptive traits. The fluidity of social and political boundaries should not blind us from noting how deeply entrenched they are becoming across the basin.

We need to remove our narrative blinders based on liberal stories about equality, fairness, and justice and begin comparing, in a systematic, rigorous, and rhetorically persuasive manner, the public practices of castelike regimes during the early modern, modern, and late modern period, focusing on the differences and similarities between hybrids and other excluded groups, including helots and metics during the classical period; untouchables in India before, during, and after the British Raj; pariahs in Nazi Germany; and colonial peoples across the periphery at the height of imperial domination.

Fourth: totalitarian regimes are in full retreat, providing us with an opportunity to rearrange our public life without constantly fearing that failures encountered along the way will necessarily endanger democratic forms of life. Inside the Atlantic basin, in Cuba and Haiti, totalitarianism remains in full force, but neither of these regimes poses a grave threat to democracy as was once the case with Stalinism and Nazism. The current stability and security enjoyed by liberal regimes offers the countries of the basin a splendid opportunity to begin the task of dismantling the castelike regimes emerging across the basin. The time has arrived to tinker with our institutional relations in ways that will make it possible to reconcile hybridness with citizenship.

Fifth: the cultural matrix from which political narratives emerged at midcentury and today differ. Arendt, Leo Strauss, and others have argued that totalitarian and Jewish stories, in spite of their obvious differences, were symmetrical in their narrative structure. Both relied on radically particularistic plots to make their case.[39] Likewise, liberalism and Marxism, in spite of their divergences, were homologous in structure, relying on abstract universalism to dispute each other's claims. These stories mirrored each other's narrative structures.

Peripheral groups were most fortunate to enter the Atlantic basin under the aegis of a liberal regime; they were tutored by liberals, not totalitarians, a distinction worth repeating. The hybrid stories that emerged from this encounter, even when flawed, remain unique in their capacity to fuse particularism with universalism, and bypassing both. Hybrid narratives are one of late modernity's defining features, providing peripheral groups with an opportunity to restructure public life.

The contributions and challenges that peripheral peoples bring to democratic regimes, north and south, provide us with an opportunity for finding novel ways of reconciling political equality with cultural differences. And yet in spite of their importance, peripheral peoples continue eluding our interpretive nets. Some of the most perceptive and palpable accounts of peripheral peoples are still found in the novels, short stories, and essays of writers in this tradition, not in political theory, where "thought and reality have parted company," to borrow Hannah Arendt's phrase.[40] Our understanding of contemporary politics will remain partial and deficient as long as we do not come to terms with peripheral peoples.[41] For all these reasons, it is important to appreciate Arendt's vision of modern politics, even if this means revising some of her specific claims. In Arendt's own words, "In this gap between past and future, we find our place in time when we think, that is, when we are sufficiently removed from past and future to be relied on to find . . . meaning . . . and [the capacity to] judge over the manifold and never-ending affairs of human existence . . . never arriving at a final solution to their riddles but ready with ever-new answers to the question of what it may be all about."[42] Whether we succeed in devising new solutions to the age-old problem of democracy and difference may be an indication of the degree of political judgment we have acquired since the last time these issues were raised.

Notes

1. Hannah Arendt, *The Origins of Totalitarianism* (New York: Harcourt Brace Jovanovich, 1979). For Arendt, the cultural roots of anti-Semitism, the symbolic core of totalitarian regimes, were to be uncovered in the "Scramble for Africa," when imperialists fashioned racist notions in order to redefine indigenous peoples into colonial

subjects. Racism eventually returned to its homeland, predisposing Nazis and their sympathizers across Europe to treat Jews as if they were "a savage native tribe of Central Africa." The end of totalitarianism brought about the creation of a newly marginalized group, "political refugees." These stateless peoples, like the European Jews before them, now embodied the essence of public life. Stripped of their citizenship, expelled from their homeland, and without a *patria* to confer and protect their rights, exiles had become among the most vulnerable, endangered peoples of the postwar period.

2. A second essay of mine—"Peripheral Peoples and Public Practices in Late Modernity"—examines the hybrid forms of civic and political life generated by peripheral peoples.

3. Brazil, Canada, and Mexico, while part of the basin, are not, strictly speaking, "postimperial" powers, even though they contain large numbers of peripheral peoples within their borders.

4. Nina Glick Schiller, Linda Basch, and Cristina Blanc-Szanton, *Towards a Transnational Perspective on Migration: Race, Class, Ethnicity and Nationalism Reconsidered* (New York: New York Academy of Sciences, 1992).

5. Judith Shklar, *American Citizenship: The Quest for Inclusion* (Cambridge, Mass.: Harvard University Press, 1991), 5.

6. Maxim Silverman, "Citizenship and the Nation State in France," *Ethnic and Racial Studies* 14, no. 3 (July 1991): 333–50; Robert D. Reischauer, "Immigration and the Underclass," *Annals of the American Academy of Political and Social Sciences* 501 (January 1989): 120–32; Gary Freeman, *Immigrant Labor and Racial Conflict in Industrial Societies: The French and British Experience, 1945–1975* (Princeton: Princeton University Press, 1979); Zig Layton Henry, ed., *The Political Rights of Migrant Workers in Western Europe* (London: Sage, 1990); Tomas Hammer, ed., *European Immigration Policy: A Comparative Study* (Cambridge: Cambridge University Press, 1985); and Mathew J. Gibney, "Crisis or Constraint: The Federal Republic of Germany's Current Refugee Imbroglio," *Government and Opposition* 28, no. 3 (Summer 1993): 372–93.

7. Mark J. Miller, "Dual Citizenship: A European Norm?" *International Migration Review* 23, no. 4 (Winter 1989): 945–51; Jean Leca, "Welfare State, Cultural Pluralism and the Ethics of Nationality," *Political Studies* 39, no. 3 (September 1991): 568–75; and Raymond Aron, "Is Multicultural Citizenship Possible?" *Social Research* 41 (1974).

8. Schiller, Basch, and Blanc-Szanton, *Towards a Transnational Perspective on Migration*; and Alejandro Portes, "Contemporary Immigration: Theoretical Perspectives on Its Determinants and Modes of Incorporation," *International Migration Review* 23, no. 3 (Fall 1989): 606–31.

9. Ivan Light, Parminder Bhachu, and Stavros Karageogis, "Migration Networks," in Light and Bhachu, eds., *Immigration and Entrepreneurship* (New Brunswick, N.J.: Transaction, 1993), 25–50; Alejandro Portes, "Caribbean Diasporas: Migration and Ethnic Communities," *Annals of the American Academy of Political and Social Sciences* (May 1994): 48–70; Sasskia Sassen, "Women Workers and Global Restructuring," *Signs: Journal of Women in Culture and Society* 19, no. 3 (Spring 1994): 831–35; Russell A. Berman, Azade Seyhan and Arlene Akiko Teraoka, eds. "Minorities in German Culture," *New German Critique* 46, special issue (Winter 1989); and Czarina Wilpert, "Migration and Ethnicity in a Non-Immigrant Country: Foreigners in a United Germany," *New Community* 18, no. 1 (October 1991): 49–62, and "From Guest Workers to Immigrants: Mi-

grant Workers and Their families in the FRG," *New Community* 11, nos. 1–2 (1983): 137–42.

10. For a discussion of "central institutions," see Edward Shils, "Center and Periphery," *The Constitution of Society* (Chicago: University of Chicago Press, 1982), 93–105.

11. On citizenship identity, see Edward B. Portis, "Citizenship and Personal Identity," *Polity* 18, no. 3 (1986): 457–72; Jeremy Hein, "Rights, Resources and Membership: Civil Rights Models in France and the United States," *Annals of the American Academy of Political and Social Science* 530 (November 1993): 97–109; Evan Wolfson, "Civil Rights, Human Rights and Gay Rights," *Harvard Journal of Law and Public Policy* 14, no. 1 (Winter 1991): 21–39; and Pamela Johnson Conover, "The Nature of Citizenship in the United States and Great Britain: Empirical Comments on Theoretical Themes," *Journal of Politics* 53, no. 3 (August 1993): 800–832.

12. Jeremy Hein, "The Emergence of Ethnic Minorities in France: Market, State and Life Course Needs among Immigrants and Refugees," *Ethnic Groups* (October 1992): 135–50; Paul Gilroy, *There Ain't No Black in the Union Jack* (London: Hutchinson, 1987); John Rex and Sally Tomlinson, *Colonial Immigrants in a British City* (London: Routledge and Kegan Paul, 1979); Vaughan Robinson, "The New Indian Middle Class in Britain," *Ethnic and Racial Studies* 11, no. 4 (November 1988): 456–73; Russell A. Berman, Azade Seyhan, and Arlene Akiko Teraoka, eds., "Minorities in German Culture"; Czarina Wilpert, "From Guest Workers to Immigrants"; and Abdil Jazouli, *L'action collective des jeunes maghrebins de France* (Paris: C.I.E.M.I./L'Harmatann, 1986).

13. For Italy: Giovanna Campini, "Immigration and Racism in Southern Europe: The Italian Case," *Ethnic and Racial Studies* 16, no. 3 (July 1993): 507–36. For Spain: Alfonso Pérez Agote, *La reproduccion del nacionalismo: el caso vasco* (Madrid: Centro de Investigaciones Sociológicos, 1984). For Ireland: Jeffrey Prager, *Building Democracy in Ireland* (Cambridge: Cambridge University Press, 1986).

14. Michael Omi and Howard Winant, *Racial Formation in the United States from the 1960s to the 1980s* (New York: Routledge and Kegan Paul, 1986); Franke Wilmer, *The Indigenous Voice in World Politics* (London: Sage, 1993); Carlos Muñoz, *Youth, Identity, Power: The Chicano Generation* (New York: Verso, 1989); Edward Said and Christopher Hitchens, eds. *Blaming the Victims* (London: Verso, 1988); and Gary Y. Okihiro, *Margins and Mainstream: Asians in American History and Culture* (Seattle: University of Washington Press, 1994).

15. Ceri Peach, "The Muslim Population of Great Britain," *Ethnic and Racial Studies* 13, no. 3 (July 1990): 414–20; Yvonee Yazbeck Haddad, ed., *The Muslims of America* (Oxford: Oxford University Press, 1994); Elena Lappin, *Jewish Voices, German Words: Growing Up in Post-War Germany and Austria* (North Haven: Catbird Press, 1994); Cornel West, "Black Anti-Semitism and the Rhetoric of Resentment," *Tikkun* (January–February 1992): 15–17; Rogers M. Smith, "One United People: Second Class Female Citizens and the American Quest for Community," *Yale Journal of Law and the Humanities* 1 (1989): 229–93; Edith Hoshino Altbach, Jeanette Clausen, Dagmar Schultz, and Naomi Stephen, eds., *German Feminism* (Albany: SUNY Press 1984); and Jeffrey Weeks, *Coming Out: Homosexual Politics in Britain from the Nineteenth Century to the Present* (London: Quartet Books, 1977).

16. Alejandro Portes, "Gaining the Upper Hand: Economic Mobility among Immigrants and Domestic Minorities," *Ethnic and Racial Studies* 15, no. 4 (October 1992): 491–523.

17. For Europe, see Ronald Inglehart, *The Silent Revolution* (Princeton: Princeton University Press, 1977); Suzanne Berger, *Organizing Interests in Western Europe* (Cambridge: Cambridge University Press, 1981); Peter Hall, *Governing the Economy* (New York: Oxford University Press, 1986); J. H. Goldthorpe, ed., *Order and Conflict in Contemporary Capitalism* (Oxford: Oxford University Press, 1984); Paul Ginsberg, *A History of Contemporary Italy: Society and Politics, 1943–1988* (London: Penguin Books, 1990); Vivien A. Schmidt, *Democratizing France* (New York: Cambridge University Press, 1990); Claus Offe, *Contradictions of the Welfare State* (Cambridge, Mass.: MIT Press, 1984); and Charles Sabel, *Work and Politics* (Cambridge: Cambridge University Press, 1982). For the U.S., see Judith Shklar's *American Citizenship: The Quest for Inclusion*; Daniel Bell, *The Cultural Contradictions of Capitalism* (New York: Basic Books, 1976); Alan Wolfe, *America at Century's End* (Berkeley and Los Angeles: University of California Press, 1991); David Green, *The Language of Politics in America* (Ithaca: Cornell University Press, 1987); Michael J. Piore and Charles F. Sabel, *The Second Industrial Divide* (New York: Basic Books, 1984).

18. My understanding of narrative identity draws heavily from the work of Paul Ricoeur: "Narrative Identity," 188–201, and "Life in Quest of Narrative," 20–33, in *On Paul Ricoeur*, ed. David Wood (London: Routledge, 1991); "The Narrative Function," *Hermeneutics and the Human Sciences*, ed. John B. Thompson (Cambridge: Cambridge University Press, 1981).

19. Michael Walzer, "Liberalism and the Art of Separation," *Political Theory* 12, no. 3 (1984), 315.

20. Samuel Bowles and Herbert Gintis, *Democracy and Capitalism: Property, Community and the Contradictions of Modern Thought* (New York: Basic Books, 1986), 16–19.

21. Michael Walzer, "The Idea of Civil Society," *Dissent* (Spring 1991): 293–304; and Jean Cohen and Andrew Arato, *Civil Society and Political Theory* (Cambridge, Mass.: MIT Press, 1992).

22. Quentin Skinner, "The Idea of Negative Liberty: Philosophical and Historical Perspectives," in Richard Rorty, J. B. Schneewind, and Quentin Skinner, eds., *Philosophy in History* (New York: Cambridge University Press, 1984); Benjamin Barber, *Strong Democracy: Participatory Politics for a New Age* (Berkeley and Los Angeles: University of California Press, 1984); and Pierre Rosanvallon and Patrick Viveret, *Pour une nouvelle culture politique* (Paris: Éditions du Seuil, 1977).

23. For the U.S.: Michael Sandel, *Liberalism and Its Critics* (New York: New York University Press, 1984). For Spain: Carlos Thiebaut, *Los limites de la comunidad* (Madrid, 1992). For Germany: Herbert Kitschelt, "The 1990 German Federal Election and National Unification," *West European Politics* 14, no. 4 (1991): 121–48.

24. For English debates: Ludwig Wittgenstein, *Philosophical Investigations* (New York: Macmillan, 1958); J. L. Austin, *How to Do Things with Words* (Cambridge, Mass.: Harvard University Press, 1962); and James Tully, *Meaning and Context: Quentin Skinner and his Critics* (Cambridge: Polity Press, 1988). For German debates: Jürgen Habermas, *The Theory of Communicative Action*, vols. 1 (Boston: Beacon Press, 1984) and 2 (Boston: Beacon Press, 1987); Karl-Otto Apel, *Towards a Transformation of Philosophy* (London: Routledge and Kegan Paul, 1980); and Seyla Benhabib and Fred Dallmayr, eds., *The Communicative Ethics Controversy* (Cambridge, Mass.: MIT Press, 1990).

25. Richard Rorty's "antifoundationalism" is offering liberalism with new vistas, although his writings, in my view, do not yield a social and political narrative.

26. Just as there are flat and melodious fugues, so, too, liberal commentators can be divided. The "Liberal-Communitarian" exchange illustrates how simple, categorical binaries hinder thinking. Mary Douglas warned us of this many years ago: "Binary distinctions are an analytic procedure, but their usefulness does not guarantee that existence divides like that. We should look with suspicion on anyone who declared that there are two kinds of people, or two kinds of reality or process." "Judgements on James Frazer," *Daedalus* (Fall 1978): 161.

27. Alasdair MacIntyre, "Epistemological Crises, Dramatic Narrative, and the Philosophy of Science," *Paradigms and Revolutions*, ed. Gary Gutting (Notre Dame: University of Notre Dame Press, 1980), 54–74.

28. G.W.F. Hegel, *Phenomenology of Spirit*, ed. A. V. Miller (Oxford: Oxford University Press, 1971); and Alexandre Kojève, *Introduction to the Reading of Hegel* (New York: Basic Books, 1969).

29. The first generation of postimperialist writers include, among other, Franz Fanon, Albert Memmi, Octave Mannoni, and those associated with the journal *Presence Africaine*. For an introduction, see Bill Ashcroft, Gareth Griffiths, and Helen Tiffin, eds., *The Empire Writes Back: Theory and Practice in Post-Colonial Literature* (London: Routledge, 1989).

30. Gilles Deleuze's *Nietzsche and Philosophy* (London: Althone Press, 1983) gives centrality to the slave, whereas other neo-Nietzcheans favor a "master-driven" narrative; see David B. Allison, ed., *The New Nietzsche* (Cambridge, Mass.: MIT Press, 1985).

31. Stuart Hall, "Ethnicity: Identity and Difference," *Radical America* 23, no. 4 (October–December 1989): 9–20.

32. Some of these themes are discussed in Emmanuel Levinas, *Totality and Infinity* (Pittsburgh: Duquesne University Press, 1969), 40–46, 52–55, 73–87; William E. Connolly, *Identity\Difference* (Ithaca: Cornell University Press, 1991), 36–63, 64–94, and 158–97; and Paul Ricoeur, *The Conflict of Interpretations* (Evanston: Northwestern University Press, 1974).

33. The sources for most prophetic narratives are the following books from the Bible: Exodus, Numbers, and Deuteronomy. Michael Walzer, *Exodus and Revolution* (New York: Basic Books, 1985), discusses them. Keith D. Miller, *Voice of Deliverance: The Language of Martin Luther King and Its Sources* (New York: Free Press, 1992); Cornel West, *Prophesy Deliverance! An Afro-American Revolutionary Christianity* (Philadelphia: Westminster Press, 1982); and Suzanne Berger, "Religious Transformation and the Future of Politics," *European Sociology Review* 1 (1985).

34. Richard Rorty outlined how this occurred in his field: "When Carnap came to the United States he imported the belief that philosophy had to be defended from historicism and Nazism by avoiding thinkers like Plato, Hegel, Heidegger and Nietzsche. Karl Popper presented the same view in England in his book *The Open Society*, which was also . . . extremely influential. . . in America." Giovanna Borradori, *The American Philosophers*, trans. Rosanna Crocitto (Chicago: University of Chicago Press, 1994), 108. Stephen Holmes does the same for political theory: "The Permanent Structure of Antiliberal Thought," *Liberalism and the Moral Life*, ed. Nancy L. Rosenblum (Cambridge, Mass.: Harvard University Press, 1989), 227–54. His essay is also a fine example of liberal purism.

35. Richard Rorty's "antifoundationalism" is the most sustained assault on these stories; see his *Philosophy and the Mirror of Nature* (Princeton: Princeton University

Press, 1979) and *Objectivity, Relativism and Truth* (Cambridge: Cambridge University Press, 1991).

36. Mary Douglas, *Purity and Danger* (London: Routledge and Kegan Paul, 1966).

37. For a discussion of these types see: Hannah Arendt, *Totalitarianism* (London: Andre Deutsch, 1986); *The Jew as Pariah: Jewish Identity and Politics in the Modern Age*, ed. Ron Feldman (New York: Grove Press, 1978).

38. Alasdair MacIntyre, *After Virtue* (Notre Dame: University of Notre Dame Press, 1981).

39. The debate over the nature of Jewish thought is far from settled, but its lineaments, as far as I know, can be understood by studying the following: Leo Strauss, "Jerusalem and Athens: Some Preliminary Reflections," in *Studies in Platonic Political Philosophy*, ed. Thomas L. Pangle (Chicago: University of Chicago Press, 1983), 147–73; Emil Fackenheim, "The Holocaust and Philosophy," *Journal of Philosophy* 82, no. 10 (1985): 505–14; Zygmunt Bauman, *Modernity and the Holocaust* (Cambridge: Polity Press, 1989); and the very provocative and thoughtful revisionist attempt by Gillian Rose, *Judaism and Modernity: Philosophical Essays* (Oxford: Blackwell, 1993), esp. 1–32.

40. Hannah Arendt, *Between Past and Future* (New York: Viking, 1954), 6.

41. In reflecting on peripheral peoples, I have followed the sensible advice of Judith Shklar, *American Citizenship: The Quest for Inclusion*, 9: "Theorists who ignore the best current history and political science cannot expect to have anything very significant to contribute to our political self-understanding. They stand in acute danger of theorizing about nothing at all except their own uneasiness in a society they have made very little effort to comprehend." I have also relied on the work of anthropologists and sociologists, fields that Shklar did not tap for her work.

42. Hannah Arendt, *Thinking*, vol. 1 of *The Life of the Mind* (New York: Harcourt Brace Jovanovich, 1978), 209–10

Part Four

DOES DEMOCRACY NEED FOUNDATIONS?

Seventeen

Idealizations, Foundations, and Social Practices

RICHARD RORTY

WE NEED to distinguish between idealizations of our practices and foundations for those practices. Idealizations answer the question "How can we make our present practices more coherent?" by downplaying some of the things we do and emphasizing others. Political debate at high levels of abstraction is, typically, debate between competing idealizations, and thus between competing visions of the utopian future of our community.

The difference between Rawls and Nozick, for example, is the difference between two idealizations of present practices in the liberal democracies. Rawls and Nozick formulate principles that function as what Daniel Dennett has called "intuition pumps." Such pumps suck up and concentrate intuitions about the importance of certain components of our practices. They thereby suggest that these practices might become more coherent if these components played a more central role. To put it very crudely, Rawls's principles remind us of what we do in our appellate courts of law, whereas Nozick's remind us of what we do in our marketplaces. Competition between the two men's idealizations is a matter of playing certain of our practices against others.

Foundations, by contrast, are supposed to answer the question "Should we be engaging in our present practices at all?" Foundationalists think that intuition pumps are not enough. They think that we not only must adjust our practices so as to render them more coherent but also must have regard to something that exists independently of those practices. Typically, this thing is called "human nature" or "rationality" or "morality," and is conceived of as an object that can be studied without any special reference to what we are currently doing and hoping. When principles are treated as foundations rather than as idealizations—as appeals beyond our practices rather than reminders of particular features of our practices—they are typically put forward as descriptions of some such object.

To be antifoundationalist about a social practice is to urge that criticism or commendation of it be confined to comparison with other actual and possible social practices. The antifoundationalist's central claim is that attempts to ground a practice on something outside the practice will always be more or less disingenuous. As we antifoundationalists see it, the object outside the practice, the purported foundation, is always just a hypostatization of certain

selected components of that practice. In particular, "human nature," "rationality," and "morality" are abbreviations for the kinds of human conduct we
wish to encourage. To say that a certain course of conduct is more in accord
with human nature or our moral sense, or more rational, than another is
just a fancy way of commending one's own sense of what is most worth preserving in our present practices, of commending our own utopian vision of
our community.

Antifoundationalism is identified with emotivism and irrationalism by
those who still accept a moral psychology that distinguishes between reason
and the passions. But this psychology has been in trouble since Darwin, as has
the idea of "human nature." Antifoundationalist Darwinians like Dewey differ
from amoralist Darwinians like Nietzsche in wanting to reconcile familiar
moral intuitions with a naturalistic sense of ourselves as simply clever animals.
Dewey wanted to reconcile Christian ethics with Darwin and Mendel, just as
Kant had wanted to reconcile Christian ethics with a morally indifferent, cor-
puscularian, physical universe.

The reconciliation Dewey wanted is best achieved by treating reason not as
the name of a source or judge of truth but as the name of our ability to use
language, and thus to employ persuasion as well as force. Conceiving of reason
in this way, however, makes it impossible to say that one language of moral
and political deliberation, and the set of social practices intertwined with that
language, is more rational than another. It also makes it impossible to say that
one such language or set of practices is truer to human nature than another.
For humanity no more has a nature, or rationality a structure, independent of
the accidents of history than life has a nature independent of the accidents of
biological evolution. Human history is simply biological evolution continued
by other means—a competition in which what is at stake is the survival of
languages, rather than of genes.

To ask for a foundation of democracy is, typically, to ask for a reason why
we should be inclusive in our moral and political concerns rather than exclusive—why, for example, we should try to broaden our moral and political
community so as to include nonlandowners, nonwhites, nonmales, non-
straights, and so on. This request is equivalent to asking for a reason why the
language of communities influenced by the Christian ethic of love is more
worthy to survive than that of communities dominated by the notion of
honor, or by pride in gender or in race. From a Darwinian point of view, this
demand is as pointless as asking for a reason why the primitive mammals were
more worthy to survive than the giant reptiles. Worthiness does not come into
it, because there is no standpoint outside of the accidents of evolution from
which to judge worth. We antifoundationalists think that once we give up on
the answer "God wills that we love each other," there is *no* good answer to the
question about the worth of inclusivity and love. So we see the foundational-

ist's question as a symptom of what Santayana called "supernaturalism," defined as "the confusion of ideals and power."

The problem foundationalists face is how to argue exclusivists into being inclusivists, racists into being democrats, by finding premises they share. By contrast, the problem faced by us antifoundationalists is how to get rid of the idea that democracy is somehow enfeebled unless such shared premises exist. I think that the best solution to our problem is to play down the Greek idea that what makes us clever, language-using animals special is our ability to know, conceived of as our ability to rise above the contingencies of culture and history. We antifoundationalists should try to substitute the idea that what makes us special is our ability to feel for, cherish, and trust people very different from ourselves. We should think of language as a tool for breaking down people's distrust of one another rather than as one for representing how things really are. To make this substitution, we have to persuade people to desert Athens for Jerusalem. We have to get them to appreciate Kierkegaard's suggestion that, *pace* Hegel, the whole point of Christianity was that God wants lovers rather than knowers.

If nowadays we find the term "love" too contaminated or too quaint, we can substitute Annette Baier's term "appropriate trust." The attempt of Baier and other feminists to substitute the notion of appropriate trust for that of "obligation" as the central moral concept seems to me the most promising contemporary antifoundationalist initiative. This is because it completes an anti-Greek train of thought that Kant began. Kant undermined knowledge to make room for moral faith—faith in the idea of unconditional, nonempirical, non–historically conditioned obligation. But by insisting on the importance of unconditionality he reinforced the supernaturalist temptation to confuse ideals with the putative power of the unchangeable and atemporal. To avoid this temptation it would help to follow Baier in taking the *family* as our model for moral and political community, rather than the schoolroom, the law court, or the marketplace. Baier suggests that it is in the family, and in particular in the child's trust in its mother, that all our moral ladders start. Accepting her suggestion might help us see the search for foundations of democracy as a mere distraction from debates between competing idealizations of current practices.

Eighteen

Democratic Theory and Democratic Experience

ROBERT A. DAHL

DOES DEMOCRACY need foundations? Professor Rorty's renowned challenge to philosopher's claims about foundations[1] encourages me to respond to the question simply as a political scientist who has been concerned with both democratic theory and practice for some time. What strikes me at the outset is that we can understand this question in many different ways, depending on how we interpret its main terms. We should ask ourselves what we mean by "foundations," by "democracy," and by "need."

As to the term "democracy," the inquiry may be interpreted as asking three very different questions:

1. Do democratic *systems* or *regimes* or *governments* need foundations in order to exist, or to function properly—and if so, what are they? Or
2. Does democratic *theory* need foundations? Or
3. Do democratic *systems* need democratic *theory* as a foundation?

Notice that the first of these poses an *empirical* question, not what I would call a philosophical one. What is more, the empirical problem it presents is hellishly difficult. To begin with, we need to decide whether we mean the inquiry to extend to all democratic systems throughout history, or only to modern democratic systems. If we mean to include all more or less democratic systems, including those of Classical Greece, the Roman republic, and medieval democracies and republics, then a reasonably satisfactory answer will probably always elude us. If, for example, one of the foundations of a democratic system is some set—or sets—of beliefs with a certain substantive content that are distributed in certain ways among leaders and citizens, then I do not quite see how the evidence needed for a satisfactory answer will ever become available, though of course we can continue to offer more or less plausible conjectures.

Suppose, then, that we restrict our attention to modern democratic systems, that is, those that in ordinary parlance we have come to call democratic since the eighteenth century, and particularly during this century. Even here a satisfactory answer is, to put it mildly, extremely difficult to arrive at. To get some kind of handle on the problem, suppose we develop criteria according to which countries like the United States, the U.K., and France, let us say, can be said to have democratic political systems. Although these countries are certainly not fully democratic in an ideal sense, ordinary speech as well as journalistic and scholarly usage authorizes us to call them democracies. Suppose we agree, then, that any country that reaches a threshold of democracy comparable to theirs will also be said to have a democratic political system. It appears that a total of twenty-one countries reached that threshold by 1950 or earlier and have maintained democratic political systems uninterruptedly since that time. Let us call this set the older democracies. Although these older democracies have been much studied in the last several decades—surely far more and far more systematically than any political systems in human history—it is doubtful whether even today we have sufficient comparable data to allow a reasonably rigorous answer.

The problem is complicated even further by the fact that as of 1993 at least thirty more countries, and on some counts as many as forty, have also attained this somewhat arbitrary threshold. Although most of these countries have acquired their democratic institutions for the first time, in several cases, such as Argentina, Chile, and Uruguay, they have regained them after a period of authoritarian rule. This extraordinary increase in the number of democratic countries—in, so to speak, the number of cases available for study—provides a historically unparalleled opportunity for the sort of comparative analysis that might some day provide a reasonably satisfactory answer to our question. But that comparative task has barely begun. It is without doubt interesting, challenging, exciting, important, and rapidly moving forward; but it is a long way indeed from completion.

Moreover, a satisfactory answer, I should think, would require a comparative analysis of both democratic successes and failures. According to the fullest count I am aware of, between 1900 and 1985 nondemocratic regimes replaced democratic regimes fifty-two times (not counting cases in which democratic governments were replaced strictly as a consequence of foreign invasions).[2] As in medicine and surgery, so too in political science, disease, dysfunction, affliction, and tragedy can provide useful evidence about how healthy systems can be maintained and afflicted ones restored to health. From studies of earlier democratic breakdowns much has already been learned. Unhappily, more may be learned from the breakdowns yet to come.

Taking a long view, then, perhaps a reasonably satisfactory answer to my first interpretation of the main question might become available in—what shall we guess? Twenty years? Fifty?

Let me turn to the second interpretation of the question before us. Does democratic *theory* need foundations?

Ignoring the question of what we mean by "need" (in particular, do we mean necessary, sufficient, or both necessary and sufficient?) I can readily

think of at least two reasons for saying that democratic theory needs foundations. First, we might feel that a theory without foundations is simply not a
good or adequate theory. However, I do not see that this takes us very far, for
it seems to be no more than one way of defining what we mean by a good
theory. One might reasonably ask whether we approve of such a definition on
purely aesthetic grounds or because such a theory provides us with a satisfying
sense of closure. Or is there more at stake than aesthetic pleasure or some
other psychological satisfaction?

In my view a better reason for attempting to develop satisfactory foundations for democratic theory is the likely consequences of not having any. By
foundations I now mean simply a set of reasonable assumptions that provide
grounds for believing that democracy is desirable, for judging whether and to
what extent a given system is democratic, and for judging what political practices or institutions would be required in order to satisfy the assumptions. The
reason why we want foundations for democratic theory, then, is that they can
help to improve our political judgments and choices.

But do democratic systems need democratic theory, or a democratic theory,
as a foundation? The answer is, I confess, not at all clear to me. Again, a
satisfactory answer would seem to depend predominantly on very difficult
empirical judgments, both historical and comparative, about the relations in
democratic systems between intellectual elites, political leaders, intermediate
opinion leaders, and mass publics. I do not believe these relationships are at
all well understood. What is more, they probably differ from country to country, and within a given country from one era to another.

However, let us imagine a country with democratic political institutions in
which intellectual elites are in the main convinced that democracy *cannot* be
justified on reasonable and plausible grounds. The prevailing view among
them, let us suppose, is that no intellectually respectable reasons exist for
believing that a democratic system is better than a nondemocratic alternative.
As long as the political, social, and economic institutions of the country are
performing adequately from the perspective of the general population, perhaps most people will simply ignore the querulous dissent of their intellectuals; and political leaders and influential opinion makers may in the main go
along with the generally favorable popular view. But in times of serious crisis—and all countries go through times of serious crisis—those who try to
defend democracy will find the going much harder, while those who promote
nondemocratic alternatives will find it that much easier.

Or consider a country with nondemocratic institutions in which the conditions are otherwise favorable for a transition to democracy. Suppose, however,
that intellectuals, including opposition intellectuals, believe that no serious
intellectual justification exists for democracy.

While it would be a misleading to attribute extraordinary influence to the
role of intellectuals or to assume that the political beliefs and ideologies of

intellectuals are necessarily any more rationally grounded than those of other people, reflections like these lead me to the conclusion that among the complex historical factors that contribute to democratic stability, breakdown, and transformation, a body of democratic theory reposing on reasonable assumptions is by no means of trivial importance.

Notes

1. In *Philosophy and the Mirror of Nature* (Princeton: Princeton University Press, 1979), chap. 8.

2. Frank Bealey, "Stability and Crisis: Fears about Threats to Democracy," *European Journal of Political Research* 15 (1987): 687–715. This fits tolerably well with Samuel Huntington's forty-seven cases of democratic reversal in *The Third Wave: Democratization in the Late Twentieth Century* (Norman: University of Oklahoma Press, 1991), table 1.1, 26.

Nineteen

Democracy, Philosophy, and Justification

AMY GUTMANN

DOES DEMOCRACY need foundations? We cannot adequately answer the foundationalist question without first asking how democracy is best defended. When we answer this question, however, the foundational question becomes moot. Democracy needs justifications, not foundations—at least, not foundations in the strict sense suggested by Richard Rorty and other antifoundationalists. If we cannot justify democracy, then neither can we know what kind of democracy is worth defending. If we can justify democracy, then we should not worry about whether our justification is, in the strict sense, foundationalist. Justifications need not be foundationalist or antifoundationalist. I will first suggest some reasons why this is so, and then briefly sketch a justification of deliberative democracy that is neither foundationalist nor antifoundationalist.

Foundationalism in political philosophy, if it is not to be trivially identified with any reason-giving defense of a conception of politics, is the claim that justification must rest upon truths about human nature, human rights, rationality, or politics that are self-evident, rationally incontestable, or axiomatic. Does an adequate theoretical defense of democracy need foundations in this nontrivial sense? Before answering this question, we should be clear not to confuse it with the more practical question of whether actual democracies need to rely upon philosophy in addition to, or instead of, education, elections, legislation, constitutions, and force, if necessary, in order to defend themselves against threats to their well-being that variously come from intolerance, apathy, corruption, and violent aggression. We are rather asking the theoretical question of what it takes to sustain the claim that democracy is a justified (or the most justified) form of government.

First, let us consider democracy as it is often understood today to describe an increasingly common set of political institutions the world over, for which Robert Dahl coined the term "polyarchy." Polyarchies, or what we might call nonideal democracies, are characterized, at minimum, by guarantees of free political speech, press, association, and equal suffrage for all adults, the right of all adults above a certain age to run for political office, the rule of law, and frequent, competitive elections that are procedurally fair. How can nonideal democracy best justify itself against undemocratic forms of government?

Democracy, Winston Churchill noted, is the worst form of government except all the others. He was referring to actual, nonideal democracies and comparing them to nonideal nondemocracies. Many people today, many of whom were raised in nondemocratic societies, defend nonideal democracy on Churchillian grounds even though their nascent democratic governments are falling far short of satisfying many of their basic needs. Why are nonideal democracies better than their nonideal alternatives? Political philosophers have offered several practically compatible (yet theoretically distinct) reasons, the first having to do with the centrality of democratic liberties to human dignity, the second with the instrumental value of democratic liberties in resisting political tyranny, and the third connecting democratic liberties with the maximization of social welfare. The moral and intellectual force of these (contestable) reasons notwithstanding, the Churchillian defense of democracy is largely negative and therefore uninspiring to many citizens of nonideal democracies who take for granted the basic accomplishments of democratic government and are aspiring for something more. The Churchillian defense of nonideal democracy is also doubly inadequate to the aspirations of political philosophy. Because it stops short of articulating a full-fledged democratic ideal, it does not expect enough of democracy and also fails to tell us what *kind* of democracy is most justified. It therefore provides only a partial defense of even nonideal democracy.

Nonetheless, to say that nonideal democracy is better than the available nonideal alternatives is to say something practically and theoretically important. The Churchillian defense offers some insight into why, despite the failures of every existing democratic government to secure for all its citizens some basic goods such as an adequate income, employment, health care, and education, most citizens of nonideal democracies, including many who are deprived of these basic goods, support them over their undemocratic alternatives.

Notice that the Churchillian defense of democracy is neither foundational nor antifoundational. It is agnostic on the question of whether democracy rests on certain rationally undeniable facts about human nature and politics. (We could say the defense is foundational in the loose sense of offering reasons for defending nonideal democracies against their undemocratic alternatives, but this is to confuse foundationalism with reasonableness. Antifoundationalists do not deny the need to give reasons in defense of democracy against undemocratic—or less democratic—alternatives.) Despite its lack of what we might call Cartesian foundations, the Churchillian defense of democracy is as salient in today's world as it was in Churchill's, and its force is not limited to any particular culture, or a few idiosyncratic ones.

Why should anyone think that the Churchillian position constitutes even a partial justification of nonideal democracy, as opposed to an indication of what "we democrats" just happen (without any reason) to believe in by virtue of our socialization? Ordinary people, not only political philosophers, think

about whether and why they should support nonideal democratic governments rather than undemocratic ones. The theoretical question of whether
nonideal democracy is justified is typically connected to a practical question:
is this nonideal democracy deserving of support? Now, what else could justify
the precarious support for democracy among former subjects of Soviet-style
communism but the comparative advantage of nonideal democratic governments over nonideal autocratic governments? And what else but the value of
civil and political liberties could account for the moral strength of nonideal
democracy? The short-run economic benefits of democracy have been con-
spicuous by their absence. The claim that the long-run benefits of democracy
outweigh its short-term costs is doubly dubious, first for sacrificing the well-
being of present people for future ones, and second for its unwarranted confidence in such long-term social forecasting and calculating. Democracy needs
to be justified to the people who are bound by its practices and policies.
Long-term benefits may be there; yet without the basic liberties that democracy brings, those benefits would be insufficient to justify nonideal democracies to people here and now.

Consider this typical story about the extraordinary economic problems
facing the new Baltic republics, featured on the front page of the *New York
Times*, April 10, 1993. This story happened to be about Lithuania, whose
citizens had experienced over the past year one of the worst economic situations of their lifetimes. Inflation in consumer goods was over 600 percent, and
inflation in agricultural products over 700 percent. Industrial output had declined over 50 percent, and new housing had declined by over 20 percent.
Unemployment was estimated at 200,000 (out of 3.7 million), an enormous
shock to a citizenry completely unaccustomed to worrying about job security.
Not surprisingly, Lithuanian citizens have voted out of office the more liberal
president (Landsbergis) and voted in a former communist, newly turned social
democratic president (Brazauskas). What is surprising is that they did not vote
for a return to authoritarian rule.

The story featured an ordinary citizen, Rimantas Pirmaitis, who had, along
with many of his compatriots, joined the protests of 1989–90 that led to Lithuania's democratization and independence from Soviet rule. Pirmaitis was
employed under the communist regime as a construction engineer, where he
made a decent living. But under the new democracy he has been reduced to
selling flowers from a street stand in central Vilnius to support his family. He
nonetheless remains a democrat, notwithstanding runaway inflation. "But we
are past the time for marches and anthems," he says. "What we need now is
something real, something we can eat and touch."

Were it not the case that the civil and political liberties of a democratic
society are as real as economic benefits, the belief in a *democratic* Lithuania
would be considerably less defensible. Although liberties are inedible and un-

touchable, they are not always overlooked by people who are struggling to survive. An appreciation of basic freedoms and their centrality to human dignity, self-respect, and well-being often makes nonideal democracy both apparently and really better than its alternatives. An understanding of the degrading experience of people living under the undemocratic alternatives to nonideal democracies may be sufficient for a nonfoundationalist defense of nonideal democracy. This defense is distinct from that of an ideal conception of democracy, but the favorable comparison with available nonideal alternatives is a strong defense nonetheless. The comparison provides reasons to people who doubt that democracy is better than the alternatives, as well as to people who are drawn to democracy but wonder why. Although much more may be said in defense of nonideal democracy, this much should suffice to show that justification, at least at the nonideal level, need not be either foundationalist or antifoundationalist to be reasonable, and useful as well.

But political philosophers aspire to something more than the defense of nonideal democracy as we now know it. We try to construct out of our inheritance, and imagine beyond it, a more fully justifiable set of social and political institutions, which we can call democracy without qualification, or at least without neologism. Political philosophers who defend a democratic *ideal* may therefore seem committed to some form of foundationalism. What else but some self-evident or rationally incontrovertible truth could support our claims for an ideal conception of democracy, which would (if democratically instituted) realize the political ideal of collective self-government? How else are we to interpret and defend such an ideal?

Suppose that a fully justified democracy authorizes all adult members of society to share, either directly or through their accountable representatives, in deliberatively shaping their collective life in a way that is consistent with respecting the basic liberties and opportunities of all individuals. Suppose also that deliberation is the give-and-take of argument in a public form (not necessarily a legislature) that aims at, and results in, provisionally justified decision-making, decisions that are respectful of the basic liberties and opportunities of all members of society. Deliberation also helps shape our understanding of basic opportunities and liberties. But if the results of democratic deliberation are to be provisionally justified, they must respect the basic liberties and opportunities of all citizens on some reasonable understanding. The arguments offered in a public forum also should be reasonable by some public standard. Deliberation at various levels of government and in different political arenas is, as far as I can discern, the most legitimate means of settling principled conflicts over social justice, conflicts that are inescapable in any free society.

This is an abbreviated outline of one interpretation of deliberative democracy. An interpretation of deliberative democracy as a political ideal, suitably expanded and more fully defended, is bound not only to be incomplete and controversial but also to be reasonably contested. Prominent among its democratic contesters are what might be called populist democracy, participatory democracy, perfectionist liberal democracy, and ultraconstitutionalist democracy. Deliberative democracy has two important advantages over these and other democratic alternatives that bear on the foundationalist question.

The first advantage of deliberative democracy is its recognition of the provisional nature of justification in politics. The empirical and moral understandings of citizens change not only over time and social space but also by virtue of deliberative interchange, the give-and-take of sometimes complementary, often conflicting, political insights and arguments (including conflicts over what counts as the political realm). Deliberative democracy therefore leaves a lot of room for "difference." Differences in practices and policies that result from deliberation among an inclusive citizenry are democratically legitimate, even if no one knows whether they are just in the strict foundational sense. Whether or not foundational claims are metaphysically possible is a moot point as far as the ideal of deliberative democratic politics is concerned. The alternative is not antifoundationalism, but fairly conducted collective deliberations that yield provisionally justified practices and policies.

A second significant advantage of deliberative democracy is its compatibility with some other conceptions of democracy, insofar as these conceptions result from democratic deliberations. Upon deliberation, citizens may decide to institute some form of perfectionist democracy. But if they decide to reject perfectionist policies, then what can philosophy divorced from democratic deliberation say in their favor? Perfectionist critics can say that the standpoint of deliberative democracy is not neutral among democratic (or undemocratic) alternatives. Of course it is not, and it need not claim to be. Critics can also say that deliberative democracy lacks incontestable foundations. Of course it does. There is neither a neutral substitute for foundationalism, as some liberal philosophers have claimed, nor a foundationalist substitute for democracy, as some perfectionist philosophers have suggested.

Defenders of deliberative democracy can offer only a moral and political argument (with the hope that it catches on). The argument, in brief, might be that the legitimate exercise of political authority requires justification to those people who are bound by it, and decision-making by deliberation among free and equal citizens is the most defensible justification anyone has to offer for provisionally settling controversial issues. This justification, once elaborated, would be compatible with respecting many moral and cultural differences within and across societies. If citizens deliberatively decide to constitute themselves as a participatory or perfectionist liberal democracy, then those forms of democracy are also provisionally justified, provided they respect the basic liberties and opportunities of all individuals and leave citizens free to deliberate in the future. (The freedom to deliberate in the future is necessary to ensure that provisional justifications are not treated as foundationalist truths.)

This defense of deliberative democracy is not an example of either foundationalism or antifoundationalism. Foundationalism tells us that we must defend democracy on the basis of human nature, natural rights, or self-evident reason; antifoundationalism tells us that reason has nothing to do with defending democracy. Both perspectives presuppose a metaphysical truth without warrant.

The foundationalist defense, sometimes attributed to Aristotle, bases deliberative democracy on an alleged truth about human nature, that human beings are rational, deliberative animals. According to this defense, only a deliberative democracy expresses the true, rational nature of individuals and offers all people the opportunity to perfect their natures through public deliberation. Every other form of government falls short of this foundational standard, because other forms of government encourage only one or a few people to deliberate on political questions, whereas all human beings are by nature deliberative beings in political as well as personal realms. Is this true? Are all people natural deliberators in politics? Maybe so, maybe not. We really do not know. The claim that people are by their very nature deliberative beings in the strong sense claimed by some Aristotelians is not self-evidently true (or false). It is subject to reasonable doubt (and defense). Far from being axiomatic, such substantive claims about human nature are reasonably contestable, and contested. This foundationalist defense of deliberative democracy does not satisfy foundationalist standards; its claims about human nature are not self-evident, rationally incontestable, or axiomatic. The claim that human beings are natural deliberators is as subject to reasonable doubt as nonfoundationalist claims about democracy. Saying that democracy is grounded in human nature cannot therefore substitute for showing that democracy gives actual people something that is valuable to them, where what is valuable includes a wide range of liberties and opportunities as well as economic well-being.

Saying that democracy needs no foundations does not leave us with anything more than a critical stance toward foundationalists, who claim or expect too much from philosophical argument. To show that democracy does not need foundations does not tell us what we need to say in its defense. We need to say something more than what is suggested by the strong antifoundationalist view, which runs roughly as follows: if we, the members of a democratic cultural community, believe in democracy but democracy happens not to satisfy the best philosophical conception of human nature or basic human needs, then so much the worse for philosophical justifications of democracy. I do not see how our widely shared belief in democracy can suffice to justify imposing a democratic government on disbelieving minorities. We need to say something to them about the political virtues of democracy. Besides, most of us believe in democracy, and in a particular kind of democracy, because we think there are good reasons to defend it against the alternatives. Our reasons will of course come from within some social understandings, but this is not to say that our reasons are therefore unnecessary, or merely a reflection of our upbringing about which we cannot critically reflect. "Our" believing in democracy is not a substitute for our offering arguments in favor of some conception of democracy. Nor is our offering good arguments a substitute for our believing in democracy. The truth in antifoundationalism is that much of what we say is going to be contestable, subject to reasonable doubt. If we take such doubt to be devastating of the philosophical case for democracy, then we capitulate to critics of democracy without good cause.

All anyone can do is try to address the doubt. Few political philosophers actually argue that democracy can be defensibly dissociated from a form of deliberative self-government that secures the basic liberties and opportunities of all members of society. Most neglect the importance of deliberation. The neglect of deliberation is untenable because the defense of democracy against traditional hierarchy, enlightened autocracy, liberal perfectionism, ultraconstitutionalism, and other credible political alternatives is weakened to the extent that we imagine a democracy that does not collectively deliberate over controversial matters of political importance. Briefly and roughly, one might say that populist democracy reduces citizenship to formal political rights and majoritarian procedures; participatory democracy not only takes too many meetings but also disrespects those people who would, quite reasonably, rather be represented than represent themselves; ultraconstitutionalism identifies justice with a comprehensive set of substantive principles, as if someone could design a government that institutes the comprehensive set of just policies, known prior to deliberative decision making among citizens or their accountable representatives.

Suppose that, with regard to the many politically controversial matters that divide democratic societies, some philosophers think that they know what is just and do not need to deliberate with other citizens who see things differently in order to figure out what is just. It is quite another question, however, as to whether, in the absence of collective deliberation, their supposedly just policies, which are meant to be socially binding, can be justified to all those other people who are to be bound by them. And it is yet another question as to how a society, without deliberating, can distinguish the philosopher who really knows what is just from all those who are no less convinced that they know, but do not.

If all foundationalists claim is that democracy can be defended by publicly accessible reasons, then we are (almost) all foundationalist. If all antifoundationalists claim is that democracy cannot be deduced from self-evident truths, then we are (almost) all antifoundationalists. But if some kind of deliberative democracy is defensible, then democracy does not need either foundationalism or antifoundationalism. It needs to be liberated from this dead-end debate. Political philosophers can contribute more to both political philosophy and democracy when we stop metatheorizing and start arguing about the substantive problems that animate contemporary politics, including the continually contested question of what *kind* of democracy is most defensible.

Twenty

Foundationalism and Democracy

BENJAMIN R. BARBER

THE LEADING political philosophical question of the eighties—Does democracy have foundations?—may not be the leading political philosophical question of the nineties. But it remains critical in that it compels an ongoing debate about the meaning of democracy itself. Whatever the merit of foundationalist approaches, they tend to mandate a construction of democracy that favors natural liberty and absolute rights. I wish here to ask not only whether democracy has foundations but what sort of democracy it is that can do without foundations or, indeed, repudiates foundations precisely because of what it requires politically.

The very question, "Does democracy have foundations?" is dangerous for democrats of my tendencies, because it mandates a discussion on the turf of epistemology that leans toward an answer in the affirmative, and yields an understanding of democracy hostile to what I believe are its necessary participatory attributes. But if democracy is concerned with a form of knowledge (say, knowledge of political things such as power, or political values such as rights, or political ends such as justice) or constituted by institutions and procedures that rest on knowledge (say, constitutions or the principle of majoritarianism), then unless we wish to invite an abject politics of relativism or arbitrariness, to the question of whether democracy has foundations we are perforce obliged to reply, "Well, yes, democracy must have foundations in truths antecedent to and not dependent upon it." How, after all, can any cognitive moral or political system function without roots in a prior understanding of what constitutes true knowledge?

By my lights, however, it is the character of politics in general, and of democratic politics in particular, that it is precisely *not* a cognitive system concerned with what we know and how we know it but a system of conduct concerned with what we *will* together and *do* together and how we agree on what we will to do. It is practical not speculative, about action rather than about truth. It yields but is not premised on an epistemology and in this sense

An early version of this essay was prepared for the international meeting of the Conference for the Study of Political Thought at Yale University, April 1993. It appeared in revised form in V. Gerhardt et al., *Politisches Denken Jahrbuch* 1993 (Stuttgart: Verlag J. B. Metzler, 1993).

is necessarily pragmatic. Where there is truth or certain knowledge there need be no politics, even though (as Plato warns) politicians and citizens may wantonly ignore truth and certain knowledge in pursuit of base interests or raw power. But democratic politics begins where certainty ends. As I suggested in *Strong Democracy*, the political question always takes a form something like: "What shall we do when something has to be done that affects us all, we wish to be reasonable, yet we disagree on means and ends and are without independent grounds for making the choice."[1]

This, then, is the sense in which politics is ineluctably pragmatic and so, as William James says of pragmatism, turns its back resolutely and once and for all "upon a lot of inveterate habits dear to professional philosophers . . . away from abstraction and insufficiency, from verbal solutions, from bad a priori reasons, from fixed principles, closed systems, and pretended absolutes and origins."[2] As democratic politics are pragmatic, so pragmatism is democratic: "See already how democratic [pragmatism] is," James rhapsodized; "Her manners are as various and flexible, her resources as rich and endless."[3]

Politics occupies the domain of practical action. As Dewey suggests, "the distinctive characteristic of practical activity . . . is the uncertainty that attends it."[4] The philosophical quest for certainty inspires a longing "to find a realm in which there is an activity which is not overt and which has no external consequences. 'Safety first' has played a large role in effecting preference for knowing over doing and making." Like the Greeks, our foundationalists continue to believe that the "office of knowledge is to uncover the antecedently real, rather than, as is the case with our practical judgment, to gain the kind of understanding which is necessary to deal with problems as they arise."[5]

What Bertrand Russell said ruefully about the quest for mathematical truth seems to me to fit perfectly the quest for political truth in the form of foundations antecedent to democratic politics:

> Real life is, to most men, a long second-best, a perpetual compromise between the ideal and the possible; but the world of pure reason knows no compromise, no practical limitations, no barrier to the creative embodying in splendid edifices of the passionate aspiration after the perfect from which all great work springs. Remote from human passions, remote even from the pitiful facts of nature, the generations have gradually created an ordered cosmos, where pure thought can dwell as in its natural home, and where one, at least, of our nobler impulses can escape from the dreary exile of the actual world.[6]

Politics is not an ordered cosmos in which our nobler impulses can be given expression; it is how we try to govern ourselves in "the dreary exile of the actual world." Here we are, to use a metaphor favored both by Charles Saunders Peirce and Michael Oakeshott, afloat on an open and endless sea where, in Peirce's words, we must rebuild our ship "on the open sea, never able to dismantle it in dry dock and to reconstruct it out of the best materials."[7]

Notice already how, despite my intentions, in replying pragmatically to the imperatives of epistemology I am entrapped by its language. Because philosophy always seeks to "create the world in its own image" (Nietzsche), its tyranny is to transform the discussion of politics into a discussion of knowledge, even among those wishing to defend the autonomy and sovereignty of politics. In order to make my case for democracy as a foundationless commitment to a certain form of politics, then, I will shift the argument from the pragmatic/ philosophical critique of philosophy, which can only remind us of the power of philosophy, to a political discussion in which the sovereign force of politics becomes evident. Since (Daniel Webster reminds us) governments are instituted for practical benefit and not for subjects of speculative reasoning, let us turn away from the epistemology and toward the politics of democracy. The question is not which politics is legitimated by a certain epistemology, but which epistemology is legitimated by a certain democratic politics.

If epistemological concerns enjoin a definition of democracy in terms of its root values and antecedent normative foundations, democratic politics defined by active citizenship and ongoing deliberation moves in a different direction. Politically, we may define democracy as a regime/culture/civil society/ government in which we make (will) common decisions, choose common conduct, and create or express common values in the practical domain of our lives in an ever-changing context of conflict of interests and competition for power—a setting, moreover, where there is no agreement on prior goods or certain knowledge about justice or right and where we must proceed on the premise of the base equality both of interests and of the interested. Voting involves not a discretionary decision about what is true but a necessary decision about what to do. This political definition suggests certain attributes of democratic politics that help explain why democracy cannot and does not rest on "foundations" in the way that (say) natural law or Platonic justice do. These attributes include:

> 1. the revolutionary spirit of democracy, which is tied to its spontaneity, its creativity, and its responsiveness to change;
>
> 2. the autonomy of democracy, which entails a commitment to engagement, participation, and empowerment; and
>
> 3. the commonality or publicness of democratic judgment (decision-making with respect to common action) in a democracy, which mandates some form of democratic communitarianism and common willing.

Revolutionary spirit. We need to distinguish several aspects of "revolution" in assessing the role of a zealous revolutionary spirit in democracy. Revolutionary resistance, for example, often is rooted in foundationalist claims that are used to assail an illegitimate or arbitrary politics. Thus resistance to seventeenth-century British absolutism was couched in natural rights rhetoric with a strong foundationalist flavor—the absolute monarch understood as a transgressor of inviolable rights antecedent to all political convention. Here revolution is quite literally—in consonance with the astronomical use of the term—a return to an original starting point: the recovery of a foundational prepolitical moment to challenge an illegitimate present politics. Tom Paine thus argued that the American Revolution was actually a "counter-revolution" aimed at recovering ancient British rights violated by a tyrannical monarch.

While this captures an important moment in revolution, I am concerned here rather with the revolutionary spirit associated with political spontaneity—that sense of fresh ownership that each generation brings to a constitution or political order by reembracing its principles.[8] The object here is to make revolution a *permanent* feature of the political landscape rather than just a founding mechanism for a new, more legitimate politics of stasis (the locus classicus of law and order!).

Benjamin Rush reminded would-be democrats that though in the American system "all power is derived from the people, they possess it only on the days of their elections."[9] Thomas Jefferson, who always loved "dreams of the future more than the history of the past,"[10] had a special sensitivity to the centrality (and fragility) of this dimension of revolutionary ardor. He warned against looking "at constitutions with sanctimonious reverence, and deem[ing] them like the ark of the covenant, too sacred to be touched,"[11] and he is known famously for his insistence that "the tree of liberty must be refreshed from time to time with the blood of patriots and tyrants. It is its natural manure."[12] These sentiments were linked both to his conviction that constitutions must change with the times[13] and to his belief that "the earth belongs in usufruct to the living" and "that the dead have neither powers nor rights over it."[14] But it was finally the preservation of the revolutionary spirit itself that was at issue: a "little rebellion now and then," he had argued, was a "good thing" in and of itself.[15]

There is of course a paradox here, since a revolution is always a founding (and thus a foundation) as well as the kindling of a certain spirit of spontaneity hostile to foundationalism. As Hannah Arendt has observed, in America the revolutionary spirit founded a constitution that in time came to be at odds with that spirit—as social contracts and fixed laws are always likely to grow at odds with the spirit of innovation that creates them.[16] Jefferson saw democracy itself, more particularly ward government and active participation by citizens in self-governance, as the remedy to the ossification of the democratic constitution. Like Rousseau before and Robert Michels after him, Jefferson worried that representative government could swallow up a people's liberties and lead to an elective despotism, the worse for being legitimized by a social contract rooted in the very notion of consent being violated by representation.

The call for ward government and full participation by citizens "not merely at an election one day in the year, but every day" was to Jefferson the key to the preservation of revolutionary ardor.[17]

The lesson taught by Jefferson is that original consent, derived from the foundational principles of natural right (the essence of social contract reasoning), is inadequate to the democratic mandate—which is why I have spent so much of my career trumpeting the benefits of strong, participatory democracy. By this logic, it is not just foundationalism but foundings themselves that imperil the democratic orders they establish. The tension between constitutional order and the revolutionary spirit has been the subject of two recent books that pointedly capture the contradictions between founding and democracy: Gordon Wood's *The Radicalism of the American Revolution* (winner of the 1993 Pulitzer in history) and, even more suggestively, Bruce Ackerman's *We the People: Foundations*.[18] In the latter book, Ackerman offers a provocative version of "dualist democracy" in which "Rights Foundationalists" face advocates of the actual exercise of popular sovereignty in a contest over the meaning of democracy and of the revolution that made it. Ackerman sees in historical moments like the Founder's rejection of the Articles (and the procedural principles the Articles mandated), or Roosevelt's New Deal, revolutionary emblems of the nation's true democratic spirit. Foundationalism, even where it represents an authoritative establishing of the credentials of democracy, tends then to undermine democracy, and democracy both requires and entails an immunity to its own foundations if it is to flourish.

Michael Oakeshott once said rationalists are "essentially ineducable," by which he meant that, wedded to formal models of truth and cognition, they were closed to the evidence of their senses about the here and now, and the common-sense conversation of those around them.[19] In a similar way, foundationalists may be said to be ineducable and thus immune to democracy for they know their truths up front and have nothing to learn from the democratic process. Foundations immobilize whatever rests on them: that is their purpose. Democracy enjoins constant, permanent motion—a gentle kind of permanent revolution, a movable feast that affords each generation room for new appetites and new tastes, and thus allows political and spiritual migration to new territory.

Autonomy. The autonomy necessary to democracy reinforces the sense of foundationalism's incompatibility with democracy. There is always something heteronomous about roots, antecedents, and a prioris even when they belong to democracy's genealogy. They tell us what is what and order us what to do ("Make no laws abridging speech! Respect private property!") rather than permit us to choose or create by willing into existence (Kant's realm of ends) our values and common objectives, or, minimally, to test fixed rules against changing reality ("Is advertising to count as speech? How about child pornography? Are slaves property?") It is in the name not just of revolution but of autonomy that Jefferson insists that the earth belongs always and first of all to the living.

The principle of liberty, often grounded in foundational reason, nonetheless demands liberty from its foundations. Minimally, the free must freely choose (rechoose) their principles to make them their own. Foundations dug up, reconsidered (perhaps redesigned), and replanted (perhaps in new or different soil) are not exactly what foundationalists mean when they speak of foundations. And while in seeking common ends democracy processes prospective norms, values, and rationales that may be rooted in metaphysics, religion, or foundational ethics, their *legitimacy* is a function not of their genealogy but of their status as products of democratic choice. In this sense, their origins are neither arbitrary nor relativistic, just irrelevant to their democratic legitimacy.

This is an important point: John Rawls validates principles of justice through the contractualist (consensualist) logic of the original position, which, nevertheless, have independent intuitive and historical status in conceptions of the person. Equal liberty and the difference principle can be argued from a number of persuasive perspectives: but their political validity for Rawls derives from their capacity to survive the consensualist test of reasoning in the veil of ignorance. Likewise, democratic principles originate in historically important, psychologically pertinent, and morally admirable ways: but their legitimacy—how we *know* them politically—depends on the democratic process. Political knowing here meets Dewey's standard: "Knowing," he writes, "is not the act of an outside spectator but of a participator inside the natural and social scene [so that] the true object of knowledge resides in the consequences of directed action."[20] The criterion by which this form of knowledge is judged "lies in the method used to secure consequences and not in metaphysical conceptions of the nature of the real."[21] The method turns out to be democracy itself. Dewey thus concludes that "the method of democracy . . . is to bring . . . conflicts out into the open where their special claims can be seen and appraised, where they can be discussed and judged in the light of the more inclusive interests than are represented by either of them separately."[22]

Dewey is portraying something like a general will, where the coincidence of particular wills describes a common good that can be willed on behalf of the community. The process modifies and legitimates as "public" not only the interests and principles that adjudicate them but the process itself. Hence Article V of the American Constitution renders the Constitution itself subject to revision via a difficult but specified democratic procedure. The operating principle of democracy produced by the imperatives of autonomy is then reflexivity: democratic rules, the definition of citizenship, the character of rights—however they originate—become legitimate only when subjected to reflexive scrutiny—democratic deliberation and decision.

This means that democracy is self-correcting: its insufficiencies are corrected democratically rather than by the imposition of externalities on the
democratic process. The process is dynamic because it is self-transforming:
educative. Dewey not only links democracy and education but suggests that
"popular government is educative as other modes of political regulation are
not. It forces a recognition that there are common interests, even though the
recognition of *what* they are is still confused; and the need it enforces of
discussion and publicity brings about some clarification of what they are."[23]
Clarification can take a long time, but democracy holds out to those with
the patience to struggle through rather than against it the promise of reform
from within. It took nearly 150 years for American citizenship to be extended
from propertied white males to all adult Americans. But the struggle that led
to the gradual expansion of the civic ambit was a democratic struggle in which
the rules of democracy were used to modify the rules of democracy. A benevolent king or a Platonic Guardian seeking to secure greater equality would
have acted far more quickly and decisively, but at the expense of the liberty of
those in whose name democracy was evolving. Jefferson's notion that the
remedy for the ills of democracy is more democracy speaks to its self-correcting character.

Commonality of political judgment. Perhaps the clearest way to differentiate
democratic from foundationalist reasoning is to contrast cognitive judgment
and political judgment; the former reverts to epistemological modes of understanding while the latter is firmly rooted in politics and publicity. I will not
rehearse the arguments I have offered in defense of political judgment as an
enterprise distinct from other forms of judgment elsewhere,[24] but there is
much to be said for the view that political judgment is defined by activity in
common rather than thinking alone and is hence what democratic politics
produces rather than (as with foundations) what produces democratic politics. Democratic political judgment can be exercised only by citizens interacting with one another in the context of mutual deliberation and decision-
making on the way to willing common actions. What is required is not
foundational mandates or individual mental acumen in rigidly applying fixed
standards to a changing world but such political skills as are necessary to
discovering or forging common ground. What is right, or even what a right is,
cannot in itself determine political judgment. Rights themselves are both constantly being redefined and reinterpreted *and* dependent for their normative
force on the engagement and commitment of an active citizen body.

Bills of Rights, Madison warned, are parchment parapets from which real
liberty cannot be defended—more covenants without the sword! In any case,
the citizen wishes only to act in common in the face of conflict, not to know
with certainty or to uphold ancient norms that claim to be foundational. The
object is to resolve or find ways to live with conflict, not to discover the
grounds of bliss or a path to eternity. Civic judgment is thus always provi-

sional, constrained by a sense of uncertainty. It is a form of judgment made uneasy by every form of absolutism, including foundational rights absolutism. Democratic politics is what men do when metaphysical foundations fail rather than metaphysical foundations reified as a constitution.

My earlier argument is apposite here: "If political judgment is understood as artful political practice conducted by adept citizens, then to improve our judgment we must strengthen our democratic practices. To think aright about politics, we must act aright, and to act aright calls for better citizens rather than better philosophers. If we find our political judgment defective, it may be the fault of too little rather than too much democracy."[25] Democracy may be established by a foundational logic but it is sustained only by a logic of citizenship. It is made in Athens but enacted and practiced in Sparta (the Athenians, said Rousseau, knew how to think aright; the Spartans how to act aright). Citizens are men and women who have learned to live freely and in common under rules they make for themselves, and who are thus capable not just of survival but of flourishing both in spite of the foundations that have supported their birth and in the absence of all foundations. Like every political system, democracy too has a birth mother, and thus rests on foundations. Unlike every other political system, however, democracy is necessarily self-orphaned, the child who slays its parents so that it may grow and flourish autonomously. This may dismay those like Burke who believe that in hacking up its aged parents democracy destroys its soul; but it will be seen by all those who wish to assure the sovereignty of the political in a setting of equality and liberty as a melancholy necessity. Reflexivity once again turns out to be democracy's great virtue. Democracy is the debate about what democracy is; democratic citizenship entails an argument about who democratic citizenship includes; democratic politics debates and ultimately defines the limits of the democratic polity, thus adjudicating issues of private and public, society and state, individual and community. Courts may enforce "natural" or "higher" rights but do so finally at the pleasure of the democratic sovereign. If that sovereign believes the judiciary has become overzealous in its exercise of independent judgment it can amend the judiciary's constitutional position (as Roosevelt threatened to do in his first term).

Persuasive as these three elucidations of nonfoundational democracy may be, to critics in the liberal tradition of natural rights hegemony they may nonetheless seem something of an evasion. To be sure, spontaneity, flexibility, autonomy, and commonality are features of democracy that seek to elude foundations; yet surely, it will be argued, they describe a set of democratic values that condition and so cannot originate in the democratic process. This puzzle, which threatens to return us to the turf of epistemology, needs addressing. Is it not obvious, goes the objection, that democracy's procedures and institutions, which constitute and guarantee the creativity, autonomy, and commonality of democracy and manifest themselves as the principles of equality, right, and liberty, require a grounding in something antecedent to democracy? If democracy is not to become an arbitrary choice in a relativized political cosmos, must it not be anchored in something other than its own procedures? After all, even William James acknowledged that pragmatism has "no dogmas, no doctrines, *save its method.*"[26] And even Jefferson, for all his devotion to changeability and popular will, wrote that "nothing is unchangeable . . . except the inherent and unalienable rights of man."[27] Might we not say that democracy, while foundationless with respect to public judgment and political outcomes, rests on procedures whose legitimacy is a function of prior arguments and agreements? And that those procedures, resting firmly on the idea of equality as an expression of the equal worth of individuals and their interests, are justified by recourse to principles antecedent to the democratic politics they engender, principles that are hence foundationalist? Is not equality, as democracy's guiding value, best thought of as the application to debate about public action of the foundational premise that all human beings, born free, are equal and have a right to equal opportunity and treatment? Finally, is this not simply another way of formulating what philosophers call the lexical priority of liberty?

No, it is not. In a democracy, living popular will is always trump. It operates under constraints, to be sure, but these constraints are themselves conditional: the product of a will to self-regulation by a prudent popular sovereign. Engines can be prevented from turning at too high a speed (rpm) through the installation of a governor, to be sure, but the governor can be removed by those who installed it. Democracy's most sacred values surely do have status and being prior to politics. However, in Dewey's formulation, "we come back to the fact that the genuine issue is not whether certain values . . . have being already . . . but what concrete judgments we are to form about ends and means in the regulation of practical behavior."[28] In pursuing concrete judgments and regulating practical behavior, values are themselves subject to democratic validation and revision. Democracy is for the living, and the living are always democratically empowered to change their founding democratic constitution. Democracy's decisions are validated post hoc.

Russian President Yeltsin's refusal to acknowledge the constraints of the 1977 Russian (ex-Soviet) constitution, and his insistence on turning to a popular referendum (in April 1993) to validate his "illegality" is a potent instance of how democracy justifies itself (although his use of force in October 1993 or his subsequent cancellation of Presidential elections is another matter: when democracy is the subject and a people unschooled in citizenship is the pupil, tanks make poor tutors). Yeltsin's earlier action, however, is redolent of the 1787 Philadelphia Convention's illegal decision to revise fundamentally the Articles of Confederation that it was supposed only to modify and amend and then, against instructions, to permit ratification by the vote of only nine of the thirteen states. These are instances of democracy's post hoc legitimacy, aptly described in Gordan Wood's *The Radicalism of the American Revolution*.

Thomas Jefferson, we noted earlier, thought constitutions should not be objects of reverence, and in practice they rarely have been. Even noble democratic principles like the priority of liberty and equal rights are constantly subject to political debate and adjustment. Whose liberty? Which equality? Current debates about abortion, AIDS, the death penalty and even NAFTA are at least in part debates about these questions. That the Declaration of Independence declared, "All men are created equal" did not preclude a bloody history of struggle for enfranchisement first by white non–property holders, then by blacks and finally by women. The "equality" Americans actually established was a product not just of a presumptive logic of natural rights but of political (and military) struggle in the name of rights not just recognized by but brought into being by that struggle, which in time led to a gradual redefinition of the inclusiveness of the democratic body politic. Exactly who the "men" were who were created equal had to be determined by democratic struggle. Justice Taney saw no incongruence between natural rights and Negro slavery because the *political* issue was not whether humankind had natural rights but who was included in humankind (African-Americans were not). The question of inclusion remains democracy's most controversial question today.

Democracy both does and must define its categories (including the category of democracy itself) through democratic struggle. There is a sense in pragmatism in which all knowledge—all reality—"depends on the ultimate decision of the community."[29] We need not necessarily accept Peirce's more radical intersubjectivity, to recognize that *political* or *public* reality has this character, *by definition*. Rights arise out of a politics of liberty, and liberty itself is a product of social struggle. That we are "born free" is a useful fiction in opposing the empirical realities of natural (physical, genetic) inequality and was a crucial weapon in the war against absolute authority. That was its great power as a premise of dissent ideology in the seventeenth century, when it first manifested its modern revolutionary potential. But in fact rights gain substance and credibility only as they are clothed in civic garments. Ironically, the rights by which we claim access to citizenship are themselves given force only by citizenship. Natural rights *are* paper parapets, and are defensible only when manned by citizens willing to pay for them with their civic engagement, their social responsibilities, and often their lives. This was once a familiar argument in the defense of positive liberty by writers like T. H. Green. The recent penchant for rights absolutism has led many to neglect or forget such arguments.[30] The simple fact is, whatever its historical genealogy and intellectual heritage, as a system of legitimacy, democracy produces itself. Democracy is the regime within which the struggle for democracy finds legitimacy—legitimates itself, that is to say, without the help of foundations, whose purposes can only be to explain but never to justify a democratic polity.

Notes

1. Benjamin R. Barber, *Strong Democracy* (Princeton: Princeton University Press, 1984), 120–21.

2. William James, *Pragmatism and the Meaning of Truth* (Cambridge: Harvard University Press, 1978), 31.

3. Ibid., 44.

4. John Dewey, *The Quest for Certainty* (New York: Capricorn Books, n.d.), 6.

5. Ibid., 19.

6. Bertrand Russell, "The Study of Mathematics," in *Mysticism and Logic* (New York: Doubleday Anchor, 1957), 57–58.

7. Peirce cited in Israel Scheffler, *Four Pragmatists* (New York: Humanities Press, 1974), 57. Michael Oakeshott's imagery is equally captivating: for him too, we are sailors "on a boundless and bottomless sea; there is neither harbour nor shelter nor floor for anchorage, neither starting-place nor appointed destination. The enterprise is to keep afloat on an even keel." *Rationalism in Politics* (New York: Basic Books, 1962), 133.

8. I am working on a project on the revolutionary origins of democracy that discriminates between at least four distinctive moments in revolution, of which only one is highlighted here. I call it the moment of "release."

9. Cited by Hannah Arendt, *On Revolution* (New York: Viking, 1965), 239. Also see Robert Michels, *Political Parties* (London, 1915).

10. Letter to John Adams, August 1, 1816; note that this was later in his life, when some claim his revolutionary ardor had cooled off.

11. Letter to Samuel Kercheval, July 12, 1816.

12. Letter to Colonel William Stephens Smith, November 13, 1787.

13. "I know also that laws and institutions must go hand in hand with the progress of the human mind. . . . We might as well require a man to wear still the coat which fitted him when a boy, as civilized society to remain ever under the regimen of their barbarous ancestors." Letter to Kercheval.

14. Letter to James Madison, 1789.

15. As Jefferson suggested in his letter to James Madison of January 30, 1787.

16. "Paradoxical as it may sound," wrote Arendt, "it was in fact under the impact of the Revolution that the Revolutionary spirit in this country began to wither away, and it was the Constitution itself, this greatest achievement of the American people, which eventually cheated them of their proudest possession." Arendt, *On Revolution*, 242.

17. Letter to Joseph Cabell, February 12, 1815.

18. Gordon Wood, *The Radicalism of the American Revolution* (New York: Knopf, 1992); Bruce Ackerman, *We the People*, vol. 1: *Foundations* (Cambridge, Mass.: Harvard University Press, 1990).

19. Oakeshott, *Rationalism in Politics*, 32.

20. Dewey, *The Quest for Certainty*, p. 196.

21. Ibid., 220.

22. Dewey, *Liberalism and Social Action* (1935; reprint, New York: Capricorn Books, 1963), 79.

23. Dewey, *The Public and Its Problems* (New York: Holt, 1927), 201–2ff.

24. In *The Conquest of Politics* (Princeton: Princeton University Press, 1988).

25. Ibid., 211.

26. James, *Pragmatism and the Meaning of Truth*, 31–32. Emphasis added.

27. Letter to Major John Cartwright, June 25, 1824.

28. Dewey, *The Quest for Certainty*, 46.

29. *Philosophical Writings of Peirce*, ed. Justus Buchler (New York: Dover Books, 1955), 249.

30. The political dimensions of this argument about rights in their relationship to democracy are argued in my "The Reconstruction of Rights," *American Prospect* (Spring 1991): 36–46.

List of Contributors

BENJAMIN R. BARBER is Walt Whitman Professor of Political Science and director of the Whitman Center for the Culture and Politics of Democracy at Rutgers University. Among his books are *Strong Democracy* (1984), *The Conquest of Politics* (1988), and *Jihad versus McWorld* (1995).

SEYLA BENHABIB is Professor of Government at Harvard University. She is the author of *Critique, Norm, and Utopia* (1986), *Situating the Self* (1992), and *The Reluctant Modernism of Hannah Arendt* (1996). She is a co-author of *Feminist Contentions: A Philosophical Exchange* (1994), co-editor (with Wolfgang Bonss and John McCole) of *On Max Horkheimer: New Perspectives* (1993), co-editor (with Fred Dallmayr) of *The Communicative Ethics Controversy* (1990), and co-editor (with Drucilla Cornell) of *Feminism as Critique* (1987). She and Andrew Arato edit *Constellations: An International Journal of Critical and Democratic Theory*.

JEAN L. COHEN is Professor of Political Science at Columbia University, where she teaches contemporary political theory. She is the author of *Class and Civil Society: The Limits of Marxian Critical Theory* and the co-author of *Civil Society and Political Theory*. Her current project is on sex, law, and the Constitution. She is widely published in a variety of journals and serves on the editorial boards of a number of these, including *Constellations*, *Dissent*, and *Thesis Eleven*.

JOSHUA COHEN is Professor of Philosophy and Arthur and Ruth Sloan Professor of Political Science at MIT, and editor of *Boston Review*. He is a co-author (with Joel Rogers) of *Associations and Democracy* (1995), co-editor (with Archon Fung) of the four-volume *Constitution, Democracy, and State Power: The Institutions of Justice* (1996), and editor of *For Love of Country: Debating the Limits of Patriotism* (1996).

ROBERT A. DAHL, Sterling Professor Emeritus of Political Science at Yale University, is the author of *Democracy and Its Critics*, *Who Governs*, and other works on democratic theory and practice.

FRED DALLMAYR is Packey Dee Professor of Political Theory at the University of Notre Dame. Among his publications are *Beyond Dogma and Despair* (1981), *Twilight of Subjectivity* (1981), *Language and Politics: Why Does Language Matter to Political Philosophy?* (1984), *Polis and Praxis: Exercises in Contemporary Political Theory* (1984), *Critical Encounters: Between Philosophy and Politics* (1987), *Margins of Political Discourse* (1989), *Between Freiburg and Frankfurt: Toward a Critical Ontology* (1991), *G.W.F. Hegel: Modernity and Politics* (1993), *The Other Heidegger* (1993), and *Beyond Orientalism: Essays on Cross-Cultural Encounter* (1996).

CARLOS FORMENT is Assistant Professor in the Department of Politics at Princeton University and a researcher in the Faculty of Political and Social Science at the Instituto Torcuato di Tella. He is completing a book manuscript, "Democracy in Spanish America: Civil Society and the Invention of Politics, 1760–1890," and is beginning a second one, tentatively entitled "Peripheral Peoples and the Language of Political and Social Theory."

NANCY FRASER is Professor of Political Science in the Graduate Faculty of the New School for Social Research. She is the author of *Unruly Practices: Power, Discourse, and Gender in Contemporary Social Theory* (1989), the co-author of *Feminist Contentions: A Philosophical Exchange* (1994), and the co-editor of *Revaluing French Feminism: Critical Essays on Difference, Agency, and Culture* (1992). Her new book, *Justice Interruptus*, will be published in 1996.

CAROL C. GOULD is Professor of Philosophy at Stevens Institute of Technology and a research associate at the Center for Research in Applied Epistemology (C.R.E.A.) in Paris. She is the author of *Rethinking Democracy* (1988) and *Marx's Social Ontology* (1978) and is currently completing a book manuscript entitled "Hard Questions in Democratic Theory." She has edited several books, including *Women and Philosophy*, *Beyond Domination: New Perspectives on Women and Philosophy*, *The Information Web: Ethical and Social Implications of Computer Networking*, and the forthcoming collection *Gender*.

AMY GUTMANN, Laurance S. Rockefeller University Professor of Politics and Dean of the Faculty at Princeton University, is the author of *Democratic Education* (1987), *Liberal Equality* (1980), the forthcoming *Democracy and Disagreement* (1996) with Dennis Thompson, and the forthcoming *Color Conscious* (1997) with Anthony Appiah. She is the editor of *Multiculturalism: Examining the Politics of Recognition, Democracy and the Welfare State*, and *Ethics and Politics* (with Dennis Thompson). Her essays on moral and political philosophy have appeared in *Ethics*, *Philosophy and Public Affairs*, *Political Theory*, *Dissent*, and other journals.

JÜRGEN HABERMAS is Emeritus Professor of Philosophy at the University of Frankfurt and the author of numerous works of philosophy and social theory. His most recent book, *Faktizität und Geltung*, has been translated into English as *Between Facts and Norms* (1996).

BONNIE HONIG is Associate Professor of Government at Harvard University. She is the author of *Political Theory and the Displacement of Politics* (1993), editor of *Feminist Interpretations of Hannah Arendt* (1995), and the author of articles on feminist and political theory published in the *American Political Science Review*, *Political Theory*, *Social Research*, and elsewhere. She is currently writing a book, tentatively entitled "'There's No Place Like Home': Democratic Politics in Cosmopolitan Times."

WILL KYMLICKA is Research Director for the Canadian Centre for Philosophy and Public Policy at the University of Ottowa. He is the author of *Liberalism, Community, and Culture* (1989), *Contemporary Political Philosophy: An Introduction* (1990), and *Multicultural Citizenship: A Liberal Theory of Minority Rights* (1995), and the editor of *The Rights of Minority Cultures* (1995).

JOAN B. LANDES is Professor of Women's Studies and History at Pennsylvania State University. She is the author of *Women and the Public Sphere in the Age of the French Revolution* (1988) and co-editor of the exhibition catalog *Representing Revolution: French and British Images, 1789–1804* (1989). She has published widely in feminist and political theory, most recently "*Novus Ordo Saeclorum*: Gender and Public Space in Arendt's Revolutionary France," in *Feminist Interpretations of Hannah Arendt*, ed. Bonnie Honig (1995), and the forthcoming "Mary Does, Alice Doesn't: The Paradox of Female Reason in and for Feminist Theory," in *Mary Wollstonecraft: Two Hundred Years of*

Feminist Theory, ed. Eileen Yeo. She is currently editing a volume of essays on feminism and the public sphere, and completing a study tentatively entitled "Visualizing Freedom: Essays on Politics, Culture, and Gender in Eighteenth-Century France."

JANE MANSBRIDGE is the Jane W. Long Professor of the Arts and Sciences in the Department of Political Science at Northwestern University and a faculty fellow at Northwestern's Center for Urban Affairs and Policy Research. She is the editor of *Beyond Self-Interest* and the author of *Beyond Adversary Democracy*, *Why We Lost the ERA*, and articles on feminist and democratic theory. Her current work, based on interviews with working-class white and black U.S. women, explores the effects of feminism, as a social movement, on nonactivists, and vice versa.

CHANTAL MOUFFE is Senior Research Fellow in the Center for the Study of Democracy at the University of Westminster in London. She has lectured widely in Europe, North America, and Latin America and is a member of the Collège International de Philosophie in Paris. She is the co-author (with Ernesto Laclau) of *Hegemony and Socialist Strategy: Toward a Radical Democratic Politics* (1985), the editor of *Dimensions of Radical Democracy* (1992), and the author of *The Return of the Political* (1993).

ANNE PHILLIPS is Professor of Politics at London Guildhall University. She has written extensively on feminism, liberalism, and democracy, and her works include *Engendering Democracy* (1991) and, co-edited with Michèle Barrett, *Destabilizing Theory: Contemporary Feminist Debates* (1992). The ideas developed in this essay form the basis for her most recent book, *The Politics of Presence* (1995).

RICHARD RORTY is University Professor of the Humanities at the University of Virginia. His books include *Philosophy and the Mirror of Nature* and *Contingency, Irony, and Solidarity*.

SHELDON S. WOLIN has been a faculty member of the University of California at Berkeley, Oxford University, and Princeton University. He is the author of *Politics and Vision* and *The Presence of the Past* and the founding editor of *democracy*.

IRIS MARION YOUNG is Professor of Public and International Affairs at the University of Pittsburgh, where she is also affiliated with the departments of philosophy and political science. She is the author of *Justice and the Politics of Difference* (1990) and of many articles on feminist theory and political philosophy. She is currently working on a book on democratic theory.

Index _____